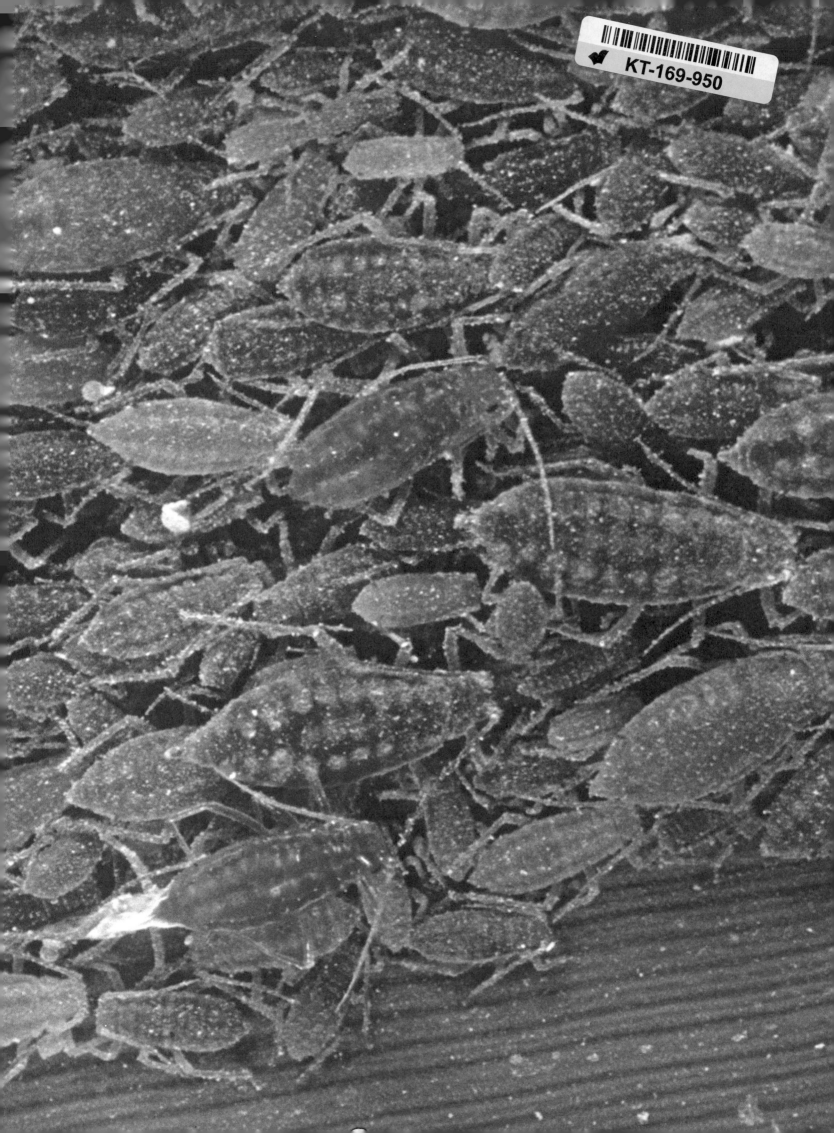

# ENCYCLOPEDIA OF
# INSECTS
## & ARACHNIDS

# ENCYCLOPEDIA OF
# INSECTS
## & ARACHNIDS

**Maurice and Robert Burton**

Introduction by
**Michael Tweedie**

octopus

in association with
Phoebus

# INSECTS

## Introduction

Insects are by far the most numerous group of animals on earth. There are over 750 000 different kinds of insects. This is more than all of the other animal groups combined. These six-legged, winged animals have been on earth for more than 200 million years, being very successful in adapting to life in many different places, from hot springs to the icy wastes of Antarctica.

Insects are related to crabs, scorpions, mites and spiders, all of which belong to the large group of animals with jointed legs, the Arthropoda. Insects are often confused with a number of their insect-like relatives such as spiders, which are also covered in this book.

Both insects and spiders are recognised as arthropods as they have a hard skeleton covering the whole body and jointed limbs. All insects have three parts to their body. The head, with mouth parts and a pair of feelers or antennae, is linked to a thorax, the middle section. This has three pairs of jointed legs on it and usually two pairs of wings. The thorax is linked to the very flexible abdomen. Spiders are immediately recognised as different from insects because the body is divided into only two parts. The head and thorax are all one, and four pairs of jointed legs spread out from this region. No spider has wings.

The horny covering of an insect's body is firm and inelastic, except at the joints where movement is possible. Because of this inelastic covering, made of a substance called chitin, an insect can only grow by casting off its skeleton from time to time. This is known as a moult or ecdysis. There is always a new skeleton underneath which is soft at first and so allows a short period of rapid growth before hardening. The insect must then wait for the next moult before it can grow again. The skeleton is waterproof and this prevents the drying up of body fluids, and is often strong enough to serve as a coat of armour.

The life history of every insect consists of a succession of these ecdyses. The simplest type of development is illustrated by the silverfish, a primitive and wingless insect often found in kitchen cupboards. From the eggs tiny individuals hatch, which differ from their parents only in size. These feed in the same way as the adults and grow, shedding their skins at intervals. When they reach a certain size they mate and lay eggs, and continue to grow and moult after they have started breeding. A silverfish may perform as many as 50 ecdyses in its lifetime.

A grasshopper has a rather more complex life history. The hatchling is recognisable as a grasshopper, but has no wings. In the course of growing up it moults five to eight times, and after the first or second ecdysis little flaps appear on its thorax. With each successive moult these become relatively larger until they are completely deve-

loped wings and the insect can fly. It is now fully grown and ready to breed, and it never moults again. Here again the young and the adult have similar habits and subsist on the same sort of food.

The life history of the butterfly is a good example of the third type. The creature that hatches from the egg, the caterpillar or larva, is more like a worm than a butterfly. It feeds and grows rapidly, moulting several times. When it has completed its growth the caterpillar suspends itself with threads of silk and then, after a day or two, moults again. This moult reveals not another caterpillar but the pupa or chrysalis. It is immobile and lacks any external limbs or other appendages. The chrysalis is really a fully

formed butterfly packed away in a hard envelope. This is because, just before the caterpillar's final moult, all the caterpillar's muscles and most of its internal organs dissolve into a kind of living soup which then quickly reassembles to form a butterfly. After a period of weeks or months, the time depending on the season and the species of insect, the final ecdysis takes place. The shell of the pupa splits, the butterfly crawls out and, after expanding and hardening its wings, flies away. In this case there are three distinct stages after the egg, and the insect behaves quite differently at each stage. The caterpillar crawls and feeds on leaves, the pupa neither moves nor feeds, and the butterfly flies and sucks nectar from flowers through a proboscis.

First published in 1975 by
Octopus Books Limited,
59 Grosvenor Street, London W 1

© 1968/69/70 BPC Publishing Ltd
© this compilation 1975 BPC Publishing Ltd.

ISBN 0 7064 0432 7

This book is adapted from Purnell's
'Encyclopedia of Animal Life' published
in the United States under the title of
'International Wild Life'. It has been
produced by Phoebus Publishing Company
in cooperation with Octopus Books Limited.

Printed in Hong Kong

Distributed in USA by
Crescent Books
a division of Crown Publishers Inc.
419 Park Avenue South
New York. N.Y. 10016

Produced by Mandarin Publishers Limited
Westlands Road, Quarry Bay, Hong Kong

## Classification of insects

Insects are classified on evolutionary principles and these are indicated by their mode of development. The most primitive are those with no changes or metamorphosis, like the silverfish; the most advanced are the ones which change profoundly, like the butterfly; and the grasshopper type of development is regarded as intermediate.

On this basis insects are classified in three main divisions, which are in turn divided into a number of orders. Members of most of these orders are described in the following pages and an indication of their position in classification is given at the end of each article. The following orders are included:

**Insects with no metamorphosis:**
Collembola: springtails.
Diplura: (no common name).
Thysanura: silverfish, bristletail, firebrat.
Protura: (no common name).

**Insects with partial or incomplete metamorphosis:**
Ephemeroptera: mayflies.
Odonata: dragonflies and damselflies.
Orthoptera: grasshoppers, locusts, crickets.
Phasmida: stick-insects.
Dictyoptera: cockroaches and mantises.
Isoptera: termites.
Mallophaga: biting lice.
Phthiraptera: sucking lice.
Hemiptera: bugs including bed-bugs, shield-bugs, aphids, cicadas, scale-insects, etc.

**Insects with extreme or complete metamorphosis:**
Neuroptera: lacewings and others.
Megaloptera: alder-flies.
Mecoptera: scorpion-flies.
Lepidoptera: butterflies and moths.
Trichoptera: caddis-flies.
Diptera: the two-winged or true flies.
Hymenoptera: sawflies, wasps, bees, ants.
Coleoptera: beetles.

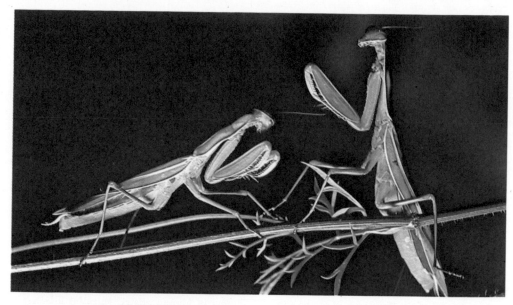

## How insects protect themselves

Insects are the natural prey of most small birds, many mammals, frogs, lizards, almost all spiders, and of predatory members of their own insect group as well. Natural selection has produced innumerable adaptations to help them to escape being eaten.

The larger insects usually have some sort of individual defence. Many of them rely on concealment, and many of these simply hide away in crevices or under debris where they are hard to find. Many night-flying moths spend the day motionless among foliage or long grass, but others rest in the open on tree trunks, and these rely on being coloured or shaped to match their background.

The remarkable case of the peppered moth *(Biston betularia)* concerns camouflage of this kind. In its typical form this moth is speckled with black and white and is well concealed when at rest on a lichened tree trunk. Up to about 1850 this was the only form known, but at that time a black variety began to appear in and around Manchester, a large town in north-western England. By 1900 it had almost completely replaced the normal form in and near all the industrial towns and cities of Britain. One consequence of industrialisation is destruction, by atmospheric pollution, of all lichen on trees and also blackening of their trunks and branches by deposited soot. Obviously in these conditions the black moths would have an advantage over the typical ones in terms of concealment from insect-eating birds, which are by no means absent from the environs of cities. A great deal of research and experiment has shown that this was really an evolutionary change brought about by natural selection favouring a variety which previously existed as a mutation so rare that early entomologists never encountered it until it began to become established.

Many insects carry the camouflage principle further by resemblance to specific objects. Some caterpillars and the tropical stick-insects look like small twigs, and can only be detected if they move. The Kallima butterfly is shaped and coloured like a leaf so it is very difficult to see when at rest.

Although most insects are edible, some have body fluids or secretions which are very ill-tasting and even poisonous. These fluids are immediately released when the insects are attacked. A pecked insect is, however, generally mortally injured; for this sort of protection to be effective the insect must advertise its distasteful properties by a distinctive appearance. A bird which has tasted one of such a species will then recognise others and avoid trying to make a meal of them; consequently only a few of them are killed. This has led to the development of 'warning colours' by insects which are protected in this way. The startling colours of the burnet and tiger moths, and of many bugs and beetles, are striking and beautiful to our eyes, but their purpose is not to please but to warn predators that they are inedible. Insects with stings, such as wasps, are protected in the same way.

Some insects that are harmless have copied harmful and distasteful insects in colour and shape to gain protection; this is known as mimicry. Hoverflies are harmless and are not protected by distasteful qualities, but many of them are marked and coloured like wasps. It is supposed that they have evolved this resemblance because birds are deceived by the warning colour and so do not attack them. Among butter-

flies there are certain groups which are poisonous or distasteful, and these are mimicked by species of other families which are palatable. Most examples of this kind come from the tropics, but the North American monarch and viceroy butterflies form a well known association of this kind. The monarch is the distasteful model and the viceroy is the palatable and deceptive mimic.

## Social insects

The communities of the so-called social insects are well known, but their extraordinary nature is not generally appreciated. In a nest of wasps or yellow-jackets as many as 25000 individuals may live and die in the course of a single summer. They will defend the nest with their stings without any regard for their individual lives, and their energies are devoted to maintaining the nest and feeding and caring for the thousands of larvae. As soon as these are mature they will devote themselves to the same selfless communal service, each wasp having a life of only a few weeks. All of the thousands of wasps which have worked in the nest are sisters, daughters of one mother or 'queen' who emerged from hibernation in the spring and founded the colony. From a few eggs laid by the queen young fertile queens and males are produced. After mating, the males and the sterile female workers die in the first frost, while the queens hibernate until the next spring.

Some species of bees and all ants also live in communities supported by sterile female workers. Ants' nests persist from year to year and the queens have long lives. A queen army ant may live four or five years and be the mother of four million or more offspring.

Termites are so like ants that they are often miscalled 'white ants', but they belong in fact to a wholly different order of insects and are related to cockroaches. Their communities resemble those of ants in many ways, but the workers are of both sexes and the young grow up gradually, without larva and pupa stages and begin to play an active part in the economy of the nest long before they are mature. The queens and males are initially winged and later shed their wings just as ants do.

## Man and insects

Most people regard insects with dislike and hostility and it is true that we have more enemies among them than friends, but it is also true that the vast majority are entirely neutral in the context of human affairs. Harmful insects fall into three categories. In the first category, some of the bees and larger wasps can sting severely, causing pain and sometimes illness. The biting of flies and mosquitos is also often found to be very distressing.

Far more important are the insect carriers of disease. Most of these are blood-suckers and inject a fluid into the blood to prevent it clotting. If they have already bitten an infected person the parasitic organisms causing the disease will be passed into the next victim. Most of the diseases conveyed in this way are specific to certain insects, the parasites requiring an alternation between the insect and man to complete their life history. Malaria, bubonic plague and sleeping sickness are examples and are conveyed by mosquitoes, fleas and tsetse flies.

The third type of insect enemy is the one which attacks cultivated plants. Almost always these insects multiply as a consequence of man providing them with an unnaturally copious food supply. The Colorado beetle and the codlin moth are examples.

A few insects are friends of man through domestication. The silkworm and honeybee have been the controlled servants of man for several thousands of years, and in North America they have recently been joined by certain small solitary bees which are bred in millions to promote pollination of alfalfa or lucerne for the production of seed.

Many insects are frequently the natural enemies of other insects or plants whose appetites or proliferation are a threat to man's interests. Some of these, for example ladybirds, are bred and then released to prey on the harmful species in the sort of operation known as biological control.

Michael Tweedie

# Alder-fly

*A primitive insect whose larvae live in water. It is not a true fly, like the housefly, but belongs to a group of insects which includes the lace-wings and ant-lions. This group already existed during the times when the coal measures were being laid down, 300 million years ago.*

*The adult insect has a body about 1 in. in length, long antennae and dull, heavily veined wings. When the insect is at rest the wings are folded over the back and ridged like a house roof. They are little known, if not wholly unfamiliar to most people, but are well known to the fly fishermen as one of the 'flies' used for trout.*

### Habits

The adult insect flies little – almost reluctantly – but when it takes off the flight is direct. More usually it rests or crawls on plants or stones near a water's edge. Its life is short – merely long enough to ensure the laying of a batch of eggs. The most striking feature of the larvae is its gills, designed for breathing under water, of which there are seven pairs on the abdomen. They look like extra legs, each being made up of a series of five joints clothed with bristles, except that they are held upwards and backwards. A further un-paired gill is carried at the end of the body. The larva spends much of its time under stones and pebbles but can swim freely by undulating its body. When the oxygen content of the water is low the larva will undulate its body in the same way while remaining stationary, so causing a current of water to flow over the gills. This is of considerable value, especially to those species of alder-fly that live in muddy or stagnant water, which lacks the aeration of a running stream.

### Life cycle

In March each female lays up to 2,000 brown, cigar-shaped eggs on plants or stones near water. These stand on end in flat masses, each of 200–500 eggs, like commuters on a station platform. They hatch in two weeks and the larvae make their way to water. The larval stage of life usually lasts for two years, during which the brown larva grows to 1 in. long. During May and June the full-term larvae leave the water and may travel some distance before making an oval cell in mud or vegetable debris in which to pupate. One was seen to travel 6 yd, apparently having climbed over a concrete wall and through a cotoneaster thicket to an open flower bed. Three weeks later the pupa leaves its cell and from it the adult insect emerges.

In many insect pupae the legs and wings are inside the pupal case. In the alder-fly pupa they are already free of the body but in special sheaths; as is usual in pupae that have to make their way to the surface before the adult insect emerges, there are spines on the abdominal ridges.

*Alder-fly on alder leaves. It never eats during its few days of life as its larva has lived and eaten for at least a year.*

Anglers use the larvae of alder-flies as bait. But they are valuable to fishermen in another way, as well as to the economy of the streams, for they and other insect larvae make possible the existence of fish such as trout. They are an important link in the food chain of water creatures, being converters of protein. Plants manufacture food; small animals feed on plants; the larvae of alder-flies feed on these vegetarian animals such as the larvae of caddis-flies; thus trout and bass, which eat the alder-fly larvae, gain protein. So the larvae are the main support of the fishes which the fisherman catches even though he uses the adult as bait. Normally adult alder-flies alight on water only when they fall from overhanging vegetation – when suddenly disturbed by a bird flying near, or when blown down by a gust of wind.

A second point of interest is one that applies to many insects – the adult is short-lived. It serves only for reproducing and dispersing the species. The male, having fertilised the female, serves no other purpose except as food for other animals. It is the same with the female once she has laid her eggs. The 'real' life of the insect is in the larva, which is longer-lived and is adapted to an entirely different way of life.

### Feeding

The adult does not feed. The larva is carnivorous and seizes any small animals that come its way with its vicious, pincer-like mouthparts, or mandibles.

△ *The alder-fly larva is divided into segments, each with a pair of jointed appendages (x12).*

## Reluctant flier

When authors write of a reluctance on the part of the adult alder-fly to take wing, they are referring to the manner in which the insect will, on being disturbed, run quickly up a leaf or a stem, then fly directly to a nearby leaf or stem, and merely repeat this manoeuvre whenever disturbed.

It is very likely that this behaviour of the alder-fly gives us an important clue to the origin and evolution of flight in insects. The alder-fly is primitive in other ways and

▽ *The female alder fly lays her eggs in close-packed rows, like commuters on a station.*

it is not unreasonable to suppose that its flying behaviour is also primitive. We have seen how the larvae live for a year or two while the adult has only a short-lived existence, taking no food and living just long enough to mate and for the female to lay her eggs. Flight can have no value for food capture, because no food is eaten. There is no question of migration. Consequently, the two primary purposes of flight in the alder-fly are to bring the sexes together and to make possible evasive action to escape enemies long enough for the eggs to be fertilised and laid.

In the course of insect evolution other functions have been added. For example, bees, wasps and dragonflies use flight to get food. Many insects migrate—some butter-

flies migrate from the Sahara to Scotland. Nevertheless, it must be emphasised that the two primary purposes of flight in insects are to ensure mating and to provide protection from enemies, with a subsidiary function—that of spreading the species.

All this contrasts strongly with the function of flight in birds and bats, where it plays such a large part in food capture and security and is often a way to avoid the worst rigours of climate by migration.

| class | **Insecta** |
|---|---|
| order | **Neuroptera** |
| sub-order | **Megaloptera** |
| genus | *Sialis spp.* |

# Aphis

*Aphides or 'plant lice' are a group of the Hemiptera (bugs) order of great importance to agriculture as they do considerable harm to crops, both directly, by sucking the cell-sap, and indirectly, by transmitting certain virus diseases, such as potato leaf-roll and sugar-beet yellows, from one plant to another. There are many species, some 500 in the British Isles alone, for example, but probably the best known are those referred to as greenfly and blackfly by the gardener who finds them, often in depressing numbers, on his roses and broad beans. Aphides have soft, oval bodies, small heads, compound eyes, long 6- or 7-jointed antennae, and a jointed beak or rostrum adapted for piercing plant tissues. Some have transparent wings, the first pair being much the longer. Aphides are usually about 2—3 mm long; rarely more than 5 mm.*

## Clouds of insects

Though most familiar as pests of cultivated plants, aphides begin their life on various wild trees and shrubs from which they migrate at intervals to other plants, both wild and in gardens. After mating in late summer or autumn, the black bean aphis *Aphis fabae* for example, lays eggs on the spindle tree or guelder rose. These hatch the following spring as winged females which fly to bean crops where they reproduce by parthenogenesis (that is, without mating). These are called 'stem mothers' as they are the beginning of a new population. Although they may reach the bean plants only singly in many cases, they breed at a tremendous rate forming large colonies, which explains the apparently quite sudden appearance of an infestation where none was visible a day or so previously.

How such a weak, delicate creature as the aphid manages to migrate so successfully from its host plant to another has been investigated thoroughly in recent years. The winged females usually leave the plants where they hatched in two main waves, one in the morning, one in the afternoon. But conditions must be favourable for the movement to take place. It never takes place at night or at temperatures below 17°C/62°F. Once airborne, the aphides are carried up on air currents, often to a great height. After several hours, descending air currents bring the aphides down and they seek out suitable plants. Sample catches taken in nets on balloons at heights up to 2,000 ft show that 30% of clouds of insects floating high up consists of aphides. They may be carried hundreds of miles over land and sea.

In preparing for flight, aphides appear to go through a kind of take-off procedure, which may be repeated several times before actual launching takes place. The centre pair of legs is raised and tucked into the hollow formed by the constriction between thorax and abdomen. Then, balancing on the remaining four legs, the aphid unfolds its wings and takes off. In spite of their apparent fragility, aphides are not easily

*A winged black aphid being tended by an ant. Ants will farm large numbers of aphides, tending them carefully and milking them for the honeydew which is secreted by the aphides (approx × 12).*

blown off plants.

The winged females settle on the alternative plants and produce mainly wingless offspring, but some winged individuals are produced at intervals, and these daily leave to seek out other uninfested plants.

## Piercing and sucking feeders

As a family, aphides feed on many kinds of plants, but while some species may be catholic in their tastes, others can exist only on one species. The mouth-parts are modified for piercing plant tissues and sucking up the cell-sap, especially from the phloem, the main food stream of the plant. The mandibles and maxillae (mouth-parts) work together as extraordinarily fine needle-like stylets which are thrust deep into the soft parts of the plant. The labium or tongue takes no part in the operation but has a groove in which the stylets are sheathed when not in use. Before feeding actually begins, a salivary secretion is injected into the wound made by the stylets. This prevents the sap coagulating as it flows up the stylets.

While many aphides feed externally on plants, others, far less familiar to us, form 'galls' or enclosed receptacles in which they are able to feed while hidden from the attacks of predators. Examples of aphid gall-makers may be found on trees such as poplars, elms, limes, spruce and cultivated currant bushes. Frequently, the galls form a refuge for passing the winter. In spring and summer a new generation may seek out quite different plants on which to feed without making a gall. In some species, there is simply a migration back and forth from one part of the tree, the leaves and shoots, to the roots. An example is the notorious woolly aphis or American blight of apple trees, which makes a characteristic fluffy 'wool' in which it feeds.

Oddly enough, it is their excretory habit which is undoubtedly the most striking and significant fact about aphides. In feeding, aphides take up large quantities of sap in order to get sufficient protein. The rest, the fluid rich in sugar, is given out through the anus as honeydew, often in great quantities. Being rich in sugars honeydew is much sought after by ants and some other insects.

### Young without mating

For most of the year, aphid populations consist only of females which reproduce parthenogenetically at a great rate. Later in the year, winged females fly back to their primary host plants—usually trees—and lay eggs which hatch as males and females. These mate and lay eggs in crevices in the bark, which hatch in the following spring, producing only females.

A single parthenogenetic female may produce as many as 25 daughters in one day, and as these themselves are able to breed in about 8–10 days the numbers of aphides produced by just one female in a season can reach astronomical proportions. It has been estimated that if all the offspring of a single aphid were to survive, and each reproduced and multiplied, there would be in the

*▽ Greenfly bearing young actually giving birth. The offspring's body is just free of the mother (approx × 20).*

course of one year sufficient to 'equal the weight of 500,000,000 stout men'. Breeding is slowed down by adverse conditions, especially cold. If aphides are kept warm in a greenhouse, parthenogenetic females are produced continuously without a single male ever seeing the light of day.

### Enemies everywhere

Many small insect-eating birds, such as tits and flycatchers, eat aphides. Ladybirds, lacewings, bugs, spiders and hover-fly larvae prey on them. In addition, certain parasitic wasps of the family Braconidae lay their eggs in aphides. The larvae consume the tissues of their hosts and eventually pupate inside the empty husk.

Some aphides have, however, evolved defensive mechanisms to guard against attack from these wasps. The aphides' blood cells secrete a capsule which envelops the parasite larva, arresting its development completely within 24 hours. Others form no capsule but appear to secrete some substance which stops the wasp larva's progress within a short period.

Aphides are also able to deter insect enemies by exuding a kind of wax from a pair of chimney-like stumps, called cornicles, on the rear end. This temporarily paralyses the attacker. Some aphides, too, are apparently so distasteful that a ladybird larva will vomit if it tries to eat one.

Ants, who rear aphides for the sake of their honeydew, also protect their charges from attack by predators. One way they do this is to eat the eggs of potential predators, such as those of ladybirds and hover-flies, which have been deliberately laid near an aphid population.

### Ants' aphid farm

Long before history, man tamed and domesticated certain animals for his own uses: for pulling loads, for hunting, for companionship, but especially as food. Ants have been doing much the same thing with aphides for infinitely longer. They rear or at least closely associate with them, eating the honeydew and taking it back to the nest for the larva. Just as man is able to stimulate the production of milk in cows and goats, so too can ants encourage production of honeydew in aphides by improving conditions for their existence. This they may do by a variety of means, apart from repelling predators. They may 'herd' their charges, by forcibly confining them to the growing tips of plants which are the most nutritious, thus stimulating growth and breeding and, of course, the emission of honeydew. Where there are no ants present, the honeydew may eventually cover large areas of the plant, causing its death by wilting, by suffocation or by attracting fungi. By removing the aphides' honeydew, the ants ensure their charges' food sources.

Ants also take aphides into their nests, where they may lay eggs, or they may carry the eggs themselves from the plants on which they are laid. After emerging, the young aphides are carefully tended and 'milked' by the ants while they feed on the roots of various plants. Some aphides live only in ants' nests, and never see the light of day. For others, special shelters are built where the aphides can feed, protected from predators. Comparison with the human farmer's cattle-sheds is irresistible.

Presumably, the ants' habit of 'farming' aphides started haphazardly by attacking and killing them for food or simply by licking the drops of fluid which appeared periodically at the insects' vents. Honeydew is not produced continuously and the drop of liquid produced is in normal circumstances discarded by a flick of the aphides' hind leg. Under stimulation from an ant, however, the aphid does not discard the fluid but allows the ant to remove it, and goes on doing so, seeming to enjoy the caressings of the ant's antennae.

Under continued stimulation very large quantities of honeydew may be produced. One large aphid can produce nearly 2 cu mm in an hour, and a colony of the common ant *Lasius fuliginosus* can, it has been estimated, collect about 3–6 lb of honeydew in 100 days.

Control of aphides is something of paramount importance, but always difficult, and it is depressing for the gardener to know that the presence of ants in an aphid colony contributes directly to the increase of the problem. It has been calculated that in accelerating growth and reproduction in aphides and protecting them from predators, ants can indirectly double the loss in the yield of bean plants as compared with when aphides alone are present.

| class | **Insecta** |
|---|---|
| order | **Hemiptera** |
| sub-order | **Homoptera** |
| family | **Aphididae** |

*The beautiful apollo butterfly, **Parnassius phoebus**, resting with wings outstretched.*

*Apollo showing its bright spot markings.*

# Apollo butterfly

*One of the family of butterflies known as the swallowtails, not unlike them in shape, but lacking the tail-like appendages on the hind wing which give the family its name. The apollo and its relatives are not brightly coloured, most of them being white, with spots and eye-like markings of black and red. They are nevertheless elegant and beautiful.*

### Range and habitat

The common apollo is found in mountainous regions of Europe, from Scandinavia to the Alps and Pyrenees. It flies at fairly low altitudes. There is, however, a related species, the alpine apollo, which occurs at higher altitudes. About 30 species of apollo butterflies are known, ranging through Europe and Asia to North America. Many are mountain butterflies and some species range up to 20,000 ft in the Himalayas. Owing to their inaccessible habitat some of the Central Asiatic species are extremely rare and highly prized by collectors.

### Life history

The caterpillar of the common apollo feeds on orpine, a kind of stonecrop. The caterpillar is black with red spots and, when fully grown, spins a cocoon in which to pupate. Growth is slow and it takes 2 years to complete the life-history. So far as they are known the early stages of all the species are similar, and the larvae feed on stonecrops and saxifrages. The habit, very unusual among butterflies, of spinning a cocoon is no doubt correlated with the need for protection from frost at high altitudes.

Only the common apollo habitually flies at low altitudes, and there are indications that some of the bodily structures of apollos as a whole may serve as an alpine kit. The body is covered with hairs, like a fur coat. It is dark in colour, which may help to absorb heat from the sun. The wings, white with black spots, are proportionately larger than in other butterflies, so exposing a greater surface to the sun's rays, and also assisting the butterfly in its unusual soaring habit. Moreover, they are so thinly covered with scales as to be almost translucent, which probably assists the absorption of the sun's heat.

### God-like butterflies

Apollo butterflies have been seen in the Alps soaring above hillsides on uprising wind currents with wings outstretched and motionless. Soaring flight, common in birds, is rare among insects. Apollo was a Greek god of the mountains and the vegetation and later the sun god. All this makes the choice of name for these butterflies singularly apt. The god-like character is, however, marred by a North American species, *Parnassius autocrator*. The caterpillar, brilliant orange in colour, gives off a most unpleasant odour from just behind its head whenever danger threatens. All apollo larvae (and swallowtail too) have an organ (the osmeterium) behind the head that gives off an odour, but this is usually faint and at any rate not unpleasant to the human nose.

| class | **Insecta** |
|-------|-------------|
| order | **Lepidoptera** |
| family | **Papilionidae** |
| genus | ***Parnassius*** |

*Pyrenees mountains where the alpine apollo can be found at high altitudes. The common apollo lives at much lower altitudes in mountainous regions from Scandinavia to the Alps and Pyrenees.*

*Caterpillar of European apollo **Parnassius apollo**, which takes nearly 2 years to grow.*

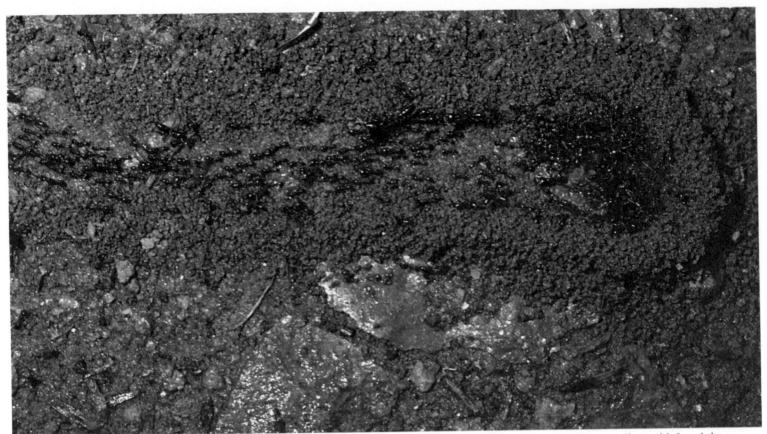

*Antics of army ants have led to tall stories about their ferocity, but they are still to be feared. A tethered horse will be eaten alive and left a skeleton.*

# Army ant

*Army ants, or driver or legionary ants, as they are also called, are often very large, more than an inch long. There is often so much difference between male, female and worker that early naturalists sometimes classified each as separate species, usually as a result of the insects having been found separately or away from the main colony. The queens are wingless. The males, by contrast, are winged and distinctly wasp-like in appearance, and there may be more than one kind of worker, showing marked differences, some being very large with powerful jaws and acting the part of soldiers or skirmishers. Although colonies may have vast numbers of individuals, there are relatively few species and genera. The main groups are the driver ants of Africa, and the army ants (**Eciton**) from South America.*

### Advancing columns drive all before

Army ants are confined mainly to tropical regions in India, Africa and South America, although in America they are found as far north as the Mississippi Valley and as far south as Patagonia. Unlike the complicated, settled existence of more familiar ants, army ants are nomadic, continually moving about the forests. They have no permanent nest and they are constantly scouring large areas in more or less regular columns, driving every living thing, large and small, headlong before them. The column may be many yards long, one writer telling of one in Nicaragua which he fol-

lowed for several hundred yards without finding the end. In some places warning of the ants' approach may be given by birds that prey on them, for example antbirds or by the buzz of parasitic flies which lay their eggs in prey carried by the columns of ants.

The sight of a colony of army ants on the march is surely one of the great wonders of nature, and the resemblance of such a column to a human army is striking. In addition to the main body of small workers, larger, huge-jawed workers flank the main columns and continually scout ahead, laying scent trails to mark the way for the main body. Quite often, the press of the column is so great that new columns may split off, so that any slow-moving prey is often surrounded and engulfed. The activity of the column alternates equally between foraging, usually at night or on dull days, and resting, the nest being moved every day. Some species of army ants are averse to light and build long tunnels as they march, the main body of ants keeping out of sight within them. This does not slow them down, because the tunnels are built so rapidly that both the rate and secrecy of advance are maintained.

### Victims eaten alive

While feeding mainly on other insects, little or nothing that is too slow to escape or insufficiently protected is safe from the attacks of army ants once they are on the march. Slow-moving animals often fall victim, such as snakes that are gorged with food and so will not move quickly. Even man will not always escape unscathed if he is foolish enough to let his curiosity or bravado mislead him into thinking the ants would not dare attack him. There are

many stories of the intrepid white hunter's adventures with army ants, although these often grossly exaggerate the ants' intelligence and ferocity. Sometimes, in fleeing from the advance of the ants, it has been impossible to rescue horses or other livestock, and these if unable to flee themselves rarely survive. A tethered horse will simply be eaten alive and left a skeleton. A horde of African army ants was once seen to eat 3 dead goats in 3 days.

Despite their terrible depredations, however, army ants often perform a service to man by ridding his dwellings of vermin. Rats, mice, spiders, cockroaches, bugs, beetles, none survives an invasion of army ants and when the owners return again their houses will be free of these unwelcome squatters. It occasionally happens, however, that the marching column arrives while the owners are still asleep. Hundreds of ants crawl over you within seconds. In Africa a widespread belief is that driver ants do not attack until they have swarmed all over your body, and then bite all at once at a given signal!

Army ants feed by simply cutting up and rending the victim on the spot, carrying the pieces back to the temporary nest and also filling their crops with juice and pulp. Very large amounts of food are needed by an army ant colony. It has been estimated that in an average-sized colony of some 80,000 adults and perhaps 30,000 larvae, half a gallon of animal food is needed for its daily subsistence. With such great quantities of food needed, it is not surprising that army ants are only in the lush tropics.

### 25,000 eggs in 2 days every 30 days

It is said that the sole reason for the army ants' constant restlessness is that they are always exhausting the food in one area, and so must move to another place. But this is only part of the story. Even when food is plentiful, army ants never settle for long. The pattern of their movements depends largely on the breeding cycle. Every 30—40 days, the huge queen produces a vast quantity of eggs, perhaps some 25—35 thousand in 2 days. Several days earlier, the colony stops and gathers in a vast swarm, individual ants being held together by their hooked legs, the spaces between them forming rough and ready chambers for the queen and her forthcoming brood. The swarm may form in a hollow tree, hang from a branch, or simply lie in a cavity in the ground.

After the eggs are hatched, the community remains static, while the workers get food for the larvae. Fragments of food are handed direct to the larvae and not regurgitated in the form of a mush as in more advanced ant communities.

About a week later, the pupal cocoons, in which the previous generation of larvae have been carried, hatch almost simultaneously, producing workers and males. It is the movement of the newly-emerging ants which excites the older ants into beginning another cycle of nomadism. This is apparently further encouraged by the larvae of the new generation which exude a secretion when licked and cleaned by the workers.

After breaking camp, the ant colony, now supplemented by vast numbers of newly-emerged workers, march and forage, carrying the young larvae and queen with them. Each night, or during the day in the dry season, they swarm to form the characteristic temporary living shelters where the larvae and queen are protected.

When the queen is ready to produce a further batch of eggs, which usually coincides with the pupation of the earlier batch of larvae, the whole community stops once more, so the crucial parts of the life cycle

△ *Safari army ants marching in column. Large, huge-jawed workers flank the main column and scout ahead, laying scent trails to mark the way for the main body of army ants.*

▽ *Army ants swarming from a branch, individuals being held together by their hooked legs. The spaces are used by the queen and her brood.*

coincide from one generation to another, reducing the time the army is stationary.

Winged males are continually leaving to seek out queens in other colonies. Sometimes it seems they pick up the trails of other army ant colonies while on the march, and, leaving the colony of their birth, follow them, but the exact means by which they find a queen is unknown. Male army ants are often quite enormous insects, with wings, large compound eyes, tremendous sickle-shaped jaws, and large abdomen and genitalia. In West Africa, where they are often found flying around lights, they are known as 'sausage flies'.

When daughter queens emerge in a colony, it may split up, each of the females gathering around her a proportion of the population and then going their different ways. In some species, however, most of the newly-emerging queens are killed, and only one queen is found in one colony, which may number up to a million individual ants.

## Regimented ants

Reports of army ants on the march, the regular columns, the division into 'rank and file' with 'officer' types flanking the main body have frequently led the more romantic writers into crediting ants with far greater intelligence than they really deserve. In fact, the apparent regulated orderliness and 'intelligence' displayed by army ants are the result of pure instinct—the fixed behaviour patterns they have evolved. The vast majority of the colony are blind and are governed by an instinct merely to follow the ant in front, the column being guided by the soldier ants who precede the main column laying down scent trails. Yet even they are hardly

seeking a path. Although best fitted to act as scouts and skirmishers, by reason of their size and armour, they take up their flanking positions merely because, being giants compared with the smaller workers, they are unable to find a footing amid the close-knit ranks of their brethren.

So it is a case of the blind leading the blind. Food is found by smell, and if there are any obstacles to the line of march, the ants have to search blindly for a way round. If a circular obstacle is placed in the centre of a colony of army ants, they will troop endlessly around it. Something similar has been seen to happen naturally. In Panama a column once became separated from the main army, described a circle by accidentally latching onto the end of its own column, and kept on marching round until the ants became weaker and weaker and eventually died.

The flanking and engulfing movements often observed in army ants are also more or less accidental in that because of the continual bustle and thrust of the main body, side-streams of new ant columns are continually being pushed out, these having the useful effect of surrounding and engulfing prey. The result of the formation of such side-streams may frequently be vast swarms of ants many yards wide: a terrifying prospect for man and beast alike.

| class | **Insecta** |
|---|---|
| order | **Hymenoptera** |
| family | **Dorylinae** |
| genera | **Eciton** (South America) **Dorylus, Anomma** (Africa) and others |

# Assassin-bug

*Some 3,000 species of assassin-bug have been described, and it is likely there are many more yet to be discovered. They vary in size, from a few millimetres to three or four centimetres, and in colour and structure. Some species are very thin and stick-like with elongated coxae (the basal parts of the legs), making them look rather like a mantis, while others are more solid and typically bug-like. Most species have two pairs of wings, although some exotic species are wingless. All assassin-bugs have a powerful, curved rostrum, or beak, with which they pierce and suck out the tissues of their prey.*

## Habits

Assassin-bugs are so called because of the speed with which they grab and poison their chosen victim. They are common and widespread throughout most of the world, more particularly in tropical and subtropical areas. Some are found in temperate climates, often in buildings. They can be found on old walls, in houses or out-buildings, and even in thatch roofed cottages. The large *Reduvius personatus* is occasionally attracted to lights on warm evenings in late summer. Others are found on flowers, deciduous and coniferous trees, sand dunes, amongst piles of faggots, under stones, and even in old birds' nests.

Assassin-bugs often produce sounds when touched and this brings us to the first surprising use of the rostrum. When not feeding, the rostrum rests against a ridged groove under the head, called the prosternum. When disturbed the insect stridulates, scraping the one against the other, the friction producing the sound. It may be that this deters predators, such as birds.

## Fearsome hunter

All assassin-bugs are carnivorous, and many of them are extremely active and efficient hunters, with a pair of powerful, jack-knife forelimbs for grasping the prey. On the end of these limbs there are adhesive pads made up of thousands of tiny hairs, covered by a thin film of oil. These adhere to the victim rather like a sticky burr. Some species have evolved even stickier pads, which enable the assassin-bug to hold fast even to the hairy body of a bee, in much the same way as a man might grasp a hedgehog between two large brushes.

Some assassin-bugs pursue their prey in a series of jerky runs, while others simply lie in wait for their victim, pouncing when it comes near enough. Others have evolved elaborate methods of enticing prey into their reach. A few species, for example, plunge their forelegs into the sticky resin exuded from pine trees and then hold them up to form alluring traps for other insects. A West Indian assassin-bug secretes fluid from its undersides which ants find very attractive. It intoxicates them so they fall easy victims to the bug.

Various assassin-bugs look very much like the insects on which they feed, so they can approach and seize their prey more easily. Some British species look like the gnats and midges that they feed on. They will also take bark-lice, attacking them through their protective web of silk. It is this that probably leads them to stealing insects shrouded in silk on spiders' webs.

Among other small creatures commonly eaten by different species of assassin-bugs are book-lice, gall-forming aphides, silverfish, flies, bed-bugs and harvestmen. These are all small insects harmful in some way to man. The huge African assassin-bug *Platymeris rhadamanthus,* is also a predator of the large rhinoceros beetle, a pest of coconut plantations, attacking this heavily armoured titan at its weak points by thrusting its beak through the joints between legs and body.

Like all carnivorous bugs, assassin-bugs feed by external digestion. They push their rostrum into the victim's body and inject into it a highly toxic fluid which acts especially on the nerves and muscles and then breaks down the body tissues. In most other bugs there is one channel in the rostrum for discharging the toxic saliva and another alongside it for sucking up the liquefied food, but assassin-bugs have one large tube that serves both purposes. With this larger tube a very large amount of digestive fluid can be rapidly injected into the victim's body, so prey many times the size of the assassin-bug can be quickly overcome.

The effects of the saliva are almost immediate. The amount injected probably varies according to the size of the victim, but a cockroach has been seen to die in 3 to 5 seconds, while the caterpillar of a moth, over 400 times the bug's weight, died in 10 seconds. When its prey is this size, the assassin-bug may live off it for days or even weeks, ignoring all passing prey. After such a feast, the bug may double its body weight.

Not all assassin-bugs feed on other insects or invertebrates. The tropical Triatominae attack mammals, birds and reptiles and suck their blood. One species is a nuisance at night, coming into bedrooms and attacking the occupants, while another's stab is said to feel like an electric shock.

## Life history

The commonest British assassin-bug, *Coranus subapterus,* mates in the autumn. The eggs, which are dark brown in colour with a paler cap, are laid in crevices, amongst leaf litter and moss, and hatch the following April or May. The larvae, which apart from size differ little from their parents, are carnivorous from the start. They moult several times during the two months before they mature.

*Reduvius personatus* mates several times and egg-laying begins about a week after the first copulation. The female lays 3 to 5 eggs daily, the final total being usually between 50 and 150, laid between mid-June and September. The eggs hatch in about 20 days and the larvae immediately camouflage themselves against predators by assuming a covering of dust, repeating this procedure after each moult.

## Assassin but not safe

While able to inflict sudden death on others, assassin-bugs are themselves preyed on by many enemies, especially birds and reptiles.

Many species, however, have a device which is often successful in repelling predators. The large, 1½ in. long *Platymeris,* for example, can use its paralysing venom as a liquid projectile, squirting a jet through its rostrum up to a distance of 1 ft with extreme accuracy. By rotating its head and depressing the curved rostrum slightly, it is even able to spit accurately over its 'shoulder' into a space above and behind it. Since as many as 15 jets can be fired successively, this can be a most effective deterrent. Certainly the effect of the saliva on humans is often extremely severe, as research workers studying these insects in laboratories have found. It can cause temporary blindness if received in the eye as well as severe irritation of the sensitive membranes in the nose.

## Darwin's illness

It is said that the hall-mark of the true naturalist is that he or she should have a lively interest in, and affection for, all forms of life, however repulsive. If we accept this principle, then even the great Charles Darwin does not quite measure up to our highest ideals. In his *Journal of a Naturalist,* Darwin tells of the disgust he felt at being afflicted by South American assassin-bugs as they crawled over his body at night. Yet perhaps we should forgive his uncharitable thoughts for he had good reason for feeling repulsion, for it is one of these bugs, *Triatoma megista,* which transmits Chagas's Disease.

In later years Darwin suffered from a strange, incurable illness which was never diagnosed. The symptoms make it seem likely that his illness stemmed from his encounter with the assassin-bugs, which are known to carry trypanosomes, minute protistans that cause disease. Trypanosomes are the agents that are carried by tsetse-flies that cause sleeping sickness when injected into the bloodstream by the latter's bites.

| class | **Insecta** |
|---|---|
| order | **Hemiptera** |
| sub-order | **Heteroptera** |
| family | **Reduviidae** |

*(1) Assassin-bug* **Prithesancus brawni.** *The long powerful jack-knife forelimbs are used for grasping prey.*

*(2) Close up of the head of* **Sirthena carinata.** *The powerful, curved rostrum, or beak, is used to pierce the prey and discharge toxic saliva and then suck up the liquefied body tissue. When not in use the rostrum is tucked away under the head. This close up also shows clearly the compound eye with its many facets, typical of insects.*

*(3) Most bugs have two pairs of wings, but some species are often wingless as seen here in* **Fitchia aptera,** *photographed at Lakehurst, New Jersey.*

*Atlas moth eggs 7½ × natural size*

*Newly emerged larva × 12.*

*Cocoon dissected to show pupa × ¾.*

# Atlas moth

*Probably the most famous of the large moths, the atlas moth belongs to the family Saturniidae which includes the British emperor moth, the North American cecropia moth and the tussah, or tussore, silk-moths of southern Asia, all of which produce a large silk cocoon, several having been used commercially.*

*The female is larger, heavier and more massive than the male, and her 'hooked' fore-wings may span ten inches. The general colour of body and wings is tawny but with a beautiful pattern, and there is a conspicuous triangular, transparent spot on each wing.*

## Habits and life-history

The atlas moth is found in the tropics and subtropics, from India, including the Himalayas, eastwards to Malaysia and Indonesia. The spherical eggs, about 2½ mm in diameter, are laid in clusters on a wide variety of tropical shrubs, including cinnamon and hibiscus. The larvae (caterpillars) are at first white but later turn a pale bluish-green. The body is ornamented with rows of spines and is covered with a white, waxy powder. Two, sometimes three months after the eggs are laid, the caterpillar, which is now 4−4½ in. long and over 1 in. in diameter, spins around itself a tough, papery cocoon of silk in which it pupates. This cocoon is attached to the foliage of the food-plant. It has no opening and the moth gets out in the same way as other cocoon-spinning insects, by secreting a liquid from the mouth parts which dissolves the silk and enables the moth to push its way out.

This moth can be kept in captivity in temperate latitudes, feeding readily on privet, willow or rhododendron, but a temperature of 21−26°C/70−80°F needs to be provided.

## The largest in the world

Atlas, in Greek mythology, was one of the Titans, therefore a giant. The atlas moth is sometimes named as the biggest moth in the world, but in New Guinea and Australia lives the hercules moth−named after another giant of mythology. Its wings are less than 10 in. across but broad and ample, giving a total surface area of about 40 square inches, probably making it, by a short head, the largest of all moths. Another candidate for the title is the great owlet moth of South America, which has the widest span, its long, narrow wings measuring up to 10in., but it is less heavily built than the other two.

At the other end of the scale is the midget spotkin, a leaf-boring moth, which is just over 1/12 in. across.

Some of the smallest insects of all are beetles known as feather-winged beetles (family Trichopterygidae) living in tropical America and Australia. The smallest of these is ¼ mm long. There is, however, a family of parasitic wasps (family Mymaridae) known as fairy flies, that lay their eggs in the eggs of other insects. The smallest of these is the smallest known insect and is only 0·21 mm long. This means that there are some insects that are smaller than the largest single-celled animals (the Protozoa) and are truly microscopic. By contrast the largest known insects are larger than the smallest vertebrates. The Luzon goby, a fish found in the Philippines, is less than ½ in. long when fully grown, so is much smaller than many insects.

| class | **Insecta** |
|---|---|
| order | **Lepidoptera** |
| family | **Saturniidae** |
| genus & species | ***Attacus atlas*** |

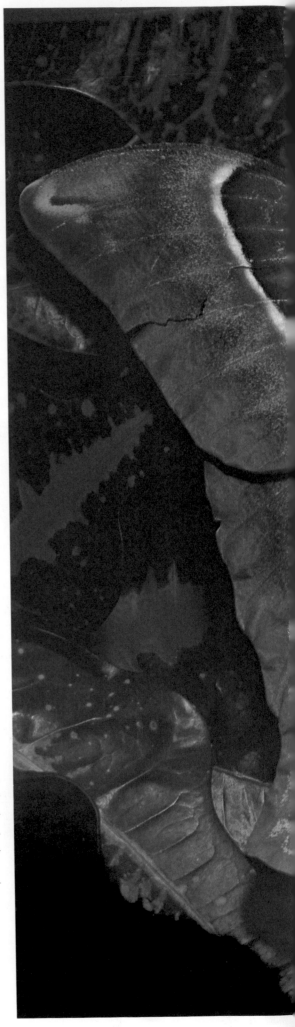

*Hercules moth **Coscinoscera hercules** has one of the largest wing areas of any insect. Although the wings do not reach the 10 in. width of the atlas moth, they are broad and ample, giving a total area of about 40 sq. in.*

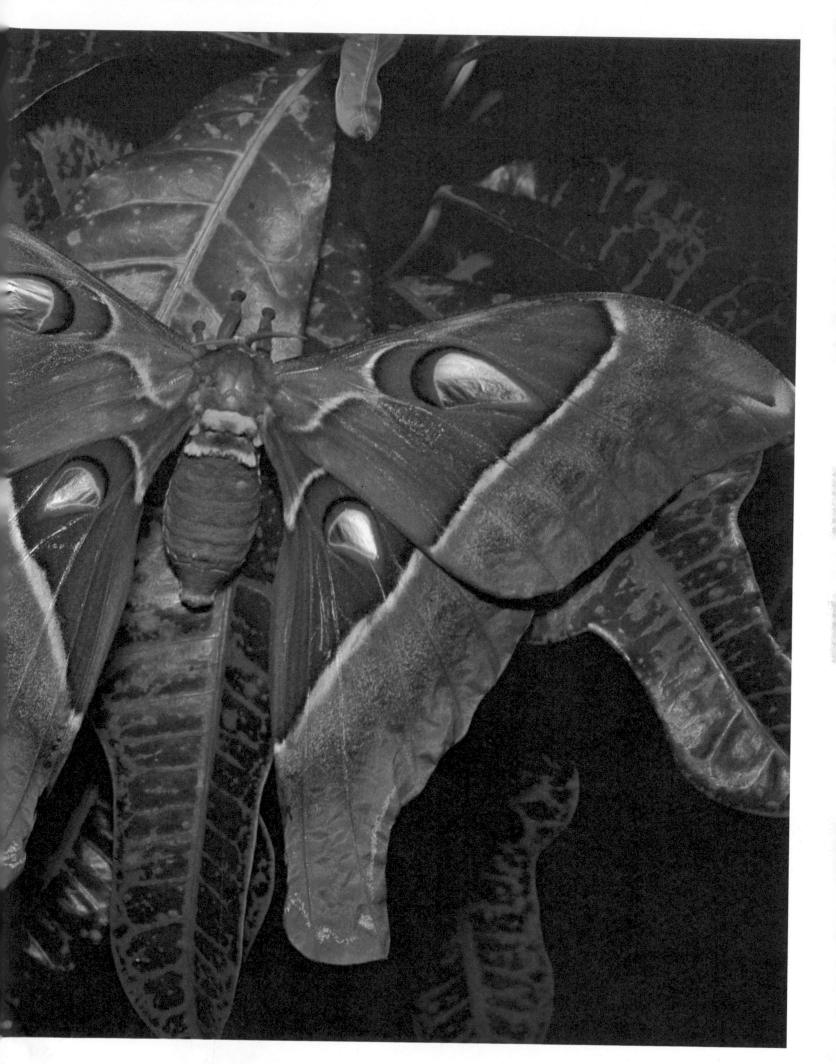

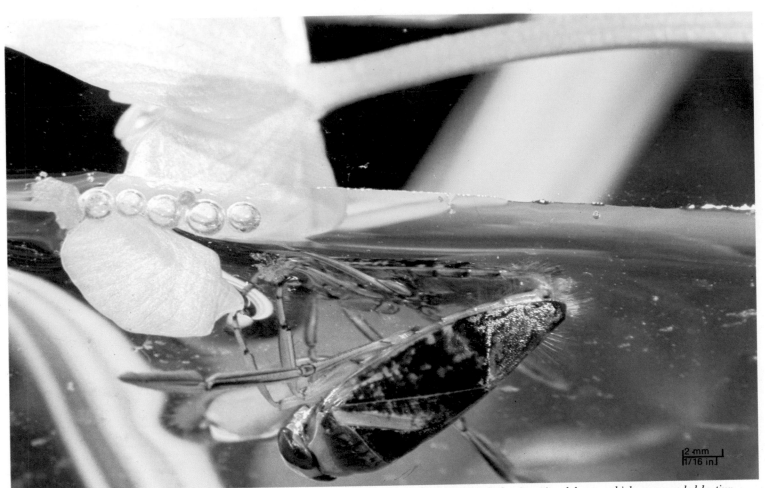

*Backswimmer or water boatman hanging upside down from water surface by two pairs of legs and the tip of its abdomen which, surrounded by tiny hairs, is trapping a bubble of air for its next dive. The third pair of legs form the backswimmer's 'oars'. The yellow flower is a kingcup.*

# Backswimmer

*A group of large-eyed aquatic bugs living in ponds, lakes and canals, including the backswimmers, boat-flies, water boatmen, or wherry-men, with a world-wide distribution. One of the commonest species is **Notonecta undulata**, which is found in sluggish water. It is about ½ in. long and brownish in colour. Backswimmers are especially conspicuous for their long, paddle-like hind legs and their characteristic habit of resting upside down beneath the surface of the water.*

## Bubble of air

The colloquial name 'backswimmer' is particularly appropriate for this insect because it does actually swim upside down. Its very long hind legs—almost twice the length of the other two pairs—are fringed by a series of fine hairs, and with a few strokes of these oar-like legs the backswimmer can propel itself through the water at a remarkably fast rate. The hind legs are, in fact, used in unison, like oars, quite unlike the tripodal method of progression used by terrestrial insects. The wing-cases of the backswimmer join to form a ridge along the middle of the back, and when the insect is seen resting just beneath the surface with its long hind legs held out sideways the impression is of a keeled rowing boat with a pair of oars over the sides.

Backswimmers are extremely wary and at the slightest hint of danger will swim down from the top of the water. This needs great physical effort because the insect is very much lighter than water and would be continually and involuntarily rising to the surface, but for a powerful swimming action or a firm grip on some submerged object. This buoyancy is largely due to a bubble of air which the backswimmer always carries pressed to its abdomen by a series of bristles.

Although it is fully aquatic, a backswimmer does not have gills and is unable to use the oxygen dissolved in the water. It must therefore get its air supply from outside, and this it does by rising periodically to the surface and sticking the tip of its abdomen out of the water. There is a channel formed by hairs on each side of the abdomen. These the insect opens at the surface, allowing air to flow in and then closes them again, trapping the air. These air-bubbles are therefore in direct contact with the backswimmer's spiracles or breathing holes which are arranged along the sides of the abdomen. The spiracles are protected by a further fringe of hairs which allows air in and keeps water out.

Although adapted to life in the water, and scarcely able to walk on land, backswimmers are strong fliers and can leave their natural element at any time; they are in consequence among the earliest colonisers of that fairly new feature, the water-filled gravel pit. During the Second World War emergency water tanks were set up everywhere, for use against fire from air-raids, and it was not uncommon to find back-swimmers suddenly appearing in a tank, far from the nearest pond or river, surrounded by tall buildings. They would appear overnight, because they fly mostly at night, and are attracted to light, reflected from the water surface.

## Voracious feeders

Backswimmers are extremely voracious feeders and it is always unwise to include them with other small forms of life in any aquarium. Mosquito and other fly larvae form a large part of their diet, but size alone does not always deter them. Large beetle larvae, tadpoles and even small fish are often attacked. The backswimmer's method of hunting is to hang motionless at the surface of the water, immediately swimming towards anything that catches its attention. It has excellent eyesight, but primarily it discovers its prey by a form of vibration-location: certain hairs on the hind legs can pick up the vibrations caused by small animals swimming nearby. Only when the backswimmer is within a few inches of its prey do the eyes play their part in securing its capture. Having captured its prey, the backswimmer then plunges its sharp rostrum (or beak) into the body of the victim, pumping in a toxic digestive fluid containing enzymes which rapidly break down the body tissues.

The carcase is then held very firmly by the prehensile fore-limbs while its internal tissues, now made fluid, are sucked out. The rostrum of the backswimmer can pierce human skin, and the toxic fluid pumped in may cause extremely painful symptoms. Fortunately, this only happens when the backswimmer is handled, and then only if handled carelessly, although the insect appears to be not over-particular what it attacks. In the days when cattle and horses drank far more commonly from village ponds, it was not unusual for backswimmers to attack their tender muzzles.

## Life cycle

Mating in *Notonecta* usually occurs between about December in one year and late spring of the next. Batches of the elongated oval eggs are inserted into the stems of aquatic plants, such as Canadian pondweed, by the female's ovipositor. The eggs hatch after several weeks, the larvae, which are at first wingless, escaping by means of the hole originally made by the female's ovipositor. By late summer, these have become young adults and the older generation dies off. Only one generation is produced each year. Like all bugs, backswimmers undergo incomplete metamorphosis. That is, from the egg hatches a larva, which resembles the adult in form. Growth then proceeds by a series of moults.

## Enemies

As a water insect, the backswimmer falls prey to the carnivorous animals present around its habitat. These include waterfowl, frogs, toads, and sometimes fish, such as trout or bass.

## Seeing wrong way up

When we are standing or walking on firm ground we know we are the right way up partly because of our appreciation of the pull of gravity but also partly through our eyes. A passenger strapped in an aeroplane and unable to look out can be flying upside down and will be unaware of it. Anyone swimming underwater and caught in a strong turbulence can, if the water is murky, lose completely any sense of which way up he may be.

A simple experiment that can be carried out on a backswimmer shows that their large compound eyes and well-developed sight play an important part in their orientation. Normally this insect rests just beneath the surface of the water, upside down. In a glass aquarium, with the top of the aquarium in darkness and a bright light shining from below the backswimmer will take up its position on the surface of the water with its lower surface directed down towards the light, so when we look at it from above it is in the position in which any other insect would be that was resting on the surface film. The backswimmer will try to live and swim in this position as long as light is maintained from below. This reaction to light is present in backswimmers even from a very early stage in their larval life.

| class | **Insecta** |
|-------|-------------|
| order | **Hemiptera** |
| suborder | **Heteroptera** |
| families | **Notonectidae, Pleidae** |
| genera | ***Notonecta, Anisops, Plea*** |

△ *The young backswimmer is a nymph which gradually develops into an adult without the larva and pupa stages of higher insects.*

▽ *Adult backswimmer and young with mosquito pupae cleverly photographed from below to show their reflections in the surface.*

# Bagworm

*The larvae of these moths make portable cases in which they live. They include the family **Psychidae**, one of several groups known collectively as bagworms, which have evolved this habit. The cases seem to act as a protection against predators, often being well camouflaged. The caterpillars of each species make a very distinctive case.*

*The adult females of the more advanced types are degenerate creatures with vestigial mouthparts and legs, while the males are active fliers with well-developed, feathery antennae. Their wings have a thin covering of hairs and very few of the scales that normally give moths' wings their rough appearance. There are rarely any markings on the body.*

*The bagworm moths are widely distributed. The exact number of species in the world is not known; 74 species were listed recently for the New World, while probably double this number are known from Europe and Asia.*

*Bagworm feeding. Only the head sticks out of bag which is temporarily attached to twig below leaf.*

## Life history

As soon as it hatches, before even eating, a bagworm caterpillar starts to make its case, or bag. Once made, it crawls in never to emerge until it changes into an adult moth. The cases are fashioned out of silk, usually with plant material, twigs, leaves and fibres cemented on to the matrix. In primitive species the case is flat but more specialised species produce cases in a variety of forms, usually tapering to a point at either end. The size of the cases ranges from ¼ in. to the 6 in. capsules made by some tropical species. There may be such a thick layer of leaves and twigs cemented onto the case that it looks like a heap of debris. As these materials will have been collected from around the larva the case will be camouflaged, blending in with the background. On the other hand, some species spin plain silk cases; *Psyche helix* of Europe having one shaped very much like snail shells.

Once in its case the caterpillar can begin feeding. While eating, its head and thorax stick out from the case, but it retreats inside to rest after securing the case to a solid object by silken threads. The rear end is left open for the disposal of its excretory products. As the caterpillar grows it merely adds more material to the front of the case, increasing both its length and diameter.

Like all caterpillars, the bagworms feed voraciously on the leaves of the particular plant which their species use as food, so much so that many bagworms are pests of fruit trees, such as oranges. Trees infested by them have their foliage left in a very ragged state, and when stripped bare, usually die, so it is vital to watch for the appearance of bagworms. It is sometimes possible to check any infection by picking off the bagworm cases by hand while their numbers are still low. Otherwise the trees must be sprayed with insecticides.

Having eaten their fill, the bagworms pupate inside their cases, first securing the case firmly to a leaf or twig.

In the pupa stage, the bagworm's body is completely reorganised, as is any caterpillar in its transformation into butterfly or moth. The bagworm's programme of change, however, depends on its sex. Males turn into adult moths that are strong fliers, but are short-lived, with incompletely developed mouthparts so they cannot feed.

Females, on the other hand, may turn out as very different creatures. In some primitive species they are very like the males, but during the course of evolution the female bagworm has become degenerate. Like the male, her mouthparts are useless and she has to subsist on food stored up when she was a caterpillar. Her legs and wings are also reduced, and sometimes completely missing. She is little more than an egg-laying machine. The females of some species can crawl out of the pupal case, and then out of the silk and fibre bagworm case. Here they wait for males to find them, probably guided by scent emitted by the females. After fertilisation, the females return to their cases, lay their eggs and die.

Females of other species cannot manage even to crawl out of the case. The common bagworm of North America stays inside her pupal shell, inside the case. The male has to mate with her through the open end. Then she dies with the eggs still within her body. When the caterpillars hatch they make their way through her body, the pupal shell and the case, and immediately set about making their own cases.

The life-history of this species shows a complete differentiation of function between the caterpillar and the female adult. The caterpillar does little more than feed and the adult is only a receptacle where the eggs can be fertilised and develop. But the function of the adults is sometimes still further reduced. In some species, the eggs will develop and hatch into caterpillars even when no male has appeared to fertilise them. This is a process known as parthenogenesis, or virgin-birth.

## Spreading the species

Summarising the life-cycle of a bagworm, the caterpillar makes its case and feeds until it is time to pupate. After an interval, the adult emerges. If female, she is fertilised, the eggs duly hatch, and the cycle starts again as the caterpillars make their cases, within a very short distance of where their mother made hers. The question that immediately arises is, how do they spread? If they do not, then all the foliage will be eaten and all the bagworms will die.

This problem is not confined to bagworms. There are many species of animal whose powers of movement are very limited, yet they are able to spread, sometimes enormous distances. This is usually done by some other agent carrying them. Water animals may get carried in mud on the feet of birds or mammals, and many small animals are carried by the wind, being swept up very high to be blown across oceans to other continents. Bagworms are spread in at least two ways. Their eggs are very hard-shelled and when a bird eats the contents of a case containing the body of a female and her eggs, the latter are passed through the bird's gut unharmed, to be dropped, perhaps miles away.

The wattle bagworm of Africa is carried in the caterpillar stage. The newly-hatched caterpillar spins a silk thread, climbs down it and stays there a few days. While hanging there it may be swept up by the wind or a passing bird and taken to another tree. These methods of spreading are obviously haphazard but quite effective.

| class | **Insecta** |
|---|---|
| order | **Lepidoptera** |
| family | **Psychidae** |
| genus & species | ***Psyche helix*** *and others* |

# Bark beetle

*Popular and often fanciful names for the various groups of bark beetles include engravers, shothole-borers, pinhole-borers, typographers and ambrosia beetles, depending on the individual habits and characteristics of the beetle in question.*

*Many countryside ramblers, naturalists and particularly foresters are familiar with the damage caused by these small beetles. Indeed, the insects themselves are less familiar than their characteristic branching tunnels seen either on the underside of tree bark which has peeled away, or on the surface of the wood proper. These are caused mainly by the feeding larvae. More than 2 000 species of bark beetle are found throughout the world and these have often been spread by the importation of foreign timbers. They are usually sombrely coloured, rarely more than $\frac{1}{4}$ in. long, and often elongated and cylindrical in shape, as befits an insect which spends most of its life either in, or making, narrow tunnels.*

### Tunnelling pests

Most bark beetles, both as larvae and adults, feed on the bark or wood of trees. Usually they make the tunnels in the bark itself, but quite often the tunnel is through the meeting layers of bark and wood. Bark beetles can be a nuisance in forests, particularly pine forests, as the attacks by the beetle allow disease-causing fungi to get in. In many instances it is an already dead or dying tree that is attacked, and some species attack only seasoned wood.

The Dutch elm disease, which has done so much damage to trees in North America and Western Europe, is a fungal disease that has been spread by a bark beetle.

To a large extent each group of bark beetles forms its own distinctive type of gallery patterning, so that in many cases it is possible to identify genera, or even species, solely from the tunnel appearance.

### Sap, sugar and fungi feeders

While most bark beetles feed on the starches, sugars and other substances in the bark and sapwood, the family Scolytidae, the ambrosia beetles, seem dependent on certain fungi which are always present in their galleries. Generally one species of fungus is associated with one species of beetle, and related species of fungi are carried by related species of beetle which suggests that the two have evolved together. The spores of a fungus are dispersed from tree to tree by being passed with the excreta, regurgitated from the female's crop or, in some species, by sticking to tufts of bristles on the female's head. In a few, the spores become lodged in a fatty secretion in pores on the front part of the beetle's body. The fungus, which is recognisable as a dark stain, has to be eaten regularly otherwise it would block the galleries, so killing the colony. In most cases, little provision is made for removing the excrement, mostly undigested wood, and this is left behind as the beetle progresses through the bark, although occasionally

*Bark beetle,* **Scolytus rugulosus,** *quite common in Britain, is found on fruit trees* ($\times 6$).

exit holes are made for ejecting material. This 'sawdust' may sometimes be seen on the ground below trees and is a sure sign of active infestation by beetles. Some bark beetles, such as the pine shoot beetle, *Blastophagus piniperda,* can be a very serious forestry problem.

### Well-adapted predators

Many birds, especially woodpeckers, nuthatches and tree-creepers, feed on bark beetles in all their stages. All have beaks which are specially adapted for getting at the beetles, either in or under the bark. An important predator, both in adult and larval form, of those bark beetles which attack pine trees, is the ant-beetle, *Thanasimus formicarius,* which feeds upon adults, pupae and larvae. Other predatory beetle larvae of the family Nitidulidae kill many bark beetles, as do various parasitic wasps which lay their eggs in bark beetle larvae.

### Flower or star patterns

In a typical species of bark beetle such as *Scolytus destructor* which attacks both trunk and branches of elms, the female first of all makes a tunnel into the bark as far as the surface of the sapwood. Here the male makes a nuptial chamber where pairing takes place. The female then goes on to make a vertical tunnel in the bark, at regular intervals placing shiny, white, oval or round eggs along its sides, protecting them with wood fragments. When the whitish, legless larvae emerge they immediately begin feeding on the wood or bark by chewing at right angles to the tunnel made by the female parent, somehow managing not to bore into each other's tunnels. As the larva grows, passing through five instars or skin changes, the tunnels naturally become larger until finally it stops feeding, makes itself an enlarged chamber just below the surface and there changes into a pupa. On emergence, the young adult bark beetle has only to cut a little of the bark above it to escape into the open and the outer surface of the tree, where it then begins to seek out a mate. Although many species of bark beetle are like *Scolytus* in creating vertical tunnels from which the larvae excavate passages at right angles, others do so in the opposite plane. Some species are bigamous or even polygamous, one male mating with several females—in *Xyleborus* sometimes more than 50. Each of the females cuts a separate tunnel radiating from the central nuptial chamber and the larvae diverge from these, the overall effect being a star or flower pattern.

### Scent signals

The means by which bark beetles find their way into a particular tree have been investigated in recent years. It differs from one type of bark beetle to another. In *Dendroctonus* species they are drawn to a tree by odours given out from the first female to bore into the tree. The attractant odour is due to a chemical in the excreta produced by the female combined with a chemical from the tree itself. The two must be combined, each having no effect on its own.

In *Ips* species, which are polygamous, the male acts as 'pathfinder'. He somehow selects a tree, and he has an attractant in his excreta. In this case the male's odour is sufficient to cause numbers of beetles of his own kind to settle on the tree.

What attracts the first beetle to a tree must largely be surmised. We have a clue, however, in the experience of foresters in North

*The mother beetle makes the central tunnel and lays her eggs along the sides. When they hatch the grubs burrow outwards—as shown here—forming characteristic patterns.*

America, where large areas of spruces and pines are often destroyed by bark beetles. A cut in the bark, even a small 'blaze' made to mark a trail, is sufficient to attract the beetles and bring about the death of a tree.

The process is self-regulatory in that in spite of the attractant, each group of larvae manages to make use of one part of the tree without overlapping the territories of other groups. Although full details are not yet known there are already some pointers. For example, the attractant generated by *Dendroctonus* ceases as feeding gains momentum. Again, there are differences in the amount of attractant given out, depending on the size of the tree and the condition of the wood, and varying with the various groups of beetles. Enough is known, however, to indicate that the odours form the basis of an efficient signalling code.

| phylum | **Arthropoda** |
|---|---|
| class | **Insecta** |
| order | **Coleoptera** |
| families | **Scolytidae, Platypodidae** |
| genera | *Scolytus, Ips, Xyleborus, Platypus, Dendroctonus* |

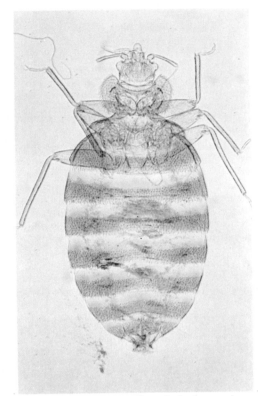

*Bed-bug, famous for its all-too-intimate association with man, whose blood it sucks. ×15.*

# Bed-bug

*Best known because of their all-too-intimate associations with man, bed-bugs are small, oval, flattish insects which pierce the skin of mammals and birds, with powerful needle-like mouth-parts, and suck up their blood for food. The commonest species in temperate and sub-tropical regions is* **Cimex lectularius,** *found in domestic houses. It is about $\frac{1}{5}$ in. long by $\frac{1}{8}$ in. broad and paper thin when starved of blood. The colour varies from rich dark brown to deep purple or red, notably after a meal, when its body becomes greatly distended with blood. The bed-bug's head is short and broad, the eyes large and conspicuous and the antennae have four joints. The whole of the body is covered with very fine short hairs. There are no wings, but a pair of flaps on the thorax represent the atrophied and useless remains of forewings. The most widespread tropical species is* **Cimex hemipterus.**

## Secret biters

Being so tiny, bed-bugs are much more often felt than seen. They come out at night and seek out their victims in the early hours of the morning, a singularly unpleasant time to be disturbed by anything, least of all bedbugs. During the day, the bugs hide away in any suitable crevice: under loose wallpaper, in the joints or cracks of walls or ceilings, in wooden furniture, in bedding and mattresses. Heavily infested houses have a characteristic odour.

Bed-bugs do not, however, confine their unwelcome attentions solely to man, although he is probably the more usual and preferred victim. Mice, rats, rabbits, poultry and other birds are often attacked. Other species of bed-bug are more selective in their choice of host. *Oeciacus hirundinis,* for example, is found only in the nests of house martins and occasionally swallows, while *Cimex pipistrelli* occurs in bat roosts. It is interesting that many, if not all, of the animals infested by bed-bugs either are or were cave dwellers, and it seems likely that man first became associated with the insects when living in such caves.

Although flightless, bed-bugs can run extremely fast, particularly in warm weather; indeed, the higher the temperature the more active the insects are, and the more troublesome they are likely to be. The bedbug can respond to even the slightest changes of temperature which it probably detects with special hairs on the antennae. It will immediately move towards any object an inch or so away from it—whether suitable host or not—if its temperature is only 1C° above that of the surrounding air. This is how it is guided towards a host. How bedbugs find their way to a host over longer distances is not entirely clear, though probably they can detect a victim's odour.

## Blood suckers

All bed-bugs feed on the blood of mammals and birds. Their mouth-parts, adapted for piercing the skin of the host, have two pairs of stylets contained in an outer protective sheath. The outer pair of stylets, which correspond to the mandibles or jaws in other kinds of insects, are barbed for piercing and sawing. The inner pair form two tubes, one of which injects saliva containing a substance that prevents the coagulation of blood, while the other, and larger, sucks up the mixture of blood and saliva. At rest, the whole of the piercing apparatus, or rostrum, is tucked away beneath the bug's head, flush with its body. When in use it is thrust forward or down, the outer protective sheath, or labium, bending and sliding up to allow the stylets to do their work. The blood is drawn up into the food-pipe and stomach by a powerful pump operated by muscles connected with the pharynx.

Bed-bugs do not always begin to feed as soon as they have discovered a suitable victim; they may test the surface of the skin repeatedly until they find a good spot. The meal may take 5 minutes, often rather longer. When full, the bug withdraws its stylets, the sheath straightening out to enclose and protect them once more. Then the insect leaves its host and runs away quickly to find a place to rest and digest its meal. Since the skin is partly transparent, a red colour clearly indicates its gorged state. Sometimes, when the food is nearly all digested, the remains of the last meal can be seen as a dark area at the tip of the abdomen.

The domestic bed-bug usually feeds most just before dawn if the temperature is above 13°C/55°F. If it is cooler than this then all activity ceases, the bugs relapse into torpidity and may eventually die if there is no subsequent rise in temperature. In certain animal houses it was found, by using special traps, that bed-bugs fed on average once every 5 or 6 days when the temperature was between 20°−27°C/68°−80°F and that they were most active between 3 and 6 a.m.

## Bizarre breeding

Mating and fertilisation in bed-bugs is so involved, difficult and bizarre that it seems almost as if nature were on man's side in trying to render the creature extinct.

On the right side of the lower surface of the female's body is a pocket-like structure known as Ribaga's organ, and it is in this that the male places his spermatozoa. This has no connection with the oviducts or ovaries. The sperms pass between the cells lining Ribaga's organ, then enter the body cavity and travel up the walls of the female's reproductive tract before finally reaching the ovaries. This is difficult enough, but it seems that Ribaga's organ and the female's body cavity contain certain cells that *eat* sperm, so that only a small proportion survive to fertilise the ovaries.

Mating and egg-laying may occur at any time of the year, so long as the temperature is high enough and the female has been able to feed. The eggs are laid on their sides in the adults' hiding places. They are very small, about 1 mm long, pearly white in colour and covered with minute spines. Just as they are being laid a kind of quick-drying mucilage, or cement, is exuded so the egg sticks to the surface on which it is placed. Each egg is curved and slightly narrowed at one end. This forms a lid which the larva pushes off when emerging. An average female lays about 150 eggs, producing about three a day, although from 12−15 a day have occasionally been recorded from large well-fed females. The time taken for the larvae to emerge depends on both the temperature and on how recently the female had fed when she laid the eggs. It can be from 1−6 weeks at average room temperature (14°C/57°F). The same factors also influence the growth of the larvae, which cannot moult until they have had a feed of blood.

Many of the eggs and larvae die if the temperature falls below about 13°C/55°F for any length of time, although the adults are more resistant to cold. As with all bugs, there is no pupal or final development stage, only a series of nymphs or larvae. The larvae differ from adults in being less round in shape with a much broader head and shorter and thicker antennae. The skin is cast five times, after each of which the larva gets a little more like an adult.

## Enemies

Being so tiny, and living so secretly, bedbugs probably have few large predators, although a number of insects and other invertebrates commonly kill and eat them. The little pharaoh's ant *Monomorium pharaonis,* a common inhabitant of kitchens, is one enemy. The assassin-bug (see page 18), *Reduvius personatus,* turns the tables on the bud-bug by sucking out blood which had previously been collected for the bed-bug's own use. Some spiders prey on bed-bugs, and another predator is the false scorpion, *Chelifer cancroides.*

| class | **Insecta** |
|---|---|
| order | **Hemiptera** |
| family | **Cimicidae** |
| genus | *Cimex* |

△ Male birdwing, **Ornithoptera priamus,** *feeding. Only the male birdwings have the attractive iridescent markings on their wings. The unfortunate females have to make do with less spectacular markings.*

# Birdwing

*Imagine a butterfly with a wingspan that is sometimes more than 10 in. and you have some idea of the size of the birdwing butterfly. This amazing wingspan of some of the genera was what provoked naturalists to dub them 'Ornithoptera' (bird-winged). The males are somewhat smaller than the females. Their wings are large and velvety and usually of a black or purplish shade. These wings are made even more attractive by their beautiful iridescent markings in blue, green, pink, orange or gold. That is the male. The unfortunate female has to make do with less spectacular markings. Her wings are speckled with a uniform white instead of the fluctuating colour ranges that make the male so irresistible.*

*The birdwing's width and size comes from its long, graceful forewings. The hindwings, by comparison, are small. One characteristic of the swallowtail family, to which they belong, is the long tail on each of the hindwings. These tails can only be seen in the birdwings on the tailed birdwing* **Ornithoptera paradisea** *and on one or two others. Butterfly collectors named several birdwings after*

*their current heroes. One was named after Queen Victoria: Queen Victoria's birdwing* **Ornithoptera victoriae;** *and one of the White Rajahs in Sarawak, Rajah Brooke, had the pleasure of seeing his name immortalised in butterfly-collecting circles by having perhaps the most beautiful of all the birdwings,* **Troides brookiana,** *called after him. Birdwings live in open woodland or forest, from southern India and Sri Lanka across to northern Australia, New Guinea and the Solomon Islands.*

### Birdwings fool the entomologists

Very little is known about some of the species. It is only recently, for example, that the life cycle of Rajah Brooke's birdwing has been described. No one has ever succeeded in finding its caterpillars in the wild, but an entomologist in Sumatra has finally succeeded in breeding them in captivity.

For a long time, entomologists listed, as one of the unusual features of Rajah Brooke's birdwing, the fact that the female was rarely seen. They even put the ratio of males to females at as much as 1 000 : 1. They based their statistics on data they got from collections made at places where the birdwings congregate, such as river banks or seepages and other damp places.

Then it dawned upon somebody that the reason they were getting these extraordinary figures was because it was only the males of the species who congregated at these spots. This explained the unusual figure of 1 000 : 1, which was quite unlike the statistics they had obtained on other species, showing the males and the females to be almost 50 : 50. Enquiries in other sources revealed, as a matter of fact, that females of the common birdwing *Troides helena* are somewhat more numerous than the males.

Birdwings live in the trees, especially in the canopy of foliage at the tops of the taller trees. When the entomologists realised this they had the answer to the mystery of the 'elusive butterfly'. They were not rare at all.

It was just that the female of Rajah Brooke's birdwing and both sexes of other species did not come down to seepages and damp places and remained totally unattracted by the bait, such as carrion, which was put out for them. This made collecting them rather tricky. The collectors found that they had to resort to shooting the birdwings with 'dust shot' as if they were birds. However, when birdwings do fly low they are easy to catch because their flight is slow, direct and unsuspecting. It makes a welcome change for the collector who is constantly being frustrated by the bouncing, weaving flight of many other butterflies.

*Above : Rajah Brooke's birdwing. It was thought that the males outnumbered the females by 1000 : 1, as only the males were usually seen. Females were then found in the treetops, making numbers equal (life size). Right : Wonderful action shot of birdwing, **Troides rhadamantus**, alighting on a flowerhead. Its long thin feeding tube, the proboscis, is already extended so it can suck the flower's nectar.*

## What they eat

Birdwing caterpillars feed on plants of the Aristolochiaceae family and on betel leaves. The adults feed on flowers. Some of the closely related swallowtail butterflies also feed on plants of the same family. These are known to be distasteful because of a chemical in the plant but it is not known whether the birdwings are also distasteful to their predators.

## Life cycle of a birdwing

The eggs of the common birdwing are laid singly on the upper sides of leaves. From the eggs hatch caterpillars bearing six rows of fleshy tubercles which run the whole length of the body. The caterpillars also have a curious Y-shaped organ, called an osmeterium, on the head. This is connected with glands in the body. When a caterpillar is alarmed the osmeterium is worked in and out, exuding an unpleasant smell.

After the caterpillars have fed for a month, they turn into chrysalises on the vertical stem of the plant where they have been living. The chrysalis has the typical form of the swallowtail family. The lower end is anchored to the plant stem by a silken pad. The body and upper end is supported by a silk thread which passes around the stem of the plant, in very much the same way that a lumberjack is secured to a tree with a safety-belt. After

three weeks the adult butterfly emerges from the pupa.

## The cost of rarity and beauty

Lots of people collect butterflies, from schoolboys with their little collections of the more common kind to professional entomologists with neat rows of specimens in glass-topped boxes marked 'Do Not Touch'. It is a hobby that can be taken to great lengths, like anything else. We are now all familiar with those tense scenes in auction rooms when paintings or postage stamps fall under the hammer for thousands, or even hundreds of thousands, of pounds. Many a non-collector has found it hard to understand why a painting suddenly becomes so amazingly valuable after being ignored by everyone for years and years.

How does one put a price on a painting or a stamp, which intrinsically is only worth the price of the materials it is made of? Two of the main criteria must obviously be its rarity or its beauty. Add to these the fanaticism of some buyers and the tension and competition in an auction room and you have some of the reasons why people pay such inflated prices.

Butterflies are just like paintings and stamps. Serious collectors have always been willing to pay for unusual specimens that they have been unable to catch themselves and the price is arrived at through a com-

bination of beauty and rarity. If a butterfly is spectacularly beautiful and rare it can be valuable. By contrast, a small, dull one, even if it is very rare, is usually not worth much. There has always been a trade in butterflies and they are even bred especially for the purpose. Not surprisingly birdwings have always been in demand. Many 'part-time collectors' supply them from New Guinea, the Solomons and Northern Australia. Good specimens of the common species are available at a pound or two, although rarer ones might cost £25 ($60) to £30 ($70).

In 1966 a large collection of butterflies was auctioned in Paris and a collector paid £750 ($1 785) for a specimen of the very rare birdwing *Troides allotei* from the Solomon Islands. It was an amazingly high price to pay for a specimen.

It should be very interesting to see, in years to come, whether this butterfly maintains its value or whether other collectors decide that even a very pretty butterfly is not worth that much and spend their money on a motor car instead.

| class | **Insecta** |
|---|---|
| order | **Lepidoptera** |
| family | **Papilionidae** |
| genera | *Troides* *Trogonoptera* *Ornithoptera* |

28

△ *Biting lice feeding on the downy parts around the base of a large feather (3 × life size).*

# Biting louse

*A parasitic insect, also called feather louse, that lives among the feathers of birds and sometimes in the hair of mammals. To the naked eye it looks much like any other insect, but the body is flattened from top to bottom and it does not have wings. The feet have two hooks by which the louse hangs on to the feathers of its host. The biting lice that live on mammals differ from those living on birds in having one hook on each foot instead of two. This is more efficient for grasping hairs.*

*Biting lice range from the size of a pin-head to about $\frac{1}{3}$ in. long.*

### Life beneath fur and feathers

As birds and mammals evolved from reptiles and developed their coverings of feathers and hair, some of the ancestral lice must have taken to living in this new and better habitat. The covering of feathers or of hair provided warmth and shelter around an unlimited supply of food. No other animal lived among hair and feathers, so the lice had no competition for any of these advantages. The biting lice became increasingly dependent on their hosts, until they had developed a way of life that allowed them to spend the whole of their life on one animal. This is how the biting lice, together with their relatives the sucking lice, which are also parasites, probably descended from free-living insects.

The biting louse leaves its host only to transfer to another host or on the death of the host. Biting lice keep away from light and move towards warmth and the smell of their host, so that normally they live well down in the plumage or fur near the skin. When the host dies, however, its smell changes and the habitat becomes cold. Now the lice can be seen wandering over the surface of the feathers preparatory to leaving the body in search of another warm object.

Sometimes the lice travel to new hosts by a process known as phoresy, or hitch-hiking (from the Greek word for 'to carry'). They attach themselves to other, more mobile parasites such as blood-sucking flies, fleas or mosquitoes or to insects that happen to alight on the dead host for a moment, for instance, bees or butterflies. If they climb on to another more mobile parasite, the lice stand a good chance of reaching a new host.

Biting lice are described as being host-specific, that is, a species of louse is found on a particular host only; sometimes on only one species of host. Another related species of host will have a different species of louse. Thus common and arctic terns are two closely related birds which are often difficult to tell apart, yet their respective lice are quite distinct. Where a species of biting louse is found on more than one host, the hosts are almost always closely related. An exception is the kangaroo louse which has, in Australia, spread to dogs.

Not only are lice specific to a host; they are often specific to one particular part of the host's body. Biting lice on the wings and body of a bird are different from those on its head. The latter are slow-moving, while the body lice are agile, as they have to escape being killed when the bird is preening itself. Body lice may be camouflaged as well. The body lice of most swans are white, but their head lice which cannot be attacked by preening are black. Conversely, the black swan of Australia has dark lice.

### Life history

Not much is known about the life cycle of biting lice. One species that has been studied in some detail is the pigeon louse.

The eggs are laid in rows along grooves between the barbs of the feathers. They are kept in place by a special cement secreted by the female as she lays each egg. In these grooves they are safe from being destroyed by the bird's bill when it is preening. On the head and neck, eggs are safe from preening and are laid at the base of the feathers.

The eggs hatch after several days, depend-

ing on the temperature of the host. The warmer the air around the eggs, the more quickly they will hatch. When the young louse is ready to hatch, it sucks air in and this blows up the eggshell until the cap is forced off. The louse then struggles out and starts to move around the feathers.

There is no complete metamorphosis, or body change, as there is in a moth or butterfly, both of which undergo radical changes from caterpillar to adult in the chrysalis. The newly-hatched louse is already similar in shape to the mature adult. It differs mainly in its smaller size and undeveloped sex organs. It reaches maturity after shedding its skin three times at intervals of about a week.

### Feathers chewed

Most biting lice feed on the small inner down feathers of their hosts or on the downy parts around the base of larger feathers. Holding on to the barbs of a feather with two pairs of legs, they guide wisps of down towards the mouth with the other pair of legs. The saw-edged mandibles, or jaws, cut the piece of feather into equal lengths, which fall into a pouch formed by the lower lip or labrum. The labrum forces the feather into the louse's mouth and it is swallowed.

Feathers are made of the same substance as hair, that is, a protein called keratin. This is very tough and special digestive agents are needed to dissolve it, but first it is broken up into fine pieces in the crop, which is lined with comb-like structures that grind up the bits of feather. The fragments are passed to the stomach where they are treated with a softening agent before being digested in the intestine.

Some biting lice supplement their diet of feathers with blood, and others live entirely on this. One of the chicken lice uses its mandibles to tear holes in the membrane that surrounds new feathers and suck the blood from the centre of the growing feathers.

Normally a bird does not suffer unduly from biting lice. Nearly every bird in the world has its colony of lice and providing it is healthy these never become a nuisance. If, on the other hand, the bird becomes sick, or if its bill is damaged so that it cannot preen properly, the louse population may multiply rapidly, and then probably causes some harm. Then, as the movement of lice is irritating, scratching may become so vigorous that the feathers are ruined and the skin broken. A high population of lice may result in patches of feathers being eaten away and the chicken louse may kill the young feathers that it sucks. Indeed, this louse can be a pest on poultry farms.

There is little evidence that biting lice spread diseases. One that lives on dogs carries tapeworms, but, as no biting louse lives on man, they pose no threat to health.

| | |
|---|---|
| class | **Insecta** |
| order | **Phthiraptera** |
| sub-order | **Mallophaga** |

# Blister beetle

*These beetles are so called because their bodies contain a substance called cantharidin that causes blistering of the skin. Merely to touch one of these insects causes a blister and a burning sensation like a bad nettle-sting.*

*Blister beetles are found throughout the world, mainly in warm, dry climates, being active in sunshine. One of the best known species is known as the Spanish fly of southern Europe. This is about ¾ in.– 1 in. long and has a shiny green body. The elytra, or wingcases, are soft and rectangular.*

### Parasitic larvae

Blister beetles have entirely different feeding habits as adults and larvae. The former live on plants: trees such as ash, willow and privet in England, while in America some of them are pests of potato and other crops. The larvae are parasites. Some parasitize solitary bees, eating their eggs and the food stored in readiness for the bee larvae. Solitary bees are those in which the female lays her eggs in a nest and abandons them. They do not form colonies with special workers to look after the larvae and to collect food. The larvae of other species of blister beetle attack the eggs of locusts and grasshoppers.

The way that the larvae of the blister beetle get to the bees' eggs is remarkable. The female beetle lays her eggs on the ground. The larvae that hatch out resemble lice but are very active. They crawl up plants and lurk in the flowers to await the arrival of a solitary bee, whereupon they seize some of the bee's hairs in their jaws and get carried away. When these larvae were first found on bees they were in fact called bee-lice.

As they will cling to any bee, or any other hairy insect, a large number of larvae are doomed to perish. It is only those who end up on a female solitary bee that survive, although some get there by indirect means, starting off on a male bee and transferring to a female when the two mate. The eggs of the Spanish fly are laid near the entrance of a bee's nest so they have a greater chance of finding the right host.

Only a few larvae ever manage to fasten onto a bee despite their being able to wait for up to ten days, without feeding. This is compensated by the thousands of eggs that a blister beetle lays. A high mortality at a crucial stage of the life cycle and an enormous output of eggs are characteristic features of parasites.

As the bee carrying a beetle larva lays an egg in a cell the larva drops off into the cell. The bee then seals it up with the egg and the nectar provided for the bee larvae. But the bee larva never appears to eat it, because the beetle larva's first action

*South African blister beetles, **Mylabris oculata**, eating canna flowers. The beetles' bright colours warn other creatures they are distasteful.*

is to eat the bee egg, so having its first meal and removing competition for the store of food.

Next the larva sheds its skin and changes its shape to a maggot-like creature with weak legs and soft, fleshy body. The spiracles, or breathing holes, are placed near the back instead of in the normal position along the sides. This prevents them from getting clogged up with nectar. The skin is shed twice more, then the larva becomes inactive, as a sort of pupa. After this there is another active stage and the proper pupa is formed, within which the adult beetle develops.

The same pattern of larval life occurs in the species that parasitize locusts. The larvae feed on the contents of the locusts' egg cases.

The larvae of insects are very much adapted in body form to utilize their food supply. If it is scarce and they have to search for it, the larvae are active creatures with well-developed legs. Alder-fly larvae (see page 11) are of this type. On the other hand, some larvae are surrounded by food, for instance blowfly larvae (see page 34), and in some of these the legs have been completely lost. The blister beetles have larvae that, at different times in their life history, resemble both these forms and this is related to the conditions of life at each stage. First, there is the searching for a host, when the larva is active, then the living amongst plenty, when it is inactive.

## Enemies

Blister beetles are brightly coloured and so easily spotted by any insect-eating animal, but the cantharidin will have unpleasant effects on any animal that does try to eat one, so that thereafter it will know that these bright creatures are best left alone.

## Early medicine

Cantharidin, or Spanish fly, is called a vesicant because its effect on skin is to raise blisters, like mustard gas (Latin *vesica* = bladder). At one time it was used medicinally when a large part of medical practice consisted of blood-letting and blistering. Cantharidin is present throughout the bodies of blister beetles but is more concentrated in the wing-cases. Spanish fly was prepared by drying the beetles in the sun, having immobilized them with vinegar vapour, but nowadays cantharidin is extracted from an Indian species which contains larger quantities.

Mustard plaster, then heat lamps and more sophisticated ointments have superseded cantharidin for external use but it has long been used internally for bladder troubles because of its diuretic effects. As Spanish fly it is best known as an aphrodisiac, so used because of its burning effect. Unfortunately one occasionally hears that its use has had severe consequences because its toxic effects were not appreciated.

| class | **Insecta** |
|---|---|
| order | **Coleoptera** |
| family | **Meloidae** |
| genera & species | ***Lytta vesicatoria***, *others* |

△ *In flight the second pair of wings are moved. The first pair, or elytra, protect these delicate wings when the beetle is at rest (3 × life size).*
◁ *The blister beetle cuts off parts of the canna bloom with its mandibles.*

△ *If handled a blister beetle secretes a fluid which causes skin to blister.*
▽ *Blister beetle, **Pamphoroea sayi**. The chemical cantharidin causes blistering and is extracted from the dried wings for use in medicines.*

# Blowfly

*These are the bluebottles and greenbottles that are so unpopular in the kitchen. Their form is very similar to that of the housefly, differing mainly in microscopic features, but they are generally larger and their bodies have a metallic blue or green sheen.*

*The name blowfly refers to their habit of laying eggs in meat, 'fly-blown' meat being decaying meat with the larvae, or maggots, of flies in it. Blown, in this context, has nothing to do with the usual meaning. It comes from an Old English usage. A fly depositing its eggs was said to be blowing.*

### Proboscis searches for putrefying food

Blowflies feed on the liquids of putrefying food and carrion or on nectar obtained from flowers. They suck these fluids up a flexible tube, or proboscis, which is formed from their mouth parts. There are organs of taste both on the tip of the proboscis and on the tarsi, or feet. If the fly walks across something edible, it will automatically feed. Experiments have shown that if a blowfly is gently lowered on to a pad impregnated with sugar solution, its proboscis uncoils and starts probing for food as soon as its legs touch the pad.

When a blowfly finds some food it begins searching in circles, and the more food it finds, the tighter becomes its circling. This is an instinctive set piece of behaviour, but it leads the blowfly to exploit food supplies to the best advantage. If food is scarce the fly searches over a wide area, but when it finds a good source it stays there to feed.

### Life cycle on carrion

The life cycle of blowflies is the same as that of most flies. Eggs are laid on suitable food, the larvae or maggots live on this food, pupate and emerge about a fortnight later as shortlived adults. Blowflies are of interest because their life histories are varied, with some species laying their eggs in strange places.

The female blowfly lays up to 600 eggs on carrion, where there is exposed flesh from a wound or in the eye-sockets, mouth and other body openings of animals. Some species are considered pests by sheep farmers as they lay their eggs in open sores and in the genital openings of ewes. They are also a serious household pest. The familiar bluebottle buzzing heavily around the kitchen or larder is probably a female blowfly in search of meat on which to lay her eggs. The coolness and darkness of a larder that deter other species of fly are no obstacle to blowflies, which seem able to get to meat despite precautions taken by the housewife. Sometimes blowflies are larviparous. If egg-laying is delayed for some reason, lack of a suitable laying place perhaps, the eggs are retained in the female's body, where they hatch out and duly leave her body as larvae, or maggots.

Normally, the eggs take a day to hatch and the larvae live for a week before pupating, when $\frac{3}{4}$ in. long. Blowfly larvae are the

△ *Bluebottles feeding and searching for sites to lay eggs on the head of a dead snake.*
▽ *Blowfly with its feeding tube, the proboscis, extended sucking up nectar from the flower head.*

▽ *Anatomy of the proboscis of the blowfly. Liquid food is collected into the numerous food canals and passed into the central canal, which leads to the alimentary canal.*

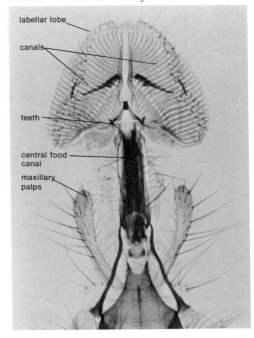

labellar lobe

canals

teeth

central food canal

maxillary palps

*Blowfly eggs are laid among the hairs of a dead mammal, which serve as food for the larvae or maggots (1). The female blowfly can lay up to 600 eggs, usually on carrion, but also on exposed flesh wounds or on other body openings of animals. Maggots, hatching from the eggs usually within a day, are little more than fleshy bags which eat and breathe (2). They feed and grow for a week, pupating when ¾ in. long. Before pupating, the larvae wriggle away from the flesh on which they have been feeding. The skin of the larva forms the pupa case (3) and within it the body is completely broken down and rebuilt. In about a week the adult forces its way out of the pupal case by sucking in air and doubling its size which splits the cap of the case open (4). The adult blowfly, a bluebottle or greenbottle, climbs out to live for about 2 weeks (5).*

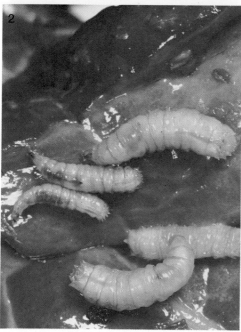

'gentles' of the fisherman, forming a good bait for many kinds of coarse fish. There are even 'gentle farms' where blowfly larvae are bred in immense numbers.

The maggots are rather different from the caterpillars of butterflies and moths or the larvae of bugs like aphids (see page 13) and assassin-bugs (see page 18). They are little more than fleshy bags that eat and breathe. They have no legs and can move only by wriggling. However, the maggots have little need to move as they are surrounded by food, which is being liquefied by bacteria and by the larva's enzymes, which are poured on to the food.

Before pupating, the larvae wriggle away from the flesh on which they have been feeding. The skin of the larva forms the pupa case and within it the body is almost completely broken down and rebuilt in the adult form. This takes about a week, and the adult forces its way out of the pupa case by sucking in air and doubling its size, which splits the case open.

Apart from the blowflies that lay their eggs in rotting meat or in open wounds, there are some that lay their eggs on healthy animals. One species, *Lucilia bufonivora*, lays its eggs on the eyes and in the nostrils of toads and frogs. The maggots penetrate the body and feed on the living tissues. The larvae of some species live in earthworms. The eggs of *Pollenia rudis* are laid in the earth in autumn and larvae invade the bodies of earthworms and hibernate. In the spring they move along their hosts' bodies devouring their tissues.

## Wounds heal quickly

During the First World War doctors working in the hospitals behind the entrenched armies were surprised to find that the wounds of soldiers that had been unattended for several days and were infested with maggots healed quickly, and often more quickly than wounds that had received immediate attention. Blowflies have a well-founded reputation of spreading infection, by picking up bacteria and spreading them by walking over food or regurgitating them in their saliva. It was surprising, then, that those unattended wounds, which probably would have become infected without any maggots present, healed so rapidly. The doctors found that the maggots were, in fact, eating away the suppurating flesh so that the suppuration did not spread and the flesh could heal.

This was well before the days of penicillin and other drugs, at a time when relatively slight wounds could become fatal, especially in the primitive conditions near a battlefield. Consequently maggots were specially bred in sterile conditions and put into suppurating wounds. Unpleasant as this may seem, it is certainly better than having an infected wound that can lead to death.

| class | **Insecta** |
|-------|-------------|
| order | **Diptera** |
| family | **Calliphoridae** |
| genera | ***Calliphora*** <br> ***Lucilia*** <br> ***Pollenia*** <br> *others* |

△ *Common blues mating, the bluish male at the top. The adult life is about 20 days (3 × lifesize).*

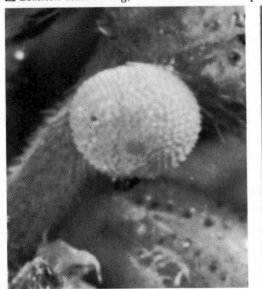

△ *Large blue single egg (45 × lifesize).*

△ *Large blue young caterpillar (24 × lifesize).*

▽ *Large blue caterpillar amongst an ant colony where it is milked by the ants for its honeydew.*

# Blues

*A cosmopolitan group of butterflies, containing several hundred species belonging to the same family as the coppers and hairstreaks. The Arctic blue ranges from Greenland across Scandinavia and Siberia to Alaska. The pigmy blue of the southern part of North America is the smallest of butterflies with a tiny wing spread of only ½ in.*

*None of the blues is large and they are generally rather fragile. Eight species are found in the British Isles, with three species arriving in Britain only as migrants. The mazarine blue bred in Dorset during the 19th century but now appears only as a summer visitor. The long-tailed and short-tailed blues, which have short 'tails' on the hind wings so that they resemble hairstreaks, are rare summer visitors to Britain, but are commonly found elsewhere in Europe, and also in Africa.*

*Although many species are blue in colour, some are whitish and brown, and a great many females are wholly brown. The undersides of the wings, usually white or brown in contrast with the uppersides, are often marked with orange or black spots. The brown argus of Europe is a brown butterfly that does, in fact, belong to the blues.*

## Cannibal caterpillar

Eggs are usually laid singly on the leaves, or tucked into the flowers of plants. Some blues will lay eggs on a variety of plants whereas others are restricted to one kind of plant. Vetches, trefoils and gorse are often used. The holly blue lays its eggs on holly, dogwood, buckthorn and other shrubs, and the eggs lie dormant over winter, hatching out in April.

When small, the caterpillars eat the outer layers of the leaves or flowers, but later they are able to chew right through them or burrow down into the flowerheads. Often the caterpillars are cannibals, devouring their fellows until only one is left on each flower head or leaf.

The caterpillars of the small blue and long-tailed blue hibernate. The small blue caterpillar retires as early as July. Having fed on the growing seed pods of the kidney vetch, it makes a shelter of a few flowers bound together with silk and hides there until the following spring; during this period it looks very much like the withered flowers around it.

The pupa is formed usually on a leaf or stem, the caterpillar first anchoring itself by a band of silk. Some emerge as adults in a few weeks, others remain in the pupal stage for the winter.

In many parts of the world, caterpillars of blues have glands on the abdomen which secrete a sugary fluid called honeydew. This is rather like the honeydew of aphides (see page 13) and it also attracts the attentions of ants which stimulate the secretion by caressing the caterpillars with their antennae and legs. The presence of ants around the caterpillars no doubt protects them from predators, but the links between ant and caterpillar are closer. The caterpillars of some species of blue, such as the chalk hill, do not flourish unless there are ants present to milk them. Ants have been seen carrying caterpillars of this species and the silver-studded blue to the vicinity of their nests, placing them on the correct food plant.

### Caterpillar preys on larvae

The silver-studded blue shows the lengths to which ants will go to get a convenient supply of honeydew, but the large blue enters into an even closer association with them. In return for supplying them with honeydew, the ants allow the large blue caterpillars to prey on their own larvae. In fact, the butterfly seems to have become parasitic on the ant and cannot survive without it.

After its second moult the caterpillar leaves the thyme where it has been feeding and becomes carnivorous, crawling across the ground looking for insects to eat. Eventually the wandering caterpillar is found by an ant, which walks round it then begins to caress it and drinks the honeydew. Then the caterpillar hunches itself up. This is the signal for the ant to pick it up with its jaws and carry it back to the nest.

The caterpillar is carried to an underground chamber where it stays for nearly a year. Here it settles down amongst the ant larvae, preying on them, and from time to time one of the worker ants visits the caterpillar to milk it. This is a departure from the ants' usual behaviour, because normally they jealously guard their off-spring, killing any intruder. But it seems that the honeydew is so esteemed by the ants that they are willing to sacrifice some of their larvae. Moreover, the ants sometimes bring so many caterpillars into the nest that in the end the ant colony dies out.

Six weeks after being brought into the nest the caterpillar, having grown rapidly, becomes fleshy, white and grub-like. In the winter it hibernates, then completes its growth the next spring and pupates in May. Three weeks later, it emerges as an adult butterfly and leaves the nest.

*This large group of butterflies, all small in size, are some of the most beautifully coloured butterflies to be seen. In the blues the sexes differ greatly, the females are usually dark sooty brown, the males show the blue colours.*

*Holly blue (3¼ × lifesize).*

*Female chalk hill blue (2½ × lifesize).*

*Female common blue (2 × lifesize).*

*Male silver-studded blu*

*Female adonis blue butterfly (4 × lifesize).*

| class | **Insecta** |
|---|---|
| order | **Lepidoptera** |
| family | **Lycaenidae** |
| sub-family | **Lycaeninae** |
| genera & species | **Cupido** *species* |
| | **Plebejus** *species* |
| | **Aricia** *species* |
| | **Polyommatus** *species* |
| | **Lysandra coridon** *chalk hill* |
| | **Lycaena** *species* |
| | **Maculinea** *species* |
| | **Celastrina** *species* |

*Cotton bollworm burrowing into a tomato. It is also called corn worm and tomato fruit worm according to the plant on which it is feeding.*

# Bollworm

*This name is applied to the caterpillars of several species of moth which attack the bolls or seed pods of cotton. The most important is the American or cotton bollworm, known in Britain as the scarce bordered straw moth, a very severe pest of cotton and the worst pest of maize in the United States.*

*The caterpillar, or worm, is light green, pink or brown, with lighter underparts. The head is yellow and there are alternating light and dark stripes running down the length of the body. The adult is a moth with wings 1½ in. from tip to tip, and variable in colour. The forewings are usually light grey-brown, while the hindwings are white with dark spots and irregular markings.*

*Another bad pest is the pink bollworm, that was once estimated to be the sixth most destructive insect in the world. The caterpillars are ½ in. long and pinkish-white on the upper surface. The adult is a small moth ¾ in. from wingtip to wingtip. It flies by night and looks like a clothes moth with narrow, pointed wings.*

*The Egyptian bollworm is the caterpillar of another small moth which flourishes in hot, dry conditions and is common in many cotton growing parts of Africa.*

## Widespread range

The cotton bollworm is widespread throughout the tropical and warm temperate regions of the world. It is occasionally found in Britain, where the moth is called the scarce bordered straw, and regarded as a great prize by collectors if found in the wild.

Adults are blown in from the Continent and caterpillars are imported in tomatoes and other fresh vegetables, but they are never able to survive the winter, so have not become established in Britain.

The pink bollworm is thought to have been a native of India but it spread rapidly to other cotton-growing countries in Asia, and to the Philippines and Hawaii. It has also been introduced to Africa, Australia, Brazil, Egypt, West Indies and Mexico.

## Not just a cotton feeder

The cotton bollworm is by no means limited to feeding on cotton or maize (known as corn in the United States). It is also a pest of tobacco, tomatoes, beans, vetch, melons, oranges and many other plants. Because of this it is given a number of names depending on the crop it is attacking. The most usual names are cotton bollworm, corn worm and tomato fruit worm. The moths feed on the nectar of many kinds of flowers, usually at dusk, but they can be seen about on warm, cloudy days.

## Life cycle of destruction

The eggs of the cotton bollworm are laid singly on the leaves and petals of the food plant, and one moth will lay 500–3 000. Each one is hemispherical and ridged, resembling a minute sea urchin, half the size of a pinhead. The eggs hatch in 10 days and the caterpillars start eating the leaves, petals and developing fruit. The damage they can cause is increased because a caterpillar does not stay in one cotton boll or tomato. It will eat its way in, then turn and bore another way out, and crawl over to another fruit and repeat the process. In this way a single caterpillar can destroy all the fruits on one branch.

The damage to the crops is caused in

several ways. Leaves and petals may wither and fall. Early in the season the blossoms may fail to open, and if the attack comes later, the fruits are made worthless, since the seeds are eaten and the fleecy cotton or lint fails to develop or becomes stunted. Where the fruits are sold for eating, the presence or mere signs of worm infestation prevent them from being sold. This is a serious problem for corn-growers, for in the worst years over 90% of the ears in a crop may be attacked and so made worthless.

When the caterpillars are full-grown, they crawl down the stem, or just let go and drop to the ground, then burrow into the ground to a depth of 2–6 in. and pupate in smooth-walled cells. The adult moth emerges from the pupa 10–25 days later, depending on the climate, and crawls back up the tunnel that was eaten out by the caterpillar.

There are three or four generations each year. The first two pass their lives on maize, tobacco and other plants. Cotton is attacked by the third generation, in August or later. The pupae of the final generation pass the winter in the soil and the adults emerge the next spring.

## Pest control problem

It is almost impossible to expect the total eradication of an insect pest, but what farmers can aim for is the reduction of the pests' numbers to such a degree that they have little effect on the crops, or they can take measures to prevent the pests spreading. The latter is more difficult now that transport is so rapid and goods are regularly shipped around the world. This is shown by the spread of the pink bollworm. It was imported to Mexico in cotton from Egypt in 1911. In 1917 it was found in Texas. The difficulty with this bollworm is that the caterpillar spends the winter in a cocoon

△ *Aerial insecticide attack on bollworm.*

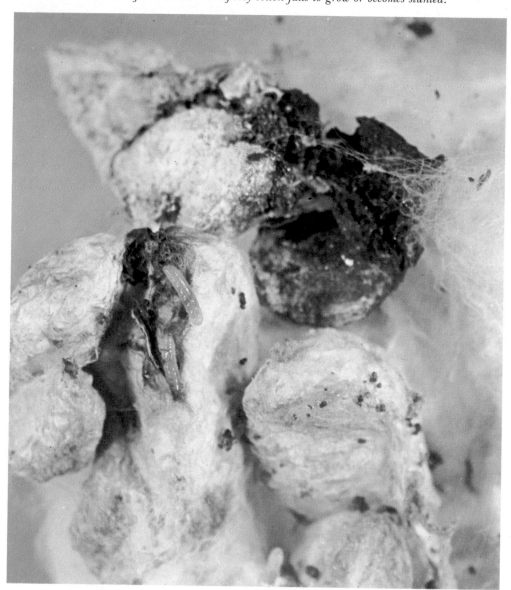

▽ *Bollworms eat seeds of cotton boll so the fleecy cotton fails to grow or becomes stunted.*

in the stored seed, or in the ground, and it can remain like this for over 2 years. Luckily, it is quite easy to control its spread by heating the seed for a short time at 55°C/131°F. This kills the caterpillar but not the seed. The caterpillars in the ground can be killed by leaving a fallow period in which no cotton is grown on infected soil.

Populations of bollworms can be kept down by deep ploughing in the winter which allows predators such as birds and rodents, as well as the weather, to destroy the resting caterpillars and pupae. The cotton bollworm's depredations can also be reduced by early planting of cotton so that the third generation of caterpillars does not have so much time to cause damage. Since the Second World War, DDT and other chemical insecticides have been used against bollworms, but once they have eaten into the bolls they are safe from the chemicals. Now, experiments are being made to find biological controlling agents, that is, predatory animals that will keep the numbers of the pests down. Spiders seem to be suitable for this as they will follow the caterpillars right into the bolls. Observations are being made as to which spiders are most suitable. It is important to find ones which feed readily on bollworms and are active when bollworms are attacking crops.

| class | **Insecta** |
|---|---|
| order | **Lepidoptera** |
| family | **Noctuidae** |
| genera & species | ***Heliothis armigera*** *cotton bollworm*<br>***Earias insulana*** *Egyptian bollworm* |
| family | **Gelechiidae** |
| genus & species | ***Platydra gossipella***<br>*pink bollworm, others* |

*The silverfish is often seen in kitchen cupboards. Looking like a small land fish it is really a wingless insect and has probably remained unchanged for 400 million years. It will eat anything from crumbs on the floor to the paste on the back of wallpaper, but it rarely becomes a pest.*

# Bristletail

*Although bristletails live throughout the world, the silverfish, found in bread or flour bins, in larders, kitchens or pantries, behind skirtings, in cupboards or among books, is the only one of these small wingless insects which is at all well-known. They get their name from the three slender bristle-like 'tails', and their antennae also are long and bristle-like but no bristletail is more than 1 in. long overall. They have small compound eyes. Their legs are long and slender, well adapted for running.*

*In places they may sometimes be a pest, but usually they are not more than little noticed scavengers.*

### Nocturnal habits

If a bristletail finds itself in the light it will scamper rapidly into cover. This strong reaction to get away from light and their need to keep their bodies from drying out means that most bristletails live in damp sheltered places: under stones or logs, among leaf litter, under dead bark. Some live in the nests of ants and termites. They come out mainly by night, and this nocturnal habit combined with their small size and neutrally coloured slender bodies, means they are seldom seen. Those most commonly seen are two that have taken to living in houses, the silverfish, already mentioned, and the firebrat, so-named because it lives around fireplaces, boilers and flues. In fact, it was given its name by bakers because it was often seen around bakehouse ovens.

### Scavenging feeders

All bristletails feed on bits of dead plant or plant products, ranging from particles of dead leaves to flour or anything containing starch. Silverfish will attack crumbs on the floor and they may eat paste from the back of wallpaper, where it has come away from the wall. They may also damage book-bindings, eating the paste. There are records of silverfish damaging artificial fabrics, but this is only when the materials have been treated with a natural plant extract.

### Nymphs lack silvery scales

The female silverfish lays 7–12 eggs. These are minute and very hard to find as they lie freely on the ground where they are laid. They hatch in 6–60 or more days, depending on the temperature. The young silverfish, known as nymphs, resemble the adults in all but size and in lacking scales—the adult silverfish body is coated with silvery scales which come away readily, as a powder, when handled. Silverfish moult several times during the 20 months or more which they take to reach maturity.

The female firebrat lays a large number of eggs but otherwise follows much the same course in development.

### Enemies

Little is known about enemies but it is assumed that bristletails are attacked by carnivorous insects, centipedes, spiders and other small predatory invertebrates.

### Ancient ancestors

It is not surprising the silverfish should not be readily recognized as an insect. It was, in fact, given the name of silverfish at least as long ago as 1703, and it was not called a bristletail until 1855, when people had begun to study insects in an organized way. It looks more like a minute land fish. To begin with it does not obviously have the body in three parts, the hallmark of an insect, and it has no metamorphosis, the newly-hatched young looking very like the parents.

It had long been presumed that silverfish, and other wingless insects like it, represent an ancestral form of all the insects. This is on the supposition that they never did have wings, unlike other insect pests such as fleas and lice, whose ancestors were winged originally but later gave up flight for a parasitic way of life.

Until 20 years ago this view about the silverfish was largely hypothetical, for the only fossils to compare with it were silverfish found in amber and a mere 40 million years old, long after fully winged insects had evolved. Then insect remains were found in rocks of the Triassic, nearly 200 million years old. These were very like the silverfish living today. The earliest insect fossils known, also of wingless insects but of a different kind, are twice that age, and we can expect that sooner or later fossil bristletails 400 million years old, or more, will come to light.

| phylum | **Arthropoda** |
|---|---|
| class | **Insecta** |
| order | **Thysanura** |
| family | **Lepismatidae** |
| genera & species | ***Lepisma saccharina*** *silverfish* <br> ***Thermobia domestica*** *firebrat* <br> *others* |

# Bumble-bee

*Bumble-bees are rather like honeybees (see page 99) except that they have a larger body which is covered with stiff yellow, orange or red hairs. The bumble-bee also has a sting which it can use to inject venom into the body of an enemy. The sting is a modified ovipositor—a tube-like organ used by other insects to deposit their eggs.*

*Bumble-bees are also known as 'humble-bees'. Both names come from the lazy humming sound made by the bee as it flies from one flower to another.*

*The bumble-bee is found all over the world. Most species live in the tropical or sub-tropical zones but they can also be found in places as far apart as Arctic Canada and Tierra del Fuego, and the equivalent of this range in the Old World. They are not native to Australasia, but were introduced there when settlers found that none of the local bees would pollinate the red clover plant which they had introduced. So the bumble-bee was brought in to do the job.*

### Buzzing around from flower to flower
Under a microscope the hindleg of a bumble-bee is an interesting sight. The outer face of the 'shin' is flat and polished but along each side there is a row of stiff bristles. These bristles make up what is called the pollen basket. If you watch a bumble-bee flying from one flower to another it is quite easy to see the large yellow balls of pollen attached to its hindlegs. When the bee forces its way into a flower the pollen is rubbed off onto its body hairs. The bee then brushes the pollen from its body, moistens it with a little nectar and sticks it onto the pollen basket. When it gets back to the nest it uses its forelegs to remove the balls of pollen from this basket and put them into the egg-cell.

The bumble-bee is attracted to the flower by the nectar, which it sucks up through a special extendible tube. The nectar is then stored away in the crop or honey stomach.

Flowers and bees depend upon each other for their existence. The bee benefits from the pollen and the flowers benefit by being 'cross-pollinated'. This cross-pollination occurs when some of the pollen from one flower is rubbed off onto another flower, thus fertilising it.

It is for this reason, to attract bees rather than people, that flowers have evolved their attractive colours and scents.

### The life cycle of a queen bee
Usually it is a pure accident if an insect meets one of her offspring. This is because most insects lay their eggs and then leave them to hatch out by themselves.

Some insects, however, are different. They are called social insects. This kind of insect stays with her offspring and they, in turn, stay with her and help look after her next brood. Wasps, honeybees and ants are all well-known examples of social insects. In their case thousands of individuals live in one nest. Most of them are sexless or, rather, under-developed females. These workers care for the breeding female, the queen, and for her eggs and larvae. Bumble-bees are social insects too, but their communal life is not as well developed as the others. There are fewer workers in the colony and they all die before the winter.

The life of a bumble-bee colony begins in autumn. A young female bumble-bee leaves the nest, mates and finds a sheltered spot where she can spend the winter hibernating. When spring comes—the actual date depends upon the species—the young queen emerges and suns herself until she is fully active. Then off she flies in search of pollen and nectar from the spring flowers. The queen needs pollen because it contains large amounts of protein which is used to build up in her ovaries the eggs to be laid later.

Soon the queen starts looking for a suitable place to build her nest. She might take over the abandoned nest of a fieldmouse, a vole, or a hedgehog. Or she might pick somewhere else: a disused bird's nest, a thatched roof, a bale of hay or even a discarded mattress. Her favourite sites are along hedgerows and banks or in old, neglected corners of fields and gardens. Nowadays it is not easy for the queen bee to find this kind of place. Modern intensive and mechanised farming demands that these unproductive corners be ploughed up so that every square foot of ground pays its way. The result is that bumble-bees, which are in a sense vital to the pollination of crops, are themselves becoming scarcer.

The queen usually builds her nest at the end of a tunnel. The tunnel may be several feet long, if she has used an old mouse nest, but some species prefer tunnels only a few inches long, so they build their nests in thatch or similar places. Some kinds of bumble-bees, known as carder-bees, even manage to build their nests on the surface. They do this by combing grass and other material into a tight, closely-woven ball.

If the queen has taken over the nest from a former occupant there is always plenty of nest material readily available. She fashions this into a small inner chamber lined with only the finest grass and roots. She stays in here for a day or two drying it out with her body heat. Insects are cold-blooded, but the larger ones generate enough heat, especially with their flight muscles, to keep their bodies a few degrees above air temperature outside the nest.

### Food in a 'honey pot'
By now the eggs are developing inside the queen bee. She begins to make an egg-cell out of wax. The wax is secreted from between the plates on the underside of her abdomen. She goes out to collect pollen which she stores in the egg-cell, in which 8–14 eggs are laid. The cell is then covered

*Male mating with queen bee **Bombus agrorum**. Young males are produced at the end of the season. After mating the queen finds a sheltered spot where she can spend the winter hibernating until the spring.*

*Bumble-bee queen, **B. hortorum**, incubating her first batch of brood which have reached the pupal stage. She stores surplus nectar in a wax 'honey pot' near the entrance of the nest to provide food in bad weather.*

with a cap of wax. The queen spends some of her time settled on top of the eggs to keep them warm. She also goes out feeding and brings home any surplus nectar which she stores in a 'honey pot' near the entrance to the nest. The 'honey pot' is made of wax and is about ¾ in. high and ½ in. across. It provides a source of food when the weather is too bad for the queen to go out foraging.

When the larvae begin to hatch out of the eggs they are just helpless maggots with very little in the way of legs or sense organs. They do nothing except feed on the pollen which has been stored in the egg-cell and on the mixture of nectar and pollen which their mother regurgitates to them. But they grow amazingly quickly on this diet. They shed their skins several times and then spin a cocoon and pupate.

At this point the queen carefully removes the wax from around the cocoons and makes it into new egg-cells. She puts these on top of the cocoons and lays the next batch of eggs in them. Eventually the first brood emerge from their cocoons as fully developed workers. They spend a day or two drying out while their wings expand and harden. Then they are ready to go out collecting food and to tend the next batch of larvae.

Before long a whole colony of several hundred workers has been built up. The queen, however, never becomes a helpless egg-laying machine as happens with ants and termites. She can still make egg-cells and feed larvae although she hardly ever leaves the nest to forage.

Towards the end of the summer, some of the eggs produce males and fertile females. The males develop by parthenogenesis — that is to say, from unfertilised eggs. The females, the next generation of queens, appear at first to be exactly the same as the sterile female workers but they grow much larger and eventually leave the nest to mate with the males. The males differ from other bumble-bees by having larger antennae,

which they use to locate the females. They do not have a sting.

Once the old queen has produced the males and the new queens she stops laying worker eggs. Gradually the whole colony dies out. After mating the males also die. It is winter again and only the young queens are left to survive through to spring.

## Bumble-bees fighting for their lives

Bumble-bees have many enemies, large and small. The worst ones are insect-eating birds like the bee-eater, but there are plenty of others. Badgers or skunks and other mammals will dig up bees' nests both for the honey and for the bees themselves.

Naturalists once observed a skunk scratching at a nest until the irate inhabitants flew out. The skunk caught each one in its forepaws and killed it by rubbing it against the ground.

Fieldmice and shrews also attack bumble-bee nests, and among the smaller animals that are enemies of the bees are robber flies. They grapple the bees with their legs and suck their blood. Then there are the 'mites' which live in the air-sacs or 'lungs' of the bees and also suck their juices. Another enemy is the wax moth. It lays its eggs in bumble-bee nests and its caterpillars ruin the egg-cells by burrowing through them.

The cuckoo-bee is a close relative of the bumble-bee and in its own way another enemy. Cuckoo-bees do not have pollen baskets with which to collect stores of pollen. So instead they invade the nests of bumble-bees and lay their eggs there. The eggs develop into males and females, but not workers, and they have to be tended by the bumble-bee workers.

In a fight the bumble-bee will defend itself by biting and stinging. It rolls onto its back, with its jaws open and sting protruding, and sometimes squirts venom into the air. Its sting is not barbed, like the sting of a honeybee, so it can be withdrawn from the corpse of an enemy and used again.

## Economic importance

Charles Darwin began many controversies with his famous book *On the Origin of Species*. One of the things he mentioned in the book was that only bumble-bees visit the flowers of the red clover. This is because the red clover has a long, narrow flower and other bees do not have long enough tongues to reach the nectar which lies at the base of the flowers.

Darwin pointed out that if bumble-bees became rare or extinct the red clover would also die out. This would have serious economic effects, he said, because cattle are fed on red clover.

He went on to quote a Mr H Newman who said that more than two-thirds of bumble-bee nests in England are destroyed by mice. He claimed that bumble-bee nests were more common near villages and towns, where cats were plentiful. Therefore a large number of cats would mean a larger crop of clover because the cats would eat the mice who killed the bees.

Later a German scientist intervened to remark that a large number of cats would be good for England's economy because he considered England's wealth to be based on her cattle.

In a true Darwinian spirit, TH Huxley then stepped in to supply the final link. He suggested that, since old-maids were very fond of cats, the sensible way to strengthen the economy of the country would be to increase the number of old-maids. Less weddings and more spinsters was the short answer, according to Huxley.

| class | **Insecta** |
|-------|-------------|
| order | **Hymenoptera** |
| family | **Bombidae** |
| genus | ***Bombus*** |

*A batch of cocoons, two of which have been cut open to show the pupae inside. These will emerge as fully developed workers and will then spend a day or two drying out while their wings expand and harden (8 × lifesize).*

*When the temperature of their nests becomes too high some of the workers fan currents of air with their wings to cool the nests (**B. ogrorum**).*

# Burnet moth

*The bright colours of the burnet moths make them very conspicuous. They are small with thick bodies, long forewings and short hindwings; the antennae are thickened near the tip and then pointed. Most are brightly coloured, the forewings dark metallic blue or green with scarlet markings and usually separate spots, the hindwings with a black border. This applies to all the British species, but in southern Europe white and yellow-spotted ones occur. In the beautiful Zygaena carniolica, of central and southern Europe and western Asia, the red spots are surrounded by white rings. Occasionally yellow-spotted forms occur as rare varieties of the normally red-spotted species.*

*Burnets from around the coasts of the Mediterranean occur in immense numbers and great variety. They extend in small numbers to temperate Asia and southern Africa and also into northern Europe. They belong to the family Zygaenidae which has many species with very metallic-looking colours and often bizarre-shaped wings. One subfamily of Zygaenidae has species where the hind wing, instead of the normal rather rounded shape, is thin and forms long trailing streamers behind the forewings.*

*Many of the brightly coloured species are day fliers, their colours warning predators that they are distasteful. In Europe some of the species are of very local distribution and many are confined to limestone districts where the soil is suitable for their food-plants to grow.*

### Moths in a meadow

Burnets usually live in colonies, often occupying only part of a hillside or a single meadow, and the colonies may persist for a few years and then die out. In a flourishing colony, the moths are often abundant, sometimes half-a-dozen or more being seen on a single flower-head.

The burnets are all day-flying moths and are most active when the sun is shining. The flight is slow and buzzing, and when at rest the moths are sluggish and can easily be captured without a butterfly net. They are on the wing at various times from June to August.

### Tubular tongues for nectar

The adult moths feed on the nectar of flowers, sitting on the flower-heads and probing the nectaries with their long tubular tongues. The caterpillars feed on the leaves of low-growing plants. The food-plants of the three common British species are trefoils and clover. The mountain burnet feeds on crowberry, and one of the other northern species on thyme.

### Annual life cycle

Normally the burnets have an annual life cycle, the caterpillars feeding during the late summer, hibernating through the winter and completing their growth during the

△ *Burnet moth,* **Zygaena trigonellae,** *drying its wings (5×life size).*

▽ *The beautiful* **Zygaena carniolica** *is found in central and southern Europe and western Asia.*

spring and early summer of the following year. The mountain burnet is exceptional in taking more than one and possibly as much as four years to complete its life-cycle. Only a short time is spent as a pupa and the adult moths probably live only two or three weeks.

The caterpillars are thick and slug-shaped, green or yellow with a regular pattern of black spots. The pupa is enclosed in a characteristic spindle-like cocoon of parchment-like silk, shining yellow or white in colour. The cocoons are usually attached to a stem of grass or some other plant, those of the commoner species being conspicuous and easy to find. After the moth has hatched the black empty pupa shell always sticks out.

## Safety in nastiness

Their habits would seem to make the burnets an easy prey for birds and other insect-eating animals, since they are slow-flying, conspicuous, and make no attempt to hide, and little to evade capture. They are all very ill-tasting, however, and to some degree poisonous, so that a bird which has pecked one of them is never likely to attack another. Their conspicuous appearance is associated with this, as it is to their advantage to be easily recognisable so that predators have no difficulty in learning to avoid them. Another day-flying moth, the cinnabar *Callimorpha jacobaeae*, of Europe and western Asia, quite unrelated to the burnets, has a

*Burnet moth caterpillar, magnified 8 times, feeding on trefoil, one of its food-plants.*

but this did not last for a very long time.

Within seconds it was almost literally running round in circles, stopping every so often to bite at cool grass blades or to rub its beak on the grass, the bare earth, or any stick or stone it came across, while saliva dripped from its beak. From time to time it spread its wings in the manner that has come to be associated with birds that have something acrid or pungent in the mouth.

Clearly the rook was agitated and going through an unpleasant experience, one it was unlikely to forget. The bill-cleaning and

agitated movement went on for some minutes. Moreover, during that time it repeatedly attacked its companion, with whom it had just been feeding harmoniously, chasing it with vicious stabs of the beak.

| phylum | **Arthropoda** |
|--------|----------------|
| class  | **Insecta**    |
| order  | **Lepidoptera**|
| family | **Zygaenidae** |
| genus  | *Zygaena*      |

*Six-spot burnet, a common European species.*

similar red and black pattern and is also protected by having a nasty taste.

The poison of the burnet moths is discharged in the form of a yellow fluid from the region of the neck, and it contains, among other substances, histamine and prussic acid (hydrogen cyanide).

## Bad taste

A rook living in an aviary with a magpie as a companion was offered a burnet moth, experimentally, to see whether it would accept or reject it. It picked up the moth, dismembered it in rook fashion, by severing the wings and biting off the head. Then it took the body of the moth into its mouth—

◁ *Turquoise Forester moth,* **Procris statices.**

*Five-spot burnet moths mating on an empty cocoon that has an empty pupa shell sticking out of it.*

# Caddis-fly

*Caddis-fly is the common name given to the insect order Trichoptera, of which between 4 000 and 5 000 species are known throughout the world. Their nearest relatives are the Lepidoptera (butterflies and moths). The antennae are long and many-jointed. The adult insects look rather like moths and fly mainly at night, often coming to artificial lights.*

*Most of the larvae are aquatic, living in freshwater and breathing by external gills on the sides of the abdominal segments. These are the well-known caddis-worms, which build tubular cases to protect their bodies, although not all caddis-fly larvae do this. All of them spin silk.*

△ *Protective tubular cases, open at one end, are built by caddis-fly larvae from pieces of plant stems and leaves, and small stones and shells, bound together with silk (3 × natural size).*
▽ *The caddis-worm **Lepidostoma hirtum** partly emerges from its tubular case to feed (×16).*

## Underwater builders

By far the most interesting feature of the caddis-flies is the life of the aquatic larvae, which varies in the different families and genera. They can be divided into two types, those which build portable cases, and are almost all vegetarians, and those which live free and are at least partly carnivorous. The case-builders use many materials in various ways to build their tubes. Members of the genus *Phryganea*, which includes the largest caddis-flies, cut pieces of leaves and stick them together with silk. The most familiar cases are probably those of *Limnophilus*, which are made of small stones, and pieces of plant stems or empty snail shells. If removed from their cases and given beads or similar objects, some of these caddis-flies will use the artificial material to make new ones. *Stenophylax* and *Heliopsyche* use fine sand grains to make their cases, the one a straight cylinder, the other a spiral tube that looks remarkably like a small snail shell. Cases made of stones or sand often have their weight reduced by a bubble of air trapped inside. *Heliopsyche* is American, all the others mentioned are found in Britain.

All the cases are tubular and open at the one end, where the larva pushes out its head and thorax to move about or feed. The rear end is closed with a silken mesh so that a current of water can flow through and aerate the gills. All caddis-larvae have a pair of hooked limbs at the back, used to hold onto the case—so tightly that attempts to pull the larva out invariably injure it. It can easily be made to leave its case, however, by pushing the head of a fairly large pin through the mesh of the rear opening.

Most of the larvae with non-portable cases live in silken tubes, in flowing water, some living under stones in swift upland streams. In the genus *Plectronemia* the larva is nearly 1 in. long and makes a silk tunnel with the open end facing upstream widely flared to form a trumpet-shaped net. Any small animal or piece of plant material carried into this trap by the current is seized and eaten by the larva, which thus gets its food in very much the same way as a web-spinning spider. A number of other stream-dwelling caddis-larvae make nets of various shapes to gather food. When they are damaged, or choked with inedible material, the larvae clean and repair them.

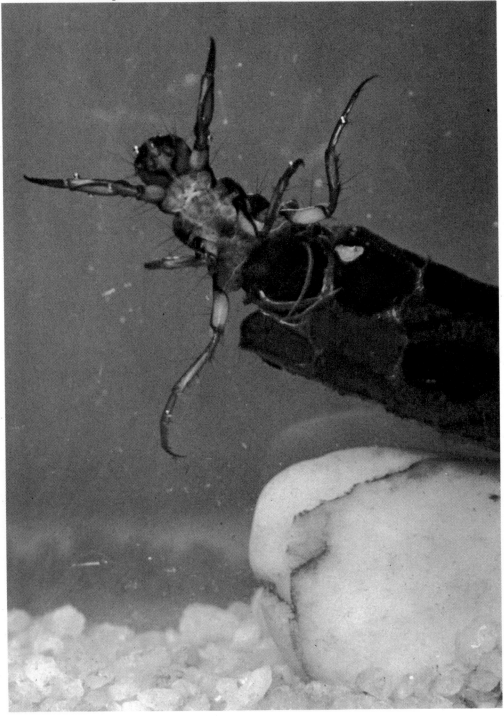

△ Adult caddis-fly **Stenophylax permistus** *has large wings and flies mainly at night. The adult is short-lived, for only a fraction of the annual life cycle (3 × natural size).*
▽ *Caddis-fly head magnified about 20 times. The compound eye's many facets can be clearly seen.*

## Adult feeds on nectar

The mouth-parts of adult caddis-flies are vestigial, and if they feed at all as adults, they can probably take in only liquid food. In the wild they probably feed from flowers with exposed nectaries, but will take sugar and water in captivity. Fed in this way they can be kept alive for 2 or 3 months, but given only water they live for less than 2 weeks. The case-bearing larvae eat mainly the leaves and stems of live plants and may be a nuisance when one is trying to establish water lilies in a pond. A cabbage leaf tied to a string, thrown into a pond and left for a few hours, will often be covered with case-bearing caddis-larvae if it is taken out carefully. The large case-bearing larvae of *Phryganea* catch and eat water insects as well as plant food. Most of the tube-dwelling or free-living larvae have a mixed diet.

## Life history

The eggs are laid by the females in spring and summer. Some kinds drop them on the surface as they are flying over, others crawl underwater and stick them to stones or plants in a jelly-like mass. Some of the larvae do not make cases or tubes until they have moulted their skins several times, others make tiny cases as soon as they hatch. When the larva is fully grown, nearly a year later, it pupates, inside the case if it belongs to a case-bearing species, otherwise in a silken cocoon. When the time comes for the adult insect to emerge, the pupa bites its way out of the case, being equipped for the purpose with strong mandibles, and swims to the surface of the water. There it splits open, releasing the adult caddis-fly, which can fly almost immediately on emergence. The life history usually takes a year to complete, of which the adult life is only a small fraction.

## Anglers and caddis-flies

These insects are of interest to anglers for two reasons. The larvae, taken out of their cases, make excellent bait for the man who watches a float. The adults, when they hatch in quantity, cause a 'rise' of trout, that is to say the fish are stimulated to come to the surface and feed, and this is of prime interest to the fly fishermen.

Entomologists always speak of caddis-flies by their Latin names, but anglers use an English terminology that is hardly ever heard except in the context of fly fishing. They are known collectively as sedge flies, the large *Phryganea grandis* being the great red sedge or murragh. There is a group of species called silverhorns, and some have names of their own such as Grannom, Caperer and Halford's Welshman's Button.

Artificial flies are made in imitation of caddis-flies. To make a murragh a piece of dark grey-black or black-claret mohair or seal's fur is used for the body, a dark brown-speckled feather from a fowl's wing is used for the wings and two dark red cock hackles (the feathers from the neck) complete the job; only the soft fibres near the base of the feather being used.

| class | **Insecta** |
|-------|-------------|
| order | **Trichoptera** |
| genus | **Limnephilus, Phryganea** |

△ *Parasitism in action: a braconid wasp has laid its eggs in a caterpillar and a hundred or so larvae have emerged and made cocoons. These in turn are now being parasitised by a chalcid wasp.*

# Chalcid wasp

*The chalcid wasp is a minute insect belonging to the order Hymenoptera, and is therefore related to the bees, wasps and ants. Some of their closest relations, the so-called 'fairy flies' (family Mymaridae) are the smallest known insects and one species, Alaptus magnanimus, is 0.12 mm long (about 1/120 in.). Over 1 500 species are known, but their minute size makes them difficult to collect and study, and many more must be awaiting discovery.*

### 'Big fleas have little fleas . . .'

*Big fleas have little fleas upon their backs to bite 'em. And little fleas have lesser fleas, and so ad infinitum.*

This old rhyme may well have been written with chalcid wasps in mind for most chalcid wasps are parasites and hyperparasites of other insects. The term 'hyperparasite' means 'parasite of a parasite'. Thus an ichneumon wasp may lay its eggs in a caterpillar and its larvae may in turn be para-sitised by a smaller wasp, such as a chalcid. Cases are even known of hyperparasites themselves being parasitised. Many chalcid wasps lay their eggs in the eggs of moths and butterflies, which gives an idea of the minute size of some of them. From one such egg, itself of pin's-head size, 20 or more fully developed and winged chalcid wasps may emerge.

Chalcids are of great economic importance as a means of control of insect pests. One species *Pteromalus puparum* lays its eggs in the newly-formed pupae of white butter-flies, destroying great numbers of them. In 1929 the small white butterfly *Pieris rapae*, one of the commonly-known cabbage whites, was accidentally introduced into New Zealand and by 1935-36 was established as a serious pest. In New Zealand it enjoyed the great advantage that the parasites which had controlled its numbers in Europe were absent. As a remedy, some 500 parasitised pupae of the butterfly were sent to New Zealand from England and over 12 000 of the wasps emerged. Most of these were released, and very soon it was found that almost 90% of pupae collected in the wild were parasitised, and the butterfly has, since that time, been well under control.

Another case of pest control by a chalcid wasp is that of the greenhouse whitefly *Trialeurodes vaporariorum* which attacks to-matoes and other glasshouse plants. It can be controlled by fumigation, but this is expensive and may be dangerous. The use of a chalcid wasp *Encarsia formosa* is cheaper and safer for the grower. Tomato leaves bearing parasitised 'scales' (the immature stage of the whitefly) are hung in bunches in the infected glasshouses. After about 3 weeks all the tiny wasps will have emerged and spread through the glasshouse in their search for further whitefly victims, and the pest is soon eliminated.

### Liquid food for adults

Adult chalcids can take only liquid food and probably confine themselves to sucking up water, nectar and honeydew. The food of the larvae depends on their habits; parasitic species feed on the tissues of their host, the others on the tissues and sap of plants.

Many of the chalcids reproduce by par-thenogenesis—the females lay eggs which hatch without ever being fertilised. In such species the males are usually rare and some-times unknown. A more remarkable method of reproduction seen in chalcids is that known as polyembryony. A single egg is laid by the parasite and at an early stage in its development it divides into a number of separate cell masses, each of which develops into a larva. The individuals formed in this way are all of the same sex and genetically identical in every way. They are formed in the same way as human identical twins, but whereas these occur as only a rare developmental accident, identical broods from one egg are normal for many of the chalcids.

Parasitic chalcid wasps usually lay their eggs in the eggs of particular host insects. Some species lay in host eggs in conifer trees, others parasitise the eggs of sawflies and other insects found in galls. Some of the fairy flies enter water and lay their eggs in those of dragonflies and backswimmers or in the larvae of caddis flies. Only one chalcid lays in any one host egg because they can smell the scent of any chalcid that has already been there.

## The wasp and the fig

In the Mediterranean region the finest edible fig is the Smyrna fig, but it bears only female flowers and will not form fruit without pollination. The wild fig or 'caprifig', whose fruit is useless, must be grown among the Smyrna fig trees if fruit is to develop, or bunches of caprifigs can be gathered and hung among the branches of the edible fig trees. This was known to the early cultivators of classical times, though they were

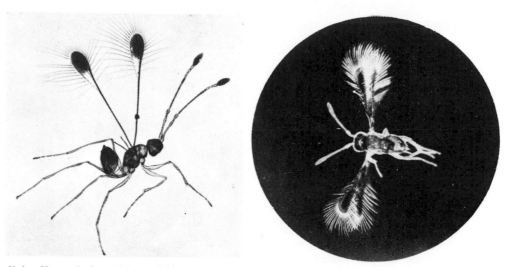

*Fairy flies: relatives of the chalcid wasps and among the smallest of known insects. They are so tiny they can parasitise the eggs of other insects.*

▽ *This feeding chalcid wasp finds itself dwarfed by the size of the flower – a daisy.*

content to regard the association as mysterious. The explanation is as follows.

Certain chalcid wasps, now known as fig wasps, family Agaontidae, live in galls on the male flowers of wild figs. The male wasps are wingless and can only crawl from one gall to another in search of females, with which they mate. The winged females then search for fig flowers in which to lay their eggs, and in this search they often enter the flowers of the Smyrna figs. They do not lay eggs in them but, having emerged from male wild fig flowers, they carry pollen on their bodies which fertilises the Smyrna fig flowers so that they develop and form fruit.

As the wasps can breed in only the wild figs, it is necessary to cultivate these, and to ensure that they are infested by fig wasps, in order to obtain fruit from Smyrna figs. Fig trees are not pollinated by the wind or by any other insects. Fig wasps had to be imported from the Mediterranean into California.

| phylum | **Arthropoda** |
|--------|----------------|
| class | **Insecta** |
| order | **Hymenoptera** |
| family | **Chalcidae** *others* |

# Cicada

*Some cicadas are among the biggest of all insects and most are fairly large. The Malayasian empress cicada **Pomponia imperatoria** has a wingspan of 8 in. Apart from their size and impressive appearance cicadas are remarkable for their extraordinarily loud 'voices', and for the very long period spent in development by some species.*

*The family Cicadidae, included in the suborder Homoptera of the order Hemiptera, is related to the aphids, frog-hoppers and scale-insects. Cicadas have a rather broad, flattened body and two pairs of large wings with a characteristic pattern of veins. The longitudinal veins do not extend to the edge of the wing but stop short of it, leaving a narrow, uninterrupted margin along the outer border of each wing. The wings are usually transparent but in some species they are coloured and patterned, the wing membrane being pigmented, so the colour cannot be brushed off as it can in butterflies and moths, whose wings are covered with loosely attached scales.*

*Cicadas are mainly tropical, extending into the temperate regions in small numbers. A few species occur in southern Europe and about 75 in North America. More than 1 500 species are known throughout the world.*

△ *Adult cicada photographed from below to show its sound-box cover just behind the third leg.*

▽ *Adult cicada emerging from the skin of its nymph phase which feeds underground.*

## Singing insects

Adult cicadas spend much of their time sitting rather high up on the trunks of trees or among the branches and foliage, singing intermittently. Some species sing during the day, others only at dusk or dawn. When approached they fly off suddenly and are difficult to catch. Their flight is fast and powerful and many of them, like moths, are active at night and fly to artificial lights.

A species found in the Amazon forests *Hemisciera maculipennis* has the basal part of both wings coloured, the forewing opaque olive green, the hindwing vivid vermilion. When the insect is at rest the forewing overlies the hindwing and only the inconspicuous dark green patch is visible, but on taking flight the cicada displays a sudden flash of bright red. This is an instance of 'flash coloration', an adaptive device which probably serves to startle and confuse a predator which finds the insect at rest.

## Artificial rain

Like all members of the order Hemiptera, cicadas have mouthparts adapted for piercing and sucking, and they feed on the sap of plant stems and succulent shoots. Most of this sap is sugar and water, so the cicadas must suck up large quantities to make an adequate meal. The result is that large amounts of a weak sugary solution are rapidly excreted. If it appears to be raining under a tree in a tropical forest when the

sky is clear cicadas are probably feeding overhead, and the 'rain' consists of drops of sugary water excreted by them.

The wingless young insects or nymphs, living underground, extract sap from roots in the same way.

## 17-year locust

The eggs are laid in slits in the twigs of trees and the nymphs fall to the ground after hatching several weeks later. They dig down with their broad, powerful front

legs and quickly disappear underground. After a variable period of feeding, the nymph digs its way to the surface and climbs up a tree. There it rests. Its skin splits, and the adult winged insect emerges. In some species the nymph builds an earthen cone or chimney projecting several inches above the ground, in which it remains for a time before its final transformation.

In the North American species *Magicicada septendecim* the nymph spends no less than 17 years underground in the course of its development. It is known as the 17-year locust. This does not mean that they appear in a district only once in 17 years, as there may be several broods in different stages of development. The cicadas, do however, appear at irregular intervals of several years, usually recurring in a 17-year cycle. The breeding period has also been checked by observation of nymphs in captivity.

## Birds are main predators

Cicadas are extensively preyed on by birds, which give a warm welcome to the great swarms of periodical cicadas that appear in North America. In that country they are also hunted by a large solitary wasp called the cicada killer *Sphecius speciosus* which stocks its nest with paralysed adult cicadas as a provision of food for its own larvae.

## The loudest insect voice

The best known insect vocalists are the grasshoppers and crickets, which produce sound by stridulating—the quick stroking of a ridge over a roughened edge or surface. Cicadas sing by a quite different and much more efficient method, if it is judged by the sheer volume of sound. Some cicadas can be heard a $\frac{1}{4}$ mile away and, close to, they can make ordinary conversation impossible.

In almost all cicadas it is only the males that sing, but both sexes are vocal in a few species. Both sexes always have hearing organs and can, of course, recognise the song of their own species.

The purpose of the song seems to be to call the local population of any one species together so that it forms a small group in which males and females can meet readily.

The singing apparatus consists of a pair of membranes at the base of the abdomen, each surrounded and held by a stiffly elastic ring. The membrane is convex when relaxed, but a muscle attached to it can pull it down and allow it to pop back, rather as a distorted tin lid can be popped in and out. In cicadas the membranes, or *tymbals* as they are called, oscillate at a rate from over 100 to nearly 500 times a second. Other muscles, attached to the ring, distort its shape, affecting the volume and quality of the sound, and the whole apparatus is enclosed in a pair of resonating chambers which amplify the sound and vary it by opening and closing.

By means of this extraordinary musical instrument the cicada can not only make a deafening noise, but each species can produce a sort of 'signature tune' of its own. A good tropical entomologist knows the songs of his cicadas just as a birdwatcher recognizes the calls of birds.

▷ *Mating cicadas.*

| phylum | **Arthropoda** |
| --- | --- |
| class | **Insecta** |
| order | **Hemiptera** |
| suborder | **Homoptera** |
| family | **Cicadidae** |

*Clothes moths are secretive and fly little, preferring to creep for shelter into cracks and folds. This mounted specimen shows its soft feathery wings.*

# Clothes moth

*Three species of small moths whose larvae damage furs and woollen fabrics by feeding on them are called clothes moths. All three belong to the family Tineidae.*
Common clothes moth **Tineola bisselliella**. *Length from head to wing-tips about $\frac{1}{5}-\frac{1}{4}$ in. Forewings (the part seen when the moth is at rest) pale buff or golden with a distinct metallic sheen and with no spots or markings. The larva is creamy-white with a brown head and about $\frac{3}{8}$ in. long when fully grown. The brown pupa is enclosed in a cocoon from which it protrudes after hatching.*
Case-bearing clothes moth **Tinea pellionella**. *Similar in appearance to the common clothes moth, but rather darker and duller and with three dark spots on each wing. The larva is more easily distinguished by its habit of making a case of silk and fibre which it drags about in the same way as the larva of a caddis-fly*

*(see page 46). The pupa is formed inside the case, which then serves as a cocoon.*
White-tip clothes moth **Trichophaga tapetzella**. *Larger than the other two clothes moths, length from $\frac{1}{4}$ to over $\frac{3}{8}$ in. The forewings are dark coloured with the basal third white and the front of the head covered with white hairs. The insect at rest, therefore, appears dark on its hinder two-thirds and white in front. It infests coarser materials than the other two, and is, therefore, sometimes called the tapestry moth.*

*Two other species, commonly known as house moths, are often encountered in houses, and their larvae feed on any organic matter that is slightly damp—neglected scraps of food, leather, wool and feathers – but they are seldom found infesting fabrics stored in dry conditions. Both belong to the family Oecophoridae.*
Brown house moth **Hofmannophila pseudospretella** *is brown speckled with dark flecks, the female (over $\frac{5}{8}$ in.*

*long) much larger than the male ($\frac{1}{4}-\frac{1}{3}$ in.). These caterpillars are known to damage man-made carpets, polythene, nylon, polystyrene. Generally they are looking for food, merely biting through the polythene; polythene bags are therefore not entirely moth proof.*
White-shouldered house moth **Endrosis sarcitrella** *is mottled greyish-brown with the head and front of the thorax white, and is much smaller than the other species, being more comparable with the clothes moth in size. Here again the female is larger (about $\frac{3}{8}$ in.).*

### Hard to keep out
Clothes moths are secretive, much more inclined to run and hide in a fold or crevice than to fly. Most of those seen flying are males, or females that have laid all their eggs. They can squeeze through very narrow crevices and will make their way into almost any cupboard or chest of drawers, however well made.

Clothes moth larvae can live on clean wool

or fur, but greatly prefer those garments that are soiled by body excretions or by food dropped on them. They bite through and scatter far more fibres than they eat, which accounts for the great amount of damage that such small creatures can do.

## Time/temperature formula

The female common clothes moth lays from 50—100 eggs which hatch in a week in very warm conditions $(27°—32°C/80°—90°F)$ but take 3 weeks or more at $16°C/60°F$. The rate at which the larvae grow varies widely with the availability of food. On raw wool or rabbit fur they may become moths in 3 or 4 months, but they often take a year to reach maturity on manufactured cloth, and a period of as much as 4 years has been recorded for their development. The adult moths live from 2–3 weeks.

Details of the breeding of the other species appear to be generally similar.

## Enemies and means of control

A small parasitic chalcid wasp *Spathius exarator* lays its eggs in the larvae of clothes moths, and the larvae of the window fly *Scenopinus fenestralis* prey on the larvae of both clothes moths and house moths.

The chief enemies of clothes moths are moth-proofing, dry-cleaning and synthetic fabrics, combined with constantly improving standards of hygiene in homes. If woollens are kept scrupulously clean and carpets regularly cleaned with a sweeper or vacuum cleaner they are not likely to become infested. Parts of carpets under heavy furniture should be sprayed every 6 months with a persistent insecticide. Bright light and good ventilation destroy the moths in all their stages, and stored blankets should be regularly aired out of doors on sunny days. Sudden changes of temperature also kill the insects, a fact that lends point to the cold storage of furs in summer.

Clothes moths are becoming rarer, so that even in conditions favourable for them, infestation is less general than it used to be.

## Before the days of cloth

Clothes moths are now very seldom found in the 'wild' state, but, of course, they must have existed before the coming of civilised man, probably before man had evolved as a species at all. At that time they must have lived in such places as old birds' nests and the lairs of carnivorous animals. There the larvae probably fed on the feathers and hair used by the birds for their nests and on scraps of skin discarded by the animals. Early in his development, man behaved very much like a carnivorous animal, and later he took to using skins as clothing. Later still he learned to spin and weave wool. Widespread regard to cleanliness is a very recent feature in human development.

▷ *European apple-tree moth alights on a flower.*

| class | **Insecta** |
|-------|-------------|
| order | **Lepidoptera** |
| family | **Tinaeidae, Oecophoridae** |
| genera | *Tineola, Hofmannophila, Endrosis* |

*Kitchen nightmare: a common cockroach has a wash and brush-up after a meal of bread. These household pests have the depressing habit of fouling far more than they actually eat.*

*Newly-moulted cockroach larvae. They may moult 6—12 times before they are fully grown.*

# Cockroach

*Cockroaches used to be classified together with the grasshoppers, crickets, stick-insects and others in one large order, the Orthoptera. This has now been split up into several separate orders of which one, the Dictyoptera, comprises the praying mantises and the cockroaches.*

*These are fairly large insects, flattened in shape, with two pairs of wings, the fore-wings being more or less thickened and leathery, serving as a protective cover for the delicate hindwings, just as the hard-ened forewings or elytra of beetles do. The hindwings of cockroaches are pleated like a fan when not in use; when expanded for flight they have a very large surface area. In the commonest European species, the black beetle as it is called, the male has very small wings, the female has*

*mere vestiges, and neither can fly. The female has reduced wings and is flightless in some of the other species also.*

*The most familiar of the 3 500 species of cockroaches are those tropical and sub-tropical forms which have taken advantage of the warmth and the opportunities for scavenging afforded by homes and premises in which food is made or stored. By this means they have ex-tended their range into temperate and cold regions, and some of them have been artificially distributed all over the world. In the wild state, the great majority of species are tropical. In the outdoor fauna of Britain they are represented by 3 small species only, belonging to one genus, Ectobius.*

*Three of the most common cockroaches are:* Common cockroach, *or black beetle* **Blatta orientalis** *length variable, averaging about 1 in., dark brown*

*(females almost black) wings not reaching the tip of the body in the male, vestigial in the female; both sexes flightless. A common pest in house. Now cosmopolitan in distribution, the region of its origin is unknown.*

German cockroach, steamfly *or* shiner **Blatella germanica** *about ½ in. long, yellowish-brown with two dark brown stripes on the prothorax, or fore-part, of the body. Wings fully developed. Almost as abundant as the common cockroach and certainly not of German origin; probably a native of North Africa.*

American cockroach **Periplaneta americana** *males nearly 1½ in. long, reddish-brown, with fully developed wings. Found mostly in sea port towns and on ships. In tropical countries it is the chief house-living cockroach. It is not an American insect and probably also originated in North Africa.*

*The young of the common cockroach are white on hatching, gradually becoming brown.*

*A brace of American cockroaches. Unlike the common cockroach, the American version has fully-developed wings. Despite its name it is not an American insect: it probably originated in North Africa.*

### They come out at night

In the wild, most cockroaches live on the ground among decaying vegetation or behind dead bark, and are coloured brown to match their surroundings. The 'domestic' species probably all lived in this way once. Some cockroaches are found among growing plants and are patterned in brown, yellow or green. The ground-living cockroaches are nocturnal, hiding away by day and coming out at night, just as the house-living ones do. Some of the large tropical species fly freely at night and are attracted to artificial light.

Their flattened bodies allow them to creep into cracks and crevices; in houses, cockroaches hide in inaccessible places and are not easy to get rid of.

Poisoned baits may be effective if used persistently, and insecticidal powders and sprays kill them if introduced well into their hiding places. Bad infestations, however, are best dealt with by professional pest controllers.

### Unwelcome scavengers

In the wild, most cockroaches are scavengers on dead insect and other animal remains, fallen fruit and fungi; the transition to scavenging in human habitations is easy and obvious. Some of the wild species feed on wood, which they are able to digest with the help of protozoans, microscopical one-celled animals, in their intestine. Termites, which are closely allied to cockroaches, eat and digest wood by the same means.

In houses, cockroaches will eat any kind of human food that they can get at. They will also eat a variety of substances not generally regarded as edible, such as book-bindings, boot-blacking, ink and whitewash. Frank Buckland, in his *Curiosities of Natural History*, tells of a gentleman on his way home from India by ship who was much annoyed by cockroaches. At night, when he was asleep they 'came and devoured the little rims of white skin at the roots of the finger nails'. The harm they do is greatly increased by their habit of fouling, with their droppings,

far more than they actually eat. The only good that can be said of them is that so far as is known they do not convey any disease.

### Breeding

The eggs are enclosed in a purse-like capsule called the ootheca. In the common cockroach this is carried for a day or two, protruding from the body of the female, and then dropped, or sometimes stuck in a crevice, after which the insect takes no further notice of it. It is white when it first appears at the tip of her abdomen, but darkens later and, when deposited, is almost black and rather less than $\frac{1}{2}$ in. long. Normally an ootheca contains 16 eggs in 2 neat rows of 8, but there may be more or less than this. The eggs hatch 2—3 months after the formation of the ootheca, which splits to allow the young to emerge. The young of the common cockroach are about $\frac{1}{3}$ in. long on hatching, and white, gradually becoming brown as they grow. They resemble their parents in form, except that the wings are lacking, and take 10 months —1 year to reach maturity. Moulting of the skin, or ecdysis, takes place anything from 6—12 times in the course of growth. The breeding habits of the American cockroach are similar.

In the German cockroach the ootheca is carried by the female until a day or less before hatching, and the eggs may even hatch while it is still attached to her. It is chestnut brown and, a few days before hatching, a green band appears along each side of it. Hatching usually takes place 4—6 weeks after the ootheca is formed and it normally contains 35—45 eggs.

*Hated and loathed as a household pest because of its habit of defiling food, the cockroach is nevertheless one of the best examples of success in surviving; and it has an important role in the teaching of entomology.*
*This close-up shows the organs of special sense: the eyes, which are compound, consisting of many small elements; the palps and antennae, which are organs of touch. On the highly mobile antennae are structures which are used for smelling. Above the front of the 'shell' are the semi-transparent elytra, or wing cases.*

## Living fossils

In a manner of speaking the world went wild with delight when the coelacanth, a living fossil, first came to light. The same intense interest would be shown if another living fossil were to be discovered. There is something in the psychology of these events which recalls the parable of the pieces of silver that were thought lost and were found again. Nobody but the most devoted scientist, however, would think of rolling out the red carpet for the roaches. Yet they are extremely interesting and primitive insects.

Many fossils have been found, showing that there were already many species and abundant populations of roaches at the time when coal measures were being deposited, 300 million years ago. These cockroaches of the Carboniferous period look similar to many of the present day ones and the family as a whole must be regarded as insects which, by adopting a simple and secure way of life at an early period of the earth's history, and never departing from it, have inherited the earth by their very meekness. As an example of success in survival they have few equals, but because they

intrude themselves on our notice in such an unpleasant manner, few people find themselves able to regard them highly. Nevertheless, there are a few people whose sole purpose in life is to rear cockroaches.

Partly because they are so easy to obtain and partly because their structure and anatomy is so simple and generalised, cockroaches are widely used to introduce students to the science of entomology, and breeding them for this purpose is one of the less well-known human occupations.

| phylum | **Arthropoda** |
|--------|----------------|
| class | **Insecta** |
| order | **Dictyoptera** |
| family | **Blattidae** |

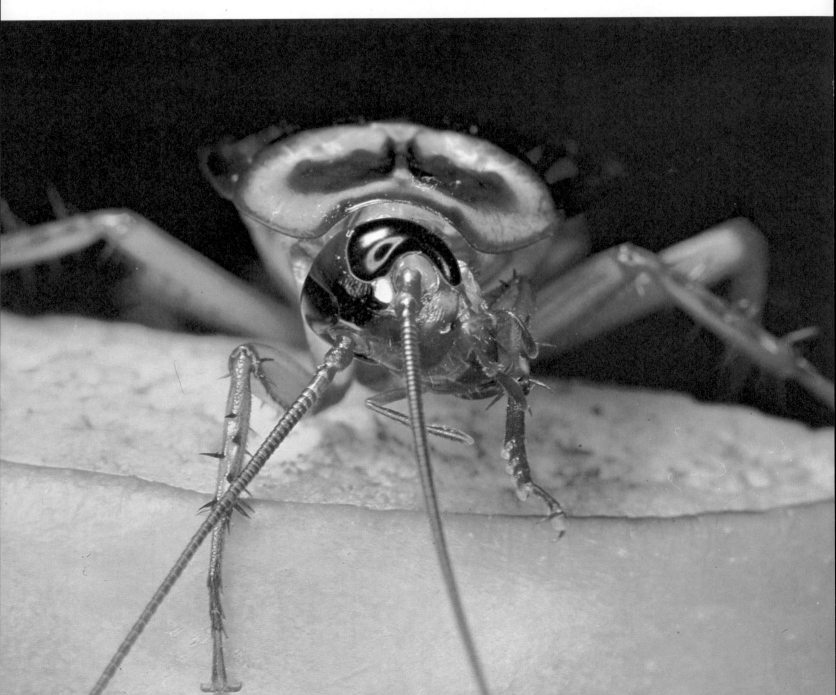

# Codlin moth

*The codlin, or codling, moth is, in the larval stage, one of the most serious pests of apples. Originally a native of Europe, it is now found all over the world where apples are grown.*

*It is a pretty moth, dark greyish-brown with a coppery iridescent patch at the tip of each forewing. The wings span about ½ in. The larva is a pale pinkish grub, about ½ in. long when fully grown, which feeds inside the fruit. When it enters through the 'eye' of the apple there is no sign of its presence and the 'maggoty' apple appears sound, but if the tiny caterpillar enters by boring through the skin, a dark reddish irregular ring often surrounds the hole. Most of the affected apples fall to the ground in late summer before they are fully grown.*

*There is much disagreement among the scientists who name and classify insects, as to the correct generic name for the codlin moth. It will be found in various textbooks under* **Laspeyresia, Ernarmonia, Carpocapsa, Cypdia** *and* **Grapholitha,** *but its specific name, the second scientific name,* **pomonella,** *always refers to the codlin moth and no other name is used.*

*The common codlin could have been a corruption of querdling or quardling.*

### Dislikes wet weather

The moth is active at night and often flies to artificial light during the summer, that is, June—August in the northern hemisphere. In Britain its numbers are affected by small climatic changes. Periods of warm dry summers and cold winters are favourable to it, while wet seasons without extremes of temperature lead to a reduction in its numbers. The climate of the United States favours the moth.

The eggs are laid on young fruit and, on hatching, the larvae enter it and pass the summer feeding inside. In August they leave the fruit and spin cocoons in crevices in bark and similar places. They overwinter as caterpillars in the cocoons, pupate in the spring, and the moths emerge a few weeks later. In normal British summers there is just one generation, but the cycle may be passed through a second time when the summer is exceptionally long and warm. In warmer climates two or more generations are the rule. The caterpillars are often found in strange places. This is due to the habit of emerging from the apples after they are picked, and wandering about to find a place to spin a cocoon. Thus in shops they may turn up in all sorts of food which have been stored near the apples.

### Feeding

As soon as they get inside the fruit, the caterpillars tunnel to the centre, where they feed on the pips as well as the flesh of the fruit. They are serious pests of pears as well as apples.

*Codlin moths have wingspans of about ½ in. The moths are active at night and often fly to artificial light during summer. Warm dry summers favour them, while wet seasons without extremes of temperature tend to reduce their numbers.*

### Small birds are fruit growers' allies

By far the most useful natural enemies of the moth are the small insectivorous birds that winter in Britain rather than migrating south. Foremost among these are the great tit and blue tit, which spend much of their time in winter searching the bark of trees for hibernating insects, and destroy great numbers of codlin moth larvae. Treecreepers feed entirely in this way but are generally less common than tits.

### Controlling the pest

In Britain, removal of all rough bark from orchard trees reduces the number of effective hiding places for the caterpillars and helps the birds to get at them. Trap banding is also useful; bands of sacking, corrugated cardboard or hay tied round the trees, just below the main branches, in August, are removed and burned in the autumn. This destroys large numbers of caterpillars which have made their cocoons in the bands. The inside walls of storage buildings and boxes need to be sprayed with a persistent insecticide in order to kill the larvae emerging from fruit that has been picked. A modern insecticide spray is used in the orchards in June to kill the young larvae as they are hatching. Spraying is, of course, useless once they have entered the fruit.

In the United States, where it is a much more serious pest than in Britain, more drastic and extremely costly measures have to be used. As many as eight sprays a year may be needed to protect the fruit effectively. If spraying is done late in the season the law very properly insists on thorough washing of the fruit before it is marketed,

and apart from the added expense of this, some fruit is always damaged during the cleaning process. In Oregon and Washington large and valuable orchards have been completely abandoned simply because the cost of control of the codlin moth proved prohibitive.

| | |
|---|---|
| phylum | **Arthropoda** |
| class | **Insecta** |
| order | **Lepidoptera** |
| family | **Tortricidae** |
| genus & species | *Cydia pomonella* |

*Inside an apple the grub eats pips and flesh.*

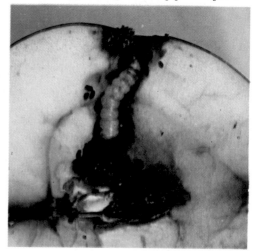

# Colorado beetle

*Familiar to many people from the pictures displayed in police stations and elsewhere, the Colorado beetle is a dreaded potato pest. It is $\frac{3}{10}$ in. long, a little bigger than a ladybird. The convex, shiny back is longitudinally striped black and yellow, and the thorax, the region just behind the head, is spotted black and yellow. The specific name decemlineata means ten-striped, as there are five black stripes on each wing-cover. The larva is equally conspicuous, orange-yellow with black markings on the head, black legs and three rows of black spots along each side. It has a characteristic hump-backed appearance.*

### Potato pests

The Colorado beetle is a serious pest, feeding on potato leaves both as larva and adult, though it may occasionally resort to other plants of the potato family.

It passes the winter as a mature beetle, hibernating underground at a depth of 10−12 in. In late spring it comes out and, if it does not find itself surrounded by potato plants, flies in search of them, often for a distance of many miles. The female lays her eggs on the leaves, usually on the underside; they are yellow in colour and laid in batches. The larvae hatch in a few days, feed voraciously on the leaves and are fully grown in about 3 weeks. They then burrow into the soil to pupate, and a new generation of beetles emerges in 10−15 days. In Britain this second brood appears in late July or August, and if the weather stays warm a third generation may be produced. As soon as bad weather sets in, the beetles burrow into the soil and hibernate until the following spring.

The damage is done to the haulm, or above-ground part of the plant, which may be completely stripped of its leaves, so that the tubers cannot develop. The large number of eggs produced by each female and the rapid succession of generations are factors which make the Colorado beetle such a formidable pest. A single individual emerging in the spring may have thousands of descendants by the autumn.

### 33 insect enemies

The Colorado beetle seems to have no natural enemies that are effective in reducing its numbers. There are at least 33 different kinds of insects that prey on it, including bugs, beetles, wasps and flies, and one fly lays its eggs in the larvae of the Colorado beetle. Yet these account for only $\frac{1}{5}$ of the total. Spraying the potato foliage with a modern insecticide is the usual method of control. The important thing is obviously to spot any infestation as early as possible and exterminate local populations before they have a chance to spread. Anyone who finds a Colorado beetle, either in a potato field or casually, should immediately report the matter at the nearest police station. The specimen *must* be taken along for its identity to be checked. This surveillance has so far proved effective.

△ *In late spring a female Colorado beetle will lay a batch of yellow eggs on the potato leaf, which hatch in a few days.*

▽ *Fully-grown larva, about 3 weeks old. It is ready to burrow into the soil and pupate for about 15 days before emerging as an adult.*

## An entomological curiosity

Like many insects which have become pests, the Colorado beetle is especially interesting. Almost all species of insects are conditioned to live in some particular type of climate. If the climate differs from that of their natural environment they will fail and die out at some stage in the life cycle. The Colorado beetle is a conspicuous exception to this rule. It can live the year round out of doors in Canada, where the winters are arctic in severity, in the hot deserts of Texas and Mexico and in the British cool wet climate. The beetle's habit of hibernating deep underground as an adult is probably the most important factor in promoting this quite unusual ability to adapt itself to any climate in which men can grow potatoes.

## A potato bridge

Among the discoveries made in the Rocky Mountains by the American explorer Stephen Harriman Long, in the early 1820's, was a pretty black-and-yellow-striped beetle feeding on a sort of nightshade called buffalo burr *Solanum rostratum*. Neither it nor its food plant were particularly abundant, and it was simply an attractive insect living in a state of balance with its environment.

The buffalo burr is a member of the potato family. The potato is native to Peru and Ecuador, in South America. It was brought to Europe by the Spaniards and later found its way to the new colony of Virginia in North America. How this happened is not known. Neither Sir Walter Raleigh nor Sir Francis Drake, both of whom are credited with discovering it, took it there. In the course of the opening up and settlement of western America in the 1850's, potatoes were introduced and cultivated by the pioneers, and in Nebraska in 1859 it was found that the 'buffalo burr beetle' was turning its attention to the potato. Its numbers increased rapidly and it began to spread. No control measures were known at that time and the beetle spread from potato field to potato field, frequently destroying the whole crop. From Nebraska in 1859 it appeared in Illinois 1864, in Ohio in 1869, and it reached the Atlantic coast in 1874. This indicates an average rate of travel of 85 miles a year. The potato fields of the United States had formed a bridge from west to east along which the beetle could travel. It also spread 400 miles northwards into Canada. The Atlantic formed a barrier, however, until 1922.

Then it was found in the Gironde region of France and from there it has extended its range all over continental Europe. It appeared in Tilbury in 1901, but the next outbreak in Britain was in Essex in 1933, where prompt control measures exterminated it. It has appeared from time to time in Britain since then, but has always been prevented from establishing itself. In 1946 there was a real danger it might become established. In 1947 infestations were discovered at 57 centres. In 1948 there were 11, and in 1949 not one was found. Prompt control measures had proved effective, much to the relief of the many British potato farmers.

| class | **Insecta** |
|---|---|
| order | **Coleoptera** |
| family | **Chrysomelidae** |
| genus & species | ***Leptinotarsa decemlineata*** |

*Adults and larvae of the brightly-coloured Colorado beetle often live together on the same plant. Scourge of potato crops the world over, the Colorado beetle is an insect with an international price on its head, but if outbreaks are reported early, prompt control measures usually prove effective.*

# Copper butterfly

*The wings of these butterflies have the colour and lustre of polished copper and are marked with dark spots and bands, sometimes with blue or purple as well. They are a group of small butterflies in the family Lycaenidae, and are thus allied to the blues and hairstreaks. They are widely distributed in the temperate and cold regions of the northern hemisphere, both in the Old and the New World. There are, however, three species in temperate New Zealand. Presumably their ancestors arose from the same stock as those in the northern hemisphere and in time became separated.*

*The caterpillars are slug-shaped and, in the majority of species, feed on various kinds of dock or sorrel. Like those of many of the blues (see page 36) the larvae of some species are attended by ants for the sake of a sweet secretion which they produce. In the case of the coppers this exudes all over the body, unlike many others of the family, which have a single orifice connected with a special gland.*

*There are nearly a dozen species known in Europe and North Africa, but only two were known to reach Britain; one is a familiar butterfly of open country in general, the other is an insect which unhappily became extinct. They are known respectively as the small copper and the large copper.*

## Small copper

This is a pretty, lively and even rather aggressive little butterfly. The males establish territories and try to chase all other butterflies away, flying out and attacking individuals of their own species and other, larger ones as well. They have no weapons and are quite incapable of injuring each other.

The small copper has an enormous range extending from Europe right across Asia to Japan, over a large part of North America and northward to beyond the Arctic Circle. It is divided into distinct subspecies in different parts of its range but they are all very similar in appearance. Some of these subspecies range into Africa. Another ranges almost as far north as any butterfly, into Ellesmere Land, and is one of the five butterflies found in Greenland.

## Three generations a year

The larva feeds on dock and sorrel and the life cycle is passed through so quickly that there may be three generations in a good summer. The caterpillar is green with a brown line along the back and clothed with short greyish hairs. It is not attended by ants. The pupa is pale brown or greenish and attached to a leaf or stem of the food plant. The species overwinters as a larva but not (as in most larval hibernators) at any particular stage of its growth. The butterfly is on the wing continuously from May to October.

▷ *Small copper at rest. These far-ranging butterflies often breed three times a year.*

△ *A small copper shows its wing pattern while taking a meal off a sprig of heather.*

▽ *One of the Dutch large coppers introduced to Wood Walton Fen on great water dock plant.*

*Small copper larvae feed on dock and sorrel.*

The small copper is exceedingly variable, and its more extreme varieties or 'aberrations' are eagerly sought by collectors. Reduction or modification of the pattern of black bands and spots produces most of the varieties, but in one of the rarest and most highly prized the copper ground colour is replaced by silvery white.

## Large copper

In this species the wing span is about $1\frac{7}{10}$ in. and the male and female are very different. In the male all four wings on the upper side are brilliant burnished copper with only narrow dark borders and small central dots. The female has dark markings not unlike those of the small copper.

The large copper was discovered in Britain a little before 1800, in the fens of East Anglia, a habitat that was rapidly shrinking due to artificial drainage. Butterfly collecting was already a popular pastime, and the coppers were persecuted without restraint. Not only did collectors visit their haunts, but dealers encouraged the local people to capture them in all their stages for sale at prices ranging from a few pence to a shilling, rich rewards for the poor of those days. The butterfly held out for half a century, the last specimens being taken in 1847 or 1848. The British large copper could probably have been saved if a reserve had been created where it could have been secure from the greed of collectors and from destruction of its habitat, but at that time the idea had not occurred to anyone that active measures might be taken to preserve rare animals from extinction.

The large copper is still found in many parts of Europe and Asia, but the British subspecies was larger and finer than any of the Continental forms. About a thousand preserved specimens of it exist, but as a living animal it has gone for ever. The great water dock is the food plant of the large copper. The caterpillar, which is attended by ants, is green and looks like a much flattened slug. It hibernates when young, feeds in the following spring, and the butterflies appear in July and August.

Two other species, the scarce copper and the purple-edged copper, were included as British by early entomologists. It is not impossible that they once lived in Britain and became extinct before collecting became methodical and widespread.

## Butterfly naturalisation

In 1915 a subspecies of the large copper was discovered in the province of Friesland, Holland, and named *Lycaena dispar batavus*. It resembles the extinct English race more closely than any other and the idea occurred to some British naturalists to try introducing it to the fenland nature reserves in East Anglia. It is rare in its native haunts, and some difficulty was experienced in obtaining living specimens. This was overcome, however, and the first butterflies were released by the Society for the Promotion of Nature Reserves in Wood Walton Fen, Huntingdonshire, in 1927. The experiment was successful and later was repeated at Wicken Fen, owned by the National Trust, in Cambridgeshire. The Dutch large copper is still maintained at Wood Walton and is bred artificially and released every year to supplement wild stock and to ensure against any accident to the small wild population.

| phylum | **Arthropoda** |
|---|---|
| class | **Insecta** |
| order | **Lepidoptera** |
| family | **Lycaenidae** |
| genus & species | ***Lycaena dispar*** *large copper* <br> ***L. hippothoe*** *purple-edged copper* <br> ***L. phlaeas*** *small copper* <br> ***L. virgauteae*** *scarce copper* |

# Corn-borer

*The corn-borer, which was introduced into North America, is a native of Europe, where it is known as the maize moth. Outside Europe it is popularly called the European corn-borer. The American name is more commonly used because it is in the United States that the moth has become a terrible pest of corn, or maize as it is called in Europe.*

*The adult corn-borer is a small moth with a wingspread of 1 in. The female is yellowish-brown with dark wavy lines running irregularly across the wings. The male is very much darker than this with markings of olive brown. Corn-borers are nocturnal and fly strongly.*

△ *Female corn-borer lays a mass of 20–30 eggs on the undersides of leaves.*

## Explosive spread

Corn-borers live in Europe and Asia. The larvae have been found on about 200 kinds of plants, including corn, beet, celery, beans and garden flowers. In England they have been found on mugwort and hops. Corn-borers lived in Europe for many thousands of years before corn was introduced from America in the 16th century, but this became a favoured food plant because it fulfilled the larvae's nutritional requirements and also provided them with shelter all the year round. As a result, when they were accidentally taken to North America they very rapidly colonised the extensive corn crops.

It is thought that the first to reach North America may have arrived about 1907, in cargoes of corn from Hungary or Italy. The first positive discovery of these moths in the United States came, however, in 1917 when crops near Boston were found to be infected. Two years after this the corn-borer appeared around the Great Lakes, and by then it had become so well established that large-scale programmes of eradication failed and the insect eventually reached the Midwest cornbelt.

Today it is a major pest in the United States and occasionally whole crops of corn are ruined because the larvae so weaken the stems by burrowing that the plants topple over. If modern insecticides had been available in 1917 the insect would probably have been checked. Compulsory burning of the remains of corn plants and weeds after harvesting proved an unsatisfactory method of control.

By 1920 about 100 species of insect pests had been introduced into the United States, although this number has now been reduced by careful controls. The ease with which introduced insects flourish in the United States is due to the absence of enemies and diseases of the insects that kept their numbers within bounds in their original homes.

## Caterpillars like to be snug

The eggs of the corn-borer are laid on the undersides of leaves in groups of 5–50, each female laying 600 or more. They hatch in about a week. The caterpillars are flesh-coloured with small brown spots. They feed until half-grown in spaces between the ears

◁ *Working its way to the top. Another corn stalk borer* **Busseola fusca** *from Africa (×4).*
▽ *Pupa of the European corn-borer (×6).*

or leaves of the corn and the stalks. Then they eat into the stalks and ears, making tunnels through the tissues until they are fully grown, at ¾–1 in. long. There is usually no more than one caterpillar on each plant, but when there is a heavy infestation the corn plants in a field may have about ten caterpillars each. Even so mortality is high before they enter the plant. Heavy rain causes many deaths of emerging caterpillars, and if the summer is very dry they perish before they can bore into plants.

The caterpillars spend winter in their tunnels then pupate the next spring and hatch out in summer.

## The perfect host

If an animal is a pest it becomes the focus of scientific studies. These studies may seem to bear little relation to the destructive habits of the animal, but it is important to investigate every facet of the animal's life.

One essential problem in the study of the corn-borer was why it preferred corn to other plants. One reason, it was found, was that the life cycle of corn fits in well with the life cycle of the moth. Corn is planted in early spring and the leaves are sprouting just in time for the moths to lay their eggs. The leaves provide a steady source of food through the year and in winter the dead stalks provide a very necessary shelter for the resting caterpillars.

Closer examination showed that the caterpillars prefer some parts of the plant more than others. At first they feed in the tightly rolled whorl of leaves wrapped around the stalk. When the flower head develops they feed there. As the flowers expand, the caterpillars move back into the leaf bases and into the husks surrounding the ears. Tests showed that this movement was due to the caterpillar's dislike of light and preference for being in crevices with as much of the body as possible against something solid. The corn-borer was used in experiments on the 'sound protection of corn'; the moth reacts to the sound of bats, so bat calls were played over a cornfield. It was found that the moths shied off–to neighbouring corn.

Even within these preferred snug parts of the corn plant, the corn-borers still exercised preferences. They move to flowers rather than leaves, to inner husks rather than outer husks because these parts contain more sugar. An unusual reason was found for the liking for sugar. Young corn plants contain a chemical poisonous to corn-borers, and sugar acts as an antidote. The chemical is the corn plant's natural remedy against corn-borers and some of them are killed by it, but the ones that can eat a sufficient amount of sugar are safe.

Once the preferences of the insects are known, it may be possible to breed corn plants in which the pests find it more difficult to survive.

| phylum | **Arthropoda** |
|---|---|
| class | **Insecta** |
| order | **Lepidoptera** |
| family | **Pyralididae** |
| genus & species | **Pyrausta nubilalis** |

# Cranefly

*Crane flies or daddy long-legs, are familiar thin-bodied insects with long thread-like legs, which are about in great numbers throughout much of the summer, flying at varying heights and often at the mercy of high winds. The male is readily recognized because the end of his abdomen is widened and clubbed, while the female's is drawn out to form a pointed ovipositor (egg-laying organ).*

*The larvae of crane flies are the troublesome leatherjackets of garden and pasture. These long, soft, fat grubs without legs feed on roots, including grasses, which is why they can ruin a lawn so easily and become greatly disliked.*

### Root pests

Adult crane flies do not feed much. Their mouthparts are modified into a snout-like proboscis with which they suck water and nectar. Most of the feeding is done by the larva or leatherjacket which, fully grown, is over $1\frac{1}{2}$ in. long, greyish and repulsive. Immediately the larvae hatch they begin to feed, using their very strong jaws to eat the roots and lower stems of plants, notably grass, but also cultivated plants such as mangolds, oats and potatoes. The effect of a heavy infestation of leatherjackets on grassland may be to produce extensive bare brown patches. Gardeners and groundsmen sometimes combat leatherjackets by placing large groundsheets over lawns. The larvae often come above ground at night to feed on grass stems, so covering the ground by day induces them to rise to the surface as if it were night.

Aquatic crane fly larvae feed on small worms, dragonfly larvae and any other insect larvae which are available.

### Larvae must have water

One of the commonest species is the large greyish bodied *Tipula oleracea* which is particularly common in late summer. They often fly low over the ground with their long legs trailing passively, and because of this many are caught in the webs of garden spiders. The males of some of the smaller species swarm in nuptial flights before mating. Eggs are laid in water, damp earth, moss or saturated wood, and the larvae and pupae are aquatic or semi-aquatic. Those species most troublesome to man which live on land also require moisture, so that periods of drought often kill off the larvae in large numbers.

Breeding may continue through much of the year. Females which lay their eggs in spring or early summer, having themselves emerged from overwintering pupae, may give rise to a further generation in a matter of weeks. On emerging from the pupa, the male *Tipula oleracea* immediately seeks a mate. Often the males emerge some time before the females and this may mean a long, drawn out search for a partner. Occasionally a male will wait as a female emerges from her pupal case and mate with her while her skin is still soft and damp.

The female lays her tiny, black, seed-like eggs by thrusting her ovipositor deep into the soil. From about June onwards she may lay up to 100 eggs which hatch in about a fortnight. The small larvae, with wrinkled and flexible skins, are exceedingly tough. The larva feeds and increases in size by shedding its skin to form the familiar leatherjacket. Finally it changes to the pupa, and as the time for emergence approaches the pupa wriggles towards the surface of the ground helped by downwardly pointing bristles on its body, and thrusts itself part way out. Then the pupal skin splits behind the head and along the lines of the wings, and the adult fly forces its way out. Dozens of delicate brownish pupal cases can sometimes be seen on a lawn.

The aquatic larvae have five pairs of false legs, lost when the insect becomes an adult, which enable them to crawl about the bottoms of ponds and streams. They breathe by taking oxygen dissolved in the water, or by rising to the surface at intervals to take in air. The pupae remain active, and have two horn-like processes on the head, with which to take in air from above the surface of the water.

### Gyroscopic flight control

Like all flies, the crane fly has only one pair of wings, the second, rear pair being reduced to two club-shaped rods called halteres. In small flies such as a blowfly or housefly, halteres are difficult to see, but in the large crane flies they are easily visible. Halteres was the name given to the two weights or bags of sand that Ancient Greek athletes held in each hand to help throw themselves forward in the long jump. The name is appropriate to the vestigal wings of flies for they are used to balance the flies in flight.

While a fly is in the air, its halteres are rapidly vibrated in the same figure of eight motion as the wings, and in doing so they act in the same way as the gyroscopes which are the basis of an automatic pilot. Rotating at great speed, a gyroscope in a plane stays level while fuselage rolls, yaws and pitches about it. Instruments attached to the gyroscope measure the degree of movement and inform the controls of the steps needed to bring the plane back on to course.

Halteres function in much the same way. At the base of each are sense organs that detect strains and stresses put on the base of the halteres as the fly changes course. If you were so callous as to cut the halteres off a fly, it would have great difficulty in flying. A housefly would be unable to remain airborne but a daddy long-legs would still be able to fly after a fashion, because its long legs and long thin abdomen help to steady it. The housefly could later be restored to normal flight by gluing a thread of cotton to its abdomen to act as a tailplane.

| phylum | **Arthropoda** |
|--------|----------------|
| class | **Insecta** |
| order | **Diptera** |
| family | **Tipulidae** |
| genus | ***Tipula**, others* |

# Cricket

*There are 900 species of cricket, found throughout the world except in polar regions. Apart from the mole crickets, of which there are two species, one in Europe and another in North America, the various kinds differ only slightly. The smallest members are wingless, $\frac{1}{5}$ in. long, and they live in ants' nests, feeding on the ants' oil secretions. These crickets are found only in parts of the northern hemisphere.*

*Typical crickets resemble grasshoppers and locusts and also the bush crickets, sometimes called long-horned grasshoppers or, in America, katydids. All have long hindlegs used for jumping. Crickets differ from grasshoppers, but resemble bush crickets, in having long, thread-like antennae. They produce sound in the same way as bush crickets and, like them, have hearing organs, or 'ears', in the form of a pit on each front leg. Crickets hold their wings flat over the back with the edges sharply bent down at the sides, and there is a pair of jointed appendages, or cerci, at the tip of the abdomen. The female carries a stiff tubular ovipositor through which the eggs are laid. Most crickets are black or brown in colour.*

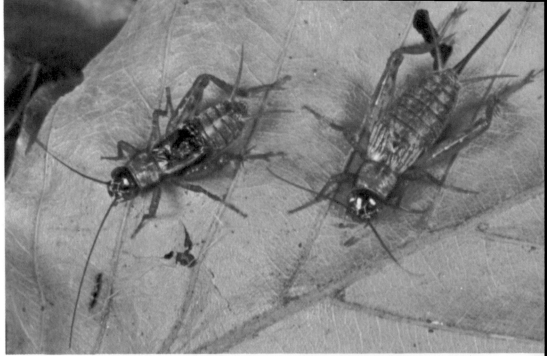

△ *Adult wood crickets (female at right). Female crickets are distinguished by their long ovipositor.*
▽ *Female tree cricket: this is one of the bush crickets or long-horned grasshoppers. The ovipositor of the bush cricket is sabre-like and curves upward. In true crickets it is straight and lance-like.*

## Crickets for all situations

The house cricket has been spread all over the world by man but is probably a native of North Africa and southwest Asia. In temperate climates it can live only indoors or in rotting refuse heaps which give continual warmth. It is brown, a little over $\frac{1}{2}$ in. long, has fully developed wings and long, angled hindlegs. It hides by day and comes out at night to look for scraps of food, when the males make their small chirping song to attract females. The field cricket is found right across Europe to North Africa. Nearly 1 in. long, shiny black with pale yellow markings at the bases of the fore-wings, it has a large head, compared with the body. The hindwings are so reduced that field crickets cannot fly. They live on heaths, preferring warm south-facing slopes. The adults hibernate in burrows dug with their large powerful jaws. The wood cricket, small and brown, less than $\frac{1}{2}$ in. long, ranges across the southern half of Europe, into western Asia and North Africa. It is found sparingly in a few southern English counties. It has no hindwings and cannot fly.

The mole cricket is found all over Europe, temperate Asia and North Africa. Dark brown and covered with a fine velvety hair, it is $1\frac{1}{2}$ in. long and lacks the long jumping hindlegs of a typical cricket. Its forelegs are modified for digging, and in action they look much like the forelegs of a mole. The hindwings are fully developed and mole crickets fly about freely.

## Eat almost anything

Crickets are mainly vegetarian but will take insect food, the proportion varying not only with the species but with circumstances.

△ *The heavy-bodied, short-winged mole cricket has powerful front legs, well equipped for digging, and armed with cutting edges for dealing with rootlets. It drives long, shallow tunnels just below the surface—and despite its subterranean tastes it is a perfectly capable flier.*

They will eat dead animal food as well as household scraps. This omnivorous diet has made it easy for the house cricket to live alongside man, and it has given, falsely, a bad reputation to the mole cricket. This is often regarded as a pest and it can sometimes do damage to root crops, but for the most part it feeds on insects.

## Calling for mates

The sound of the cricket, once welcome, tends today to be regarded as a nuisance. It is produced by stridulation, rubbing the finely toothed vein on the right forewing against the hind edge of the left forewing. A clear area on the left wing acts as a resonator. The male sits at the mouth of his burrow singing while the female wanders about, guided by his song, until she finds him. Female crickets become excited after they hear the song of a male through a telephone, showing that it is to this song and not to scent or sight of the male that they react.

The male cricket deposits his sperm in small capsules, known as spermatophores, which are taken up by the female.

The field cricket lays her eggs during the summer by inserting them into the ground with her ovipositor. The young hatch fully grown the following spring, after hibernation. The adults die in July and August. The wood cricket lays her eggs in autumn, the young hatching the following spring and hibernating to complete their growth in the second summer. Consequently adults of one year can never meet adults of the year

▽ *The sound mechanism of the cricket*
*It is produced by the rapid friction of the cricket's wings—like a man rubbing his hands together. The finely-toothed file vein on the underside of the right forewing is rubbed against the scraper on the hind edge of the left forewing. The bottom illustration shows the overlapping action of the wings during the cricket's song. This song is, in every sense of the word, a love song. Experiments have shown that it is the song—not the scent or the sight of the male—which excites the female cricket.*

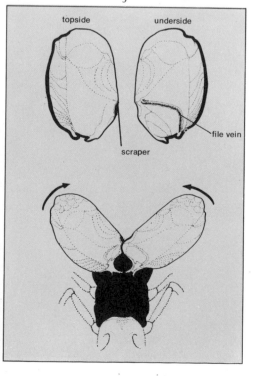

topside    underside

file vein

scraper

△ Superb camouflage: the sharply-jointed legs of a bush cricket in the field blend perfectly with the angles of the surrounding vegetation.

▽ The startling colour of a bush cricket's face. Unlike grasshoppers, crickets and bush crickets have long, thread-like sensitive antennae.

immediately past or following. This has led to 'even-year' and 'odd-year' wood crickets which seem to be different races biologically isolated from each other.

The mole cricket lays her eggs in spring in an underground nest and remains with them for up to 2 weeks until they hatch.

## The thermometer cricket

The American tree crickets of the genus *Oecanthus* are very sensitive to temperature when singing. The rate of the chirps is speeded up as the temperature rises so exactly that the temperature in degrees Fahrenheit can be calculated quite accurately by timing them. You tell the temperature by counting the number of chirps in 15 seconds and adding 39. If you have a thermometer and no watch, the cricket can be used as a timer: just multiply the temperature by 4 and subtract 160 to find the number of chirps uttered per minute.

## Fighting crickets

The Chinese have long had an interest in and sympathy for insects, which is reflected in their art. Crickets especially fascinated them by their singing and their pugnacity. Many varieties have been selectively bred for their musical qualities, and others have been specially bred for fighting. Both were kept in small bamboo cages.

The points looked for in a fighting cricket were loud chirping, big head, long legs, and broad backs. Successful fighters were pampered pets fed on special foods including a soup made from a special flower and mosquitoes gorged with blood from their owner's arm. But they were starved before a fight to step up their fighting spirit.

Fights were staged in special bowls on tables with silk covers. A referee recited the past deeds of the contestants before encouraging them to fight by prodding them with a fine hair. Bets were laid and the end usually came when one cricket bit off the other's head, to earn the victor an entry in letters of gold on an ivory scroll, as *shou lip* (conquering cricket).

At first cricket fighting was the costly pastime of the leisurely scholar of Imperial times. Later it became an entertainment of less literate people. Even 30 years ago the 'sport' had degenerated to little better than an amusing old custom, rapidly dying out. Today it is played only by children.

| phylum | **Arthropoda** |
|---|---|
| class | **Insecta** |
| order | **Orthoptera** |
| family | **Gryllidae** |
| genera & species | ***Acheta domesticus*** *house cricket* |
| | ***Gryllus campestris*** *field cricket* |
| | ***Nemobius sylvestris*** *wood cricket* |
| | ***Gryllotalpa gryllotalpa*** |
| | *mole cricket* |
| | *others* |

*Familiar to tiddler-fishing children as 'blue arrows', damselflies are never found far from the water where they breed. Their wings are long and weakly-muscled, and—as this male demonstrates—they are held over the back when the insect rests, like those of butterflies.*

# Damselfly

*A damsel was originally a woman of noble birth or stately position, elegant and well-dressed, and this is why smaller relatives of dragonflies are called damselflies. Smaller on average than dragonflies (page 73) and far more slender, they hold their wings when at rest elegantly erect over the back, like a butterfly. Their flight is weak and fluttering and many are brightly coloured, blue, red or metallic green. The wings may be colourless and transparent or variously and often beautifully tinted. In some species the males have coloured and patterned wings while those of the female are transparent. The early stages of almost all damselflies are passed in water and the eggs are laid at a depth of about a foot.*

*Although the term 'dragonfly' is often used as equivalent to the insect order Odonata, the two main suborders,*

*Zygoptera and Anisoptera, are better designated by separate English names, damselfly and dragonfly respectively.*

### Fastidious insect

Damselflies have only a weak flight and so are seldom found far from the water in which they breed. Ponds, ditches and canals with a thick growth of reeds and water plants are their favourite haunts, and bulldozers and mechanical dredgers are now their most serious enemies.

Most insects often clean the eyes and antennae with the forelegs, much as a cat 'washes its face'. Damselflies are particularly given to this. They not only clean the sense organs of the head but use the hindlegs to clean the end of the abdomen. Frequently the abdomen itself is curved and raised so as to stroke the wings and divide them from each other. The most likely reason for this is that the long and weakly muscled wings are liable to get stuck together by drifting threads of spider gossamer.

### Courtship displays

Some kinds of damselflies perform courtship displays before mating. In the banded agrion *Agrion splendens* the male waits for a female to fly past and signals to her by raising his body and spreading his wings. If this succeeds and she comes to rest near him he performs an aerial fluttering dance backwards and forwards, facing her all the time, and then comes to rest and mates with her. The banded agrion is one of the species in which the wings are conspicuously coloured in the male and not in the female, and it seems likely that this difference in the sexes is associated with courtship display.

The method of mating used by damselflies (and dragonflies) is unique among insects. The opening of the male's internal sexual organs is in the usual insect position, near the tip of the abdomen. Before mating he transfers sperm to a complicated accessory sexual organ on the underside of the front part of the abdomen, just behind the thorax. When pairing he first grasps the female's

67

head or prothorax with a pair of claspers at the tip of his abdomen. Both then bend their bodies so as to bring the end of the female's abdomen into contact with the male accessory organ, and the sperm is transferred.

The fertilised eggs are laid through a saw-like ovipositor, in the tissues of water plants. This often takes place immediately after mating, and sometimes before the male has released his hold on the female. In some species the two, coupled in this way, crawl down the stem of a reed into the water and descend together to a depth of a foot or more before the eggs are laid.

## Life cycle

The minute creature that hatches from a damselfly egg can neither swim nor crawl and is known as the prolarva or pronymph. Within a few minutes, sometimes almost immediately after hatching, it sheds its skin and the first active larval stage is produced. This larva spends its life in the water and grows in the usual insect fashion, by shedding its skin at intervals. It has a long body, not unlike that of an adult damselfly in shape, but of course no wings. At its hinder end are three leaf-like external gills. These contain a network of minute tubes, or tracheae, into which oxygen diffuses from the water. Respiration also takes place through the skin, rectum and wing sheaths.

In a temperate climate the life cycle of most of the smaller damselflies takes a year, that of some of the larger ones two years. In the tropics, development is more rapid and there may be several generations in a year. When growth is complete the larva crawls out of the water up a stone or rush stem, waits for a short time until the skin of the back splits, and the mature damselfly emerges. The wings are expanded and hardened and the insect can fly within an hour or two.

Although damselfly larvae are usually aquatic, in Hawaii there are a few species, of the genus *Megalagrion*, whose larvae spend all or part of their time on land. In one of these *M. oahuense* the leaf-like tail gills are replaced by hairy appendages and the larva is unable to swim.

## Feeding

Adults feed on small insects, both in the air and at rest, and the larvae probably eat small water insects, worms and the like. Adults, although neither swift nor strong, can 'hawk' small flying insects, as dragonflies often do. They probably feed mainly on gnats and midges.

## Spirit of the dead

People who go out collecting insects have never been rated highly by the general public. At the same time, nobody has treated them with worse than amused tolerance, except in parts of tropical America. Most damselflies are much smaller than dragonflies, but the largest damselflies are greater than the largest dragonflies. One of these huge damselflies *Megaloprepus coerulatus* is 5 in. long and has a wingspan of 7 in. When these damselflies fly in the dusk of the tropical forest they are hardly visible, except for the coloured wing tips. This ghost-like appearance has led the native people to believe that they are the departed spirits of the dead, and they strongly object to their being hunted by collectors.

| phylum | **Arthropoda** |
|---|---|
| class | **Insecta** |
| order | **Odonata** |
| suborder | **Zygoptera** |
| genera | ***Agrion, Megalagrion*** *others* |

▽ *Confused encounter: two damselfly couples, indulging in pre-mating display, form a bewildering pattern for the camera.*

# Diving beetle

The largest diving beetle is popularly called **Dytiscus**, from its scientific name. Also called the great water beetle or carnivorous water beetle, it is the joy of the small boy who goes pond-collecting and one of the worst menaces to small fishes and tadpoles.

It is oval, 1¼ in. long, olive-black above with the thorax and wing covers margined with yellow. Although able to fly, the beetle spends most of its time in water swimming mainly with the broadened hindlegs fringed with bristles. These are used like oars. It is only one of many species of water beetle, mostly of much smaller size but otherwise all very similar.

### Aqualung beetle

The best place to find the beetle is in still water containing plenty of water-weeds. Sooner or later the beetle must come to the surface to breathe. It rises hind end foremost to push the tip of the abdomen just above the surface. Then it raises its wing covers slightly so air is drawn into a pair of breathing pores (spiracles). Air is also drawn in under the wing covers and trapped among the fine bristles covering the back of the abdomen. The remaining spiracles draw upon this store of air while the beetle is submerged.

### Formidable larva

Male and female are easy to tell apart. The wing cases of the female are marked with grooves running lengthwise. Those of the male are smooth, and he has in addition circular pads on his front pair of legs. These have a sucker on the underside and also are sticky. He uses them to cling to the female in spring when mating. She lays her eggs one at a time, making a slit with her ovipositor in the stem of a water plant. The larva is one of the most formidable carnivores in fresh water. When fully grown it is 2 in. long, greenish or yellow-brown, with sharp calliper-like jaws. It may walk over the bottom or swim using its hair-fringed legs as oars. It also must come to the surface to breathe through its tail-tip. The larva crawls out onto land and makes a mud cell in which to pupate.

Each jaw of the larva is tubular and once prey, a baby fish or a tadpole, has been seized digestive juices are pumped down the jaws into the prey's body, converting its tissues into pre-digested soup which is then sucked up through the jaws. This goes on until the body of the prey is an empty husk. The adult beetle, by contrast, chews its food. Both larva and adult beetle will prey upon any small animal or dead fish, even eating its own kind at times.

### Water tiger

To say these beetles are voracious is almost an under-statement. They also attack without hesitation even to biting the fingers of the collector. The very young larvae doubt-

△ At the surface: adult beetle, prey's view.

▽ Water tiger: voracious larva has huge fangs.

less fall victim to bottom-feeding fishes but the fully-grown larva and the adult beetle can take very good care of themselves. Some idea of the force of their attack is seen in the way their jaws penetrate the bodies of other water beetles or disembowel a tadpole at the first lunge. In the United States the larva has been nicknamed the water tiger, which expresses everything about it. The adult beetle, as if not content with its own powerful jaws as a means of defence, may when handled give out an evil-smelling white fluid from its thorax, and possibly from glands near the rear end of the body a yellow fluid reeking of ammonia.

In spite of these drawbacks it seems that not only small boys are fascinated by them. More has probably been written about this beetle than any other, including a German treatise in 2 volumes of 1 827 pages.

| phylum | **Arthropoda** |
| --- | --- |
| class | **Insecta** |
| order | **Coleoptera** |
| family | **Dytiscidae** |
| genus & species | *Dytiscus marginalis* *others* |

# Doodle bug

*Doodle bug is the name given to insects of the family Myrmeleontidae, grouped in the order Neuroptera, together with the alderflies (see page 11) and which bear some resemblance to dragonflies, and more particularly to the lacewing flies (page 114) which they resemble in appearance and habits, in both larval and adult stages. The adults have long thin bodies and two pairs of slender wings of about equal size. Their heads are small with short, thread-like antennae, knobbed at the tips. The largest are little more than 3 in. The larva has a short, thick, fleshy body and dispro-portionately large calliper-like jaws which are armed with strong spines and bristles that help to grasp its prey, mainly ants. This habit of preying on ants has led to the English name ant-lion, a translation of the French name, which is 'fourmi-lion'. The name is also thought to be derived from the habits of the larva. There are several species of doodle bug in the United States, especially in the south and south-west. The student of etymology may be interested to know that this name was applied independently to the flying bomb in 1944. There are more than 600 species of doodle bugs. The typical European species is **Myrmeleon formicarius**, the adult of which is about 1 in. long with a wing span of 2 in.*

## Habits

Doodle bugs are found in woods, forests and plantations wherever there is a sandy soil. The larvae of many species burrow in the sand, the entrance of the burrow being at the bottom of a conical pit, 2 in. deep and 3 in. in diameter at the top, which is also dug by the larva. Groups of these pits can be readily seen in places in southern Europe where the soil is fine and quite dry, and sheltered from the weather, for a shower of rain would destroy the pits and smother the doodle bugs. Likely places are the entrances to dry caves, beneath over-hanging rocks and trees, below the eaves of houses, and in similar sheltered sites.

The adults are active from June to August, usually at dusk or during the night. Their flight is somewhat feeble and awk-ward. One reason why this type of insect is named after its larva is because the adults are very inconspicuous even in strong day-light, flying only when the light is failing or has gone, seldom being seen except when attracted to lights.

## Pit-trapped victims

Adult doodle bugs have been relatively little studied. They are reported to feed on fruit and on small flies, and they may possibly feed on the honey-dew produced by aphids, as do the lacewings. The larva sets and springs one of the most spectacular traps

△ *Doodle bug gripping an ant in its vice-like jaws.*

◁ *The delicate beauty of the harmless adult doodle bug is in vivid contrast with its vicious hunting larva.*

▽ *The gigantic calliper-like jaws or mandibles of the doodle bug larva which firmly seize its victim. Together with the secondary jaws or maxillae, two tubes are formed down which flows a paralysing fluid.*

in the animal kingdom. Buried at the bottom of its pit, with only camouflaged head and strong jaws exposed, it waits for grains of sand disturbed by a passing ant or spider to fall and provide a trigger to spring its trap. Immediately sand is scooped on to the head by the jaws and the larva then jerks its head forwards and upwards, catapulting a stream of sand with great force and accuracy at its intended victim. This barrage, the steep sides of the pit, and the sand being undermined by the doodle bug's digging, together cause the victim to slide down to within reach of the doodle bug's jaws where it is immediately seized.

Sometimes the doodle bug gets only an unsatisfactory grip on its prey. In this event it may toss its victim rapidly against the sides of the pit until it gets a firm hold. It may even temporarily release its victim and again hurl sand at it if it shows signs of escaping. But once firmly held, the prey is drawn partially beneath the sand and then the second function of the calliper-like jaws comes into effect. These jaws are deeply grooved underneath. When the maxillae or secondary mouth parts are pressed against them, together they form two tubes down which a paralysing fluid flows, to be injected into the victim's body. When its struggles have ceased digestive juices are then injected in much the same way. These dissolve the tissues which the doodle bug then sucks up and swallows. Finally, the empty case of the insect's body is tossed up and over the edge of the pit by the doodle bug using the same technique as when catapulting sand grains.

Although the eyes of the larva are well-developed they seem to play no part in detecting the presence of food. If a few grains of sand at the edge of the pit are dislodged so they roll down the side and strike the doodle bug larva in wait at the bottom, it will immediately begin hurling sand upwards. Since it will react in this way when no prey is visible it is a fair assumption that the eyes play little part.

Occasionally doodle bug pits are grouped so close together that there is little chance of the occupants all getting sufficient food. This is offset by the larvae being able to fast without harm for up to 8 months.

Not all species of doodle bug dig pits. Some capture their prey by speed, others do so by stealth or ambush, perhaps lurking beneath stones and rubbish. It is interesting to note that while the highly specialised and somewhat sedentary pit-making species can only walk backwards, the more active species are able to do so in any direction.

### Three-year life cycle

After mating, the female doodle bug lays her eggs singly in the sand. These are white and oval, and being sticky on the surface, immediately become encrusted with a layer of sand, which serves as a protective camouflage. Within a day of hatching, the young doodle bug has already dug a pit, of a size proportionate to itself. Thenceforth, the larva goes through three stages known as instars. At the end of each of these, the larva leaves its pit temporarily and hides beneath the sand for about a week to ten days. During this period it casts its old skin,

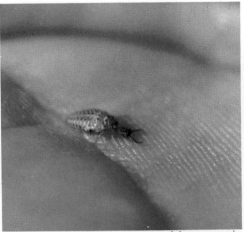
*Doodle bug larvae although very vicious are quite small. Here a larva is held in the palm, clearly showing its size.*

and then digs a new pit and begins to feed again. Probably the length of time spent as a larva depends to a large extent on the food available. But even with plenty of food it is estimated that the life-cycle from egg to adult takes from 1–3 years, and far longer under unfavourable circumstances. Once fully grown the larva pupates beneath the soil at the bottom of the pit, within a spherical silken cocoon. As in all insects of the order Neuroptera, the silk is produced by the Malpighian tubules; these structures are named after Malpighi, the 17th-century Italian microscopist who first described them. The silk is given out through the anus. This contrasts with caterpillars of butterflies and moths, for example, whose silk is produced by glands in the head. Almost as soon as the silk makes contact with the air, it hardens and, like the eggs, the cocoon is further protected by sand which sticks to its outer surface, although the innermost layers of silk never become sanded. Only when the cocoon is completed does the doodle bug larva shed its skin for the last time, revealing the cream-coloured pupa. The period of pupation to emergence of the perfect winged insect is usually about a month. Just prior to emergence, the doodle bug pupa cuts a hole in the cocoon with its pupal mandibles, and, using its 'free' pupal legs, crawls part way out of the cocoon before emerging as the perfect insect. At this stage, the pupal skin splits, and the adult works its way to the surface of the soil where it then climbs up a plant or tree from which it can hang while the body hardens and the wings expand and dry.

### Innate abilities

Before man settled down to agriculture he lived by hunting and capturing wild animals. No doubt one of the first things he learnt to do was to build a pit in which to trap his quarry. Whether he merely stumbled on the idea or thought it out carefully in the first place is something we shall never know. Whichever way it was, however, he devised various methods of using the pit. He would camouflage it with branches of trees so that the animal passing that way did not suspect a trap. He would plant pointed stakes in the bottom of the pit or lurk nearby ready with a spear to make a kill. These and many variations have been used

for thousands of years and are still in use in various parts of the world even today. All the methods bear some resemblance to the tactics used by the doodle bug. Indeed, some of the things the doodle bug does seem to be an improvement on human techniques and therefore have the appearance of intelligence. We can be fairly sure that man started using pits because his better brain capacity enabled him to see the advantages and also to improve on method. Here is the essential difference between the things that insects do and the things we do. The insect merely follows an inherent behaviour pattern. We would find if we examined the pits and the behaviour of thousands of doodle bug of a given species that each individual trapped its prey in exactly the same way as every other individual of its species. Each doodle bug larva would start with the same method and would continue to use this method throughout its lifetime as a larva, without any improvement on it. Everything it does is therefore inborn or innate.

Nevertheless, those who study insects find themselves being forced to admit that there are times when even insects appear to depart slightly from the inborn pattern of behaviour, to adjust their actions to the varying needs of the moment or to the

*Doodle bug trapping pits. Should an ant or spider walk too near this steep-sided pit, it is doomed. The doodle bug disturbs the sand so the victim slides down to be gripped by its waiting jaws.*

changing circumstances, in a way which suggests that some sort of thought or some sort of intelligence, no matter how rudimentary, is being brought to bear on it. As a result, scientists now tend to talk about insects having plastic, that is, flexible behaviour.

| class | **Insecta** |
|-------|-------------|
| order | **Neuroptera** |
| family | **Myrmeleontidae** |
| genera | ***Myrmeleon, Palpares, Hesperoleon,*** *and others* |

△ Male dragonfly **Orthetrum coerulescens**.
The female of this British species is brown
with black markings on the abdomen.

▽ African beauty of the family Libellelidae.
The wings show the complex venation supporting
the membrane which is found in all dragonflies.

# Dragonfly

*Colourful and powerful fliers, dragonflies
are among the fastest of all insects. Most
dragonflies are large insects which hold
their wings stiffly extended on each side
when at rest, whereas most other insects
fold them over the back. The wings are
capable of only simple up-and-down
movement, have no coupling device joining
the front and back wings, as in higher
insects such as butterflies, and have
a fine network of 'veins' supporting the
membrane. All these characteristics show
that dragonflies are primitive insects that
have existed with little change for a very
long time. The earliest known fossil
dragonflies are from the late
Carboniferous period, deposited about
300 million years ago. There were
dragonflies similar to those living
today in the Jurassic period, 150 million
years ago, when the giant dinosaurs were
roaming the earth.*

*The name is often used in England as an
equivalent of the insect order Odonata,
but the members of the suborder Zygoptera
are very distinct in appearance and have
been dealt with under Damselfly (page 67).
Living dragonflies consist of two very
unequal suborders, the Anisoptera (all the
familiar species) and the Anisozygoptera
(only two species known, from Japan and
the Himalayas respectively).*

*As in their relatives the damselflies,
the wings of dragonflies are usually transparent and colourless, but may be tinted or
patterned, and the body is often brightly
coloured. They differ markedly from
damselflies in having very swift, powerful
flight. Estimates of their actual speed are
difficult to obtain and vary from 35 up to
60 mph, but they are certainly among the
fastest of all insects. The antennae are
minute and the eyes enormous, occupying
the greater part of the head. Each compound eye may contain as many as 30 000
facets.*

## Territorial instincts

Dragonflies fly a 'fighter patrol' over a
fixed area. Although they are most often
seen near water, which is where they breed,
their powerful flight carries them far away
from their breeding places, and they may
be met wherever there are trees and bushes
on which they can rest. One can often be
seen flying back and forth over a definite
'beat', and when it lands it will do so on
one or other of a small number of resting
places. The beat may be an area selected
as suitable for hunting prey or, especially
if it is over water, it may be the territory
chosen by a male dragonfly, which will then
mate with any female of its own species
which flies into this area. These males defend their territories strenuously against
other males of the same species. After a
while they begin to show signs of battle in
the shape of torn wings and mutilated legs.

Whether in hunting or fighting, the sense used most is sight; a dragonfly can detect movement 40 ft away.

Some species of dragonflies are migratory and may fly great distances over land and sea. One species *Libellula quadrimaculata* sometimes migrates in spectacular swarms. In 1862 a swarm was observed in Germany, estimated at nearly two-and-a-half thousand million strong, and in June 1900 the sky over Antwerp 'appeared black' with these dragonflies. In 1947 a huge migration of another species *Sympetrum striolatum* was seen flying overhead by observers on the south coast of Ireland.

**Masked killers**

Dragonflies are predatory in all their stages. The adults catch other insects on the wing, seizing them with their forwardly directed legs and chewing them with their powerful jaws. In the southeastern United States two large species *Anax junius* and *Coryphaeshna ingens* are serious predators of honeybees.

The larvae capture their prey by what is known as a mask, a mechanism that is shared with the damselflies but is otherwise unique among insects. The labium or lower lip is greatly enlarged and armed with a pair of hooks. At rest it is folded under the head,

△ *Skimming low over the surface, a female dragonfly dips her abdomen to lay eggs.*

but it is extensible and can be shot out in front of the head, the hooks being used to seize the prey like a pair of pincers. The victim is then drawn back within reach of the jaws. Other insects, tadpoles and small fish form the prey of dragonfly larvae, and those of the larger species can make serious inroads into the numbers of young fish in a rearing pond. On the other hand, the young dragonfly larvae perform a useful service by destroying great numbers of the aquatic larvae of mosquitoes.

## The 'tandem'

Mating involves the same curious procedure described for damselflies, in which the male transfers his sperm from the primary sexual organ near the tip of his abdomen to an accessory organ farther forward, at the base of the abdomen. He then alights on the back of a female and curls his abdomen under his own body in order to seize her head (not her thorax as in damselflies) with a pair of claspers at the end of his abdomen. He then releases the hold with his legs but retains that with his claspers. The female then curls her abdomen round in such a way that the tip of it makes contact with the male accessory organ. Both before and after mating the two may fly together, with the female held by the male claspers, in what is known as the 'tandem position'. They may even maintain this position while the eggs are being laid.

Dragonflies almost always lay their eggs in water. One of two ways is used. Some insert their eggs into the stems of water plants, as damselflies do. These include the big hawker dragonflies, *Aeshna*. Others, like the golden-ringed dragonfly *Cordulegaster boltoni* force their eggs into the sand or gravel at the margins of shallow streams. The second method is to fly close over the surface of water and repeatedly dip the tip of the body, extruding eggs at the same time, so these are washed off and sink to the bottom.

## Form of jet propulsion

Most dragonflies spend their early life under water. The larvae vary in shape. Those that live in mud are short, thick-set and covered with a dense coat of hairs to which the mud clings. When such a larva is at rest, only the eyes and the tip of the abdomen are exposed, the rest being buried. The golden-ringed dragonfly has a larva of this type. Those that live among water weeds are more slender and active, but no dragonfly larvae are as slender and delicate as those of damselflies. They have gills inside the intestine a short distance from their hind opening and the larvae breathe by drawing water into the rectum and then driving it out again. This mechanism is also used for another purpose. If suddenly disturbed, the larva drives the water out forcibly, so propelling itself rapidly forward, in a simple form of jet propulsion.

When fully grown, after 2 years or more in most European species, the larva crawls up a plant growing in the water, climbs above the surface and undergoes its final moult to become an adult dragonfly.

Destruction of their habitat by pollution, drainage, dredging and infilling of ponds is the most serious threat to dragonflies and this is increasing throughout the world. As larvae, their chief natural enemies are fishes, whose own babies the well-grown dragonfly larvae prey upon. In fact dragonfly larvae probably form an important source of food for freshwater fishes. When small they are also eaten by other predatory insects, including larger dragonfly larvae, often of their own species. The adults are so swift and active that they have few natural enemies, but one small bird of prey, the hobby, feeds extensively on them.

△ *Libellula quadrimaculata* —both male and female have very similar markings on the abdomen and wings.

▽ *Dragonfly of Transvaal Lowveld, South Africa, resting. Powerful fliers, dragonflies are among the fastest of all insects.*

## Biggest insects ever

The present-day Odonata are among the largest living insects. In tropical America there are damselflies with bodies 5 in. long and wings spanning 7 in. These are slender, flimsy creatures and are greatly exceeded in bulk by a Borneo dragonfly *Tetracanthagyna plagiata* whose wings also span 7 in. and whose thick body measures about 5 in.

No modern dragonflies, however, compare in size with some which lived 300 million years ago, in the forests when our coal measures were being laid down. At Commentry, in France, fossil remains of these have been found, including impressions of wings, which show that the wingspan of the biggest of them *Meganeura monyi* was as much as 27 in., about equal to that of a crow. They are by far the largest insects known to have inhabited the earth, but it is interesting that no larval remains have yet been found.

| class | **Insecta** |
|---|---|
| order | **Odonata** |
| suborders | **Anisoptera, Anisozygoptera** |

*Top left: 'Watch it' — a threatened male raises his pincers. Top right: Birthday suit — a freshly-peeled female rests beside her old skin.*

*Above left: Female earwigs are model mothers. This one is pottering anxiously round her eggs, protecting and cleaning them.*

*Above right: Watching over a nursery of earwig toddlers, which stay with the mother until their second moult, eating their own skins.*

# Earwig

*The fearsome-looking pincers of the common earwig are referred to in its scientific name — **Forficula auricularia** — since **forficula** is Latin for 'little scissors'. Curved in the male and straight in the female, they are carried at the hind end of the flattened brown body and when danger approaches they may be raised in the air and displayed as a threat. Although not as effective weapons as they look, they are nevertheless used in defence and the insect can use them to grip with some tenacity. Those of the males vary in length and fall into two more or less distinct size ranges.*

*At first sight, the earwig seems to have no wings, but in fact there is a serviceable pair neatly folded away beneath tiny wing cases overlapping the front part of the abdomen. These wing cases or 'elytra', like those of beetles, are the hardened front pair of wings, which in dragonflies, butterflies and other insects are still used in flight. The pincers of the earwig are said to assist in folding away the wings after use.*

*The tawny earwig is only half the size but otherwise much like the adult of the*

*common earwig. There are a few other British species, including two that have been introduced, but these are much less common.*

*There are some 900 species of earwigs throughout the world, differing in size from $\frac{1}{4}$ in. to $1\frac{1}{2}$ in. but otherwise similar except that some are wingless.*

## Rarely seen on the wing

Earwigs spend the day hidden away in dry, usually upright crevices, and are often to be found under loose bark. The common earwig is also found tucked away among the petals of dahlias. Whether or not they are doing much damage is a disputed point though they are known to eat both petals and leaves. Gardeners often provide an alternative home in the form of an upturned flower pot, preferably stuffed with newspaper or straw. Earwigs are active at night and it is partly for this reason that they have rarely been seen flying although some — and the tawny earwig is one — often take to the wing on hot days. When earwigs are seen on clothes hanging out on a line overnight, however, it is easier to believe they have flown there than climbed.

The common earwig is widespread in Europe and has also been introduced and firmly established in the United States, becoming a nuisance in some places.

## Earwigs eat plant lice

The diet includes a great variety of both animal and plant matter. To a large extent, earwigs are scavengers, but they may sometimes eat large numbers of plant lice, and have been seen to capture larger insects like bluebottles with their pincers. They will also eat fruit, leaves, flowers and fungi:

## The 'broody-hen' insect

The most remarkable feature of the earwig is its family life and the 'broody-hen' behaviour of the mother. The sexes come together in September. Then, throughout much of the autumn and winter, they may be found in pairs either in chambers dug about an inch down in the earth, or sometimes just in crevices among vegetation. Late in January or towards the end of March, the male leaves — or is perhaps driven out — and the female starts to lay her oval, pearly-white eggs. Within about 2 days some 20—80 are laid, the largest females tending to produce the greatest number. At first the eggs are scattered about the floor of the chamber, but the mother soon gathers them into a pile and thereafter gives them her continual attention. One by one she picks them up in her mouth and licks them all over. At this time she is more than usually aggressive, and her only food is the occasional egg that has gone bad. The rest hatch 3—4 weeks after being laid.

The behaviour of the mothers has been subjected to scientific scrutiny. It has been found, for instance, that they recognise their eggs, when collecting up after they are laid. A female earwig will quite readily collect little wax balls or rounded stones. Later on, however, the wax balls and stones are rejected as lacking the appropriate taste or smell.

It has also been found that the eggs must be licked by the mother if they are to hatch and that the female's urge to lick them is dependent on the presence of the eggs. The urge fades in a few days if the eggs are removed, and after that it cannot be revived even if the eggs are replaced, but it will persist as long as 3 months if the eggs are continually replaced by others as they hatch.

The young earwigs are not grubs or larvae but nymphs, essentially like the parents though smaller and more dumpy, with simple straight forceps. Like domestic chicks, they stay with their mother for a while, nestling under her body. Twice they cast and eat their skins while in her care, and after the second moult they disperse, to become fully grown by about July. This cosy family picture is spoiled, however, if the mother dies, for she is then eaten by her own offspring (along with the cast skins).

The family life of the earwig represents an early stage in the evolution of a social organisation, which is developed independently and far more fully in ants, bees, wasps and termites. A relative of the earwig (Hemimerus) protects its eggs in a very different way. It behaves more like a mammal than a bird. Its eggs are retained within the body, where they are nourished by a sort of placenta and the young are born alive.

## Do earwigs enter ears?

To some people earwigs are endearing animals, for no very clear reason. To others, through a belief that they will enter the human ear, they are objects of apprehension. This belief is reflected in the name given to the animal not only in English but in other languages, *Ohrwurm* in German and *perce-oreille* in French, to name only two. It is sometimes suggested that the English name is derived from 'ear-wing' since the extended wings are somewhat ear-shaped, but 'wig' is from the Old English 'wiggle', to wriggle, and the wings are hardly likely to be seen often enough to compete with the pincers for commemoration in a common name.

Entomologists seem to discredit the notion of earwigs entering ears, but there are authentic accounts of its having happened in medical journals and in the case-books of medical practitioners. Moreover, there is a consistent note in the descriptions of the discomfort experienced by the patients, who complain of a 'noise of thunder' in the ear.

It must be agreed with the sceptics that the earwig has no special passion for ears, but it does have an instinct to insinuate itself into cracks and crevices, under loose bark or in folds of curtains—so why not on rare occasions in the ear of an unwary camper or, more often perhaps in the past, in the ears of our ancestors who lived closer to nature? For peace of mind, when sleeping under canvas, some cotton wool in the ears is a reasonable precaution. The first aid remedy is to float the insect out with oil.

It is interesting that earwigs themselves have been used in medicine, as a cure for deafness, on the principle that like cures like, or, as it is popularly known 'a hair of the dog that bit you'. The earwig was dried, powdered and mixed with the urine of a hare.

| phylum | **Arthropoda** |
| --- | --- |
| class | **Insecta** |
| order | **Dermaptera** |
| family | **Forficulidae** |
| genera & species | ***Forficula auricularia*** *common earwig* ***Labia minor*** *tawny earwig others* |

*Below left: Earwig couple. The male can be distinguished from the female by the scimitar curve of his pincers; the female's are straight. Below: Female earwig's wing pattern. Earwigs can fly quite well, but they are rarely seen doing so because they are most active at night.*

# Firefly

*Fireflies are named for the brilliant light they give out when flying. This comes from the underside of the tip of the abdomen. The more brilliant fireflies are found mainly in the tropics, in India, Burma, Thailand and Malaya, although some are found in temperate latitudes. Several occur in Europe, and in North America they are often called 'lightning bugs'. The female of the South American **Phrixothrix** has 11 pairs of green lights, and a red 'headlight'. It has been called the 'railway worm'. Fireflies are in no way related to the true flies (Diptera) but belong to two families of beetles, the Lampyridae, which also includes the glowworms (page 90), and Elateridae.*

### Light without heat

For obvious reasons, fireflies are best seen after nightfall. The short-lived adults spend the evening hours displaying their greenish, yellowish or sometimes reddish lights, usually at regular intervals which vary with the species, so these signals serve for recog-

*Fireflies swarm around a luminous lure.*

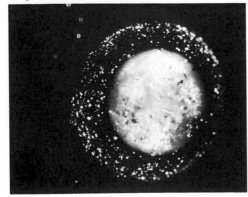

nition. Most female fireflies are flightless. They cling to foliage, flashing their lights at intervals to attract the males. Sometimes large groups of them may be seen, flashing more or less in unison. Such beautiful and highly spectacular displays are particularly common in Burma and Thailand. Moonlight seems to inhibit the fireflies, reducing their output of signals.

The light organs of fireflies consist of an area of transparent cuticle under which the light-producing chemical, luciferin, is stored. Behind the luciferin is a layer of dense tissue that probably acts as a reflector. The light production is an oxidative ('burning') process similar to respiration in which sugar is broken down by enzymes, or catalysts, in the presence of oxygen, releasing energy in the form of heat. In fireflies, the same thing happens except that the result is light – also a form of energy.

The enzyme involved in light production is called luciferase and it speeds the reaction of luciferin with oxygen to produce oxyluciferin, the light being emitted as a byproduct. Later the oxyluciferin is changed back to luciferin and the process repeated. Oxygen is supplied by the system of fine breathing tubes that spread through every part of an insect's body, carrying air to the tissues.

Firefly light is produced almost entirely without heat: a strange eerie cold light which thus effectively gives the lie to the 'fire' part of the firefly's everyday name. Because of this, firefly light is, in strictly physical terms, one of the most efficient lighting systems known, although it may be dim when compared with man-made methods of illumination. In the average electric light bulb, the efficiency is only about 3%; 97% of the energy released is wasted as heat. In many fireflies, there is more than 90% efficiency. Experiments have been tried to harness chemiluminescence – as the process

△ *In daylight the firefly is not an inspiring sight, looking like any other bug – but it is a very different story when it cuts loose with its full candle power in the dark (right).*

of light-production in fireflies is called – but the cost has so far proved far more expensive than any system in present use.

### Most adults do not feed

Many adult beetles are very voracious, and most of the firefly's feeding is done in the larval stage. Many of the larvae are carnivorous. Most lampyrids (including the common glowworm) feed on various small slugs and snails which they first break down with a special digestive fluid. Some fireflies, such as the elaterids, feed on certain vegetable materials, including roots and rotting wood.

### Mating by signal

The main purpose of the luminescence is to bring the sexes together. In fireflies both sexes are almost equally luminous and the male locates the female either by emitting a series of flash signals and noting her responses or by watching for her signals. Most species have their own well-defined flash sequences. In the common North American *Photinus pyralis* the male flashes his light for a split second, at intervals of 6 seconds, and in these intervals the female may reply. This may go on until the two sexes are near enough to make physical contact. The eggs, larvae and pupae of fireflies may also be luminescent to some extent. Nobody knows why and it is assumed that the light may be defensive. On the other hand, in the larvae, luminescence may sometimes be a way of keeping groups of them together in areas where there is a plentiful supply of food, even to attracting hungry larvae to others that have found food. While adult fireflies are mainly short-lived, the larval stage may extend over many months, or even years.

## Main enemies

Frogs and toads are the fireflies' main enemies. Frogs have been found which at first seemed to possess their own built-in light, but closer inspection has shown they had been eating fireflies. In some species it seems the light fireflies emit often has the effect of leading them to their destruction. In America, the female *Photuris pennsylvanica* emits light which will occasionally attract males of another firefly *Photinus scintillans*, which she seizes and eats. Quite often the cannibalistic female is carrying fertile eggs, and although adult fireflies usually eat little it is believed that this extra protein helps the development of her offspring. As with so many insects, artificial light is a means of attraction, leading to death or mutilation, the male fireflies mistaking such lights for possible partners, and being irresistibly drawn to them.

## Firefly candle power

Although firefly light is so remarkably efficient, its brilliance can be exaggerated. It has been shown, for example, that even the most brilliant luminous animal known, the 'cucujo' beetle *Pyrophorus noctilucus* of South America produces light equivalent to only about 1/40th of a candle power. The reason we find them so brilliant is that the light is emitted along a wavelength at which the human eye is most sensitive, and this is why the brightest fireflies give off enough light for a book to be read with comparative ease. It is perhaps hardly surprising therefore to find that in some parts of the world fireflies have been used as cheap lights. In China and Japan, for example, poor students once used them for reading at night. In Brazil, they have been used, enclosed in special perforated gourd lanterns, to illuminate huts. The native Brazilians also wore them in their hair or tied them to their ankles when on night expeditions. In the United States National Museum there is a firefly lamp from Java which is said to have been used by a burglar. It consists of a shallow wooden dish containing a layer of wax on which the fireflies were stuck. A hinged lid enabled the intruder to douse his light when it was not needed – or presumably if he was disturbed at work!

| phylum | **Arthropoda** |
|--------|----------------|
| class | **Insecta** |
| order | **Coleoptera** |
| family | **Lampyridae** |
| genera | ***Photinus, Photuris*** |
| family | **Elateridae** |
| genus | ***Pyrophorus*** |

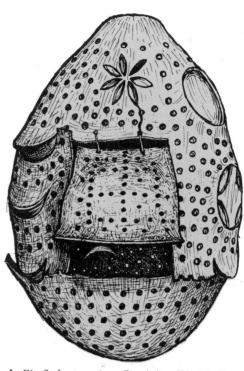

△ *Firefly lantern from Dominica, West Indies.*

# Flea

*Fleas are small, wingless insects, parasites with the body flattened from side to side, making it easy for them to slip through the fur or feathers of the host. The legs are modified for rapid movement in this environment and also for powerful jumping, and the thick, hard skin is a good defence against the host's scratching.*

*The name 'flea' is used for any member of the insect order Siphonaptera, of which a little over a thousand species are known. The order is very distinct and isolated from other insects, but there are indications of winged ancestors and a relationship with, perhaps, the scorpion flies (Mecoptera). All fleas live, when adult, as blood-sucking parasites of mammals or birds. Their larvae live on the debris and dirt that accumulate in the lairs or nests of the animals which are the hosts of the mature insects.*

*The eggs are large for the size of the insect, about $\frac{1}{50}$ in. long, and white. The larvae are small whitish maggots, legless but having a pair of short antennae and biting jaws. The pupae grow in cocoons.*

*In a few species the female is sedentary, remaining attached and feeding in one spot. She may even burrow into the skin of the host, the tropical jigger flea* **Tunga penetrans** *being an example of this.*

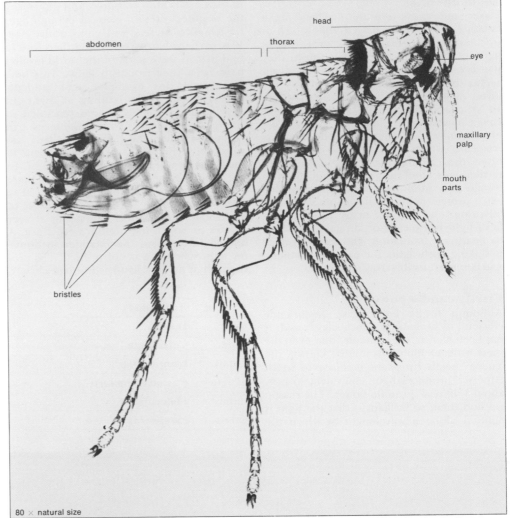

80 × natural size

△ *Flea showing the tough, bristle-covered shell – a good defence against scratching hosts.*
▽ *Prepared specimen displays powerful legs.*

▷ *Making the most of babyhood: the flea gorges itself on the blood of a blind, defenceless common shrew infant.*

## Choice of targets

Fleas usually parasitise only mammals and birds which have a lair or nest in which they live and breed, or which congregate in large numbers in regular roosts. The majority of known species are parasites of rodents, most of which live in nests or burrows, and insectivores and bats are also much infested. Apart from man, primates are never more than casually infested. Monkeys do not as a rule carry fleas at all. Aquatic mammals such as otters and coypus are also not attacked by fleas and among the hoofed animals, the pig is one of the few animals regularly infested.

Among birds fleas are most numerous on the species which nest in holes such as woodpeckers, tits and the sand martin, the last being perhaps the most flea-infested of all birds. The rock dove and its descendant the domestic pigeon have a special flea of their own *Ceratophyllus columbae* and this is not found on wood pigeons. Possibly it is because rock doves and domestic pigeons nest in holes and on ledges while wood pigeons make an openwork nest in trees. This underlines the basic requirement for infestation by fleas, which is a suitable environment in the host's nest for the non-parasitic debris-eating larvae.

It is unusual for fleas to be confined to one host. Both the flea of the rock dove and the sand martin's flea *Ceratophyllus styx* are restricted to the one species. Most fleas will feed and breed on a variety of hosts; the

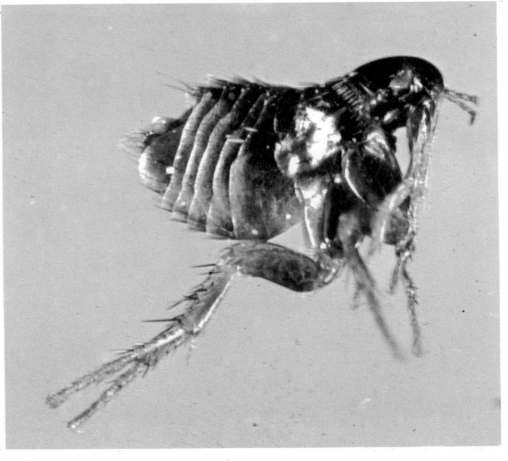

human flea *Pulex irritans* is found also on pigs, and the hen flea *Ceratophyllus gallinae* feeds on a great number of different birds and can live on mammalian, including human, blood as well.

## Carriers of disease

Fleas will also casually infest hosts with which they have no breeding association. Cat fleas, finding themselves on a human, bite readily. The incidence of the dreaded bubonic plague is mainly due to a particular flea *Xenopsylla cheopis* that normally lives on rats, leaving these bodies when they die of plague and infesting people whose hygienic standards permit rats to live in numbers in their dwellings. The bacterium *Pasteurella pestis* that causes plague affects rats and men equally severely and is conveyed from one to the other in the saliva of the fleas. In medi-aeval times practically no house was free of rats and the great epidemics of plague or 'black death' killed millions of people.

In the jigger flea, the female burrows into the skin of its human host. Both sexes start their adult life as very small fleas, hopping about in the dust around human habitations. After mating the females burrow into the skin of people's feet under the toenails and grow to the size of a pea, forming a cyst. This causes a great deal of pain and is difficult to remove without causing sores or abscesses due to secondary infection. The hen stick-tight flea *Echidnophaga gallinacea* infests poultry and the females gather on the naked skin of the birds' heads and attach themselves permanently. This flea's choice of hosts is quite unusual; it infests poultry and various small mammals, clustering on their ears, and is particularly partial to hedgehogs.

## Delayed hatching

The eggs of fleas are dropped into the nest of the host or may be laid among its fur or feathers, whence they are shaken out and many fall into the nest. Almost all fleas require a meal of blood before they can develop and lay their eggs. The tiny maggot-like larvae feed on dirt and debris, including dried blood, in the host's nest, or in dusty unswept corners in human habitations. When fully grown they make cocoons and pupate. The pupae often lie dormant for long periods and in some species, including the human flea, are sensitive to movement and vibration, which stimulates them to hatch. Campers, invading a deserted house that has been abandoned months before, may be greeted by hordes of fleas that hatch in response to the tramping and dumping of heavy luggage. This is an obvious adaptation to delay hatching of the pupae until a new host and source of blood appears on which newly-emerged adults can feed.

## Special mouth parts

Like other blood-sucking insects fleas have special sucking mouth parts. The most important part is a narrow tube formed from three needle-like stylets, an anterior and two lateral ones. They are serrated towards the tip to increase their efficiency in piercing. An anticoagulant 'saliva' is injected before the blood sucking commences. It is this which causes the irritation associated with a flea bite, and which leads to disease

organisms being passed into the blood of the host by infected fleas.

Fleas are very greedy feeders and only digest and assimilate a fraction of the blood they suck up, the rest being passed out of the intestine unchanged. It is thought that this apparently wasteful habit may have been evolved to provide a supply of dry coagulated blood for the flea larvae which are feeding in the nest of the host. If this were so it would be an example of a parent insect making provision for its larvae resembling, but far less elaborate than, that used by wasps and bees. The idea may not be as far-fetched as it appears. The larvae feed in the normal way, searching for edible particles among their surroundings and chewing them in their mandibles.

## When parasite eats parasite

Fleas are regularly caught and eaten in small numbers by their hosts, usually in the course of licking, cleaning and preening. This benefits another form of parasite. The common tapeworm of dogs and cats *Dipylidium caninum* spends one phase of its life cycle in dog fleas and depends on the fleas being eaten to get from one host to another. Far more effective enemies of fleas are certain mites which live in nests and prey on the fleas in all their stages. Small beetles of the genus *Gnathoncus* are often found in birds' nests, and they also prey on fleas and their larvae.

## Performing flea

At one time the flea circus was a familiar item of entertainment in country fairs. *Pulex irritans* was still an abundant and familiar insect 50 to 100 years ago when the forms of public entertainment were far less numerous and less sophisticated than they are now. At the present time the manager of a flea circus would be faced with two difficulties. He would probably have difficulty in finding an audience and he would certainly have difficulty in finding a sufficient supply of human fleas for his performers. He would therefore have to be content with dog or cat fleas, which are not easy to feed in captivity.

It was customary for the proprietor of one of these circuses to keep human fleas and feed them on his own arm. A large part of his skill lay in constructing tiny devices such as tricycles and 'chariots' which could be propelled by fleas attached to them in such a way that the crawling of the insect caused them to move. Another very delicate operation was the tethering or harnessing of the fleas with very fine gold or silver wire. There was never any question of the fleas being taught or trained in any way, though of course this was always claimed as part of his expertise by their owner. Advantage was simply taken of the natural movements of the insect when restrained in various ways. The real skill displayed by those who ran flea circuses lay in making the 'props'. One

was a coach, of tiny proportions, perfect in every detail which was drawn by a team of fleas.

The relatively enormous size and rapidity of the flea's jump has puzzled naturalists since the time of Socrates. It has recently been shown that in addition to the powerful leg muscles and tendons, the flea's jumping apparatus incorporates a cap of resilin, a rubber-like protein which, when compressed and suddenly released, delivers power faster than most actively contracting muscle. Resilin is generally a component of the wing-hinge ligament of flying insects, such as dragonflies and locusts, and its presence in the thorax of fleas suggests that they have adapted and modified a flight mechanism to increase their mobility while living among fur and feathers. In other words fleas are insects which fly with their legs.

Adult fleas are remarkably long-lived. Supplied regularly with blood a human flea has survived 513 days, and a Russian bird flea is said to have lived for 1 487 days or a little over four years.

| class | **Insecta** |
|-------|-------------|
| order | **Siphonaptera** |
| genera | **Pulex, Tunga, Echidnophaga** *others* |

▽ *Flea sword-fight and chariot race.*

▽ *The gadgets of a flea circus 'ring': chariots, a tricycle, a tight-rope, and sword-fighting frame.*

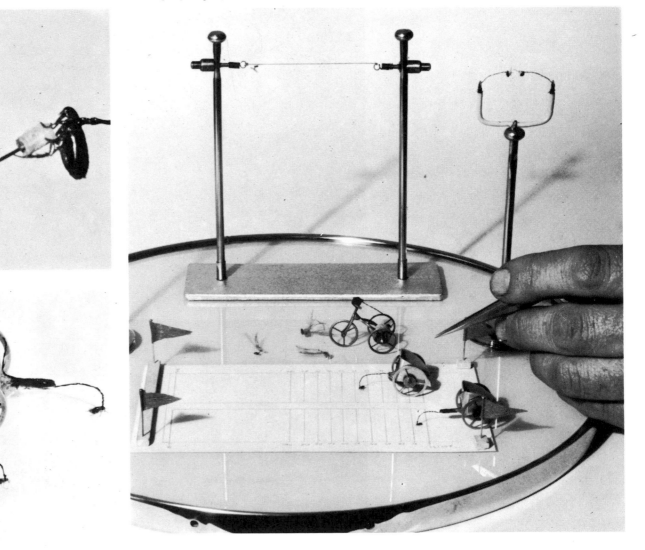

*High brown fritillary* **Argynnis adippe**.

# Fritillary

*Fritillary butterflies owe their name to a genus of plants* **Fritillaria** *whose flowers have a dark and light chequered pattern. Certain butterflies of the family Nymphalidae have a similar pattern on their wings and were named 'fritillaries' by the early entomologists. Nearly all have the upperside of the wings reddish-yellow with black spots or chequers and the underside more variously patterned. The popular usage of the name includes members of two subdivisions or 'tribes', the Argynnidi and the Melitaeidi; in America only the former are called*

*fritillaries, the latter being known as 'checkerspots', and the distinction is a useful and logical one. Most of the argynnid or 'true' fritillaries have a pattern of metallic silvery markings on the underside of the hind wings, most beautifully developed in the Queen of Spain fritillary. Metallic markings are never found in the melitaeids or checkerspots.*

*The larvae of both groups have rows of finely branched spines on their bodies and they pupate by hanging themselves up by the tail, as in all the butterflies of the large family Nymphalidae to which the fritillaries belong.*

## Localised colonies

Fritillaries are mainly woodland butterflies, the silver-washed, high brown and the two pearl-bordered fritillaries being especially characteristic of mixed woodland in which oak and birch predominate. The dark green fritillary flies on downs, moors, and open grassy country. The Queen of Spain fritillary is a very rare vagrant to the south of England; in continental Europe it is found both in woods and flowery meadows.

The scientific classification of fritillaries used by specialists is complicated and no agreement on it has yet been reached. This means that each book uses slightly different scientific names, which only adds to the confusion, especially for the amateur entomologist.

Fritillaries frequent flowers but are seldom seen in gardens unless these border on or are surrounded by woods. They are highly characteristic of the temperate and cool zones of the Northern Hemisphere.

## Distribution of fritillaries

Both groups are well represented in North America and in Europe, whence they extend across Asia to Japan. A few species are among the most northern of all butterflies. The Arctic fritillary *Clossiana chariclea* is circumpolar in distribution and has been found at 81° 42′ north latitude.

The few that occur south of the equator are nearly all mountain butterflies and are regarded as relict species which probably crossed the tropics in the cool conditions of the Ice Age. Three of these occur at altitudes of over 6 000 feet in Africa; they are members of the genus *Issoria,* related to the Queen of Spain fritillary. Another genus *Yramea* is represented by a number of species along the Andean mountain range in South America; they are intermediate in their characters between the true fritillaries and the checkerspots. There is only one truly tropical fritillary *Argyreus hyperbius* which is widespread in the Oriental Region and extends to New Guinea and eastern Australia. Frejya's fritillary in North America is found from Alaska to Labrador, and in the Rockies, at higher altitudes, is found as far south as Colorado. There it occurs above the timberline. The caterpillar feeds on bearberry in North America; in Europe and Asia its food source is cloudberry.

Other fritillaries, for example the polar fritillary, occur in Canada, Greenland and Northern Europe.

Curiously enough, although the Arctic fritillary is widespread in the more northern parts of the northern hemisphere the food plant of the caterpillar is as yet unknown.

In their choice of larval food plants the two groups differ. The true fritillaries almost all feed on violets or closely related plants such as violas and pansies. The checkerspots on the other hand range widely in their food plants, but each species is usually confined to a particular plant species or genus, a habit that must be at any rate partly responsible for their occurring in localised colonies. Of the European species the Glanville fritillary feeds on certain species of plantain, the heath on cowwheat and the marsh on devil's-bit scabious.

*Top: Queen of Spain fritillary* **Argynnis lathonia***.*
*Centre: Pearl-bordered fritillaries mating.*
*Bottom: Dark green fritillary* **Argynnis aglaja***.*

| class | **Insecta** |
|---|---|
| order | **Lepidoptera** |
| family | **Nymphalidae** |

*Species include*
| | |
|---|---|
| **Cloisiana chariclea** | *Arctic fritillary* |
| **Boloria selene** | *small pearl-bordered fritillary* |
| **Clossiana freija** | *Freja's fritillary* |
| **Argynnis pabhia** | *silver-washed fritillary* |

84

# Fruit fly

*Fruit flies are very small insects that go almost unnoticed unless they have to be fished out of a drink, but they are one of the most important laboratory animals. Fruit flies are true flies, with club-shaped halteres (modified vestigial wings) instead of a rear pair of wings. Most fruit flies are very much like houseflies in appearance, but only about ₁₀ in. long. Their bodies are bulbous, yellowish or brownish in colour, and their eyes are red. They have a slow hovering flight with their abdomen hanging down.*

Colourful cousin: the Mediterranean fruit fly **Ceratitis capitata** is from the family Trypetidae.

## Vinegar flies and wine flies

Many of the different kinds of fruit fly are so similar that careful examination of minute features under a microscope is needed to tell them apart. About 2 000 species have been found, half of which live on Hawaii. For some reason there has been a massive evolution of fruit flies on Hawaii. Perhaps they have been free to evolve in the isolation of the mid-Pacific in the same way as Darwin's finches evolved on the Galapagos Islands, only on a much larger scale. By contrast, there are 31 species in Britain, of which four are common. One arrived as recently as 1942, when it was found in London. It is now well established in the kitchens of restaurants and hospitals.

Fruit flies are also called vinegar flies or wine flies because they are attracted to weak solutions of acetic acid and alcohol, the principal ingredients of vinegar and wine respectively. They are often found in breweries, pickling plants, in bars and restaurants, where they settle on the rims of glasses and occasionally fall in. Fruit flies are also found in fruit stores where they feed on the juice, especially if it is fermenting. Other fruit flies feed on fungi or decaying plants or the sap flowing out of wounded plants.

## Eggs submerged in liquid

The eggs, larvae and pupae of fruit flies live in the semi-liquid, often fermenting, substances that the adults feed on. The eggs are spindle-shaped with hair-like filaments at one end. The filaments may be used for breathing, as the eggs are often submerged in liquid with the filaments floating at the surface. The larvae have 11 segments each with a ring of hooked spines. At the rear is a telescopic organ bearing spiracles or breathing pores that can be raised above the liquid. The pupae breathe through feathery organs at the front end of the body.

With 2 000 or so species of fruit fly, many of which live in the same places and many having almost identical features, there must be some method by which species are prevented from interbreeding. Before mating, a male fruit fly courts the female, and she will only accept him if she is mature and of the same species. She recognises a male of the right species by sight, hearing or smell, or a combination of all three. The male fruit fly approaches the female, runs round her, licks her and finally mates. If they are of different species the female flies away, kicks the male or buzzes violently. While running around, the male vibrates one or both wings, and in some species it is the buzzing emitted by the wingbeats that is important for identification of the species.

The buzzing is so faint that it has to be recorded by placing a fruit fly actually on the diaphragm of a microphone which is placed within several layers of soundproofing material. Even then it is necessary to make the recordings at night when all is quiet. All fruit flies of one species were found to buzz at the same frequency. The female is 'tuned in' to the frequency of her species, ignoring all others.

The female fruit fly lays batches of 15–20 white eggs each day, continuing until she has laid 400–900. When the larvae hatch, they burrow into the food material such as rotting fruit, staying there while they moult three times and emerging to pupate. The larvae of one species *Drosophila sigmoides* lives in the froth of the cuckoo-spit insect rather than in rotting fruit.

## Bred by the million

Fruit flies have been extensively used as laboratory animals because they breed very rapidly. They can be kept in milk bottles or other convenient containers and fed rotten bananas or other fruit. They are attracted to light so they can easily be lured to one end of the container and transferred to another vessel without any being left behind or squashed. Their generation time is a fortnight; in other words the cycle of eggs, larvae, pupae and adults to the laying of the next generation of eggs takes a fortnight. This rapid breeding made them useful subjects for the study of population growth. If a pair of fruit flies are put into a milk bottle with food they start breeding and the population rises at an ever-increasing rate until a certain density is reached, when it slows down. Eventually the population levels off. The uneven growth rate, fast at first then slowing down, has been found in populations of many species from protistans to man. The slowing-down has sometimes been found to be due to overcrowding. There is less food available for each individual and in fruit flies, as well as other animals, it has been found that females will not breed if they are constantly being disturbed.

Fruit flies have another and more important use. It was found that the cells of the salivary glands contained large chromosomes, and only two pairs of them. These are the string-like structures in the nucleus that carry the genetic information from one generation to another and which determine the hereditary characteristics of an individual. The large size of the fruit fly chromosomes made them very easy to study under the microscope. Moreover, as fruit flies bred very rapidly it was easy to study changes in the chromosomes, called mutations, and link them with corresponding changes in the bodies of the flies. One common change that occurs in fruit flies is for individuals to be hatched that have two pairs of wings instead of one pair of wings, and one pair of halteres. When body changes like this turn up, the chromosomes can be examined for changes in their structure. In this way a 'map' of the chromosomes can be made in which the pieces of genetical information, or genes, and the body character they control can be plotted. For instance, 100 genes have been found that control the eye shape.

These studies are helping us to understand the workings of heredity, and also the processes of evolution. Because of the rapid breeding rate it is possible to study the survival abilities of different forms of fruit flies, and so study the process of natural selection. Experiments have shown, for example, that light-coloured mutants do not survive as well in dry air as dark ones, but in wet air both types survive equally. Therefore, the two types live together in wet air, but if the humidity drops the dark fruit flies increase in number, replacing the light fruit flies.

| phylum | **Arthropoda** |
|---|---|
| class | **Insecta** |
| order | **Diptera** |
| family | **Drosophilidae** |
| genus & species | *Drosophila melanogaster* **D. sigmoides** **D. simulans** *others* |

# Gall wasp

*The familiar oak apples and marble galls on oak, and 'robin's pin-cushion' on wild roses are made by insect larvae. Some of these are made by the gall wasps, minute insects belonging to the order Hymenoptera and forming a superfamily, the Cynipoidea. They are closely related to the chalcid wasps (page 48). Over 80% of cynpid wasps make their galls on oak and about 7% of them affect roses. Other gall-forming insects include certain saw-flies (also Hymenoptera), the gall flies and gall midges (Diptera) and some of the aphids (Hemiptera). In most cases, as in gall wasps, particular species confine their attentions to one species or genus of plant.*

**Food and shelter for the larvae**

All gall wasps lay their eggs in the tissues of some particular part of the plant, a flower-bud, a leaf-bud, the blade of a leaf or even the root. No effect is seen until the minute larva hatches from the egg, but from this time on, the tissue of the plant surrounding the larva develops abnormally, usually swelling up and providing the insect with both shelter and food. It is believed that the plant tissues are stimulated to grow in this irregular way by some secretion given out by the larva. The swelling size, colour and shape of the gall depend on the species of wasp that laid the egg. In some cases a number of eggs are laid and the larvae grow up together enclosed in the same gall. The activities of the mature insects, as far as they are known, seem to be concerned almost solely with completing the complicated life cycles typical of gall wasps.

**Types of gall**

There are many different types of gall only a few of which can be described here.

*Oak apple.* When fully formed the oak apple is a hard, round, fruit-like object, 1–2 in. diameter and coloured light brown or pink. If opened in June and July when mature it will be found to contain a number of larvae, usually about 30, each enclosed in a little chamber in the gall tissue. The oak apple represents a stage in the life history of the gall wasp *Biorhiza pallida*, whose life cycle will be described later.

*Marble gall.* Caused by the gall wasp *Andricus kollari*, this is the most familiar of all the oak galls and is often mis-named 'oak apple'. It is green when it reaches full growth—rather less than 1 in. diameter—in August and then turns brown and woody and remains on the twig after the leaves fall, when it is very conspicuous. It harbours only one larva of the gall wasp, whose exit hole can be seen in an old gall. Often there is more than one exit hole, and this means that the gall has harboured other parasites or 'inquilines'. Males of this gall wasp are quite unknown. In an attempt to find them 1½ bushels of the galls were once collected and the wasps bred out, but among over 12 000 females that hatched not one male was found.

*Top left: Spangle galls on underside of leaf. Top right: Marble gall showing exit hole, with oak apple sectioned to show grub. Above: Ready to face the world, a wasp leaves its gall.*

*Common spangle gall.* In July numbers of little round button-like objects can often be seen on the undersides of oak leaves, attached by a central stalk, so they look like tiny, very short-stemmed mushrooms. This is one of the two kinds of gall formed by *Neuroterus quercus-baccarum*. Each contains a single larva, and in September the stems break, and the galls fall to the ground where the insects inside them pass the winter. The wasps that hatch in April (females only) climb the trees again and give rise to currant galls, which look like bunches of red currants and in no way resemble the spangle galls, which the next generation of wasps will again produce. This alternation of generations is more fully described below.

*Bedeguar gall.* Also known as the moss gall or robin's pin-cushion this spectacular gall of wild rose bushes is almost as familiar as the marble gall. The part containing the larvae is surrounded by a tangled mass of branched fibres, green at first, turning to bright red in July and August. Inside it are 50 or more cells, each containing a larva of the gall wasp *Diplolepis rosae*.

**Unusual life history**

In many gall wasps there is an 'alternation of generations', already mentioned in connection with the spangle and currant galls. The rather similar life cycle of the oak apple gall wasp *Biorhiza pallida* shows this.

When the oak apple is mature, the larvae in it pupate; the wasps hatch in July and eat their way out. They include both males and females, the former being winged, the latter wingless. After mating, the females crawl down the trunk of the tree and enter the soil, making their way to the small fibrous roots, in which they lay their eggs. When the larvae hatch, galls develop on the roots, round, dark brown and of ½ in. diameter, wholly unlike an oak apple. The wasps which emerge from these are all wingless females. They must find the tree trunk, crawl up it and seek the ends of the shoots, where they lay their eggs (without mating) in the terminal buds. When these hatch the larvae form a new generation of oak apples.

In the case of the spangle gall and currant gall wasp *Neuroterus quercus-baccarum* the female-only generation appears in April,

having overwintered in the fallen spangle galls among dead leaves under the tree. These wasps lay unfertilised eggs which form the larvae, giving rise to the currant galls and causing a bi-sexual generation.

The life history of the marble gall wasp *Andricus kollari* is something of a mystery. We have mentioned that males of this gall wasp are quite unknown, but as long ago as 1882 an entomologist claimed that the species known as *Andricus circulans,* which makes galls on Turkey oak, is really the bi-sexual generation of *Andricus kollari.* This was confirmed in 1953.

### Food always to hand
The sole food of the larvae of any gall wasp is the substance of the gall which forms round it. The mature insects probably do little more than take a drink when needed.

Woodpeckers are known to peck open marble galls to get at the larva and currant galls are sometimes eaten by birds, which probably mistake them for fruit. By far the most serious enemies of gall wasps, however, are other insects which lay eggs in the gall. The larvae of some of these are parasites or predators on the 'legitimate' larva, the parasites slowly eating it alive, the predators

killing it and eating it outright. Others are inquilines, which feed on the substance of the gall, and so rob the primary inmate but do not otherwise harm it except sometimes to starve it enough to stunt its growth. The inquilines do not have it all their own way, for they too are preyed upon by predators and parasites, and these in their turn have parasites specially adapted to afflict them, known as hyperparasites. The inquilines are usually other species of gall wasp and the parasites chalcid wasps or ichneumons.

If bedeguar galls are collected in late winter and kept in jars over damp sand, a remarkable assembly of tiny wasps will emerge. In one such experiment only a quarter of the insects were *Diplolepis rosae,* the makers of the gall, and of these (which numbered over 16 000) less than 1% were males. No alternation of generations is known in *D. rosae,* and it looks as if males are on the way to disappearing altogether.

### Make your own ink
The very common and familiar marble gall, with its wasp *Andricus kollari,* has been used in the dyeing industry and for making ink, the tannic acid in the galls being the chemical agent involved. In fact, anyone

△ *Sliced-open gall shows a mature wasp and the chamber in which it has developed.*

can make ink from marble galls. All you have to do is to bruise 4 oz of galls with a hammer, put them in a quart of boiling water and leave for 24 hours. Then take $1\frac{1}{2}$ oz of ferrous sulphate and dissolve rather less than an ounce of gum arabic in a little water. Filter the infusion of galls through cloth and add the other ingredients together with a few drops of carbolic acid.

| phylum | **Arthropoda** |
| --- | --- |
| class | **Insecta** |
| order | **Hymenoptera** |
| super-family | **Cynipoidea** |

# Ghost moth

*Swinging to and fro, as if on an invisible thread, with the white uppersides of its wings flashing on and off, this moth is aptly called 'ghost'. It is one of the Hepialidae family.*

*Hepialid moths are particularly common in Australia where many large species with wingspans of 8–10 in. occur. Most Hepialids are root feeders and are often troublesome in pasture lands. Males have the uppersides of all four wings shining white. Females have the hindwings dusky and the forewings yellow with a pattern of reddish markings, and they are generally larger than the males. Ghost moths are ¾ in. long with a wingspan of just under 2 in. They are found throughout the British Isles and all over central Europe and western Asia. The larva is a large, whitish, rather grub-like caterpillar, with a brown plate on the segment just behind the head.*

## Courtship display

Ghost moths frequent open spaces where rough grass and weeds are allowed to grow, and are on the wing in June and July. The males execute a kind of aerial dance, swinging to and fro just over the herbage as if suspended on invisible threads. As they fly they vanish and reappear as the dark underside and white upperside of the wings are alternately exposed. The dance is performed for about half an hour after sunset and again shortly before dawn; at other times the moths hardly fly at all. It is a courtship display and serves to attract the females, which fly about the countryside and are guided visually to their palely glimmering partners, their search being assisted by a scent, given off by the males, that has been likened to that of a carrot. This is one of the few cases known among insects where the females fly in search of the males. More usually female insects remain static in courtship and the males are attracted to them, in most cases by the emission from the female of a specific scent.

## Non-feeding adults

The eggs are laid at random among grass in June and early July and the larva feeds underground on the roots of various plants until May of the next year, when it pupates in the burrow that it has made. The adults have vestigial mouthparts and do not feed. There is no association with the hop, as the specific name *humuli* suggests.

## Shetland ghost moths

In the Shetlands a peculiar race of the ghost moth is found, in which the males differ in their colours from the ghost moths of both the British and the European mainlands. It is regarded as a subspecies and has been named *H. humuli thulensis*. The hindwings of the males are dusky and the forewings dull white with a brown or ochreous pattern similar to the female's.

The shining white coloration of the typical male ghost moth is not characteristic of

△ *Male ghost moth. In June and July the males execute a kind of aerial courtship dance. This serves to attract the females who fly in search of these glimmering partners.*

▽ *The female is slightly larger than the male usually being ¾ in. long with a wingspan of just under 2 in. After mating she lays eggs at random among grasses and herbs.*

△ *In the courtship dance the male swings to and fro just above the herbage as if suspended on invisible threads. The dance is performed for about half an hour after sunset and again shortly before dawn. At other times they hardly fly at all. The dance attracts the females, helped by a carroty scent given off by the males.*

▽ *Ghost moth larva — a large, whitish, rather grub-like caterpillar — it lives beneath the ground feeding on the roots of plants such as burdock, dandelion and dead-nettle.*

swift moths in general. Presumably it is maintained by natural selection, on the principle that the most conspicuous of the twilight dancers will be more readily found by females and so are most likely to leave progeny. In the almost Arctic latitude of the Shetlands, however, where there is no darkness at midsummer and the sun disappears at midnight for only half an hour, the males must perform their dance in broad daylight. They do not need the porcelain-white wing colour of their relatives farther south to make them visible to the questing females. The selection pressure being relaxed, it is supposed that the males have reverted to an appearance more characteristic of the Hepialid moths in general, probably more like that of their ancestors.

This is, however, an academic point and there is another, more practical explanation. In the Shetlands, ghost moths are heavily preyed upon by gulls, which by flying above the moths will see white individuals more readily than darker ones against the background of heather, rock or peat. In these circumstances the pure white coloration is a definite disadvantage. Here the tables are turned. The white males are more likely to make a meal for a gull than a mate for a moth, and therefore are less likely to leave progeny.

| class | **Insecta** |
|---|---|
| order | **Lepidoptera** |
| family | **Hepialidae** |
| genus & species | *Hepialus humuli* |

89

# Glowworm

*The glowworm is a beetle belonging to the family Lampyridae which also includes the fireflies (page 78). Centuries ago anything that was long and crawling was called a worm. The female glowworm lacks wings and it was this and her general appearance that was responsible for the name.*

*Male and female of the common European glowworm* **Lampyris noctiluca** *are yellowish grey-brown. The male has large eyes and two very tiny light-producing organs at the tip of the abdomen. He also has wings covered by the usual wing cases of beetles, and his length is about $\frac{1}{2}$ in. The female, slightly longer than the male, differs little in shape from the larva and the last three segments of the body, on the underside, are yellowish and strongly luminescent.*

*A second species of glowworm* **Phosphaenus hemipterus** *is widespread over continental Europe.*

△ *Fickle flasher: having attracted three males to her powerful light, a female glowworm mates with one, ignored by her disappointed suitors.*

▽ *Incandescent cousin: female African beetle of the closely related family Phengodidae waiting in the grass for response to her light.*

### The lure of the lights

Adult glowworms are most active in June and July. Preferring slightly damp places, they may be found on hedgerow banks, hillsides and in rough meadows, especially where there is a plentiful supply of snails. By day they hide in cracks and crevices. After nightfall the female climbs onto a prominent piece of foliage and takes up a position head down so her luminous end is prominently displayed. Her method of light-production is the same as in the firefly (see page 78). Beneath the light-producing bands is a whitish, opaque layer which not only prevents absorption of the light into the body, but reflects it back, making full use of all the light. The winged male homes on the female's light for mating. The light may be visible to us over 100 yd or so under suitable conditions, but may be 'doused' as we approach and switched on again after an interval. By contrast, the larvae light up as a result of being disturbed, which suggests that in them the luminescence may serve as a defence, frightening away some enemies. The larvae's light also is slightly different from that of the adults, being more intensely green.

### Short-lived adults

The pale yellow eggs are $\frac{1}{20}$ in. diameter. Usually they are laid in ones and twos over a period of a couple of days on grass stems or moss, or in or on the soil. They hatch in a fortnight, the larvae being almost exact miniatures of the adult females except for the simpler structure of the legs and a series of paler spots at the front corners of each body segment. Growing by a series of moults, the larvae reach the adult stage in three years. The pupa of the male differs from that of the female, reflecting the different appearance of the adults. Emerging from the pupae after about 8 or 9 days, usually in April or May, the adults live for only a short while after mating and egg-laying. During mating neither sex glows.

*Making the most of youth: doomed to starvation as an adult, a glowworm larva gorges itself on a tiny garden snail (12 × life size).*

## Larvae feed, parents starve

Adult glowworms take no food, although it is often asserted that they do. The larvae feed on snails which they discover by following their slime trails. They drive their hollow, curved mandibles into the mollusc and inject a dark fluid, partly paralysing and partly digestive. This rapidly reduces the snail's tissues to a pre-digested soup-like liquid which the glowworm then sucks up. Newly-hatched glowworms are only $\frac{1}{5}$ in. long. They feed on the smaller snails. Sometimes the larvae feed communally, crowding round the lip of the shell and feeding side by side. After a meal the glowworm pushes out a white sponge-like device from its anus. With this it can clean away from its head and back any remains of slime resulting from its meal.

## Lucky to survive

Glowworms fall victim to any insect-eating animal, despite the glowing lights on their bodies, but especially to toads and hedgehogs, both of which feed at night. Some are eaten by frogs and spiders, and there are mites which penetrate the soft joints between the body segments of the larvae and feed on their body fluids. The larvae are particularly vulnerable to mites when they have shed their skins at the periodic moults, making them fair game for these parasites.

## On the decline

The twinkling lights of a modern city are an irresistible attraction to the eye of young and old alike. It is doubtful, however, whether any of the artificial illumination produced by man has the same aesthetic quality as that from a well-stocked colony of glowworms seen on a moonless night. It is not surprising that poets have made so much of this. Unfortunately, the chances of seeing it today are on the whole much smaller than in times past. Glowworms, useful and attractive insects, have died out from many areas where they were once common. The reasons for this are not easy to see, but it almost certainly springs from the pressure on land for housing, factories, intensive farming, combined with more efficient draining of the land. No doubt the use of insecticides is also partly to blame. What is quite certain is that it is not natural enemies that have brought about this fall in numbers, because toads and hedgehogs are all less numerous than they used to be.

Ironically, there may be another reason. Many insects are irresistibly attracted to artificial light, and in this the male glowworm is no exception, in spite of the fact that it has its own, highly individual 'bright light' to go to—that emitted by the female. Even the weak, flickering light of a candle-flame will attract a glowworm, as Gilbert White, one of the first naturalists, records. In many areas, it seems, modern artificial lighting systems have become a serious threat to glowworm survival, in that the male glowworms are finding them far more alluring than the more modest glow produced by the females, which as a result may languish in vain and even die 'old maids'! Once attracted to the lights of large buildings the male insects may damage themselves in hitting or being burnt by them, and then fall to the ground stunned or dazzled, to be subsequently eaten by a variety of small animals; or the attraction may simply disrupt the delicate balance of nocturnal flight activity. Fortunately there are still many areas where such hazards are less pronounced, as is indicated by the fact that the greatest numbers of glowworms are found in areas which are comparatively less developed industrially.

| | |
|---|---|
| phylum | **Arthropoda** |
| class | **Insecta** |
| order | **Coleoptera** |
| family | **Lampyridae** |
| genus & species | ***Lampyris noctiluca*** |

# Goat moth

*The goat moth is so called on account of the strong and unpleasant smell of its larva, which burrows in the wood of trees. It is a large, stout insect with brown intricately mottled wings spanning 3 in. or more and is one of the species belonging to the family Cossidae. These are regarded as primitive moths related to the family of small or minute moths called the Tortricidae. They are also called carpenter moths.*

### Feeds on timber

The goat moth flies at night and is attracted to light. By day it sits on the trunks and branches of trees, where its colour and markings give it very effective camouflage. The larva burrows in the living wood, especially of willows and poplars. It is over 3 in. long when fully grown and stout in proportion, and its burrowing severely damages the timber of the tree in which it feeds. Affected trees exude a dark fluid from the openings of the burrows and this has a powerful smell, somewhat like that of a male goat. In spite of its unpleasant smell, other butterflies and moths are strongly attracted to the fluid, and an infested tree is worth keeping under observation by day and night.

The caterpillar is fully grown sometime in spring or summer, and often comes out of the tree in which it has lived and fed, to wander about seeking a place to pupate. This is the stage at which it is most often seen, the huge chestnut- and flesh-coloured larva being very conspicuous. If such a larva is taken home and put in a tin with some pieces of decayed wood it will spin a cocoon and pupate. It is useless to confine a goat moth larva in a wooden box as it will eat its way out in a very short time, and probably not all members of the household will be happy to encounter it in its subsequent wanderings.

Two other moths of the family Cossidae are the leopard moth, whose larva also feeds in trees, and the reed leopard. The latter is rather rare, confined to fens and marshes, and its larva lives in the stems of reeds. The larva of the leopard moth lives in the trunks and branches of various trees, including fruit trees, where it may do some damage. It has been introduced into the United States, no doubt in timber imported from Europe, and is a considerable pest in trees in city parks. Both these moths are also found in Japan, and the reed leopard is found in China.

In the tropics and subtropics, especially those of Australia, some very large relatives of the goat moth are found. One *Xyleutes boisduvali* has a wing span of up to 10 in. and a body that has been described as resembling a small banana in shape and size.

### Three-year larva

The eggs are laid on the bark of a tree and the larvae on hatching burrow under the bark and feed there for a year or so, eating their way into the solid wood as they grow larger. In the wild state they take up to three years to complete their growth.

### Recipe for quick growth

The proboscis of the adult moth is vestigial and it must be supposed that the insect does not feed at all. Rather curiously, however, there are records of it visiting the bait of treacle painted on to tree trunks by moth collectors.

The larva eats wood throughout its long life and must consume great quantities of it. It is a matter of interest that if young goat moth larvae are fed on beetroot they complete their growth and come to full size in only a year.

### Goat moths in history

The caterpillar of the goat moth has always attracted attention. In the 1750s a French entomologist, P Lyonnet, made a most detailed study of this larva and published a book about it. Among the facts he established were that, from the time of hatching from the egg to full growth, it increases its weight 72 000 times. Also in the course of dissecting it he discovered 4 061 muscles in its body. A second book, describing the pupa and the moth, was published after the author's death.

The Roman writer Pliny, who lived in the first century AD, wrote a monumental Natural History in 37 volumes, and one

*Young goat moth larva (6 × life size).*

*Adult goat moth. The larvae of this drab insect increase their weight 72 000 times to become fat and 3 in. long. Their voracious appetite damages poplars and willows, but their greed was repaid in kind many years ago; despite their goat-like smell, the Romans considered these repulsive larvae a delicacy, if the writer Pliny is to be believed.*

of the items he describes is a sort of large 'worm' that lived in the wood of oak trees and was highly esteemed as a luxury by gourmets of the time. The goat moth larva does sometimes live in oaks, and it has generally been assumed that this is what Pliny's edible wood-boring worms were, though there is no detailed description of them to serve as proof of this. If the ancient Romans did really eat these huge smelly caterpillars they must have had remarkably robust appetites.

| phylum | **Arthropoda** |
|---|---|
| class | **Insecta** |
| order | **Lepidoptera** |
| family | **Cossidae** |
| genus & species | ***Cossus cossus*** |

*Poplar riddled by grown larvae.*

# Grasshopper

*As their name suggests, most grasshoppers live among grass and herbage on the ground. They are variously coloured— mostly green and brown—and are protected as long as they keep still by blending with their surroundings. Grasshoppers are active by day and if disturbed jump suddenly and powerfully, using their greatly-enlarged hindlegs. They can also crawl slowly by means of the other two pairs of legs.*

*Nowadays the term 'grasshopper' is applied to the short-horned Acrididae, while the long-horned Tettigoniidae are called 'bush-crickets' because they are more closely allied to the other main family of the order Orthoptera (the Gryllidae or true crickets) than to the Acrididae. In all Orthoptera the forewings are leathery and serve as coverings for the folded, membranous hindwings which, in the flying species, are the sole organs of flight.*

*Grasshoppers are mainly ground-living insects, while most bush-crickets live in the foliage of trees and bushes. True crickets have been dealt with (page 64) while locusts, which are in fact swarming grasshoppers, will be dealt with under a separate heading (page 121).*

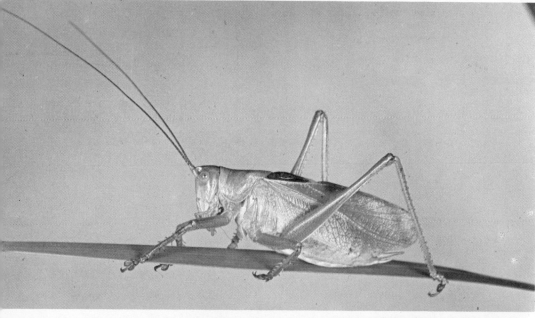

### Fiddlers in the grass

The familiar chirping chorus in the fields and hedgerows of the countryside is the result of grasshoppers' stridulation. A row of evenly spaced, minute pegs on the largest joint of the hindlegs is rubbed over the more prominent veins or ribs of the forewings. Usually, but not always, only males can sing. Each species has its own song, and these may be learned, like the songs of birds, and used in identifying the species. The colours of species of grasshoppers vary so much that their song is a better means of recognizing them than their appearance.

Apart from stridulation, both pairs of wings serve their usual function. In most of the common species the hindwings are fully developed in both sexes and the insects can fly. One exception is the meadow grasshopper *Chorthippus parallelus* in which the hindwings are vestigial; even in this species there are occasional individuals in which the wings are fully developed and functional. Among Orthoptera it is not uncommon for species to occur in two forms, winged (macropterous) or wings much reduced (brachypterous). The most usual cases are like the one described, in which occasional winged individuals occur in a normally brachypterous population.

*Top left: Bush-crickets mating. Male (right) is placing the spermatophore—package of sperm—at the base of the female's ovipositor. The blade-like structure of this organ is typical of bush crickets. Centre: Bush-cricket* **Tettigonia cantans**. *Bottom left: Short-horned grasshopper* **Chorthippus parallelus**

*Rhapsody in purple: an inch-long South African grasshopper of the family Eumastacidae.*

*Openings to the hearing organs on the foreleg of a bush-cricket—sensitive enough to pick out the calls of different species.*

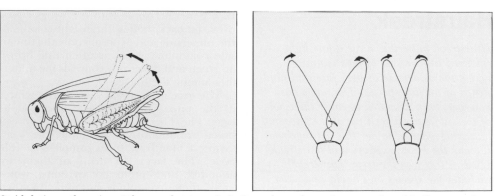

*Stridulation—the voice of the grasshoppers. Left: Long-horned grasshopper rubs a hindleg over the ribs of the forewing. Right: Bush-crickets have one of the left wing ribs adapted to form a row of teeth, which is rubbed against the trailing edge of the right forewing to produce the sound.*

## Bush-cricket crawlers

Although some species live on the ground, most bush-crickets are at home in the foliage of trees and bushes. These tend to be mainly green while the ground-dwelling ones are brown or blackish. Unlike grasshoppers bush-crickets are not lovers of the sun, but become active in the late afternoon, or may be wholly nocturnal. Their hindlegs are adapted for jumping, but they have not the prodigious leaping powers of grasshoppers, moving mainly by climbing and crawling.

## Singing a different song

They are also noisy and call by stridulating, but the mechanism is very different from that of grasshoppers. In the left forewing a rib, formed by one of the veins, has a row of minute teeth and this is rubbed against the hind edge of the right forewing. The arrangement is the same as in crickets except that the roles of the left and right forewings are reversed. Here again the species all have distinct songs, and there is good reason for this. In both bush-crickets and grasshoppers the song is mainly a courtship invitation addressed to the female, and it is important that the females should be able to recognise the call of males of their own species.

The great green bush-cricket *Tettigonia viridissima* ranges across Europe, Asia and North Africa. The female is 2 in. long, including the straight, blade-like ovipositor, and is bright green in colour. The male is a little smaller and his song is very loud and sustained, and uttered at night. In the late summer and autumn the speckled bush-cricket *Leptophyes punctatissima* is common in gardens and hedges. It is a plump, soft-looking insect, green with the wings reduced to small vestiges; the female ovipositor is broad and curved.

## Two ways of laying eggs

Both grasshoppers and bush-crickets lay eggs. In the former they are enclosed in a tough case called the egg-pod, which the female buries in the ground. Each pod has from 5 to 6 or up to 14 eggs, more or less according to the species. Bush-crickets lay their eggs without any covering and usually singly, some putting them in the ground or crevices of bark, others inserting them in stems or leaves by cutting slits with the ovi-

◁ *Rhapsody in purple: an inch-long South African grasshopper of the family Eumastacidae.*

positor. In both, the young hatch in the form of tiny worm-like larvae which moult immediately after hatching. They then resemble their parents except that they have no wings. With each moult (ecdysis) their size increases. The wings also appear and grow larger at each moult, becoming fully formed and functional, in the species that fly, at the last moult. Most of the common species have one generation a year.

## Mainly vegetarian

Grasshoppers are entirely herbivorous and can be fed in captivity on bunches of grass tied with string and lowered into their home. The floor of the receptacle should be covered with 1½ in. of slightly damp sand, and in these conditions they will breed readily.

Bush-crickets are at least partly predatory and one species, the oak bush-cricket *Meconema thalassinum,* is entirely carnivorous and hunts caterpillars and other insects in oak trees. The others feed partly on grass and leaves and partly on insects. In captivity they must be given plenty of room; if they are crowded cannibalism will occur. Lettuce leaves seem to suit most of them, but they should have some animal food as well. Small looper caterpillars can usually be found by shaking bushes and branches into an open umbrella held underneath them.

## Colour means nothing

Some grasshoppers show an extraordinary range of variation in the colour and markings on both legs and body. In the stripe-winged and common green grasshoppers *Stenobothrus lineatus* and *Omocestus viridulus* there is a small number of well defined colour varieties, but in the common field and mottled grasshoppers *Chorthippus brunneus* and *Myrmeleotettix maculatus* there is almost every shade of colour: green, brown, yellow and red are the main colours and to these must be added extremely varied patterns of stripes, spots and mottling. As a result it is hopeless to try to tell a grasshopper by its colour.

| class | **Insecta** |
|-------|-------------|
| order | **Orthoptera** |
| family | **Acrididae** |
| genera | ***Chorthippus, Omocestus, Stenobothrus, Myrmelotettix, Tetrix*** |
| family | **Tettigoniidae** |
| genera | ***Tettigonia, Leptophyes, Meconema*** |

*Standing room only: a crowd of **Phymateus** grasshopper nymphs. Wings show after moulting.*

# Hairstreak

*Hairstreak butterflies have a fine light-coloured line or row of dots running across the underside of both fore and hind wings of all five species. The name has, however, been extended to cover the whole of the subfamily Theclinae of the Lycaenid butterflies, which, under this arrangement, include the blues, coppers and hairstreaks. Used in this way the term 'hairstreak' includes the species of* **Thecla** *and other similar genera, of which there are many different kinds in Europe, North America and temperate Asia, and extend into South America. In the Indo-Australian region the Theclinae are represented by a great variety of small butterflies, many of them vividly coloured. A single genus* **Arhopala** *of metallic blue and green hairstreaks is represented between India and Malaysia by over 100 species.*

*The 'hairstreak' line is not a very constant feature of the subfamily, but in the majority of them the hindwings have appendages, usually spoken of as tails.*

*The lovely, metallic colours are a special feature of many of the exotic hairstreaks, and include vivid blue, purple, green and orange-red. In most of these the sexes are very distinct, the male being usually the more brightly coloured. The colours are not due to pigments but are of the type known as structural. That is to say they are due to the light falling onto the wings being sorted out into its different wavelengths by the same process of 'interference' that produces iridescent colours in a film of oil floating on water. In butterflies the effect is produced by ultra-microscopic grooves, ridges or other structural features on the scales.*

## Flashy in flight

In Europe the hairstreaks are seen mostly beside paths and lanes through woods and heaths and they seldom venture into gardens in populated districts as the more familiar butterflies do. In the tropics they are mainly inhabitants of lowland forest. Their flight is extremely fast and erratic and they generally settle with the wings closed over the back, hiding the bright colours of the upperside and exposing only the underside coloration, which is often dull brown or green and effectively conceals the butterflies among the foliage.

The green hairstreak spends the winter in the pupa stage, the rest spend it as eggs. The Theclinae of the tropical forests breed continuously throughout the year, taking a month or so to complete the life cycle. The larvae of many of them are attended and protected by ants, which 'milk' them like aphids, but none is known to live inside ants' nests, as some larvae of the 'blues' do (page 36).

## Back-to-front camouflage

In some of the tropical Asian genera such as *Marmessus*, the tails on the hindwings are extremely long and have twisted lobes at their bases. In addition the underside pattern of the hindwings is conspicuously chequered with black-centred spots near the base of the tails. It is thought that the effect of this distribution of pattern is to direct the attention of a stalking bird or lizard away from the front and towards the back of the butterfly. Possibly the tails simulate antennae and, together with the eye like spots, persuade the predator that this area of the insect's hindwings is really its head. The twisted lobes make a conspicuous figure when the butterfly is seen in profile and so make the device equally effective in this position. A grab at this 'false head' will probably close on the wings and miss the butterfly's body altogether. After a brief struggle the fragile wings tear away and the butterfly, left with a wing area quite adequate for flight, escapes to live a few more days and very likely to continue with the business of propagating its species.

There is some further evidence that the pattern and tails are really protective adaptations. When at rest these butterflies often perform a peculiar motion, moving the hindwings backwards and forwards and causing the tails to tremble and flutter, and so still further directing the attention of an enemy to the insect's 'expendable' parts. Also specimens are occasionally caught with the tails and a part of the hindwings symmetrically torn away, as if the wings had been seized when closed together by a beak or a pair of jaws.

## Slug-like larvae

The eggs of hairstreaks are usually round and flattened, like tiny cakes, and have geometrical sculptured patterns which differ in the different species. The larvae are slug-like in shape and crawl slowly, and the great majority of them feed on the flowers and leaves of trees and bushes rather than on herbaceous plants. A number of the northern-temperate hairstreaks are associated with various kinds of oak.

| phylum | **Arthropoda** |
|---|---|
| class | **Insecta** |
| order | **Lepidoptera** |
| family | **Lycaenidae** |
| subfamily | **Theclinae** |
| genera | **Thecla, Strymonidia, Callophrys** *European* **Arhopala, Marmessus** *Indo-Malayan* |

△ *Green hairstreak* **Callophrys rubi.**
▷ *Feeding white-letter hairstreak demonstrates how the five hairstreak species got their name.*
▽◁ *Exotic* **Zephyrus signata,** *from Japan.*
▽ *Purple hairstreak* **Thecla quercus.**

# Honey ant

*Also called honey-pot ants, these are species living in dry or desert regions, in which some of the workers remain in the nest and act as living storage vessels. They are then known as 'repletes'. The habit has been developed independently in various groups of ants belonging to two subfamilies, the Camponotinae and Dolichoderinae, living in North America, Australia and Africa. The so-called 'honey' is a sugary solution obtained by the ants from aphids and, in America, from the secretion of a gall growing on small oak trees. The habit is developed in deserts because this source of food is not available during long periods of drought.*

*A kind of half-way condition is seen in the common American ant **Prenolepis imparis**. It feeds largely on honeydew from aphids, and the workers have unusually distensible abdomens which are often seen swollen to a 'semi-replete' condition. This probably represents a stage in the evolution of the fully developed honey ants.*

## More take than give

In the nest of the honey ants some of the workers fail to go out foraging with the rest, and remain at home from the time they leave the pupa. They are perfectly normal ants, at first differing in no way from the workers which hunt for food and perform ordinary duties in the nest. But their behaviour is peculiar. Ants constantly feed each other, mouth to mouth, and these individuals accept food from incoming workers far beyond their own needs. They also give food to others when it is solicited, but on balance, when plenty is available, they take far more than they give.

As a consequence of this excessive intake the abdomen of these ants becomes more and more distended, taking the form of a globe $\frac{1}{4}-\frac{1}{3}$ in. diameter. It is translucent with narrow black bars, which are the body segments that were in contact with each other when the ant had its normal shape. When fully replete they hang from the roof of the deeper chambers of the nest. If one of them falls it cannot move, as its fantastically swollen stomach is far too heavy, even if it happens to land in a position from which its feet can reach the ground. If its overloaded crop splits and spills its burden, the other workers rush to enjoy the feast, wholly disregarding the fate of their crippled sister.

## Dies to feed others

While there is green vegetation around and food is plentiful the hanging repletes are constantly visited by incoming ants and persuaded to add more and more to their store. In time of drought, when the foragers return empty or cease trying to find food in the parched and sterile desert, visitors to the repletes solicit the mixed food and water, and their swollen bellies gradually diminish. They can never return to a normal existence, however, as the stretched skin of their

*Bulging honey ant repletes gleam like amber beads, their abdomen plates grotesquely separated.*

abdomens cannot contract. They probably die as soon as their store is exhausted.

When supplies are coming in and all the established repletes are distended to capacity, any young worker ant may accept a proffered drop from an incoming worker and then find herself besieged by more and more of them until she begins to swell and climbs for comfort to the roof of the chamber. Her fate is then sealed; instead of taking her place as an active, busy member of the community, she must spend the rest of her life as an inert, swollen barrel of syrup.

Honey ants were first discovered in 1881 by an American cleric named Henry C McCook. The scene of their discovery was the Garden of the Gods in Colorado, and the classically minded McCook gave the ant the specific name *horti-deorum*, Latin for the romantically sounding name of its home territory. It is now regarded as a subspecies of *Myrmecocystus mexicanus.*

## Edible ants

The country people of Mexico search eagerly for the nests of these ants and regard the swollen repletes as a gastronomic delicacy. It is not easy work digging them out as the ants nest on dry ridges where the soil is very hard; but the reward is worth the effort since a well-stocked nest may contain

50 repletes and sometimes as many as 300 may be found. The American entomologist Dr Alexander Klots writes of the repletes, massed along the ceiling of a horizontal gallery, as gleaming like amber beads in the rays of a flashlight. He describes their contents as 'extremely sweet and delicately flavoured, far surpassing, in our opinion, honeybee honey'. The Australian aborigines living in the Central Desert also dig out the honey ants and the smiles on their faces, showing their flashing white teeth, are eloquent testimony to the tastiness of the honey ants. They hold the ant's thorax between thumb and forefinger and nip off the honey-filled abdomen with their teeth.

| phylum | **Arthropoda** |
|---|---|
| class | **Insecta** |
| order | **Hymenoptera** |
| family | **Formicidae** |
| sub-families | **Camponotinae and Dolichoderinae** |
| genera | ***Myrmecocystus Plagiolepis, Melophorus, Leptomyrmex, Camponotus*** |

*Left: A tree-suspended nest of wild bees. Centre: A queen struggles out of her cell. Right: Each egg is laid in a hexagonal cell.*

# Honeybee

*Any of the four species of social bees belonging to the genus* **Apis** *can be called honeybees but the name is most usually associated with the European domestic bee* **Apis mellifera,** *sometimes called the western honeybee. This differs from all other social bees and social wasps of temperate climates in forming colonies that survive the winter by living on reserve stores of food, so a particular dwelling site or nest may be occupied for an indefinite length of time. In social wasps and bumble bees all the members of the colony die at the end of the summer except the fertilised females or queens, which hibernate and found new colonies in the following spring.*

*In the colonies of social bees, wasps and ants there are two kinds of females. The fertile females are called 'queens' and the sterile females are the 'workers', the latter doing all the work of maintaining the economy of the colony. In the wasps, most bees and some ants, the egg-laying organ or ovipositor of both types of female is transformed to a sting, connected with a poison gland. In the queens the eggs are extruded from an opening at the base of the sting.*

*Bees have been kept for their honey by man for many hundreds of years. Throughout most of history this has been mainly a matter of inducing them to make colonies in hollow receptacles of various kinds, such as earthenware pots, logs and straw baskets or 'skeps', and then robbing them of their honey. Until recently their breeding has been entirely uncontrolled and even now they are not domesticated in the same way as dogs, cattle, or even silkworms.*

## Household chores

The great majority of European honeybees are now living in hives although wild colonies may be found, almost always in hollow trees. In midsummer a strong colony normally contains one queen, 50 000 to 60 000 workers and a few hundred males or drones. The expectation of life of a worker bee at this time is only 4–6 weeks and her span is divided into two periods. For just under 3 weeks after emerging from the pupa the worker's duties lie within the hive, where she is fed at first by older bees, but later feeds herself from the stores of honey and pollen. Her first spell of work is as nursemaid to the developing larvae, to whom she passes on a great deal of the food she eats, partly by direct regurgitation and partly by giving them a jelly-like secretion from certain salivary glands in her head. By the time she is about 12 days old her wax glands have developed and she turns to building and repairing the comb of geometrically arranged cells in which the larvae are reared and food is stored. At this time she also goes out for short flights around the hive, learning the landmarks by which to guide herself home when she ventures farther afield.

From about 12 days to 3 weeks old she takes over the nectar and pollen brought in by returning foragers, converting the former to honey and storing it away. At the same time she helps to keep the hive tidy, carrying outside dead bees and other debris. At 3 weeks old she is ready to go out foraging herself for nectar, pollen, water and resin, which are the four substances needed for the hive's economy. The last is used to make a sort of varnish-like cement called 'propolis' with which crevices and any small openings in the hive are sealed up.

## Searching for nectar

In searching for nectar-yielding flowers the worker bee is guided by her senses of smell and sight. Bees have good colour vision but it differs from our own. They cannot see red at all but can see ultraviolet 'colour', invisible to us but revealed by photography by ultraviolet light. Bees guide themselves to and from the hive by reference to the angle of the sun, or of polarised light from the sky, and have a time sense which enables them to compensate for the continuous change in the sun's position.

Foraging is very hard work and after 2–3 weeks of it the worker is worn out and dies. Workers hatched in the autumn have a much longer life before them, as they build up food reserves in their bodies and their activity is reduced through the winter. They keep warm by huddling together in a mass and feeding on the honey that they have stored.

The queen rules her great horde of daughters, not by example or wise counsel, but by secreting from her body a substance whose presence or absence controls their behaviour. Her chief role, however, is egg-laying, and at midsummer she may be laying 1 500 eggs a day, totalling more than the weight of her own body. This enormous fecundity is needed to compensate for the shortness of the workers' lives.

## The idle drones

Mating with and fertilising the queens is the only useful part played in honeybee economy by the drones. During summer they usually live 4–5 weeks and are fed by the workers, not even seeking their own food among the flowers. In autumn the drones remaining in the colony are turned outside to die of starvation or chill.

New colonies are founded by what is known as swarming. As a preliminary to this extra queens are produced in the hive and then large numbers of workers, accompanied by some drones and usually one queen, leave the hive and fly together for some distance. Then they settle in a large cluster and search for a suitable place, where a new colony is made by some of the workers. At this stage they can easily be persuaded to settle down in artificial quarters of any kind merely by shaking the swarm, with its attendant queen, into a suitable receptacle, such as a beehive.

## Natural and artificial breeding

Queens may be produced in a hive in response to ageing of the mother queen or to the urge to swarm. In either case they fly out to seek mates when they are about a week old. A drone that mates with a queen condemns himself to death. The reason for this is that his genital organs become so firmly fixed in the queen's body that they are torn out when the two bees part, and he dies almost immediately. The sperm is stored by the queen in an internal sac called the spermatheca, and sperms are released to fertilise the eggs as she lays them. Here there is a strange departure from the condition normally found in animals. All eggs that are fertilised produce females, either workers or queens; drones are only produced from eggs that develop without being fertilised.

The larva and pupa stages of honeybees (collectively known as the 'brood') are passed in the wax cells into which the eggs are laid, one in each cell. The larvae are entirely helpless and are fed by the workers. The development of a worker bee takes 21 days, 3 as an egg, 6 as a larva and 12 as a pupa.

The natural mating behaviour of queen and drone bees makes any control of pairing and breeding impossible, but in recent years a technique for artificially inseminating chosen queens with sperm from chosen drones has been developed. It is a difficult process requiring delicate manipulation under a microscope, but by this means selected strains of bees can now be bred.

### 'Common' and 'royal' food

The natural food of bees consists of nectar and pollen, the nectar supplying the energy-producing sugar and the pollen being a source of protein. The bees also make honey from nectar and store it for food. It is untrue to say that bees suck honey from flowers; nectar and honey are chemically distinct and the latter is much more concentrated. The larvae are fed partly on a mixture of nectar or honey and pollen and partly on a secretion from various glands of the young workers, the substance that is often called 'royal jelly'. When a fertilised egg is laid in a normal sized cell the larva is fed at first on jelly and later on pollen and honey, and it develops into a worker. When production of queens is needed the workers make larger cells into which the reigning queen lays ordinary fertilised eggs. The larvae from these, however, are fed until they are fully grown on royal jelly alone and they develop into queens. Drone larvae are fed similarly to those of workers but for 2 more days, 8 instead of 6.

Bees will readily drink a solution of sugar in water and are often fed on this during the winter by bee keepers who take most of their stored honey but are also concerned to keep their bees alive.

### Enemies and disease

In spite of their stings bees are preyed upon by birds, dragonflies and some kinds of wasps. Certain moths called wax moths lay their eggs in the hives and the larvae live on wax, pollen and general comb debris, doing serious damage if they are at all numerous. The big death's-head hawk moth is said to invade colonies and steal the honey, piercing the wax comb with its short, stiff proboscis. It was called the 'Bee Tyger' by the early entomologists.

The greatest menace to honeybees, however, is disease and starvation.

### Fierce relatives

Only four species of the genus *Apis* are known, and one of them, the eastern honeybee *Apis indica*, is so similar to *Apis mellifera* it is sometimes regarded as a subspecies. It is domesticated in tropical Asia.

Both the other species inhabit the eastern tropics. The giant honeybee *Apis dorsata* is a large bee which makes enormous hanging combs in the open. An overhanging surface is chosen at a considerable height from the ground. Large branches overhanging cliffs and buildings, especially water towers, are favourite sites for colonies. These bees may be dangerous if molested and there are records of people being attacked and stung to death. Nevertheless the Dyaks of Borneo climb by night with smoking torches, throw down the combs and gather the honey.

The little honeybee *Apis florea* is by contrast an inoffensive little insect, reluctant to use its sting. A colony consists of a single comb the size of the palm of a man's hand, which contains only 1 or 2 oz. of honey.

In tropical America stingless bees of the genus *Trigona* (not closely related to the Old World honeybees) make large colonies in hollow logs and similar places and they used to be domesticated for their honey by the Maya Indians of Mexico.

| phylum | **Arthropoda** |
|--------|----------------|
| class | **Insecta** |
| order | **Hymenoptera** |
| family | **Apidae** |

*A drone makes landfall beside the queen, who is surrounded by workers. From her body the queen secretes a substance whose presence or absence controls the behaviour of the great horde of her daughter-workers, who supply the hive or colony.*

*Method in their madness: this is a workers' conference, carried out in dance language. To tell each other where flower-nectar is to be found, worker bees have evolved two sorts of dance: a round dance for nearby nectar and a tail-wagging dance for distant nectar.*

*△ Elevation . . . side view of a gaily coloured leafhopper* **Graphocephala coccinea** *▽ . . . and plan:* **Cicadella viridis** *shows its pastel wing cases.*

# Hopper

*There are several thousand species of hoppers belonging to the families commonly called froghoppers, leafhoppers, treehoppers, plant hoppers and jumping plant lice. These insects are related to cicadas and aphides. Most are rather small, many minute. They are, however, of great economic importance because they suck sap from plants, causing them to wilt, and many inject viruses into the plants, causing diseases.*

## Froghoppers and cuckoo-spit

In Britain the cuckoo arrives in April on migration from Africa. Soon after it arrives blobs of spittle begin to appear on plants. An ancient belief, still held today in some rural districts, is that the cuckoos have been spitting, giving the name cuckoo spit to these blobs of bubbly froth. In America these are called spittlebugs. Inside each blob of foam is a froghopper nymph, a tiny pale-brown insect with a large head. Sinking its proboscis into the skin of the plant it sucks sap at such a rate that the liquid quickly passes through its digestive tube and out at the other end. There it mixes with a soapy

fluid given out from glands on the underside of the abdomen. The sides of the abdominal segments are extended to curve beneath the body enclosing a cavity into which the spiracles open. This chamber opens to the rear through a valve and the froth or spume is caused by expelled air coming into contact with the fluid passing over the valve.

The adult froghopper does not make any froth but leaps from plant to plant. Its large head and jumping powers strongly resemble those of a frog, and earn it the name froghopper *Philaenus spumarius*. Most froghoppers are sombrely coloured but some species are vividly coloured, for example, *Cercopis vulnerata*, living on sallows and alders, which is a striking black and red. Froghoppers are about $\frac{1}{4}$ in. to $\frac{1}{2}$ in. or more long.

## Leafhopper sharpshooters

These are small insects, rarely more than $\frac{1}{2}$ in. long, but they are serious pests in many parts of the world, damaging a wide variety of cultivated plants, including fruit and other crops. Most of them are powerful jumpers. Some are known as sharpshooters from the way they shoot drops of clear liquid, or honeydew, from the tip of the abdomen, regularly every second for as long as 2 minutes. Because the liquid is

sweet ants are attracted to it. Leafhoppers are also known as dodgers. Instead of leaping to safety when disturbed a leafhopper may run round to the other side of a leaf or twig then return quickly to see if all is clear, retreating rapidly again if it is not. Leafhoppers are pests on rice, potatoes, beet, grain, grass and soft fruits. The females use a sharp ovipositor to lay eggs in long rows just under the skin of plants.

## Lerps—the jumping plant lice

Another bothersome type of insect, especially on apple and pear trees, is the lerps or jumping plant lice, *Psylla pyricola* and *P. mali*. After passing the winter as eggs, laid the previous autumn on leaf scars, the nymphs, by sucking sap, damage fruit blossom and stunt shoots. They give out their honeydew in long slender waxy tubes. When these break up the honeydew spreads over the leaves of the food-plants. In Australia the Aborigines collect and eat the honeydew of the lerps that live on mimosa and eucalyptus.

## Plant hoppers

There are over 5000 species of insects under this heading which are sometimes grouped as one family, sometimes split into a number of families. Collectively they

△ *Either a mobile lump of bark, the head of another animal or a treehopper.*

▽ *A treehopper shows disruptive camouflage.*
▽▽ *A leaf? A plant hopper, genus **Acanalonia**.*

have been known as lantern flies because one of the most striking of them, *Laternaria phosphorea*, was supposed to be luminous. The Chinese candlefly *Fulgora candelaria* is also said to be luminous. In fact, none of them is luminescent. Many have large heads, often grotesquely shaped, and some are brightly coloured while others are covered with white wax that may hang like wool on their bodies. *Laternaria* has a head like a peanut, almost the same size as the body, with the eyes set far back, and the markings on it make it look like a miniature crocodile's head. There is almost certainly protection in the colours of the African species of *Flata*. These have two colour forms, green and red, that live together. Moreover they arrange themselves on a plant stem in a row, the red individuals lowermost looking like blossoms, the green ones above looking like unopened buds.

## Hoppers in the trees

The last group in this cavalcade of hoppers is the treehoppers. Like the froghoppers and the others in this series they feed on sap as nymphs and adults and are noted for their jumping ability. Most of them are not present in large enough numbers to be pests. One, the buffalo treehopper *Ceresa bubalis*, may damage fruit trees through laying eggs in holes in the bark. Each hole is made by the female's ovipositor. As nymphs most treehoppers are inconspicuous but many, especially those in tropical America, have grotesque shapes. The external skeleton of the front part of the thorax becomes much enlarged and takes on fanciful shapes. In the thornbug *Umbonia crassicornis* it has the shape of a large rose thorn. Sometimes these bugs line up on a twig and can hardly be distinguished from a row of thorns.

## Evolution run wild

Is it useful to the treehopper to look like a thorn? Even if the lantern fly does not deceive its enemies by looking like a miniature crocodile, perhaps its outsize proboscis may be protective, by making enemies hesitate before attacking. Treehoppers like *Membracis expansa* have a huge boldly and garishly coloured shield covering the body like a large cap so the insect resting on a plant looks like a flower. In others this outgrowth of the skeleton becomes truly monstrous, forming all manner of odd shapes decorated with spines, or forming a circular arch high above the insect's body. The limit seems reached in one that has an arm rising from the thorax, curving over the head to end in a slender stalk bearing three balls, like the pawnbroker's sign. It is hard to see how such elaborate ornaments benefit the insect, and no acceptable theory has yet been put forward.

| | |
|---|---|
| phylum | **Arthropoda** |
| class | **Insecta** |
| order | **Hemiptera** |
| sub-order | **Homoptera** |
| families | **Cercopidae** *froghoppers* |
| | **Psyllidae** *jumping plant lice* |
| | **Fulgoridae** *plant hoppers* |
| | **Cicadellidae** *leaf hoppers* |
| | **Membracidae** *treehoppers* |

*Face to face with a hornet. Despite its intimidating look, this European hornet does not seek trouble and is less aggressive than the common wasp.*

# Hornet

*The name 'hornet' should really be used for a large species of social wasp known as the European hornet, **Vespa crabro**. In North America the name is applied to a large native wasp, the white-faced hornet, as well as to the European species, which has been introduced. The common American social wasps of the genus **Dolichovespula**, popularly known as yellowjackets, and large social wasps in the tropics are also sometimes called hornets. In the rest of the English-speaking world 'hornet' has lost all precise meaning and is applied to any large social wasp, rather as 'tarantula' is used by the majority of people when referring to any large spider.*

*The European hornet is distinguished from the two almost identical common wasps, **Vespula vulgaris** and **Vespula germanica**, and other similar species, by its larger size and distinct coloration, which is dull orange and brown instead of bright yellow and black. Worker hornets are rather larger than queen wasps, and the queen hornet is even larger, being over an inch long.*

## Papier-mâché nests

The European hornet resembles the common wasps in that it makes a 'paper' nest of wood chewed to a paste, but the nest is usually built in a hollow tree, occasionally under a bank or in an unfrequented building and for this reason alone often escapes notice. Wasps use hard sound wood to make their paper, but hornets are less particular and content themselves with soft decayed wood sometimes mixing it with sand or soil. The resultant paper is yellowish and rather coarse in texture. The nest is of the usual wasp type, made up of a series of tiers or layers of cells, separated by interspaces, with the cells opening downwards. The cells in a hornets' nest are larger but less numerous than in a wasps' nest, and the total population of a hornet colony is smaller.

Its large size and alarming appearance have led to the hornet acquiring a reputation for ferocity which does it great injustice. It is in fact less aggressive than the common wasps and will not sting unless seriously molested. It has the unusual habit among wasps of remaining partly active at night. It sometimes goes to the treacle bait that collectors paint on tree trunks to attract the moths that fly at night, giving the collector quite a surprise when he finds a colourful hornet in his trap instead of a drab moth.

## Laying the foundation

The life-history of the hornet is essentially the same as that of the common wasp. Fertile females or queens appear in the nest towards the end of summer. They mate and then find a sheltered place in which to hibernate, while all the other inhabitants of the nest, males and infertile females or workers, die. In the spring the queens become active again and search for nesting sites, each one founding a separate nest or colony. The queen begins the paper nest by building a single tier of downward-pointing cells hanging by a stalk from the roof of a cavity. In each cell she lays an egg and the eggs hatch into larvae which she feeds until they grow to full size and pupate, each in its own cell. These pupae produce a small brood of workers.

From then on the energies of the queen are devoted to laying more and more eggs in cells built by the workers, which enlarge the nest as their numbers increase. They also forage for themselves as well as for the larvae and the queen. In the late summer queens and males are reared and the cycle begins all over again. As in other social wasps the larvae are fed on animal food, such as flies and caterpillars, and the adults live mainly on nectar, honeydew and other sweet juices from plants.

## Moths mimic hornets

A familiar theory of protective mimicry, originally founded on the study of tropical American butterflies, can be given here. Two moths, the hornet moth *Sesia apiformis* and the lunar hornet moth *Sphecia bembeciformis*, of the family Sesiidae or clearwings are as big as a hornet, have transparent wings and yellow and brown banded bodies. They look so like hornets that few people will touch them and birds are probably deceived as well. Birds avoid eating wasps and hornets not only on account of their stings but also because both of them have an unpleasant taste.

| | |
|---|---|
| phylum | **Arthropoda** |
| class | **Insecta** |
| order | **Hymenoptera** |
| family | **Vespidae** |
| genus & species | ***Vespa crabro*** European hornet ***Vespula maculata*** white-faced hornet others |

▷ *What the proverbial 'hornets' nest' looks like: an irregularly-ridged papier-mâché ball suspended in the undergrowth, patrolled by its outsize inmates.*
▽ *Solitary diner: European hornet **Vespa crabro** feeding on a flower.*

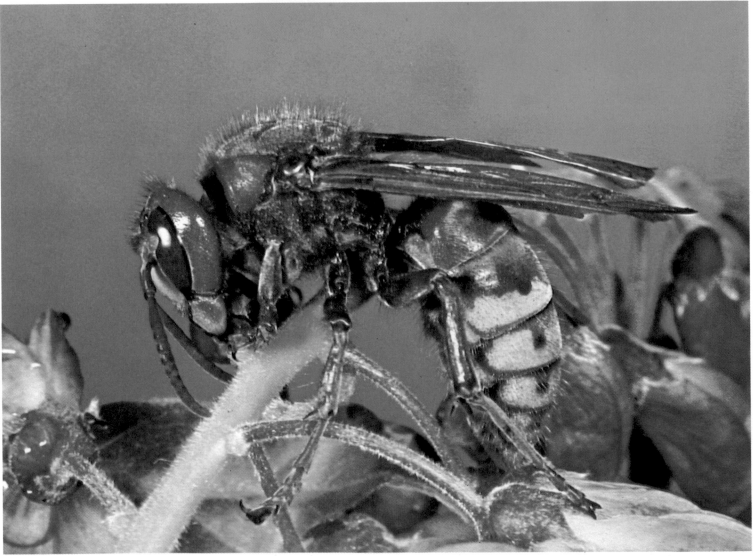

104

*Beauty in life: the face of a deerfly* **Chrysops caecutiens**. *The brilliant colours fade after death, and are lost in preserved specimens.*

# Horsefly

This name is given to certain large flies belonging to the genera **Tabanus** and **Haematopota**.. *The females feed on the blood of animals, especially horses and cattle, the males on nectar from flowers.* The name horsefly is often used to describe all the flies of the family Tabanidae, all of which feed in the same way. Among them are the well-known flies called 'clegs' which greatly relish human blood and can be a serious nuisance in warm weather on moors and in woodland. The deer flies **Chrysops** also belong to the Tabanidae. The true horseflies are sometimes called 'stouts', probably on account of their size; the largest British species **Tabanus sudeticus** may be an inch long and have a wing span of nearly 2 in. Horseflies and clegs are dull grey or brown with clear or mottled wings, but the equally bloodthirsty deer flies are handsome insects, brown and yellow, the wings clear with distinct brown markings. In many tabanids the eyes are wonderfully beautiful, with rainbow-like bands of gold, red and green. Unfortunately these colours fade after death and are not seen in preserved specimens.

Horseflies are not important as carriers of disease, but are nevertheless very harmful to cattle, causing disturbance and loss of grazing time, and consequent deterioration in health. In some parts of the world herdsmen drive their cattle out to graze through the summer night and keep them in shelter by day, simply to protect them from horseflies.

*The real menace: most people are shy of wasps and hornets, but once in damp pasture horse-flies are the most painful and persistent of biters. Above: **Tabanus bromius** takes a rest. Left: The piercing mouthparts of a deerfly.*

horsefly makes quite a big hole, and when the fly withdraws its mouthparts a drop of blood oozes out. It feeds both by licking up the drop and by sucking from the wound. It has been estimated that a single grazing beast may lose as much as 100 cu cm of blood in this way in the course of a summer day.

Our knowledge of horseflies' habits is based mainly on females that come to bite. Males are seldom seen and are comparatively rare in entomological collections. They are known to feed on nectar from flowers but are seldom observed doing so.

In the tropical rain forest of Africa some of the commonest flies of the forest floor are biting horseflies, but for a long time only females were known. Then, as part of a programme of entomological research, scaffolding and platforms were put up, so scientists could go up and watch near the treetops or jungle canopy. In and above this hitherto inaccessible environment were found swarms of male horseflies, together with occasional females. Presumably these females fly up to find a mate and then descend again to resume their quest for blood. Another curious habit of male horseflies is darting down to take water from lakes and streams in the same way as swifts and swallows do.

## Cannibalistic larvae

Although about 3 000 species of horseflies, in the broader sense, are known (28 in Britain) we know very little about their life histories. Such larvae that are known live in shallow water, in mud and sand by streams or in damp soil. They are elongate creatures with rather leathery skins and a breathing tube or siphon at the tip of the abdomen. Those of the big *Tabanus* horseflies are carnivorous and will eat any other insects, worms, snails, tadpoles and even each other! A number kept together in one container is soon reduced to one well-fed larva. They catch their prey with a pair of strong, curved, vertically moving jaws. The larvae of the pretty marble-winged deerflies live on vegetable rubbish and can easily be reared in numbers in a shallow-water aquarium. All horsefly larvae tend to seek drier surroundings to pupate; even aquatic larvae leave the water and pupate in mud or damp soil.

## Once seen . . .

An insect collector in Africa once came upon a swarm of horseflies of both sexes, evidently just emerging from their pupae. He collected a large number, and they proved to be a new species. He was generous in distributing his specimens and the species is now well represented in collections—but it has never been seen alive since by the collector or anyone else!

## Bloodthirsty females

Horseflies may sometimes be seen sitting and sunning themselves on tree trunks and fence posts, but are far more often seen feeding on cattle or horses, or flying around them. The clegs and other smaller tabanids may often be discovered on the clothing or exposed skin of a companion on a walk, or located on oneself by the sharp, painful prick that accompanies their bite. The big horseflies fly with quite a loud hum, but clegs and deerflies arrive silently on the victim's coat collar or sleeve and then stealthily make their way to the nearest area of exposed skin. They are not very quick and wary and one can usually swat a cleg that has bitten, but where they occur they are numerous, and are in no way deterred by casualties among their fellows.

Tabanid flies have sharp, blade-like mandibles and maxillae and use these to pierce the skin of their victims. The bite of a large

| phylum | **Arthropoda** |
|---|---|
| class | **Insecta** |
| order | **Diptera** . |
| family | **Tabanidae** |
| genera | ***Tabanus, Haematopota*** *clegs* ***Chrysops*** *deerflies* |

*A housefly cleans itself by rubbing its first pair of legs together. This common fly spreads disease mainly as a result of its indiscriminate feeding habits. Bacteria may be carried on the legs or body, or in the proboscis and so be exuded onto food with the next flow of saliva.*

# Housefly

*Many different kinds of flies come into houses. Some are accidental intruders that buzz on the window panes trying to get out into the open air again. Others enter houses in the autumn to hibernate in attics and roof-spaces. But there are two kinds that make our houses their home. One is the housefly, the other is the lesser housefly. The first is stoutly built and in both sexes the abdomen is yellowish or buff. Lesser houseflies are smaller and more slender, the females dull greyish, the males similar but with a pair of semi-transparent yellow patches at the base of the abdomen. The two are also distinguished by a difference in the veins of the wings which can easily be seen with a lens. This difference separates the two species regardless of sex.*

*Both have a wide distribution, the housefly being found throughout the tropics as well as in almost all inhabited temperate regions.*

## Kiss-in-the-ring flight

Houseflies pass their adult lives in houses, flying about the rooms and crawling over food that is left exposed. Both species breed in the sort of refuse that accumulates around the dwellings of people who live unhygienically, but their habits differ in detail. Lesser houseflies appear earlier in the season than houseflies, which build up their numbers rather slowly after the winter and are not usually abundant until July. The males of lesser houseflies fly in a very distinctive way. They choose a spot in a room, often beneath a hanging lamp or similar 'landmark', and fly as if they were following the sides of a triangle or quadrilateral, hovering momentarily at the corners and turning sharply at them; a single fly will continue to follow the same course for long periods. If, as often happens, more than one fly is patrolling in the same area, one of them will intercept the other and the two whirl together for an instant and then part again. The expression 'playing kiss-in-the-ring' aptly describes this activity, but they are in fact all males, and always lesser houseflies.

## Flies in summer — and winter

The breeding habits of the two species are similar but the larva of the lesser housefly prefers food rich in nitrogenous compounds, such as urine or bird droppings. These flies are nearly always abundant where chickens are kept. The larvae of the housefly are less particular. Manure and compost heaps, the night soil from old-fashioned privies and house refuse of any kind all provide them with breeding-grounds.

The eggs are laid on the larval food, and the adult flies also feed in places of this kind. The eggs are white, about $\frac{1}{25}$ in. long and a female housefly may lay as many as 900 in batches of about 150. They hatch in as little as 8 hours if it is very warm, otherwise in 1–3 days. The white legless maggots feed rapidly and may reach full size in under 2 days, but can live for 8 weeks in colder and less favourable conditions. At 15°C/60°F houseflies will breed continuously throughout the year, taking about 3 weeks from egg to adult, but in the tropics the cycle is completed in a week. The pupa is formed in an oval brown capsule called the puparium, which consists of the last larval skin; instead of being shed at pupation this is retained and plays the same part as the moth cocoon.

The lesser housefly has a similar life cycle, but its larva is very different in appearance, being flattened and beset with rows of short branched tentacle-like processes on the upper surface of the body.

Flies disappear in winter time, and the question where they go is often asked — and it once formed the theme of a popular song. There seems no simple answer to it. Houseflies may hibernate as adults or continue breeding slowly in warm places, especially in buildings where cattle are kept. Probably the fly has different adaptations for wintering in different parts of its range. In warm regions it breeds all the year round.

## Sucking up their food

Adults of both species feed by settling on moist organic matter of almost any kind and sucking up nutrient liquid from it. If the material is dry the fly regurgitates a drop of liquid on to it and sucks up the resultant solution. Crude sewage and a bowl of sugar are equally attractive and the insect may fly straight from one to the other. The feeding apparatus consists of a short sucking proboscis expanded at the end into a sponge-like organ with which the fly mops up its liquid food. Flies that have overfilled their stomachs will often regurgitate on any surface on which they happen to be resting, leaving little dirty spots.

People will sometimes assure you that they have been bitten by a housefly. The mistake is excusable because the stable fly *Stomoxys calcitrans* looks almost exactly like a housefly. Its mouthparts are, however, very different, consisting of a stiff piercing organ, and they feed, as horseflies do, by sucking blood. Their bite is quite painful and they can penetrate one's skin through a thick sock. The stable fly breeds in dung mixed with straw and is far less common now than when horses were kept in large numbers.

## Bearers of disease

The most important disease-carrying insects are those which feed on our blood, taking micro-organisms from infected people and injecting them into the blood of healthy ones. Examples are the tsetse fly and some mosquitoes. Houseflies do not feed in this way, but by feeding on excrement and exposed foodstuffs they are potential carriers of gastro-intestinal diseases such as dysentery. Houseflies taken from a slum district have been found to carry on average over $3\frac{1}{2}$ million bacteria per fly, and over a million in clean districts. These are not all disease bacteria, but some of them are very likely to be. Infants and small children seem to suffer most from fly-borne disease. In a tropical village infant mortality dropped in one year from 22·7 to 11·5 per cent when flies were controlled by an insecticide.

It is not difficult to kill flies in vast numbers by spraying such substances as DDT and chlordane on the places where they feed and breed but they have a remarkable capacity for developing resistance to specific poisons. No individual fly develops resistance during its lifetime, but some will almost always survive a spraying and these will include individuals having, by an accident of nature, some degree of immunity to the pesticide being used. This immunity is inherited by their offspring, in varying degrees, and the most resistant of these will again survive and breed. Selection of this kind continues with every generation until the insecticide is useless in any concentration at which it is safe to use. The process is exactly the same as the natural selection through which evolution has taken its course. These examples of acquired resistance in insects are in fact examples of very rapid evolutionary change, and they form one of the most compelling arguments against relying too much upon pesticides in our efforts to control harmful insects.

Control of houseflies is best achieved by depriving them of breeding places. The modern civilised way of life has already gone a long way towards doing this with water-borne sanitation, the use of covered dustbins and the decline of the horse as a means of transport.

| class | **Insecta** |
|---|---|
| order | **Diptera** |
| family | **Muscidae** |
| genera & species | ***Musca domestica*** *housefly* <br> ***Fannia canicularis*** *lesser housefly* |

*Top right: Photomicrograph of a leg. The last segment has a pair of claws and two suction pads which help the fly to walk on smooth surfaces (× 60).*
*Bottom right: Housefly just about to land.*
*▽ Wings of housefly (top) and lesser housefly (bottom). The differences in venation can be used to distinguish the two types of fly.*

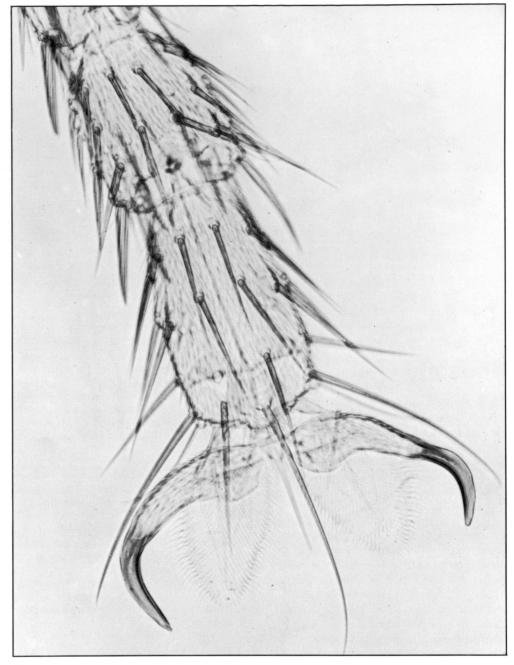

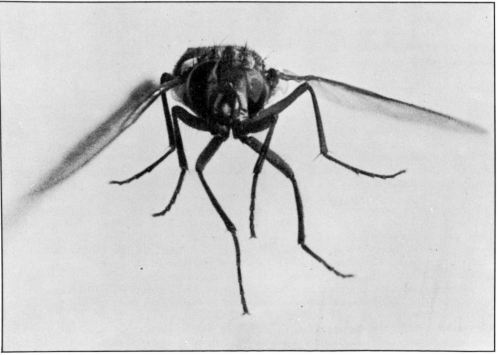

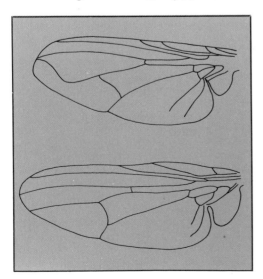

108

*Syrphus feeding. Adult hoverflies live entirely on nectar and honeydew which they suck up through their proboscis with its sponge-like tip. This makes them important as flower pollinators, second only to bees, which they also closely resemble with their striking black and yellow markings ( 10 × life size).*

# Hoverfly

*Hoverflies are probably the most skilful of all insect flyers. They can hang suspended in the air then glide rapidly to one side or forwards or backwards, or move up or down to hang suspended once more. They are two-winged flies belonging to the family Syrphidae. Many visit flowers in large numbers to feed on nectar and in America they are also known as flower flies. They are second only to bees in importance as flower pollinators.*

*Most hoverflies have a superficial resemblance to wasps and bees, being either marked with black and bright colours in contrasting patterns or covered with a coat of short, dense hairs, also variously patterned. In some cases there is such*

*close resemblance between certain species of hoverflies and the wasps and bees living in the same area that there seems no doubt mimicry is involved.*

*Most of the two-winged flies are unattractive to us, including as they do the mosquitoes and houseflies. Hoverflies are almost all harmless and many are useful as well as being attractive to look at. Two common varieties of the hoverfly are the little yellow-and-black striped species* **Syrphus balteatus** *and* **S. ribesii,** *and the large bee-like* **Eristalis tenax.** *They are mainly seen towards the end of the summer.*

## Living helicopters

Hoverflies are most active in sunshine and warm weather. They can be seen in large numbers hovering over flowers with exposed nectaries, and feeding from them.

When hovering they sometimes make little rocking movements while accurately maintaining their position. This is a more remarkable feat of controlled flight than it first appears, for the air in which the fly is poised is not motionless. There is almost always some lateral drift or 'wind', as well as eddies caused by rising air currents and the breeze passing around branches and other obstacles. The insect must therefore be constantly making minute adjustments of its wingbeats to avoid being carried up and down or to and fro.

It seems most likely that the hoverfly maintains its position through its sense of sight. Insects' eyes are less efficient than ours at forming images, but much more efficient at detecting small movements. The slightest shift in the fly's position is thus instantly perceived and as quickly corrected, so it remains motionless in relation not to the air around it but to the solid objects within its field of vision. Occasionally it is

109

slightly displaced and recovery from this is shown in the rocking movements already mentioned.

The eyes of hoverflies are relatively enormous. Other insects with very large eyes, such as the dragonflies and robber flies, need efficient vision to hunt winged prey in the air, but hoverflies feed from flowers and the need for accurate control of their hovering provides the only explanation of their very highly developed sense of sight.

Why do they hover? In a few cases it seems to have some connection with courtship and mating, but in most of them both sexes constantly hover without taking any notice of each other at all. It seems stretching a point to suggest that hoverflies hover because they enjoy doing so, but there is no better explanation at present.

Another curious habit hoverflies have is of continuing to buzz or 'sing' after they have settled and ceased to move their wings. The sound seems to be produced by vibration of the thorax, but why they do this is not known.

## Many kinds of larvae

Most hoverflies have a short proboscis that has a sponge-like expanded end with which they mop up sugary liquids. They can feed only on flowers in which the nectaries are exposed, such as those of ivy. Others have a kind of snout which they can push into bell-shaped flowers, and one Oriental genus *Lucastris* has a long proboscis and can feed from tubular flowers. As well as taking nectar, hoverflies also take aphid's honey-dew from leaves.

The feeding habits of the adult hoverflies are fairly uniform but those of the larvae are extremely diverse. They may hunt aphids or greenfly, feed on decaying organic matter—often in very foul surroundings, feed on the juices oozing from wounds in trees, burrow into stems or roots of living plants, or feed on the rubbish in the nests of bees, wasps and ants.

The aphid killers include some of the most abundant and familiar hoverflies. Their larvae are slug-like with the body tapering to a kind of neck at the front end. They have no eyes and the head is small and no broader than the neck. They hunt the swarming aphids by touch, crawling among them and swinging the trunk-like neck from side to side. The aphids make no attempt to escape so this method of hunting is very successful. Starting when very tiny with 3—4 aphids a day, a hoverfly larva may be eating 50 or 60 a day when fully grown.

One of the most interesting of the larvae living on decaying matter is that of the drone fly *Eristalis tenax*. The larvae, often called 'rat-tailed maggots', live in the puddles that collect around manure heaps, in water containing little oxygen. At the hind end of its body the rat-tailed maggot has a breathing tube or siphon which is extensible like a telescope. Its length can be adjusted to reach 4 in. to the surface or a small fraction of this when the larva is only just immersed.

Hoverflies that feed on juices from wounded trees do not belong to familiar species and those that burrow into living plants provide exceptions to the rule that

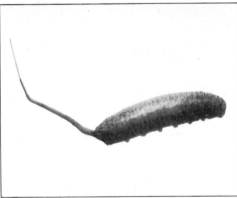

△ *Syrphus luniger* hovering (8 × lifesize).
◁ *Rat-tailed maggot*—the larva of **Eristalis** (1½ × lifesize). The siphon is an extension of the posterior spiracles, an obvious adaptation to life in water or decaying matter. The larva can creep about under water and reach to the air with its extensible breathing tube.
▷ **Volucella zonaria** is often mistaken for a hornet because of its yellow-banded abdomen. It breeds in wasp and hornet nests (× 16).
▽ *Syrphus* larva—an aphid-eater. The larva raises the front end of its body and swings from side to side until it touches and seizes its victim which is literally a sitting target (7 × lifesize).

hoverflies are harmless. The narcissus fly *Merodon equestris* spends its larval stage inside bulbs of narcissus and daffodil plants, eating their substance and destroying them. In places where bulbs are cultivated on a large scale they may cause considerable losses. The adult fly is large and hairy and looks like a bumble-bee.

### Feeding on bees' litter

The big handsome hoverflies of the genus *Volucella* provide the larvae that feed on rubbish in the nests of bees, wasps and ants. The females enter the nests and lay their eggs, and the larvae from them live in the 'rubbish heap' space beneath the nests where dead bee larvae and adult bees are thrown, living on the bodies and any other edible debris. The exact pattern varies according to the type of nest invaded, but in all cases the egg-laying females and the larvae are accepted by the bees and wasps, which are generally most intolerant of trespassers. In the case of the common species *Volucella bombylans*, which usually lays in the nests of bumble bees, the adult flies closely resemble the bees; furthermore the species occur in two distinct forms, each of which looks like a particular species of bumble-bee. It is tempting to think this helps them get into the nests, but this is far from certain, since they also breed in the nests of wasps which they do not at all resemble.

### The Samson legend

The resemblance of hoverflies to wasps and bees led to a queer belief that persisted from the dawn of history right up to the 17th century. We meet it in the writings of the classical Latin and Greek scholars and in the Old Testament, in the story of Samson and the lion, and the riddle, 'out of the strong came forth sweetness'.

People believed that a swarm of honeybees could be engendered by leaving the carcase of a large animal to rot. An ox was usually recommended, and in the Samson story it was a lion. The truth is that drone flies *Eristalis* breed in a decaying, liquefying carcase, and after a time large numbers of these bee-like flies emerge from it.

Drone flies have only two wings, bees have four; drone flies do not sting, bees do—and not a drop of honey can ever have been obtained from 'bees' conjured up in this way. In those days, however, all learning was in the hands of classical scholars, and their authority prevailed over any kind of evidence. If Aristotle and Ovid said that carcases produce bees, then the insects that appeared had to be bees. Anyone questioning this would risk his reputation and livelihood, possibly his life.

| class | **Insecta** |
|---|---|
| order | **Diptera** |
| family | **Syrphidae** |
| genera & species | *Syrphus balteatus* |
| | *S. ribesii* |
| | *Eristalis tenax* |
| | *Merodon equestris* |
| | *others* |

# Kallima

*This, from a Greek word meaning beautiful, is the generic name of certain butterflies belonging to the family Nymphalidae which are also called leaf butterflies or, more commonly, dead-leaf butterflies. This same family includes the fritillaries, purple emperor, white admiral, and butterflies such as peacock, red admiral, tortoiseshell and Camberwell beauty, all brilliantly marked and powerful in flight. The dead-leaf butterflies share these qualities but with the exception that when they close their wings they are transformed. The several species of* **Kallima** *range from New Guinea through southeast and south Asia to India and Sri Lanka, with species in Madagascar and also in Africa.*

*The Indian and far eastern species* **Kallima inachus** *and* **K. paralekta** *are 3½ in. across the spread wings. The upper-side of the wings is patterned with dark brown, blue and bright orange but in the Sri Lanka species* **K. philarchus** *the orange is replaced with white. The other species are variously coloured but all have this kind of colour combination.*

### Bogus foliage

The shape of the wings of kallima butterflies when closed over the back, together with the colours and patterns of their undersides, give the appearance of a dead leaf. Many members of their family have 'tails' on the rear margins of the wings. These are short and blunt-ended. The dead-leaf butterflies have one such tail and when the butterfly comes to rest on a twig this touches the twig and looks like a leaf stalk. The tip of the leaf is represented by the pointed and curved tips of the forewings as they lie together. Between this tip and the bogus leaf stalk runs a dark line, across both fore- and hindwings, which looks just like the midrib of a leaf.

### Trembling like a leaf

Less distinct dark lines run obliquely upwards from this central line to the margins of the wings, and these look exactly like the veins of a leaf. To complete the illusion, and this is especially true of *K. inachus*, the species most often seen in museums or books, there are patches on the wings just like the holes and tears, the fungal growths and other blemishes found on dead leaves. The body, head and antennae are tucked away between the wings when the butterfly is resting and the whole effect is such that once the butterfly has settled it is almost impossible to see it against the background of leaves and branches. No two butterflies of the same species are patterned alike on their underwings, just as no two dead leaves are exactly alike. And immediately the butterfly settles it turns and faces down the stem, as a dead leaf would hang, and it starts to sway gently as if in a breeze. It looks so much like a leaf that it is surprisingly hard to find and is a very effective camouflage against its predators.

The celebrated British naturalist AR Wallace met *K. paralekta* in Sumatra in 1861 and he describes in his book, *The Malay Archipelago*, how he had the greatest difficulty in finding the butterfly, once it had settled, even when he had watched it fly in and marked the spot with his eye.

## Only flies when it must

Dead-leaf butterflies live in regions of heavy rainfall, in thick forests in hilly and mountainous districts. They are seldom seen in the open and never fly far, spending most of their time resting on bushes. When they do fly, as when they are disturbed, they fly off rapidly on an erratic course, the bright colours on the uppersides of their wings making them very conspicuous. The result is they are often chased by birds, but once the butterfly settles and closes its wings the bird chasing it is baffled. The butterfly has done the perfect disappearing act.

## Flaunting its colours

The butterflies often settle on sweet sap exuding from trees or on over-ripe fruit or on damp patches on the ground to drink. At such times they hold their wings partly open and move them up and down, with no attempt at concealment.

## The disappearing trick

The orange oakleaf, or Indian leaf butterfly, as *K. inachus* is called, is double brooded. One breeding season is from April to June and the other is after the rains. Its caterpillar feeds on flowering trees and shrubs *Strobilanthus* and *Pseuderantheum*. It is golden brown with nine longitudinal rows of fine spines. Its head and legs are black and on the head are two long red 'horns' set with minute branched spines.

The remarkable resemblance the settled orange oakleaf butterfly bears to a dead leaf has led to this species being used as the last word in perfect protective resemblance. A few entomologists have questioned whether this may not be a mistaken idea because the butterfly usually settles among green foliage, not among dead leaves. We are on more certain ground in using *Kallima* to illustrate two other principles. The first is that known as *coincident disruptive pattern*. The line which represents the midrib of the leaf runs across the fore- and hindwings, and only forms the unbroken line required for its camouflage effect when the wings are held in the natural position of rest, and this is also true of the leaf-like outline formed by the wings. Any alteration in the relative position of the wings largely destroys the illusion. The other principle is that of *flash coloration*. The upper surface of the wings of *Kallima* are attractively coloured orange and blue. When the butterfly suddenly flies there is a startling explosion of bright colour, and when it alights a large blue and orange butterfly apparently disappears, the detailed camouflage of the undersides of its wings seeming to transform it into a dead leaf. Both effects are puzzling and confusing to a predator (or collector) searching for the butterfly, more so than if it had inconspicuous coloration on both upper- and undersides of the wings.

△ Now you see it: few predators drawn to the bright, flashes of **Kallima inachus** in erratic flight can distinguish between butterfly and dead leaf once it has landed.

◁△ Museum specimen of **Kallima inachus**, uppersides of its wings flaunting the beauty that gave it its name.

◁ The underside of the same butterfly—each wing a perfect imitation dead leaf, even to the 'veins' and 'fungus holes' all over it.

▷ Photographer's reconstruction of **Kallima inachus** in typical pose, showing the peak of perfection reached by this insect's camouflage.

| phylum | **Arthropoda** |
|---|---|
| class | **Insecta** |
| order | **Lepidoptera** |
| family | **Nymphalidae** |
| genus & species | **Kallima inachus, K. paralekta, K. philarchus** |

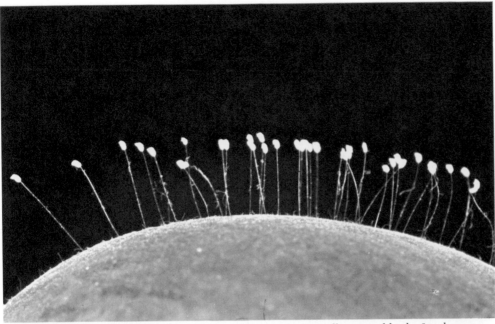

△ *Eggs aloft: eggs of lacewing **Chrysopa** on the hardened gum stalks secreted by the female.*

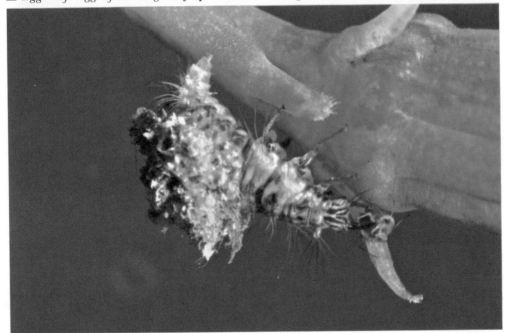

△ *Mobile litter basket: when the aphid has been sucked to a husk by this chrysopid larva its skeleton will join the remains of previous meals on its bristly back.* ▽ *Chrysopid cocoon.*

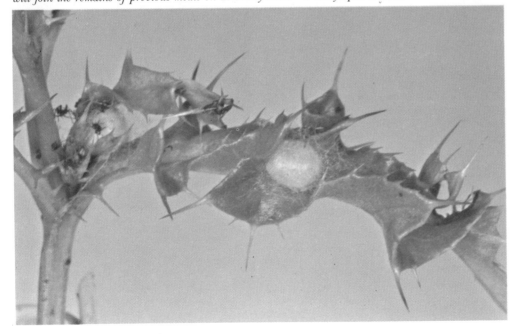

# Lacewing

*The lacewing's delicate gauzy wings and rather feeble flight could well have influenced artists who were portraying fairies. Several insect families of the order Neuroptera are given this name. The most familiar in Europe are the green lacewings Chrysopidae, most of which have a green body and metallic golden eyes. All this beautiful coloration fades after the insect is dead. The brown lacewings Hemerobiidae, smaller and brown or grey, are quite common among bushes and rank herbage. The spongilla flies or sponge flies Sisyridae are small lacewings whose larvae are aquatic and live as parasites on freshwater sponges. The largest of all is the giant lacewing **Osmylus fulvicephalus**, which has a 2 in. wingspan and is found near woodland streams. The tiny 'dusty-wing' lacewings Coniopterygidae are inconspicuous but of economic importance as their larvae prey on the red spider mite, a serious pest of fruit trees.*

## Malodorous beauty

Most lacewings fly at night and are attracted to artificial light. Green lacewings often fly out by day when bushes and low branches are disturbed, and the small brown Hemerobiidae can be found by shaking leafy branches over an inverted umbrella. Some may fly up but most will fall into the umbrella. The beautiful giant lacewing is best found by searching in culverts and bridges through which small streams run. It is a local and not very common insect. The giant and some of the green lacewings have a strong and unpleasant odour, which protects them against birds and other predators.

The larvae of the giant lacewing live in wet moss beside streams and those of the spongilla flies are wholly aquatic, breathing by means of gills. Most other lacewing larvae live among foliage.

## Pincushion eggs

Lacewings undergo a complete metamorphosis, with larva, pupa and imago stages. The female green lacewing has the amazing habit of laying her eggs on the ends of long, hair-like stalks which she makes herself in groups in leaves. She first dabs a drop of gummy liquid from the tip of her abdomen onto the leaf and then, raising her abdomen, draws it up into a slender stalk which immediately hardens. The egg is then laid at the top of this stalk. The larvae are predatory, feeding largely on aphids. When fully grown each spins a cocoon of white silk given out from a spinneret which is at the hind end of the body, not on the head as in the silk-spinning caterpillars.

The cocoons are usually attached to leaves or bark. Most of the young spend the winter as larvae inside the cocoon. They pupate the following spring, but one very common species *Chrysopa carnea* hibernates as an adult. Although it is green before hibernation, it turns brown soon after it settles down, becoming active and green again in the spring. These brown hibernating lacewings can often be seen inside houses in autumn and early winter.

The aquatic larvae of the spongilla flies *Sisyra* leave the water and spin cocoons in bark crevices and similar places. The giant lacewing spends the whole of its larval life, and spins its cocoon, in wet moss.

## Hypodermic feeding

In captivity brown lacewings have been seen preying on aphids. As larvae, all are predators and share with the ladybird and hoverfly larvae the task of keeping within bounds the swarming aphids or greenfly. Lacewing larvae are flattened, louse-shaped creatures with sharp-pointed, hollow jaws resembling a pair of callipers. They mostly live among foliage and crawl actively about searching for aphids and other insects. The victim is seized and pierced by the jaws through which a digestive juice is injected, liquefying the body contents. The resulting 'soup' is then sucked back by the larva. In both the injection and the suction the hollow jaws act like miniature hypodermic needles. The larvae of the larger species feed on small caterpillars and other insects as well as on aphids, and those of the giant lacewing eat any insects in their moist habitat. The smallest species prey on microscopic mites and their eggs, and in doing so may render as valuable a service as the aphid-eaters.

## Unusual disguise

The larvae of some of the green lacewings set a wonderful example in what to do with the wrappings after an open-air meal. When one of them has sucked an aphid dry it does not throw it away but holds the husk in its jaws and presses it down onto its own back, which is covered with stiff, hooked hairs. These hold the husk in place, where it dries and shrivels. After a time the larva is covered with a mass of husks, which makes it look more like a small heap of dried rubbish than a living insect. When it moults its skin the accumulation of husks is lost, but the larva starts to replace it as soon as it begins feeding again. Most of us must have seen these disguised larvae at some time or other, on the leaves of rose bushes or other foliage, but without noticing them. Almost certainly insectivorous birds also miss them when they are searching among the leaves.

| phylum | **Arthropoda** |
|---|---|
| class | **Insecta** |
| order | **Neuroptera** |
| families | **Chrysopidae, Hemerobiidae, Sisyridae, Osmylidae, Coniopterygidae** |
| genera & species | *Chrysopa carnea, Osmylus fulvicephalus, Sisyra,* others |

△ *Aphids beware: a chrysopid lacewing creeps down a branch in search of food.*

▽ *As remarkable for its pungent smell as its size, a giant lacewing* **Osmylus fulvicephalus**.

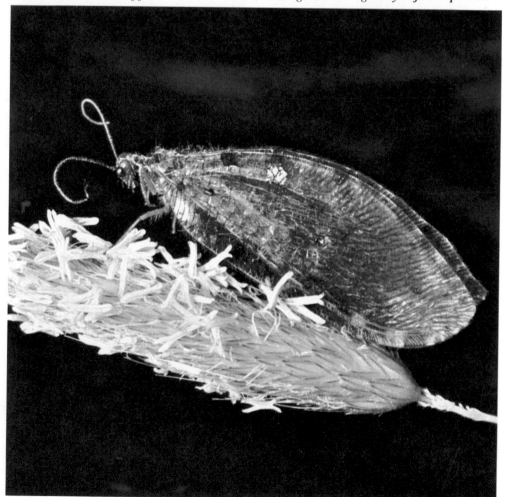

115

# Ladybird

Small, brightly coloured beetles, oval or almost circular in outline, ladybirds were regarded with affection long before it was realised they are useful as well as pretty. The name ladybird (sometimes ladybug or lady beetle) dates from the Middle Ages when the beetles were associated with the Virgin Mary and called 'beetles of Our Lady'. Their coloration is generally red or yellow with black spots and the pattern tends to be variable, extremely so in some species. A few, like that known as **Coccidula rufa**, are brown without conspicuous markings, and are not usually recognised as ladybirds. The colourful species have a strong and unpleasant smell and they taste equally bad. Their bright colours doubtless serve as a warning to predators not to try to eat them. Both ladybird adults and their larvae prey on aphids, destroying them in great numbers.

The four commonest species in Europe are the two-spot, ten-spot, seven-spot and twenty-two-spot ladybirds. The first is red with a single black spot on each wingcase but black specimens with four red spots are common, and the beetle is sometimes yellow with black spots. The underside and legs are black. The second is reddish or yellow, usually with five black spots on each wingcase, but the ground colour may be black as in the last species. The underside is brown and the legs yellowish. The seven-spot is larger than the first two species and its colours hardly vary at all. It is orange-red with a black spot on the line dividing the wingcases and three others farther back on each side. The last is much smaller with 11 black spots on each side on a bright yellow ground. One of the largest and most handsome species is the eyed ladybird **Anatis ocellata**, which has black spots on a red ground, each spot being

▷ △△ The lunate ladybird of the South African high veld **Chilomenes lunata** laying a batch of eggs. There are 5–50 in a batch, but the beetle lays several batches, usually to a total of about 150 eggs, though 1 000 has been recorded. To provide for the young, the female lays them in an aphid-infested place. They hatch in about 3 weeks.

▷ △ Eggs of the lunate ladybird. The larvae will start their aphid massacre, made easy by the mother's consideration and the soft, defenceless prey, straight away. The massacre continues even after pupation. Some idea of the extent of aphid and scale insect control by ladybirds can be had from the record of a single larva's eating 90 adult and 3 000 larval scale insects. This appetite, and the high rate of reproduction, make it a very beneficial beetle.

▷ Scourge of the aphids: larvae of the S. African ladybird **Cryptolaemus** hunting. Protected by a waxy secretion, then by warning colours, and a vile taste as adults—an easy life at all stages.

surrounded by a halo of yellow. It may be ⅖ in. long and lives among pine foliage.

The first four of these have been given the scientific names **Adalia bipunctata**, **A. decempunctata**, **Coccinella septempunctata** and **Thea vigintiduopunctata** respectively. Even scientists sometimes jib at long names so these four ladybirds are usually referred to as **2-punctata**, **10-punctata**, **7-punctata** and **22-punctata**.

### Winter hibernation

In summer ladybirds fly actively about among foliage. In winter they hibernate as adults, often in large groups. Sometimes 50 or 100 of them can be found crowded together under a piece of loose bark, on a post or in a porch. They often congregate in houses and usually go unnoticed until they come out in spring. In California crevices and caves on certain hilltops are well known as hibernation resorts where ladybirds gather in their thousands.

### Hordes of ladybirds

Ladybirds usually lay their orange-coloured eggs on the undersides of leaves, in batches of 3–50. Several batches are laid by one female, totalling 100–200 eggs, sometimes more. Because the beetles themselves feed on aphids or greenfly they tend to choose places where these are abundant in which to lay, so the larvae find food handy from the start. The eggs hatch in from 5 to 8 days, turning grey shortly before they do so. The larvae are active, bristly and variously coloured in patterns of black, orange, blue and red. Like the adult beetles they feed on aphids, but since they are growing rapidly they are far more voracious. The larval stage lasts 3 weeks or so, during which time several hundreds of aphids are eaten.

When thousands of aphid-eating ladybirds are each laying hundreds of eggs and every larva is consuming hundreds of aphids, it can be imagined that very large numbers of greenfly are destroyed, and the benefit to plants, both wild and cultivated, is enormous. The pupa is usually attached to

◁ △△ *A pupa, the ladybird's only lull in feeding.*

◁ △ *Full circle: adult lunate ladybirds feeding on a liberal supply of aphids.*
Even man, for hundreds of years, has contributed to the ladybirds' mollycoddled existence by recognising the need to keep them alive. They have even taken their place in English folklore with the rhyme 'Ladybird, ladybird, fly away home, your house is on fire, your children alone', a reference to the custom of burning hop vines at the end of the season, no doubt with many larvae on them. The second stanza, 'Except little Nan, who sits in a pan, weaving gold laces as fast as she can' concerns the colourful larva weaving a pupal case. These lines, spoken when a ladybird landed nearby, must have saved many an extremely useful insect's life.

◁ *The black sheep: one of the few vegetarian ladybirds* **Epilachna dregei** *which spoil the group's fine reputation by feeding on potato leaves.*

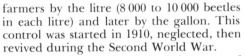

a leaf. The whole life cycle takes from 4 to 7 weeks, so several generations of ladybirds may be produced in a summer.

One small group of ladybirds are not predatory but feed as larvae on plant food. For example, there is a species, the twenty-four-spot ladybird *Subcoccinella viginti-quatuorpunctata* (certainly better written *24-punctata*), which eats clover.

## Ladybird farms

The principle of using one species of insect to control the numbers of another is now well known, and is often advocated as being preferable to the use of poisonous insecticides. An early example of an operation of this kind concerns the use of a ladybird. Towards the end of the last century the Californian citrus orchards were devastated by the cottony-cushion scale insect, which was accidentally introduced from Australia. A brightly coloured ladybird *Rhodalia cardinalis* was found to be a natural enemy of the scale insect in Australia, and in 1889 some of these ladybirds were brought to California and released in the orchards. They effectively controlled the scale insect there and they have since been introduced to South Africa.

The Californian citrus growers were also troubled by aphids and other plant bugs, and use was made of a native ladybird, a species of *Hippodamia*, that hibernates, as mentioned earlier, in caves in the hills. These were collected and sold to the citrus

farmers by the litre (8 000 to 10 000 beetles in each litre) and later by the gallon. This control was started in 1910, neglected, then revived during the Second World War.

Even this is not the end of the story of useful ladybirds in California. In the 1920s the orchards were attacked by another scale insect *Pseudococcus*. Again a ladybird was brought from Australia, by the name of *Cryptolaemus montrouzieri*. This failed to breed under natural conditions in Western America, so huge ladybird factories were maintained where they were bred, with careful control of temperature and other conditions, on potato shoots infested with *Pseudococcus*. In 1928 alone 48 million ladybirds of this species were set free in the Californian orange orchards.

*(1) Searching every nook and cranny of a rock face for prey **Propylea 14-punctata**.*
*(2) The writing on the wings: the unusual markings of **Coccinella hieroglyphica**.*
*(3) Beauty as well as usefulness: the black and yellow **Thea 22-punctata**.*
*(4) The lighter colour variation of **Calvia 14-guttata**.*
*(5) Mopping up the plant parasites on a leaf, a dark colour variety of **Calvia 14-guttata**.*
*(6) Not all ladybirds have spots: a striped ladybird **Paramysia oblongoguttata**.*
*(7) One of the best-known ladybirds, the two spot **Adalia bipunctata**.*

| class | **Insecta** |
|-------|-------------|
| order | **Coleoptera** |
| family | **Coccinellidae** |

# Leafcutter ant

*Leafcutter ants are famous for their habit of cutting out pieces of leaves and carrying them away to their nests. Large numbers of them may be seen walking on well-defined trails leading to the nest, carrying pieces of leaf larger than themselves. They hold them in their jaws, well over their heads, like flags or umbrellas, and because of this they have sometimes been called parasol ants.*

*The ants themselves are large and long-legged with spines on their bodies. The queen may be up to $\frac{7}{10}$ in. long, the male $\frac{1}{2}$ in. The workers are of very different sizes, from tiny small-headed ants $\frac{1}{10}$ in. long to relatively gigantic large-headed ants $\frac{1}{2}$ in. long. For convenience they are divided into three grades called maxima-, media- and minima-workers.*

*In Brazil they are known as **saubas** and in the neighbourhood of orchards or plantations they may do a great deal of damage by defoliating the trees. Leafcutter ants, of which the chief genus is **Atta,** are confined to the tropics and subtropics of the New World.*

## Underground colonies

Leafcutter ants nest in gigantic underground colonies. The earth excavated from the galleries accumulates over the nest as a mound, which has been estimated to contain as much as 280 cubic yards of soil. A colony of this size may be made up of well over half a million ants, including a number of queens. Even with modern insecticides and bulldozers such nests are extremely hard to eradicate.

The ants cut and carry pieces of leaves to the nest to provide themselves with food. In special chambers within the nest the workers chew the leaves to make a compost on which a special kind of fungus is grown. By meticulous 'weeding' the ants keep their 'mushroom beds' pure, so only one kind of fungus is grown in spite of the fact that they must constantly be contaminated by fungus spores of other kinds. Although leafcutter ants as a whole grow several kinds of fungus, each species keeps to one particular kind, either one species, or those species belonging to one genus. The fungi themselves are peculiar and appear to have evolved in association with the ants. Under the care of the ants the fungi produce peculiar rounded bodies called 'bromatia', and the ants feed solely on these.

## Founding new colonies

New nests are established in typical ant fashion: a fertilised queen flies for some distance, comes to earth and breaks off her wings. She then seeks a sheltered place in the soil in which to lay her eggs and rear her first brood. The *Atta* ants have, however, a special addition to the usual routine. Most ants have a small pocket below the mouth, known as the infra-buccal pocket, in which masticated food is squeezed and kneaded. The liquid from this is swallowed and the remaining solid is rejected as a pellet. When

△ *Fighter cover: a minima worker perches on her defenceless sister's load ready to ward off attacks by the **Apocephalus** fly.*

▽ *Food for the fungus: a pair of leafcutter ants live up to their name as they slice leaves for their underground 'mushroom farm'.*

the *Atta* queen leaves her nest she always carries in her infra-buccal pocket a pellet made up of the hyphae or living threads of the fungus. As soon as she settles down in the crevice in which she will found her nest, she ejects the pellet and then carefully cherishes and cultivates it, using her own excrement as fertilizer. The fungus grows and provides the culture without which no *Atta* colony can exist.

## Division of labour

Within each colony of leafcutter ants there is a division of labour. The large workers, the maximae, defend the nest. The mediae workers collect the leaves, and the minimae tend and cultivate the fungus beds. Recently, however, a remarkable discovery was made on the island of Trinidad of an additional task carried out by the minimae.

When the mediae are out collecting leaves they are exposed to attacks by a small fly called *Apocephalus*, which circles above the ant and tries to settle on the back of its neck. This fly belongs to the Phoridae, the family to which the coffin fly belongs. If it succeeds it lays an egg which hatches into a parasitic larva that eats out the ant's brain. These flies are the leafcutter ants' most serious enemies.

At the Tropical Research Station of the New York Zoological Society in Trinidad somebody noticed that very often the piece of leaf carried by a home-coming media

had a tiny minima riding on it like a hitch-hiker. It usually sat near the top of the leaf, facing upwards in a threatening attitude, with wide-open jaws. A similar thing was seen when the media-workers were cutting the leaves. A long and careful watch was kept and finally the reason for this became clear.

When the media is unencumbered she can protect herself against the attack of the *Apocephalus* fly by snapping upwards with her big scissor-like jaws, but if cutting or carrying a leaf she can do no more than kick up with her legs, and this is often ineffective. The minima acts as a bodyguard; if a fly approaches the leaf on which her big sister is at work, she runs actively about, snapping her jaws and effectively intercepting its attack. Ants are known to have all sorts of curious tricks of behaviour, but nothing quite like this had ever been seen before.

| phylum | **Arthropoda** |
| --- | --- |
| class | **Insecta** |
| order | **Hymenoptera** |
| family | **Formicidae** |
| subfamily | **Myrmicinae** |
| genus | **Atta** |
| | *others* |

# Leafcutter bee

*There are a number of bees known by this name from their habit of cutting neatly rounded pieces out of leaves to line the cells of their nesting burrows. They belong to a large group of solitary bees which have the 'pollen baskets' — receptacles formed of bristles, for collecting pollen — on the underside of the abdomen. In honeybees and bumble-bees the pollen baskets are on the hindlegs. Leafcutter bees also have large heads and well developed jaws.*

### Habits and life cycle

The smoothly rounded cut-outs in the leaves of rose bushes and other plants, which so often mystify and infuriate gardeners, are a sure sign of the activities of leafcutter bees. They use the sections they snip out of leaves to line their burrows and to separate the cells. The breeding habits of the leafcutters are basically the same as those of other solitary bees. After mating, the female bee digs a burrow or finds one ready made, and builds a row of compartments, known as cells. In each of these she stores a mixture of honey and pollen, then lays an egg on it. This food is enough for the whole development of the larva. Oval pieces of leaf are cut for the sides of the burrow, and arranged to overlap. The cells are divided, and the last cell is capped by circular pieces of leaf. The final result is a series of cells in the burrow, looking like small cigar stubs laid end to end.

In species which produce only one generation a year, the bees hatch from their pupae in the autumn but do not come out as perfect insects until the spring. When they do so the one in the outermost cell, and therefore the youngest by a narrow margin, comes out first and the rest follow in succession. Some unknown mechanism restrains each bee from attempting to burrow out through an occupied cell. The outer cells almost always contain male bees, the inner ones females.

Leafcutter bees can be studied by drilling holes in logs or dead trees, or putting out lengths of hollow plant stems. Sometimes they will accept accommodation provided in this way, so their nesting can be watched.

### Bees and alfalfa seed

Lucerne or alfalfa is one of the main forage crops in the United States, but there has long been a problem about its seed production. When a bee visits a lucerne flower it prises apart the petals which enclose the anthers and stigma and which form what is known as the keel of the flower. This releases a sort of trap by which the reproductive parts of the flower spring up and hit the bee on the underside of the head. Honeybees learn to avoid this rude reception by manoeuvring their tongues straight to the nectar without parting the enclosing petals. Their caution results in anthers and stigmas being avoided altogether, the flowers are not pollinated, and no seed is produced.

Certain solitary bees are somewhat less sensitive and ignore their rough reception. They are, however, not nearly numerous

△ *A leafcutter bee on a rose leaf.*

▽ *Putting a piece of leaf into the nest.*

enough to pollinate effectively the hundreds of square miles of alfalfa that are grown for seed. Professor WP Stephen of Oregon State University has perfected methods of breeding huge numbers of two species of solitary bee artificially in the alfalfa growing districts, thereby increasing the yield of seed as much as tenfold. One of the species, the alkali bee *Nomia melanderi*, does not concern us here, but the other is a small species of leafcutter, apparently an accidental introduction from Europe. It is a species that likes nesting in ready-made burrows and is gregarious. The closer their burrows are together the better the bees are pleased. After a lot of experiments with drilling holes in wood it was found that paper drinking straws, packed in their original containers, but glued to the bottom to stop them dropping out, were readily used by the bees. The straws are closely packed, but each female appears to have no difficulty in locating her own nest among the 200-odd identical circles which she sees facing her as she flies

in towards a full container. In many cases almost all the straws become occupied. The bees seem to prefer straws $\frac{1}{5}$ in. in diameter and 4 in. long.

The culturing of this bee is now well established, and the seed producers make box-like homes for the bees, roofed and protected against birds with wire netting, and packed with large numbers of drinking straws in their containers. One such domicile, if well stocked with bees, is sufficient for about 5 acres, and the beauty of this method is that the bees can be moved from place to place as required.

| phylum | **Arthropoda** |
|---|---|
| class | **Insecta** |
| order | **Hymenoptera** |
| family | **Megachilidae** |
| genus & species | ***Megachile centuncularis*** *others* |

# Locust

*Although the term 'locust' is loosely applied to any large tropical or subtropical grasshopper, it is better restricted to those whose numbers occasionally build up to form enormous migrating swarms which may do catastrophic damage to vegetation, notably cultivated crops and plantations.*

*Africa suffers most seriously from locust swarms and three species are of special importance. These are the desert locust, the red locust and the African subspecies of the migratory locust.*

*Both the red locust and the African migratory locust have their own regional control organisations which effectively prevent plague outbreaks. The desert locust, however, presents a real international problem which has yet to be solved and is the main subject of study of the Anti-Locust Research Centre in London. It will therefore be the main subject of this entry.*

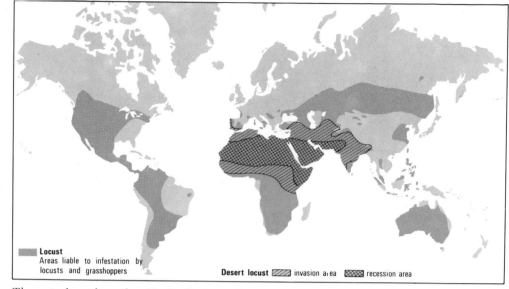

**Locust**
Areas liable to infestation by locusts and grasshoppers

**Desert locust** ▨ invasion area ▨ recession area

*The map above shows the wide distribution of locusts. In some places, like North America, cultivation of their breeding grounds has reduced their numbers. In Africa, however, the desert locust is public enemy number one. Other locusts are easier to control, because after their migrations they recede to small areas; the desert locusts' outbreak area is very wide, as indicated.*

## Locust or gregarious grasshopper

The vast plagues of locusts which periodically create such havoc in many regions of the underdeveloped world are really nothing more nor less than hordes of gregarious grasshoppers. For locusts can exist in two phases: a solitary, grasshopper phase, or a swarming locust phase. When the grasshoppers are crowded together they change their behaviour, and, if kept like this for a generation or more, also change their shape and colour to that of the swarming form.

Solitary locusts come together only for mating and then behave very much as other grasshoppers do. The eggs, the size of rice grains, are laid down to 4 in. below the surface of the ground. They are held together by a frothy secretion which hardens to form an egg-pod 1½–2 in. long, which usually contains 80–100 eggs. Above the pod the

froth forms a plug which helps prevent the eggs from drying out and stops sand falling into the hole, so the hatchlings can escape. The egg stage lasts about 10–14 days in the main summer breeding areas but may be up to 70 days in the colder North African spring. The insects that hatch grow through a series of moults or skin-changes in the course of which they become gradually more like adult locusts and in the final 2 moults the wings form, becoming functional after the last moult, when the insect is adult. This takes 30–50 days, mainly depending on temperature. In a swarm the adults are pink at first, but after a few weeks or months, usually coinciding with the rainy seasons, they mature sexually and become yellow. The flightless immature locusts are traditionally known as 'hoppers'.

When they first hatch young solitary locusts disperse and unless some environ-

mental factor forces them together they never do begin to associate in bands but settle down to the solitary life of grasshoppers. These are usually green or brown, blending well with their surroundings.

## Jekyll and Hyde phase-change

Under certain conditions, depending on many variable factors, often associated with the weather, scattered solitary locusts may become concentrated into favourable laying sites. With every female locust laying two or three batches of 70–80 eggs each the numbers after hatching will have multiplied at least 100 times. With many more hoppers crowded into the same area, groups coalesce and they are then well on the way to the all important phase change from solitary to gregarious type which leads eventually to hopper bands and locust swarms.

When crowded together their colour

*Left: Immature pink adult female. Millions of these exist in vast swarms, which follow the wind to arrive in new breeding grounds soon after rain.*
*Right: Hopper bands on the march, eating all the way. At first they move only a few yards a day, but in the later stages they hop for up to a mile.*

changes to a bold pattern of black and orange or yellow stripes which probably helps them see one another and so keep together. The brightly patterned, crowded hoppers grow into pink adults which turn yellow at sexual maturity, solitary adults being sandy-coloured. Moreover, in the adults there are structural differences between the solitary and gregarious phases, notably in the wing, which is relatively longer in the gregarious phase. It is known that structural changes between one phase and another are associated with relative differences in the insects' hormonal balance.

Mutual stimulation leads to greater activity and they start to 'march'. Because an urge to keep close together is induced by development in the gregarious phase they march together in bands.

As adults they continue to migrate, and the urge to crowd together is maintained, but they are now airborne and move much faster. Weather conditions too can lead to the development of gregarious locusts and swarm formations. Scattered flying locusts fly downwind towards frontal systems of converging airflow and thus tend to accumulate in rainy areas. As the region inhabited by the desert locust is mainly arid, the result of persistently flying with the wind is to concentrate large numbers of locusts in areas when rain is likely to fall and provide them with food in the form of a flush of desert plants springing up after the rain. The gregarious phase develops in the offspring and migration then takes place in the usual way, following the prevailing wind and the favourable weather.

## Locust plagues

When the swarm descends the locusts devour everything green. After mating takes place each female lays several hundred eggs. The young that hatch are still crowded and behave in just the same way, but the swarm that results can be many times larger. This swarm continues to migrate and again descends and multiplies its numbers. In this way a swarm may cover vast areas and build itself up into an aggregate of thousands of tons of locusts resulting in plague conditions. Plagues eventually come to an end due to adverse weather. The few survivors revert to the solitary phase, in which they are relatively harmless.

Perhaps the most important discovery made by the Anti-Locust Research Organisation has been that the African migratory locust and the red locust change from the solitary to the gregarious phase only in certain limited outbreak areas. These areas are effectively policed by regional locust control organisations and plague outbreaks have been prevented since 1944.

The desert locust is the locust of the Bible, and now by far the most damaging of all. It is hard to control because it has no geographically determined outbreak areas. It ranges over a vast area, from southern Spain and Asia Minor, the whole of northern Africa, through Iran to Bangla Desh and India, an area comprising about 60 countries. Between plagues lasting 6 or more years there are equally long recessions when only solitary locusts are to be found. The last plague ran from 1950 to 1962 and another showed all the signs of building up rapidly after the spring rains of 1967. In 1968 the situation looked very serious but by mid-1969 it was much quieter than expected 6 months previously. The last outbreak was in 1973–4 in New South Wales, Queensland and Victoria.

## Natural enemies

If all the locusts in a swarm only 2 miles square were to breed successfully, in only four generations there would be a severe infestation of the whole 196 million square miles of the earth's surface. Fortunately there is enormous mortality from natural causes. Winds may fail to carry the locusts to a suitable breeding area. The soil may not be moist enough for the eggs to hatch. Or they hatch to find insufficient plant growth for their food or to protect them from the heat of the midday sun. There are also many predators, parasites and diseases of locusts. A little fly *Stomorhina* lays its eggs on top of the locust egg pods as soon as they are laid and the fly's grubs eat up the eggs. Larvae of the beetle *Trox* can destroy an egg field completely and ants have been seen waiting at the top of an egg froth plug and carrying away all the hatchlings. Flocks of birds often accompany both hopper bands and adult swarms and they can account for enormous numbers of hoppers. At this stage hoppers are particularly vulnerable and their predators take advantage of the feast.

## Control by man

Concentrated insecticides and highly efficient spray gear using both aircraft and ground vehicles are used in enormous campaigns against desert locusts. One of the most effective, because it is simple and cheap, uses the exhaust gases from a Land Rover to produce a fine spray of poison. This will drift over the vegetation in the path of hoppers and is a very quick and economical way of killing hopper bands. Aircraft can match the mobility of a migrating swarm; searching greater areas, finding and following swarms and spraying them in the morning and evening when they fly low and are most vulnerable to spraying. A single light aircraft carrying 60 gallons of insecticide can destroy 180 million locusts.

Migrating swarms of locusts commonly travel between 1 000 and 3 000 miles between successive breeding areas and naturally cross many international frontiers. Regional locust control organisations within the desert locust invasion areas pool resources and facilitate the movement of supplies across frontiers. These organisations in turn are coordinated by the Food and Agriculture Organisation (FAO) of the United Nations with its headquarters in Rome. FAO cooperates with the Desert Locust Information Service run by the Anti-Locust Research Centre in London.

| phylum | **Arthropoda** |
| --- | --- |
| class | **Insecta** |
| order | **Orthoptera** |
| family | **Acrididae** |
| genera & species | ***Austroicestes cruciata*** |
| | *Australian plague grasshopper* |
| | ***Chortoicetes terminifera*** |
| | *Australian plague locust* |
| | ***Locusta migratoria manilensis*** |
| | *Oriental migratory locust* |
| | ***Locusta migratoria migratoria*** |
| | *Asiatic migratory locust* |
| | ***Locusta migratoria migratorioides*** |
| | *African migratory locust* |
| | ***Melanoplus spretus*** |
| | *Rocky Mountain locust* |
| | ***Nomadacris septemfasciata*** |
| | *red locust* |
| | ***Schistocerca gregaria*** |
| | *desert locust* |

*Left: Close-up of a yellow and black hopper. Right: Trio of swarming hoppers. These come together to form dense groups, which join others to become a massive band.*

# Longhorned beetle

*The name used to describe the beetles of the family Cerambycidae, which number about 15 000 species, the great majority of which are tropical.*

*The most obvious feature of longhorned beetles is the very long antennae, to which the name 'longhorn' or 'longicorn', as it is sometimes spelt, refers. An extreme form is seen in the genus* **Acanthocinus** *in which the antennae are four or more times the length of the body. When longhorned beetles settle they hold their antennae out like a pair of the large callipers used for measuring tree trunks. For this reason foresters call them 'timbermen'. Some of the tropical species are among the largest insects:* **Xixuthrus heros** *from Fiji is 6 in. long with its antennae as long again. The New World species of* **Macrodontia** *are equally large in the body but have rather short antennae and enormous spiky jaws, rather like those of a stag beetle.*

*The longhorned beetles are of economic importance as pests of timber, as the larvae of many of them burrow in living or seasoned wood, making large tunnels which weaken it and spoil it for structural purposes.*

*Among the European species are the spotted longhorn, often seen on flowers in summer and the two-banded longhorn. The musk beetle lives in old willows and is noted for its pleasant scent. It is now far less common than formerly.*

### Creaking beetles

Adult longhorn beetles are usually found on or near the trees in which the larvae feed, often hiding under loose bark. They also visit wild flowers on which they sun themselves and feed on the pollen. Many of them fly well, and they may be attracted to lights at night. Some of the large tropical species bite quite effectively if handled, and there are also species which make a creaking noise (stridulation) which is doubtless a defence reaction. This may be done either by moving the thorax up and down, producing friction between it and the abdomen or by scraping the hindlegs against the edges of the wing-cases.

### Exceptional wood-eaters

The larvae of most longhorn beetles feed inside the stems of plants and often inside trees, either under the bark or burrowing in the solid wood. Most species are attached to one or a few kinds of tree; in Europe poplar, willow and oak suffer most from the attention of longhorns. The eggs are laid on the bark and the tiny larvae burrow in. As they grow they develop into large white or yellowish grubs with round instead of the usual flattened heads and extremely powerful jaws with which they can rasp away the hardest heartwoods. Most insects which feed on wood cannot directly digest the cellulose: either they must devour great quantities of wood, like the caterpillar of the goat moth

*Geloharpya confluens attacked by ants from the lowveld of South Africa ($\frac{2}{3}$ natural size).*

to get the non-cellulose protein, or they have bacteria or protistans in the alimentary canal which break down the cellulose as in termites and stag-beetles. The grubs of longhorned beetles are exceptional in having a digestive enzyme that breaks down cellulose.

Most of the larvae take 2–3 years to reach full size and some take a good deal longer. When nearly ready to change into the pupa the larva makes a tunnel to the exterior and then stops it up with a plug of wood fibres or a cap of hardened chalky mucus. When the beetle emerges from the pupa it pushes or bites its way out. The adult beetle is quite unable to gnaw its way through solid wood but it can bite through the plug made by the larva.

The grubs that live in the heartwood are fairly safe from enemies, but those that live under bark or in decayed wood are favourite prey of woodpeckers. There is a large longhorn beetle found in New Zealand whose grubs, known by the name of 'hu-hu', are regarded as a delicacy by the Maoris.

### Camouflage and mimicry

The longhorned beetles are extremely varied in colour and marking, and some of them show adaptive coloration in great perfection. The big African species *Pterognatha gigas* lies along a twig with its antennae extended in front and is coloured and mottled to look exactly like a patch of moss. Perhaps more remarkable are the numerous cases of longhorned beetles which have come to resemble other insects that are distasteful or poisonous, and so are left alone by predators. Many examples of mimicry of this kind are known from the tropics, and there is one quite common British species, the wasp beetle, whose black and yellow stripes give it a strong resemblance to a wasp. Its antennae are abnormally short for

a beetle of this family; they are in fact hardly longer than a wasp's antennae.

### An insect Methuselah

The larvae of the house longhorn live in dry, seasoned softwoods and are a pest of structural timber in some parts of Europe where a large percentage of buildings are infested. The beetle is greyish-black with two lighter grey marks across the wing-cases. It is covered with hair except for two areas on the thorax, which are bare and shining and look like eyes. The larva grows to an inch in length, and in warm weather the rasping of its jaws, as it feeds, is distinctly audible. Its dry and austere diet makes it very slow-growing, and it seldom reaches full size in less than 3 years and not uncommonly lives for ten. One case is known of a larva that lived for 32 years before the beetle emerged from the wood; this is probably the longest life span known for any insect.

| phylum | **Arthropoda** |
|---|---|
| class | **Insecta** |
| order | **Coleoptera** |
| family | **Cerambycidae** |
| genera & species | ***Aromia moschata*** *musk beetle* ***Clytus arietis*** *wasp beetle* ***Hylotrupes bajulus*** *house longhorn* ***Rhagium bifasciatum*** *2-banded longhorn* ***Strangalia maculata*** *spotted longhorn* *others* |

# Louse

*A louse is a small wingless insect which lives as a parasite on the outside of a mammal or a bird. Lice fall naturally into two distinct groups which are regarded by entomologists as separate orders.*

*The sucking lice (suborder Anoplura) are parasitic on mammals only and feed by sucking their blood. The biting lice (suborder Mallophaga, see page 30), which are mostly parasites of birds although a few live on mammals, feed mainly on the feathers or hair of the host. The members of both orders have a similar appearance. They are small, pale in colour and flattened, and they have tough, leathery skins. The last two features are adaptations to protect them against scratching and other attempts by their hosts to dislodge them. Their bodies have undergone many changes linked with the parasitic way of life. Their legs are short and so are the antennae. The eyes are very small, sometimes almost non-existent. The segments of the body, so noticeable in the abdomen of a normal insect, are often not very clearly marked. There is no metamorphosis. Both types pass the whole of their lives on the body of the host, and one species of louse is often confined to one species of mammal or bird or to a group of related species.*

*The so-called book-louse is neither a true louse nor a parasite, but belongs to the order Psocoptera. It lives among books and furniture in damp, badly ventilated rooms.*

## Sucking lice

The hollow, piercing mouthparts and the way in which the claws of the legs are adapted for gripping hair distinguish this order of only 230 known species. The human louse can be used as a typical example. Not only is it confined to man as a host, but there are two varieties: the body louse and the head louse. The former lives on clothing next to the skin and the latter among the hair of the head. The two varieties differ slightly in structure as well as in habits; they can be persuaded to interbreed under experimental conditions, but there is no evidence that they do so naturally. They have very similar life cycles. Their eggs, known as 'nits', are cemented on to the hair or fibres of the clothing. An adult louse lays about 10 eggs every day and in the course of its life lays about 300. At body temperature the eggs hatch in about a week, and the insects hatching from them are miniatures of the adults. They feed throughout their lives by inserting the hollow, piercing mouthparts into the skin and sucking up blood. They shed their skins three times before they are fully grown. Lice live for about 7 weeks.

The only other louse parasitic on man is the so-called crab louse which lives among the pubic hair. Its mode of feeding and life history are similar to those of the head louse.

## Scratching can be fatal

In spite of its unpleasant associations, the crab louse does not convey disease, but this is very far from true of other species. By far the most serious disease carried by the human louse is epidemic typhus, which is caused by a virus-like micro-organism called *Rickettsia*. The body louse is the carrier and, rather curiously, the disease is not transmitted by its bite but by the entry of infected louse-excrement and the body fluids of crushed lice into abrasions in the skin. Scratching and seeking out lice and squashing them are therefore dangerous practices in conditions where typhus is likely to occur.

Such conditions are found in places where people are crowded together and have no opportunity to change and wash their clothes, or customarily fail to do so.

## Flowers and fever

Up to quite recent times, gaols crowded with unfortunate people awaiting trial were subject to terrible epidemics of typhus. The hazard even extended to the courts of justice, because infected lice dropped out of the ragged clothing of the prisoners and transferred themselves to the court officials, witnesses and anyone else present. This risk was recognised, though no one associated it with lice, and judges were provided with a bouquet of flowers whose scent was believed to keep away the 'evil humours' of the disease. It is still traditional in some courts for the judge to receive a nosegay of flowers. The terribly crowded conditions of the crew on ships, especially naval vessels, also led to typhus epidemics, and both 'gaol fever' and 'ship fever' were among the names by which the disease was known.

In the First World War, when conditions in the trenches were very conducive to louse infestation, a curious disease called 'trench fever' occurred. It was conveyed by lice and seems to have been a sort of mild and seldom fatal variant of typhus. After the war it completely disappeared, and so has never been investigated by modern techniques.

Our own horror at the idea of being infected with lice is, of course, salutary, but it is quite a modern attitude. In mediaeval times the sanctity of holy men was enhanced in proportion to their lousiness. When the body of Thomas à Beckett was disrobed after his murder the lice in his hair-cloth garment, in the words of a contemporary chronicler, 'boiled over like water in a simmering cauldron'. The onlookers, far from being disgusted, were overcome with 'the joy of having found such a saint'.

Absence of lice from one's body used also to be regarded as a sign of lack of virility, and even today the religion of large numbers of people forbids them to kill a louse, though it is permitted to remove one from one's own person and deposit it unharmed on that of a neighbour. Evidently it will be some time before typhus goes the same way as trench fever.

Another quite distinct disease called relapsing fever is carried by human lice. It is easy to cure and not very prevalent.

| class | **Insecta** | |
|---|---|---|
| order | **Phthiraptera** | |
| sub-order | **Anoplura** | |
| genera & species | *Pediculus humanus* human louse *Phthirius pubis* crab louse others | |

▽ *Photomicrograph of female human louse (× 20).*

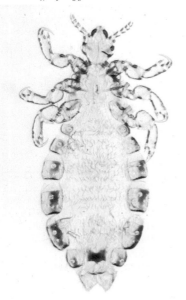

▽ *Eggs or 'nits' cemented onto human hair (× 25).*

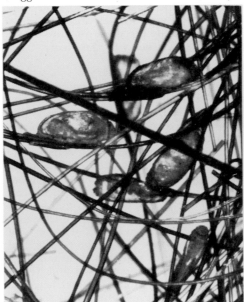

▽ *De-lousing in the fifteenth century.*

*Like an unknown monster from outer space the mantis cradles a day-flying moth in its spined forelegs and delicately and neatly eats its live victim.*

# Mantis

*The name Mantis is derived from a Greek word meaning 'prophet' or 'soothsayer' and refers (as also does the epithet 'praying') to the habitual attitude of the insect – standing motionless on its four hindlegs with the forelegs raised as if in prayer – it is waiting for unwary insects to stray within reach. The forelegs are spined and the joint called the tibia can be snapped back against the femur, rather as the blade of a penknife snaps into its handle, to form a pair of grasping organs which seize and then keep a hold on*

*any unfortunate victims.*

*Mantises, or praying mantises as they are often called, feed mainly on other insects, and are found mostly in tropical or subtropical countries. Most of the smallest are about an inch long. They have narrow, leathery forewings and large fan-shaped hindwings, which are folded beneath the forewings when not in use. Most mantises can fly, but they do not readily take to flight and seldom go far.*

*About 1 800 species are known, the most familiar species being the European mantis* **Mantis religiosa**, *which lives in the Mediterranean region and has been introduced into eastern North America.*

## Hidden terror

Most mantises spend their time sitting still among foliage, or on the bark of trees, waiting for insects to stray within reach of a lightning-quick snatch of their spined forelegs. Nearly all are shaped and coloured to blend with their surroundings. Many are green or brown, matching the living or dead leaves among which they sit, but some have more elaborate camouflage which serves two purposes. First, because they do not pursue their prey but wait for it to stray within reach, they need to stay hidden. Secondly, their grasping forelegs, although formidable to other insects, are usually useless against birds and lizards, and since mantises are slow-moving, they must be concealed to avoid being caught and eaten.

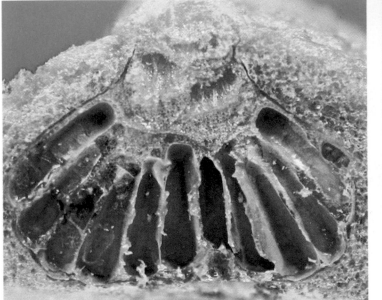

Mantises never take plant food. They seize their insect victims in their spined forelegs and eat them alive, neatly and delicately. Some of the largest species occasionally catch and eat small birds and lizards in the same way.

## Unusual mating habits

To a female mantis a male is no more than just another piece of food. He must, therefore, be careful in his approach if he wishes to mate, rather than be the next meal. On seeing a ripe female, the male, justifiably enough, freezes, then starts to creep up on her with movements almost too slow for the eye to follow—sometimes taking an hour or more to move 1 ft. Once within range, he makes a short hop and clasps the female, to mate. If the pair is disturbed or the female sees her suitor, she will eat him, starting by biting off his head. As he loses his head, so he loses his inhibitions, because mantis copulation is controlled by a nerve centre in the head which inhibits mating until a female is clasped. If this nerve is removed (by an experimenter, or by a female mantis) all control is lost, and the body continues to copulate. The female, therefore, has much to gain from attacking and eating males; she ensures both fertilisation of her eggs and nourishment for her developing ovaries.

## Eggs in a bag

The female lays 80–100 eggs at a time in tough, spongy capsules which she attaches to twigs, and she may produce 20 capsules in her lifetime. While laying her eggs she gives out a liquid which she stirs into a froth by movements of her body. The eggs become enclosed in this while it is still plastic, then it quickly hardens and dries.

The young mantises hatch together and at first hang from the egg capsule by silken threads which they give out from the hind end of the abdomen. After their first moult they can no longer make silk. They grow by gradual stages, moulting up to 12 times before becoming adult. The wings, tiny at first, grow with each succeeding moult.

The egg capsules are a protection against insectivorous animals and birds, but they are no protection against parasitic wasps of the ichneumon type, which are probably the most serious enemies of mantises.

## Fatal flowers

Some mantises are even more deceptive, taking on the appearance of flowers and so luring insects such as bees and butterflies within reach. The orchid mantis of Malaysia and Indonesia, in its young or subadult stage, is coloured pink and the thigh joints of the four hindlegs are widely expanded so they look like petals, while the pink body resembles the centre of the flower. When the mantis reaches the adult stage, however, its body becomes white and elongated as in a normal mantis. It still has the expanded, petal-like legs but its resemblance to a flower is largely lost. The African 'devil's flower' has expansions on the thorax and the forelegs which are white and red. It hangs down from a leaf or twig, and catches any flies or butterflies attracted to it.

When they are frightened, many mantises will suddenly adopt a menacing posture, rearing up and throwing their forelegs wide apart. One African species *Pseudocreobotra wahlbergi* improves on this display by spreading its wings, on which there are a pair of eye-like markings, so the enemy is suddenly confronted with a menacing 'face'.

| class | **Insecta** |
|---|---|
| order | **Dictyoptera** |
| suborder | **Mantodea** |
| family | **Mantidae** |
| genera & species | **Hymenopus coronatus** orchid mantis **Mantis religiosa** European mantis **Idolum diabolicum** African devil's flower, others |

# May bug

*A large beetle, also known as the cockchafer, which is seen and heard flying about on summer evenings. It is a member of the scarab family and related to the dor beetles and dung beetles. Nearly 1 in. long, it is a very 'square' beetle with a broad and deep abdomen. The elytra, or wing cases, are reddish-brown and do not cover the whole of the abdomen. A conical 'tail' protrudes from under them. The head and thorax are black, and under the body there is a dense layer of hair-like bristles. A feature of the May bugs and their relatives is the elaborate antennae, which end in a fan of thin plates. These structures give rise to the name Lamellicornia, or leaf-horns, for a superfamily of beetles, as the fan resembles the leaves of a half-opened book.*

*Many beetles of this family are known as chafers, a name derived from the Anglo-Saxon for beetle. In the British Isles, there is the garden chafer, or June bug, with green head and thorax and a dark yellowish red abdomen. The rose chafer has a bright golden green and white-spotted abdomen with copper underside and black legs and antennae—an attractive combination when found among the petals of a rose. In North America, other chafers are especially noticed because they bang into lighted windows or strike motor-car windscreens. In Assam there lives the giant May bug, 2 in. long with rather long front legs. Each leg has two sharp spurs.*

## Pests as adults . . .

Both larval and adult May bugs damage plants. The larvae attack the roots while the adults eat the leaves and petals or suck sap and nectar. They are called May or June bugs because, although the adults emerge from pupation about October, they do not start to fly until early summer but may be as early as April. May bugs can then be seen in large numbers on fine evenings as the light is fading, sometimes climbing up grass stalks and vigorously pumping their abdomens in and out, presumably to warm the body before takeoff, in the same way as an athlete warms up before a race. They then fly off through the grass with the same ponderous, meandering flight as a bumble bee, and also producing a humming noise with the very rapid wingbeats, although the wingbeat of the May bugs is slow, 46 beats/second, compared with 130–240, that of bumble bees. At other times they can be seen flying around trees such as oaks or flowering chestnuts.

The adults feed on the foliage of trees, and when abundant can cause serious damage by stripping all the leaves. The rose chafer, a day-flyer, lives on the petals of flowers, especially roses. The giant chafer feeds on nectar.

## . . . and as larvae

The females lay several batches of eggs in the early summer. Each batch numbers a dozen to 30, totalling about 70. The eggs are laid in burrows 6–8 in. deep, and hatch in 3 weeks. The larva is familiar to anyone who has dug the garden as a large white grub with a brown head and three pairs of legs very near the head.

The larvae of some May bugs live in rotten trees and logs through which they burrow, grinding up the wood with their strong, horny jaws and digesting it with the help of bacteria in the gut that can break down cellulose, the main constituent of wood. They are probably important in helping the breakdown and conversion into humus of dead trees, but they also cause considerable damage in timber plantations. The larvae of the rose chafer also live in dead trees, and because these are no longer

△ *May bugs mating. The female lays several batches of eggs, totalling about 70.*

▷ *A May bug drones in for a landing on young leaves. Large numbers of May bugs can cause much damage to trees by stripping them of foliage.*

△ *May bug larva. Armed with powerful jaws, they spend 3 years in the soil before pupating.*

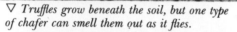

▽ *Truffles grow beneath the soil, but one type of chafer can smell them out as it flies.*

·△ *Breaking surface: a May bug digs its way out after pupating. This happens about October.*

▽ *Complex fan antennae make for sensitivity, and the May bug uses them to seek food.*

tolerated in highly efficient agricultural areas, the rose chafer is becoming less common.

The larva of the May bug spends 3 years in the soil before pupating, but this period depends on the climate. Each winter it burrows down, avoiding the frost, and returns to the surface in spring to feed on roots of grass, wheat and other plants including trees, often causing great damage. At the end of their third summer the larvae burrow down and pupate in a cocoon some 2 or 3 ft beneath the surface, emerging as adults a few months later. The larvae are sometimes called white grubs or rookworms, rooks being a particular enemy.

## Careful enemy

The manner in which a rook deals with the grub is of special interest. It holds the grub under one foot and bites off the head so getting rid of the grub's strong jaws. Next, the bird pulls off the spiky legs and discards these also. Then it squeezes the soft body with its bill, eats the semi-liquid contents that ooze and finally discards the tough skin.

## Truffle hunters

Antennae are sensory organs, reacting to airborne vibrations and to chemicals or, in plain language, to sound and smell. By examining an insect's antennae we can easily see whether it has great or small powers of hearing or smell. If the antennae are well-developed, then the chances are that the insect is highly sensitive. For instance, we find that male mosquitoes have well developed antennae but females have only small ones, and experiments have shown that male mosquitoes' antennae are 'tuned in' to the hum of the female's wingbeats. In this way the sexes are drawn together for mating. The May bugs also have elaborate antennae, the fan being spread out when it is in use, but they are well developed in both sexes, so it would seem that their main use is not as a device to lead the males to the females. Both sexes must make use of their antennae, and it seems they are used for finding food.

There is one May bug that feeds on truffles, which are fungi that grow under the surface of the soil. The May bug will suddenly stop in flight, drop to the ground and dig down to where a truffle is buried.

To be able to scent something buried in the ground is, to us, a remarkable achievement, but many animals feed on truffles including squirrels, mice, badgers and deer. Truffles are also esteemed by gourmets and in various parts of Europe, dogs, especially poodles, and pigs have been used to hunt them.

| phylum | **Arthopoda** |
|---|---|
| class | **Insecta** |
| order | **Coleoptera** |
| family | **Scarabaeidae** |
| genera & species | ***Melolontha melolontha*** *May bug* ***Phyllopertha horticola*** *June bug* ***Cetonia floricola*** *rose chafer* *others* |

# Mayfly

*Mayflies make up one of the most distinct and peculiar of insect orders. They have features which are not found in any other group of insects, and all the species in the order are very much alike.*

*The adult has large forewings and its hindwings are small, sometimes absent altogether. Each wing has a fine network of veins, and when the insect is at rest all four wings are held close together over the back in the manner of a butterfly. The legs are small and weak and the tail ends in three, sometimes two, long filaments or cerci. The eyes are large, especially in the males. In some genera,* **Cloeon***, for example,*

*the males have two pairs of compound eyes, one pair with small facets on the sides of the head and one pair with large facets on the top. The antennae are reduced to tiny bristles, suggesting that the insect is aware of its surroundings mainly through its sight. The jaws and other mouthparts are vestigial and functionless and adult mayflies never feed. They only gulp down air until the stomach becomes distended like a balloon. This reduces the insect's overall specific gravity and makes the mating flight easier.*

*About 1 000 species are known, but only those of Europe and North America have been thoroughly studied and there must be many species still undescribed.*

## Guiding light

The adult life of mayflies is concerned solely with reproduction. They nearly always hatch in great numbers together, and the males gather in dancing swarms over

the land. The compact mass of moving insects attracts the notice of females, which fly into the swarm. Each is at once seized by a male, the pair then leaving the swarm to mate. The males die almost immediately after mating and the females soon after laying their eggs, although they may have spent several years as aquatic nymphs.

The female mayfly always lays her eggs in water, but in some species she drops them from the air as she flies just above the surface. In many species the eggs are provided with fine threads which anchor them to water plants or pebbles. A few give birth to living young which have hatched from eggs retained in the mother's body. In the egg-laying species one female may lay several hundred, or several thousand, eggs.

The nymphs are always aquatic; breathing is supplemented by gills set along each side of the abdomen. Unlike the adults, the nymphs show many differences from species to species. Some are adapted for swimming actively among water plants, others to living on the bottom, burrowing in the mud or clinging to rocks in rapidly flowing water. Nearly all are vegetable feeders, and they take from a year to as much as 4 years to reach full size. A recent discovery about free-swimming mayfly nymphs is that they orientate themselves in the water not by a sense of balance based on gravity, as had been supposed, but by the direction from which the light reaches their eyes. In an aquarium with a glass bottom, lit from below, they swim upside-down.

## They mate and die on land

The event in the mayfly's life which sets the Ephemeroptera, as they are collectively called, wholly apart from all other insects is the change from a subimago to an imago. Before this happens, however, the fully grown nymph rises to the surface of the water and floats there, or crawls out onto

◁◁ *The egg patches of a mayfly* **Baetis** *laid under a submerged rock in a stream.*
◁ *Hatchling: the nymph of the largest British mayfly* **Ephemera danica** *(approx 8 × life size).*

△ *The nymph forms a subimago. The anglers' Green Drake is shown* **Ephemera danica.**
▽ *From dun to spinner: leaving behind the subimago case, an imago* **Baetis rhodani.**

a stone or reed. Its skin splits and a winged insect creeps out, resting for a time before making a short, rather laboured flight to a bush or fence or to a building near the water. Although it is winged, this insect that creeps laboriously out of the water is not the perfect insect or imago, as the final stage is called. After a few minutes or hours, varying with the species, the subimago moults again, shedding a delicate skin from the whole of its body, legs and even its wings. Then it flies away, much more buoyantly than before, but it will live at most for a few days and, in many species, only for a few hours. A subimago can be recognised by the wings which appear dark and dull due to the presence of microscopic hairs, which form a visible fringe along their hinder edges.

### The fisherman's fly

Mayflies are of great interest to anglers, both on account of the part they play in supplying fish with food, and by their direct connection with the sport of fly-fishing. The hatching of a swarm of mayflies excites the fish, especially trout, and stimulates their appetites, so they take a lure more readily than at other times. The swarming is known as a 'hatch' and the fish are said to 'rise' to it. They feed both on the nymphs as they swim to the surface and on the flies, both subimagoes and adults, which touch or fall into the water.

A mayfly is far too delicate an object to be impaled on a hook like a maggot or a worm, and the flyfisherman's practice is to make replicas of the flies by binding carefully prepared scraps of feathers onto the shaft of a hook. These are then 'cast' and allowed to fall onto the surface of the water. A lure so used is called a 'dry fly', as opposed to a 'wet fly', which sinks under the surface.

The more exactly the artificial fly duplicates the species of mayfly which is hatching, the greater are the chances of success, so anglers study mayflies carefully and they have their own names for them. Any subimago is known as a 'dun' and the imagoes are called 'spinners'. Those of the species *Procloeon rufulum* are called the Pale Evening Dun and the Pale Evening Spinner respectively. *Rhithrogena semicolorata* are the Olive Upright Dun and the Olive Upright Spinner. The two stages of *Ephemera danica* have separate names, the Green Drake and the Spent Gnat.

If a well made artificial fly is swung, by means of a rod and line, into a swarm of the males whose species it represents, numbers of them will pursue it, losing interest only when actual contact reveals to them that they have been heartlessly deceived.

◁ *A short life but a gay one: having passed through all the hazards of a year or more of aquatic larval life this adult* **Ephemera vulgata** *will live only long enough to reproduce.*

| class | **Insecta** |
|---|---|
| order | **Ephemeroptera** |
| families | **Ephemeridae** |
| | **Caenidae** (hindwings absent) |
| | *others* |

# Meadow brown

*This is the common name of a butterfly* **Maniola jurtina** *of the family Nymphalidae. It is found in areas of waste ground with uncut grass, bushes and hedgerows, and in woodland clearings. Where this type of habitat is allowed to persist it may be very common.*

*The sexes are very distinct, the males being smaller and dull coloured, the females larger and brighter with an area of dull orange on the forewings which is much less extensive in the male. Like other butterflies of the family Nymphalidae the male has a patch of scented scales on each forewing, which are important in courtship. Their scent has been described as resembling that of an old cigar box.*

*The meadow brown ranges over the whole of the British Isles, Europe, North Africa and eastward to northern Persia and, in the USSR, as far east as western Siberia. There are local variations in its coloration over the whole of its range and several distinct forms occur.*

## Unobtrusive caterpillars

In midsummer meadow browns are on the wing, ready for mating. The male approaches the female and the scented scales on his wings, known as androconia, make the female responsive. After mating the female lays whitish green eggs shaped like minute barrels with vertically ribbed surfaces. They are laid on the blades of meadow grass and other grasses, which are the food plant of the larvae. The caterpillar is green with short white hairs and with a darker line along the back and a lighter one on each side. There are two short points or tails at the hind end, a feature almost universal among larvae of the subfamily Satyrinae. The larvae are seldom seen as they feed only at night, hiding at the base of the grass stems by day. They have a long life, from early August to the following April. The green pupa is suspended by the tail from a stem or blade of grass, and the butterfly emerges 3 weeks to a month after pupation.

## Races of the meadow brown

The meadow brown butterfly belongs to the subfamily Satyrinae, popularly known as 'browns' from their sombre colouring. However, this was applied by entomologists unfamiliar with the 'browns' of the tropics and subtropics. While the majority fit the name – although often having intricate patterns in brown and orange–there are many brightly coloured tropical species. In South Africa, for example, there are Satyrinae which are blue, and would easily pass as Blue butterflies (Lycaenid). One rather gorgeous satyrid is silver–and is most

▷△ *A meadow brown caterpillar cuts the ground from under its own feet as it eats away a leaf.*
▷ *Insect buds. The pupae of the meadow brown, which will soon burst into butterflies, are attached to the plant by a tail at their bases.*

unusual in appearance. In the depths of the Amazon forest there lives a curious transparent satyrine butterfly; it has been described as being like the delicate petal of a flower floating in the deep shade in which it lives.

Many butterflies alter their position when they land in bright sunshine in order to cast the smallest possible shadow, helping to make themselves less conspicuous. This can be seen in the European grayling butterfly which generally sits on rather exposed ground. On landing here, it can often be seen to lean forward towards the sun's rays, thus reducing its shadow length. In the tropics, some of the satyrine butterflies are out at dusk, unlike the more usual sunloving image they have: these are the evening browns.

Species of the subfamily Satyrinae are worldwide, ranging from the tropics to the Arctic Circle and high up on the mountains. This butterfly has become separated into local populations or races throughout its range probably because it seldom flies far and is rather sluggish in its habits.

## Perfumed courtesy

The most complete study of the courtship of butterflies in the subfamily Satyrinae has been of the grayling. This shows the use of the scent patches. The male chases the female through the air until she lands, when the male takes up position facing her and so close that her antennae overlap his head and front part of the thorax. The organs of smell are in the antennae. Once settled into this position the male courts the female, ending in an elegant bow. At the same time he closes his wings which, up to then, have been spread or halfspread. In doing so he catches her antennae between his forewings and they are pressed against the scent patches. Male grayling butterflies that have had the scent patches removed, which can be done without further injury, can court females as ardently as they may, but without the scent organs the chances of getting a mate are extremely small.

▷ *A meadow brown butterfly takes a drink of nectar before flying off, perhaps to pollinate another flower.*

| phylum | **Arthropoda** |
|---|---|
| class | **Insecta** |
| order | **Lepidoptera** |
| family | **Nymphalidae** |
| British genera & species | ***Aphantopus hyperanthus*** *ringlet* <br> ***Coenonympha pamphilus*** <br> *small heath* <br> ***C. tuilia*** *large heath* <br> ***Erebia aethiops*** *Scotch argus* <br> ***E. epiphron*** *mountain ringlet* <br> ***Eumenis semele*** *grayling* <br> ***Maniola jurtina*** *meadow brown* <br> ***M. tithonus*** <br> *hedge brown or gatekeeper* <br> ***Melanargia galathea*** <br> *marbled white* <br> ***Parage aegeria*** *speckled wood* <br> ***P. megaera*** *wall butterfly* |

△ *Adult specimen of* **S. gemmarum** *with eggs.*

# Midge

*Although midges are usually associated with painful bites and irritation, many of them do not bite. There are three families of these small mosquito-like flies that can be properly called midges: the non-biting midges of the family Chironomidae, the biting midges which used to be classed as Chironomidae but are now placed in a separate family, the Ceratopogonidae, and the gall midges, the Cecidomyidae.*

*There are some 2 000 species of Chironomidae midges, sometimes called harlequin flies. They look very like mosquitoes but are paler and do not suck blood. The biting midges are sometimes barely detectable by the naked eye, but they can produce wounds that itch painfully. They are particularly common in northern regions, and in North America they are called 'no-seeums'. Some species attack other insects. The gall midges often cause damage to crops; the Hessian fly is a serious pest of wheat in North America and southern Europe.*

*Also known as midges are the phantom midges* **Chaoborus,** *close relatives of mosquitoes. The phantom or glass larvae are almost transparent with dark, air-filled bladders, one at each end of the body.*

## Dancing midges

The tiny insects that can be seen on summer evenings dancing up and down in clusters, usually over water, are non-biting midges, performing their mating dance. The males gather in groups and fly up and down; females are attracted to the groups and each mates with one of the males. Most species lay their eggs in water but others lay in rotten wood, dung and decaying plant matter. The larvae are the familiar, small 'worms' that can be seen wriggling energetically in water butts and ponds. Some larvae live near the surface of the water, others at the bottom, burrowing in the mud or making tubes of mud and silk in which to live. Chironomid (non-biting midges) larvae have been found at the bottom of Lake Geneva in Switzerland and Lake Superior in North America, and some species live in the sea, at depths of up to 120 ft. The pupae also live at the surface or at the bottom. Those living at the bottom extract enough gases from the water to float to the surface when the adult is due to emerge. The larvae of one of the marine species builds tubes of sand and pieces of seaweed. It lives between high and low water and the adults emerge when the pupae are exposed by the falling tide.

## Biting midges

The biting midges are minute, vicious bloodsuckers. The adults attack a wide variety of animals, from man to mosquitoes, and feed on their blood, although some feed on nectar. The species that attack mosquitoes suck the blood that the mosquitoes have already extracted from mammals. Other species suck the blood of caterpillars and some pierce the wing veins of adult butterflies and dragonflies to get their juices. The attacks of biting midges on man can be a serious nuisance, particularly in the evening and in hot weather when the skin is bathed in perspiration. They can penetrate clothing to pierce the skin and, apart from causing severe irritation, some species carry parasitic worms that cause diseases in man and animals. There are two groups of biting midges. In one the adults have hairy wings and the larvae are terrestrial, living under

the bark of trees in manure heaps and similar damp places. The adults of the other group have naked wings and their larvae are aquatic, living in mud or at the surface of the water and swimming by undulations of the body. The minute flies of the family Ceratopogonidae can be easily distinguished from non-biting midges because they carry their wings folded one above the other when they are at rest.

## Gall midges

Gall midges are so-called because most of the larvae live in galls on plants. Within the galls, which are formed by the gall midge larvae stimulating the plants to grow abnormally (see gall wasp page 86), the larvae feed on the plant tissues. The larvae of each species of gall midge produce galls of exactly the same pattern, a feature which helps identification. The adults of many species also lay their eggs on only certain host plants. Not all gall midges, however, make galls. Some feed on plants without causing galls and others feed on other insects or decaying matter. The most notorious of the gall midges is the Hessian fly, so-called because it is thought to have been introduced to the United States in the straw for the horses of the Hessian troops serving there during the War of Independence. The larvae of the Hessian fly bore into stems of wheat, weakening them, so they fall over. They are extremely difficult to control and cause millions of dollars' worth of damage.

## Larval cannibals

A peculiar feature of the life cycles of some gall midges and chironomid midges is that their eggs develop when they are still larvae. This is called paedogenesis and is a form of neoteny, which is the ability to reproduce at the larval stage. The eggs are not fertilised but develop into larvae within the mother's body. They feed on her tissues, killing her and eventually breaking free. The cycle of larvae producing larvae may be repeated many times until overcrowding or a rise in temperature causes them to revert to the normal four-stage cycle.

## Unusual bloodworms

The larvae of chironomid midges are red, black or yellow. Red larvae, or bloodworms as they are called, are found at the bottom of ponds where they live in mud. The red colour is due to haemoglobin, the same pigment that colours our blood and is used for carrying oxygen. Haemoglobin is rarely found in insects but its presence in chironomid larvae is linked with their ability to live in mud where there are only the minutest traces of oxygen. It was originally suggested that the haemoglobin stored oxygen for use when the larvae were in poor oxygen conditions, but they have only enough haemoglobin to store oxygen for 12 minutes. It now appears that the haemoglobin acts as an oxygen mop. It has

◁ *'Big bud' on Juniper. The galls are opened to show the cecid larvae of* **Schmidtiella gemmarum.** *Since the larvae have such tiny, insignificant mouthparts, it has been a puzzle how they could feed from plant tissues. It has to be assumed that they suck the juices, since they can scarcely be thought to bite and chew.*

a great affinity for oxygen, combining with it very readily. When a midge larva is in mud with little oxygen in the surrounding water, the haemoglobin sweeps up such oxygen as there is, concentrating it so it can be used in body processes. As a result chironomid midge larvae can live in water, often badly polluted, where no other animals can.

| phylum | **Arthropoda** |
|---|---|
| class | **Insecta** |
| order | **Diptera** |
| family | **Chironomidae** *non-biting* |
| genera | ***Chironomus, Tanytarsus****, others* |
| family | **Ceratopogonidae** *biting* |
| genera | ***Culicoides, Forcipomyia****, others* |
| family | **Cecidomyidae** *gall midges* |
| genus & species | ***Mayetiola destructor*** *Hessian fly others* |

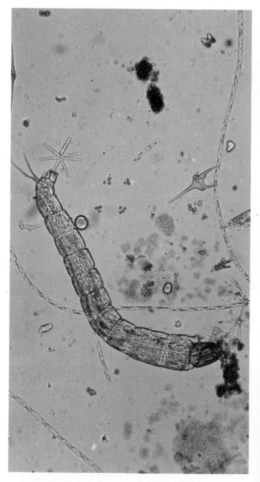

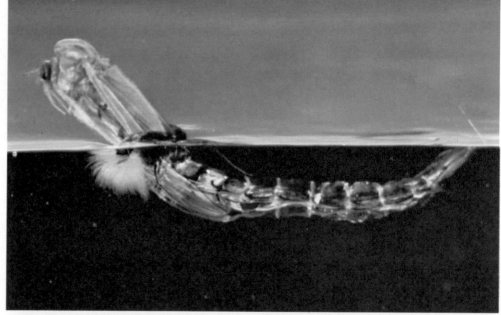

△ *Larva of* **Chironomus** *in freshwater plankton; the T-shaped dinoflagellate is* **Ceratium**, *the star-shaped organism is a primitive plant* **Asterionella**. *The worm-shaped, plump larva is a very abundant creature in freshwater mud and is important as food for fish. 2 700 specimens of midge larvae have been collected from ½ square metre.*
*Top right:* **Chironomus** *pupa. The feather 'anal gills' regulate the body fluids which contain red haemoglobin (approx. 10 × life size).*
*Centre: Emergence: the adult leaving its pupa case.*
*Bottom: Male midge* **C. plumòsus**. *Note the large antennae with their long, sensitive hairs.*

# Monarch

*A wanderer among butterflies, the monarch is native to both North and South America, the three subspecies inhabiting the northern, central and southern parts respectively of the New World continents. It has spread westwards across the Pacific and is established in Hawaii, Tonga, Samoa and Tahiti and in Australia and New Zealand. The fact that the extension of its range has taken place within the last 120–130 years suggests that it has been helped by shipping, and the butterfly has sometimes been seen on ship's rigging. It now seems certain that it may occasionally fly the Atlantic, to Europe, helped on its way by persistent westerly winds.*

### Far-flying migrant

The monarch is the most celebrated of all migratory butterflies. It is the only one which makes a definite journey in one direction each year and returns along the same route the following year. In North America it is found in summer all over southern Canada and the northern United States. In autumn the monarch butterflies in the north gather in groups and begin to move south. As they go, the groups are joined by other monarchs, so they get larger and larger until there are thousands of butterflies on the move. Each night they settle on trees, moving on in the morning. When they get as far as Florida in the east, and southern California in the west they settle in great numbers on trees and pass the winter in a state of semi-hibernation, occasionally flying round on warm, sunny days. The inland streams fly into northern Mexico. The same trees are used as resting places year after year, and in some places, where the butterfly trees are regarded as a tourist attraction, the hibernating insects are protected by law from disturbance.

In spring the butterflies of both sexes fly northward, the females laying eggs as they go, but on this return migration they fly singly and in quite a dilatory manner, so their movement is far less easy to observe. During the summer two or three generations are passed through, and the butterflies of each generation continue to press northward. They do not reach Canada until June, when, if they have travelled from the north to south of their range the journey may be as much as 2000 miles.

### Unfit for consumption

Like other members of its family, the monarch is distasteful and poisonous to birds and other insectivorous animals; they leave monarch butterflies severely alone after one or two experiences of trying to eat them. The few monarchs that fall foul of predators are sacrificed for the sake of the many.

The larvae are conspicuously coloured with white, yellow and black stripes and have two pairs of black fleshy filaments on the fore and hind parts of the body, which make them even more unmistakable. They feed on various plants of the milkweed

△ *Migrating monarchs gather in profusion before moving off in ones and twos on the long journey to their summer home. Several generations will be born on the way.*

▽ *Turning it on and brushing it off: the scent patches on the hind wings and the scent brushes on the tip of the abdomen of an African monarch butterfly,* **Danaus chrysippus.**

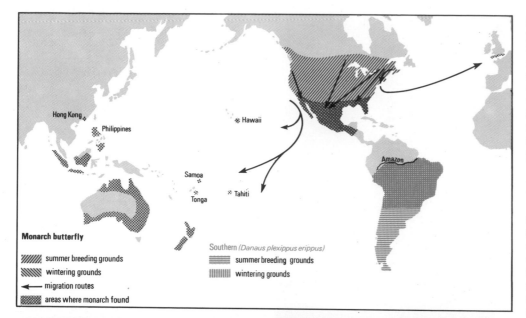

**Monarch butterfly**

///// summer breeding grounds

\\\\\ wintering grounds

→ migration routes

▦ areas where monarch found

Southern *(Danaus plexippus erippus)*

≡ summer breeding grounds

|||| wintering grounds

family (Asclepiadaceae), all of which are poisonous. They derive a two-fold benefit from this; firstly, the plants are avoided by grazing animals so the caterpillars do not run the risk of being accidentally eaten or otherwise destroyed, a fate that may overtake insects feeding on ordinary plants. Secondly the toxins of the plant are kept in the haemolymph or 'blood' of the insect, so it is poisonous in all stages. The rounded pupae, often brightly coloured and with metallic gold markings, hang from a twig or some other support by a cord of silk from the tips of their tails.

The butterfly is strikingly marked and coloured on both the upper and under sides of the wings, so it is conspicuous both when flying and when at rest. This contrasts with what we find in most colourful butterflies, which are brightly patterned only on the upper side and this is concealed when they are resting. The monarch is a good example of warning coloration. Instead of concealing it, its colours make it conspicuous, so predators quickly learn to recognise and avoid it. The caterpillar's coloration protects it in the same way. The poison is a heart poison or 'cardenolide'. If retained in the predator's body it may be fatal, but it also acts on the stomach, so a bird swallowing the insect generally vomits it up after 10–15 minutes. In either case it is unlikely to make a meal of another one.

### Resistant to injury

The monarch and other Danaid butterflies have another interesting feature which has developed in association with this form of protection. They are extremely leathery and resistant to injury. Most butterflies can easily be killed by pinching the thorax, but it is almost impossible to kill a monarch in this way. Birds catch them, peck them and then, realising their mistake, release them, and the insect almost always flies away unharmed. An ordinary palatable butterfly, caught in this way, would be pecked to pieces and eaten.

### Similar markings

There is another American butterfly, the viceroy *Limenitis archippus*, which belongs to another family, the Nymphalidae, and is related to the European white admiral *L. camilla*. Although it is not distasteful to birds, it is coloured and patterned very like the monarch and is much the same size, so the two are difficult to tell apart except by close inspection. In America captive jays, that have never before seen a butterfly, will readily kill and devour viceroys. If, however, they are experimentally offered monarch butterflies they may eat the first, and possibly a second, but soon learn to leave them alone. Moreover, they will then avoid any viceroys offered them.

▽ *The beginning of the saga. A monarch laying her eggs in the wild in Australia. The larvae produced by this butterfly are as brightly coloured as the adults.*

△ *To discover the distribution tagged butterflies are released.*
▽ *The larva of a monarch **Danaus chrysippus** prior to pupation.*

| phylum | **Arthropoda** |
|---|---|
| class | **Insecta** |
| order | **Lepidoptera** |
| family | **Danaidae** |
| genus & species | **Danaus plexippus**, *others* |

139

# Morpho

*For every person who has seen living morpho butterflies there must be tens of thousands who have seen their wings in brooches, lockets, plaques, trays and objets d'art. It is the brilliant blues of the males that are particularly attractive.*

*Morphoes are among the largest and most brilliant of butterflies and like many other brilliant butterflies they spend much of their time in or above the forest canopy, though some even fly in towns.*

*There are less than 50 species, all from tropical America, from central Mexico to southern Brazil. The largest of all, **Morpho hecuba**, is 7 in. across the wings. The upper surface of its wings is black with a broad band that shades from an intense orange brown to light yellow. **M. rhetenor** is a deep blue on the upper wing surface. **M. neoptolemus** is a rich blackish brown with broad bands of blue shot with a delicate violet. **M. sulkowskyi** has a more delicate colouring like mother-of-pearl, and the iridescent wings change with the angle of the light. These are the best known species and in all of them the upper surfaces of the wings are iridescent, while the undersurfaces of the wings are patterned with browns, greys, blacks and reds to harmonize with the background instead of standing out. In all species the females are less showy, their wings being cryptically patterned above and below.*

## Beauty out of reach

Morpho butterflies fly through forest clearings flapping their wings lazily. Their wings are very large in proportion to their body and will carry them along at a fair speed. As each shaft of sunlight strikes the butterfly, its upper wing surfaces flash and then lose their brilliance as it goes into the shade. When it turns, the undersides of the wings show, hiding the iridescent colours so the butterfly temporarily disappears, only to flash into sight again as the sunlight catches its upper wing surfaces. This must be as disconcerting to an animal

△ *Captured beauty.* **Morpho hecuba hecuba** *above,* **Morpho hecuba cisseis** *below, sub-specific variation.*

pursuing it as it is to the butterfly collector trying to net it. Probably if pursued the butterflies melt into the foliage when danger threatens.

## Butterfly farming

The caterpillars of the morpho butterflies are covered in hairs which are irritating to human skin. They live together in a web spun communally, but not in harmony because they are strongly cannibalistic. Those that survive eventually pupate together in the web. For gregarious caterpillars to be cannibalistic is most unusual. It suggests that the butterflies have few enemies at any stage in their life history and that this is the means whereby the population numbers are controlled. The communal webs doubtless protect the caterpillars from such enemies as there are. Caterpillars of one species of morpho that are not protected by a web bunch together when they rest, looking exactly like an orchid.

Despite their irritating hairs large num-

bers of caterpillars are bred and reared commercially, the butterflies being farmed to supply the demands for the iridescent blue wings that are used in jewellery, pictures and other fancy articles. This is the only way to get large quantities of a butterfly that normally lives in such inaccessible places.

## Fast colours

The trade in iridescent blue butterfly wings would never have flourished as it has done had the colours been likely to fade. The colours are 'fast' because they do not depend on pigments but are structural colours. In the early days of the microscope it was soon discovered that the wings of butterflies and moths were covered with scales. These are arranged like tiles on a roof. They form the powder that is left on one's fingers after handling one of these insects. As microscopes were improved and better lenses were made, it could be seen that the scales were not, like tiles or slates, flat pieces with smooth surfaces. They have a pattern of ridges, 35 000 to the inch, which give a rigidity to each scale, like the corrugations in roofing materials. The patterns of ridges on the scales are much more complicated than originally thought. Each ridge is made up of many thin layers slightly separated from each other. These layers are inclined at an acute angle to the plane of the scale. It is as if each ridge were a complicated set of Venetian blinds whose surfaces break up the white daylight into its various colours because they reflect back only light of a certain wavelength. It is this which, among other things, gives the iridescence, so the colours, being due to the physical structure of the ridges on the scales, are permanent.

| phylum | **Arthropoda** |
|--------|----------------|
| class | **Insecta** |
| order | **Lepidoptera** |
| family | **Nymphalidae** |
| genus | *Morpho* |

▽ *A lighter shade of pale. A series of morpho butterflies showing the changes in colour as the angle of the light alters.* **Morpho sulkowskyi sulkowskyi.**

△ *Resplendent in its lifesize beauty. Underside of* **Morpho hecuba hecuba,** *one of the largest of the morphos, with a wingspan of about 7 in.*

▽ *The overlapping scales on a morpho's wing, magnified 200 times.*      ▽ *A single corrugated scale with thousands of tiny ridges;* × 2 000.

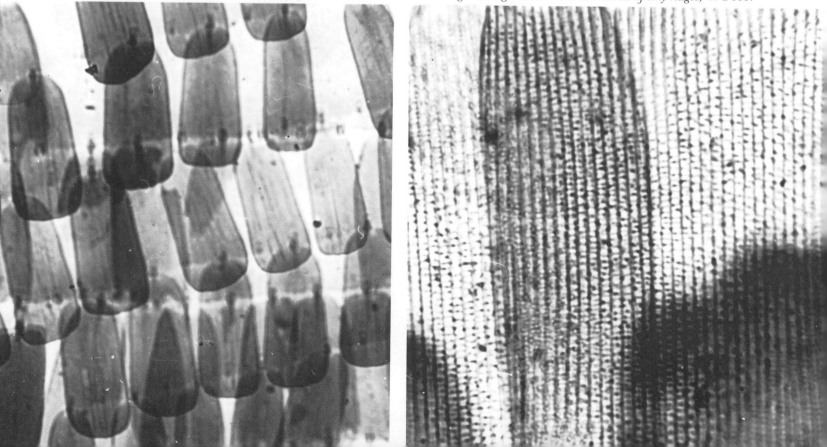

# Mosquito

There are 2 000 species of mosquito living everywhere from the Tropics to Arctic latitudes, often in enormous numbers. While not all are troublesome to man, some species are notorious bloodsucking pests which transmit distressing diseases such as malaria, yellow fever, elephantiasis and filariasis.

Mosquitoes are slender-bodied insects, about $\frac{1}{4}$ in. long, with a single pair of narrow wings and long slender legs. In most of them the wing veins and the rear edge of each wing are decorated with small scales. The antennae are hairy in the female and copiously feathered in the male, except in members of the subfamily Dixinae. In most species the female has a sharp tubular proboscis adapted for piercing and sucking fluids, usually blood. Exceptions to this are again found in the Dixinae, which are also unusual in having transparent larvae, known quite appropriately as phantom larvae.

Basically 'mosquito' and 'gnat' have the same meaning, the first being Spanish, the second Old English. Today many people speak of small insects that 'bite' as mosquitoes, and similar but equally small, harmless insects, especially those seen in dancing swarms, as gnats. The confusion is the same among scientists—judging from popular books on the subject—who speak of **Culex pipiens,** the commonest mosquito in Europe, as the common gnat, but otherwise restrict the use of the word 'gnat' to the Dixinae.

There are two main groups of mosquitoes, the culicines and the anophelines, represented by the genera **Culex** and **Anopheles** respectively. The wings of culicines are transparent or slightly tinted, while the wings of anophelines are usually marked with dark and light spots or patches. Another difference is that the female culicine has a pair of very short palpi beside the long proboscis while the palpi of the anopheline female are as long as the proboscis. The best way of distinguishing the two is that when resting the culicine holds its body horizontal to the surface on which it is standing and the anopheline tilts its body upwards.

### Eggs in any water

Mosquitoes lay their floating eggs in water, which may be fresh, brackish or salt, according to the species. With few exceptions each species chooses a particular kind of

▷△ Blood transfusion. An adult mosquito **Culex pipiens** sucks up blood through its tubular proboscis. Most of them are specialised in their habitat also at this stage, each species usually preferring a particular type of host. (14 × life size)
▷▽ Bloated with blood. A female mosquito **Culex pipiens** has just taken her last blood meal before she lays her eggs.

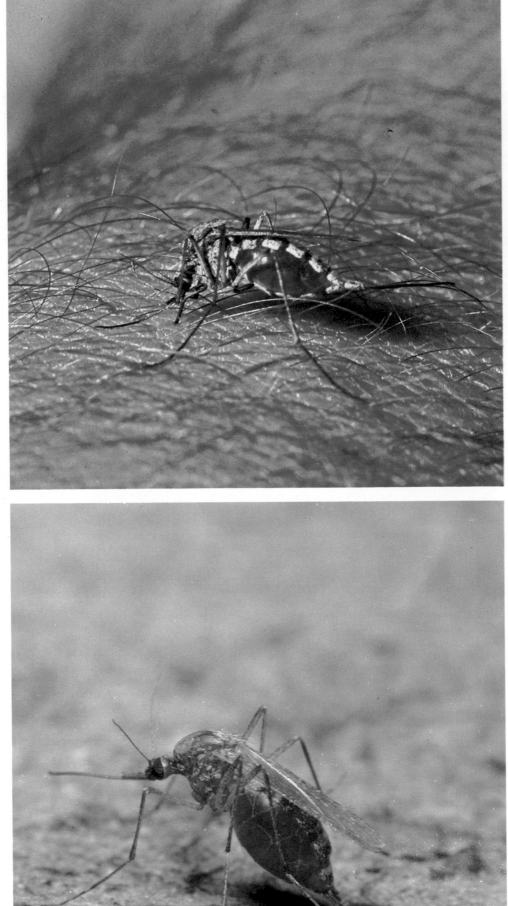

△ *The feathery antennae of the male (×60) are sensitive to sound vibrations, but only when the long hairs are erect. Some species keep them permanently erect so are always ready to mate while others erect them only at certain times of the day.* △ *Impending doom? A swarm of mosquitoes.*

watery situation, which may be the margins of ponds or lakes, in ditches, seepages, waterfilled cart ruts or hoofprints, polluted waters, water collected in holes in trees — usually at the top of a hole where branches fork — in aerial plants growing on trees or in pitcher plants. Water butts are often homes for mosquito larvae, but the eggs have even been seen in the water bowl put down for a pet dog. *Anopheles* lays single eggs, while *Culex* lays its eggs in compact masses or egg-rafts.

Each larva has a broad thorax in which all three segments are fused and an abdomen of 9 segments. The head bears the simple larval eyes and a pair of developing compound eyes. Brushes of bristles either side of it sweep fine particles of animal or plant food into the mouth, except in those larvae that extract dissolved food from the water, or prey on other insect larvae, usually other mosquito larvae. The thorax and abdomen are also decorated with long bristles. At the tip of the abdomen are four gills and a breathing siphon which can be pushed through the surface film of water to take in air. Some larvae feed on the bottom, others nearer the surface. They swim with twisting movements of the body, coiling and uncoiling spasmodically. Mosquitoes rest just beneath the surface hanging down more or less vertically. At the slightest disturbance of the water they quickly swim down but, after a while, they must return to hang from the surface film in order to breathe.

### Lively pupae

Larval life lasts about a week in most species, depending on temperature, but in those feeding on other insects it is prolonged, with usually only one generation a year. The pupae are active but do not feed, and the pupal life is short, at the most a few days. Pupae are typically bulky, having a large rounded head and thorax combined, with a pair of breeding siphons on top, and the abdomen more or less curled around it. In the last stages of development the pupa rises to the surface of the water, its hard outer skin splits, and the adult mosquito pulls itself out of the pupal husk and takes to the air.

### The love call

Soon after leaving their pupal skins, the adults mate, after which the males die. The females must take a meal for their eggs to develop, either of blood or, in some species, nectar or sap. A few can manage on food stored during the larval stage. Some species of mosquitoes take the blood of mammals, others the blood of birds or even of amphibians. Sometimes a female will take another drink of blood after laying.

In the interval between leaving the pupal skin and mating the mosquitoes must rest. If a male takes to the wing too soon, his wings do not beat fast enough to proclaim him a male and other males will try to mate with him. He may lose some of his legs in the process. If a female takes off too soon, her wingbeats will be so slow the males will not recognize her until she has been in the air for a while and the pace of her wingbeats has quickened.

### Surviving hard times

In temperate latitudes the females of some species pass the winter in sheltered places, such as caves, hollow trees or houses, especially in cellars. A few species lay their eggs in dry places which will be flooded in late winter or spring. These eggs can withstand

dry and cold conditions, and in some instances will not hatch successfully without them. When the female of *Anopheles gambiae*, a malaria-carrier, lives in desert areas, she gorges herself with blood and then shelters in huts, cracks in rocks or in rodent burrows, until the rains come. The dryness delays her egg-laying. Other species of desert mosquitoes lay thick-shelled eggs able to hatch even after 1—2 years, and in some cases up to 10 years later.

### War on mosquitoes

Mosquitoes have many enemies. Airborne mosquitoes are eaten by birds such as swallows and flycatchers hunting on the wing. The larvae and pupae are eaten by small fish. The guppy, called the millions fish because of its large numbers in its native home, is used to control mosquito larvae and has been introduced into rivers in infested areas to keep down their numbers. Another control is to spray oil on waters of ponds and swamps. A small amount of oil will spread to cover a wide area with a thin film which prevents the larval mosquito from breathing at the surface of the water.

### Homing on victims

When a female mosquito takes blood from a malarial patient, she will pass the malaria parasite by her saliva on to the next victim whose blood she sucks. It is the same with yellow fever, although a different species of mosquito is involved, and with elephantiasis, filariasis, and other mosquito-borne diseases. There are several defensive measures which can be taken to keep the mosquitoes away. This is usually achieved by netting or by deterrents, or by killing the larvae or the mosquitoes, or changing the habitat and reducing the number of people carrying the disease who act as a reservoir for further infection. The use of deterrents depends on the behaviour of a mosquito in homing on its victim. An increase in the carbon dioxide in the air, as from human breathing, makes a female mosquito take off and fly upwind. As she draws near her victim the slight increase in temperature and humidity directs her more certainly towards her target until she can see where she needs to land. In these later stages the concentration of carbon dioxide is also greater, but certain chemicals (deterrents) will confuse her and make her swerve away.

## Mysterious outbreaks

The ague was once prevalent in Europe but was stamped out largely by the draining of the marshes. When soldiers serving in the tropics during the First World War returned home after contracting malaria, it was feared they might act as a reservoir for malaria (or ague). With the air traffic of today there once again is the fear that infected mosquitoes may be introduced into countries at present free from their diseases, and steps must be taken against them. Thirty years ago an African mosquito *Anopheles gambiae* found its way to Brazil, and 60 000 people died before the malaria was brought under control. In the Second World War, in Colombia, yellow fever suddenly struck villages where it had been unknown. In due course it was traced to the monkeys living high in trees which formed a reservoir, the carrier being a mosquito whose larvae lived in water in aerial plants growing in the tree tops. Woodmen felling some of these trees were attacked by mosquitoes from pupae in the aerial plants. The disease was then spread by a species of mosquito living at ground level.

## Odd behaviour

Not all mosquitoes are troublesome; some are highly interesting. The larvae of *Mansonia* do not need to swim to the surface of the water to breathe. They have a saw-like apparatus for piercing water plant roots and drawing off the air contained in them. The females of another species *Leicesteria* lay their eggs onto their hindlegs which they then push through small holes in bamboo stems where water has collected. The eggs fall into the water and later hatch. A New Zealand mosquito *Opifex* has unusual mating behaviour. The males fly over water waiting for pupae to come to the surface to release the females within. They then mate with the females before they can get out. A mosquito *Harpagomyia* of Africa and southern Asia settles on tree trunks waiting for ants to pass. It then flies over to an ant, holds the ant's body with its front pair of legs and does not let the ant go until it has brought up a drop of food from its crop. The oddest story of all is, however, of a tropical American carrier of yellow fever which seems to prefer laying its eggs in water in flower vases, even those in hospital wards. In dealing with an outbreak of yellow fever in New Orleans it was found that the mosquitoes were breeding in the water in flower vases placed on the graves of the unfortunate yellow fever victims.

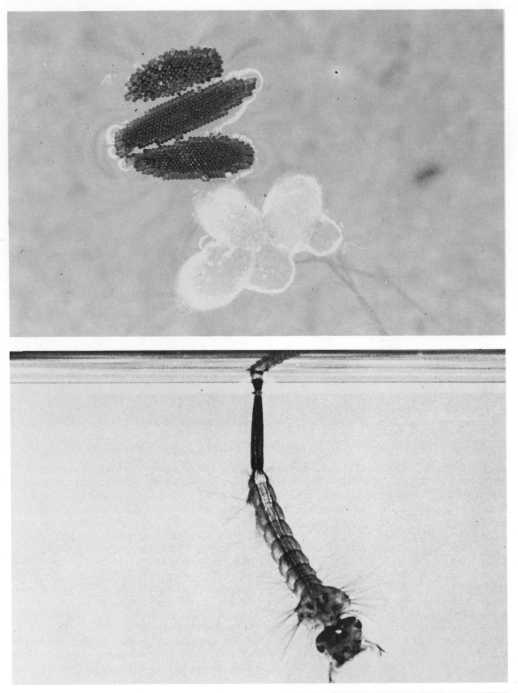

△△ *Life afloat. Compact rafts of the eggs of the common gnat* **Culex** *beside a duckweed plant. Between them mosquitoes lay their eggs in almost every type of water, although the majority live in fresh water. Each individual species is, however, very limited in its habitat.*
△ *Living down under? A mosquito larva hangs from the surface in still water. It breathes through the respiratory tubes which reach up to the surface. The head, thorax and abdomen are clearly visible as are the mouth brushes which hang like a drooping moustache and sweep particles into the mouth.* (7 × *life size*)
▷ *Bulky but active. Mosquitoes spend only a few days in this pupal stage, whether the life cycle lasts a year or 10 days.* (13 × *life size*)

| | |
|---|---|
| phylum | **Arthropoda** |
| class | **Insecta** |
| order | **Diptera** |
| family | **Culicidae** |

△ A female oil beetle **Meloë proscarabaeus** with a mass of orange eggs she has just laid. These hatch in 3–4 weeks.

▷ A ½ in. long **Epicauta velata** feeding on grass pollen. Oil beetles are often pests, feeding on the foliage of crops, but the beetles of this genus perform a useful function in attacking locust egg pods.

# Oil beetle

*These small beetles get their name from their habit of exuding an oily fluid from the joints of their legs when disturbed. They belong to the blister beetle family (page 31), and have the same complicated life-cycle, but unlike the brightly-coloured blister beetle, oil beetles are dully-coloured and ugly. They were described by the famous French entomologist Fabre, as 'uncouth beetles . . . their wing cases yawning over their back like the tails of a fat man's coat that is far too tight for their wearer.' This describes the very short wing cases that do not cover the abdomen and which overlap in a way most unusual for a beetle. The wing cases are, in fact, functionless as oil beetles have no wings. A common European oil beetle **Meloë proscarabaeus** is 1 in. long and bluish-black.*

*In the deserts of the southwest United States and Mexico there are some unusual oil beetles, about 1–1½ in. long with very hard bodies and wing cases. The wing cases are fused together and are larger than usual. They reach over the abdomen to form an air chamber. The air in this chamber acts as an insulating barrier against the sun's heat, while the hemispherical shape presents a relatively small surface area for the absorption of heat, and the hard, thick body armour prevents evaporation of the body fluids into the dry desert air.*

### Dependent on bees

Only a very few oil beetle larvae survive to adulthood as the larval life is extremely complicated. To survive, the larva must manage to hitch a lift, usually on the body of a solitary bee, and then to drop into a cell of its honeycomb. The stout antennae of the adult males of some species, resemble the forceps of an earwig, and are used to clasp the female during mating. As the thousands of eggs develop within her abdomen, the female becomes extremely swollen. Eventually she lays several batches of 3–4 thousand eggs in cracks or holes in the ground. They hatch in 3–6 weeks and thousands of tiny larvae emerge to swarm up the stems of surrounding plants.

The hatchlings are like lice, with long, narrow bodies, and when they were first discovered hanging to the bodies of bees they were called bee lice. They are very active and scramble up plants to sit in the flowers until a solitary bee visits them. When a bee alights the larvae grip it with their jaws and are carried away. Unfortunately for the larvae they show no discrimination and grasp any hairy insect. Consequently they are often borne away on beetles, flies, butterflies and honeybees. Any that do are doomed, but if they catch hold of the right species of solitary bee, they are eventually carried to the bee's nest. Here they drop off and enter a cell where they devour the bee's egg.

The rest of the larval life is spent in this cell, feeding on the nectar and pollen intended for the growing bee. The louse-like larva undergoes a radical transformation and becomes a soft, helpless creature with short legs, rather like a May bug grub. All it does is feed. The spiracles, or breathing holes, are placed high on the back to be clear of the sticky fluid on which the larva is floating. While in the bee's nest the larva sheds its skin several times. At the third moult it is known as the 'pseudo-pupa' and has only minute legs. Two moults later it becomes the true pupa which resembles the adult in form.

The adult oil beetles emerge from the bee's nest in the spring after they entered it as larvae and the complicated cycle starts again. When adult, these beetles feed on plants and are sometimes pests of crops such as potatoes and tomatoes. This very complicated cycle of events with two very different kinds of larvae—one active and one passive—is known as hypermetamorphosis. In other words the oil beetle undergoes more changes in form than the usual larva-pupa-adult stages of other beetles.

In the United States some oil beetles have a simpler, less 'hit-or-miss' life history. The louse-like larvae just run about until they find a mass of locust eggs which they settle in and devour.

### Oily fluid

An oil beetle crawling sluggishly through the grass would seem to be utterly defenceless but when handled it exudes an oily, caustic fluid containing cantharidin (see blister beetle, page 31). This fluid is the oil beetle's blood; the beetle's reaction to disturbance is to compress its abdomen and raise its blood pressure so much that the thin skin of the joints is ruptured and blood squirts out. Once the pressure is released, the blood clots quickly. This behaviour is known as 'reflex bleeding' and is practised by several insects, including the ladybird *Coccinella* and certain grasshoppers. Some grasshopper larvae can squirt fluid as much as 2 in. and one produces a foam as air is mixed with the blood. One beetle *Timarcha tenebricosa* is called the bloody-nosed beetle because it ejects red fluid from its mouth when alarmed.

| phylum | **Arthropoda** |
|---|---|
| class | **Insecta** |
| order | **Coleoptera** |
| family | **Meloidae** |
| genera & species | *Meloë proscarabaeus* *Apulus muralis, others* |

# Paper wasp

*Paper wasps are closely related to the
common wasps and hornets of the genus
**Vespula** and **Vespa**. There is little to
choose between them in appearance, but
the thorax and abdomen of the paper wasp
are pear-shaped where they join, more like
an hourglass than the rounded thorax and
abdomen of the other wasps. In habits
paper wasps differ by making small nests
that are not enclosed by a papery sheath,
and the cells containing eggs and larvae
are open.*

*Paper wasps are found all over the world
in tropical and temperate regions. They
are very common in North America.*

### Cup-shaped nests

The life of the paper wasp is very easy to
study because the nest is built above the
ground, it is open so that all the activities
can be watched and the colony is comparatively small. Some nests may number up to
500 wasps but there are usually less than 100.
In small nests it is quite easy to mark all
wasps with individual paint marks and to
watch and record their behaviour.

In tropical regions the nests survive the
year round but in temperate climates the
workers and males die in the autumn,
leaving the queens to survive the winter by
lying dormant in a shelter. In the following
spring the queens emerge and seek a suitable place for their nests. As the nests are
open the site must not be exposed to
strong winds or strong sunlight. A common
place for nests is under eaves of houses and
sheds, or on branches, but as these places
often get warm, the nests are kept cool by
the wasps fanning their wings, and they may
bring water to regurgitate over the comb.

The queen paper wasp constructs the nest
from paper which she makes by rasping
wood from a tree with her jaws, chewing it
and mixing it with saliva. The first stage in
building is a flat foundation on the underside of a roof or branch. From this grows a
short stalk that holds the main part of the
nest—the brood cells which make up the
spherical comb.

### Family planning

Sometimes in warmer regions several queens
combine to build a nest and lay eggs, but
eventually one queen asserts her authority
and the others stop laying. If, however, the
senior queen dies, one of the others will
take her place. The ovaries of the lesser
queens are small in comparison with those
of the senior queen, but if they do lay eggs
she destroys them. The senior queen is also
looked after more carefully by the workers
than the other queens. How she manages to
dominate the nest is not really known but it
is probably by means of pheromones, chemicals given off from her body which affect
the behaviour and body functions of the
other paper wasps.

The queens are fertilised before their
winter retreat and the sperms are stored
until the eggs are laid. The workers develop
from fertilised eggs, but are infertile them-

selves because they are reared on a reduced
diet. Only later in the season are new
queens raised by feeding larvae on a rich
diet. At the same time males are reared
from unfertilised eggs.

The first batch of larvae are reared by the
queens but once they have emerged from
cocoons as fully fledged worker wasps they
are left to tend the next generation. The
larvae are fed on a paste of caterpillars
and other insects that have been chewed up
by the adults. The larvae grow fat on this
diet and after a few weeks the entrances
of their cells are sealed with a thin layer of
paper and pupation takes place. After
emerging from their cells the new workers
take a meal from other workers then start
their life's work of raising new generations.
The nest gradually increases as new cells
are added, but in autumn larvae start to die,
probably because of a failing food supply,
and the colony dies off. Before this happens
the males and queens will have set out on
their mating flights. The colonies cannot
survive in temperate regions as wasps do not

*The queen paper wasp builds the small globular
nest from paper which she makes by rasping
wood from a tree and mixing it with saliva.*

▷ *Hibernation between mango tree leaves;
female S. African wasps **Polistes fastidios**.*

store food as honey bees do. In the tropics
and near tropics, however, the workers can
hibernate through the brief period of bad
weather and then become active again.
The life of social insects—bees, wasps and
ants—is a hard one and individual workers
do not live long. The ways of these insects
have been held up as shining examples of
industry, but some species let the side down,
and exploit the industry of their relatives.

| phylum | **Arthropoda** |
|---|---|
| class | **Insecta** |
| order | **Hymenoptera** |
| family | **Vespidae** |
| genus & species | *Polistes annularis P. gallicus* others |

*Fan dance: a long legged plume moth* **Pterophorus pentadactylus** *looks rather ghost-like with its 'feathered' wings spread out at right angles to its body.*

# Plume moth

*The plume moths make up a comparatively small family whose wings are divided into 'feathers'. The forewings which are very long are divided into two or three parts and the hindwings into three or four parts. A few have wings without clefts, such as the European genus* **Agdistis***. The bodies of plume moths are very long and slender, as are the legs which have prominent spurs. The wingspan ranges from ¼ – 2 in. The flight is feeble and with their long body and legs, plume moths look rather like crane flies (page 63). When at rest the forewings are rolled around the hindwings and usually held straight out at right angles to the body.*

*There are about 600 species of plume moths, found in most parts of the world. Closely related are the feather-winged moths of the family Alucitidae, most of which are found in Asia. The many-plume moth, with ½ in. wingspan, is found in Europe and the temperate parts of North America. The fore- and hindwings are divided into six and look like a pair of feather fans.*

### A watery death
During the day a sudden glimpse may be caught of a disturbed plume moth as it flies out of a plant in which it has been resting. Usually plume moths are active only in the evening or at night. They make themselves very inconspicuous when at rest among the herbage or hedgerows. Adults of *Agdistis* hold their rolled wings pointing forward in a line with the body, so they resemble the dried grass on which they rest. This camouflage is improved by their blackish

markings which look like moulds.

Plume moths live on a variety of food plants but are only occasionally pests. The grape vine plume of the United States attacks the sprouting leaves of vines but is not as serious a pest as *Exelastis atomosa* of India which burrows into pods and eats the growing peas. The pupa is later formed within the pod. The leaves and sometimes the flowers of a plant are the usual food of plume moth caterpillars. The caterpillars bore into the leaf and flower stems making them wither, or they bind the leaves into a rosette with silk strands so they are protected while they eat. The caterpillars of *Stenoptilia pneumonanthes*, which feed on marsh gentians, are sometimes drowned by rain when they feed in the cup-shaped flowers. The caterpillars of *Agdistis bennetii* are liable to suffer the same fate. They feed and hibernate on the leaves of sea lavender, and it is believed that they can survive submergence.

### Mobile pupae
Eggs of plume moths are usually laid on the leaves of the food plants and the caterpillars feed on these leaves or flowers, or bore into the stems and buds. There are often two generations in one year, the second hibernating as caterpillars in stems of the food plants. The pupa is soft and hairy and hangs from a leaf or stem like the chrysalises of some butterflies. Some species weave a cocoon that is no more than a few strands of silk thrown around the body. The caterpillars of the triangle plume, which has black triangles on its forewings, hatch in June and feed on coltsfoot. The adults emerge and are on the wing from August to September then a second generation of caterpillars becomes active in September. They feed on the leaves of coltsfoot, before burrowing into the stems to hibernate. In the spring they feed on buds and flowers then pupate in the seed

heads, binding the seeds with silk so they do not fall. The adults emerge in May.

The pupa of *Leioptilus lienigianus* jerks sharply if disturbed, perhaps startling a predator. That of *Platyptilia calodactyla* is also mobile. It often wriggles to the surface of its burrow in a leaf but retreats if disturbed. It is prevented from emerging too far by an anchor rope of silk attached to its hind end and the inside of the burrow.

### Preying on the predator
Adults of *Trichoptilus paludum* can sometimes be seen during the day, flying over boggy heaths and moors. They lay their eggs on sundew, a peculiar bog plant that captures and devours insects. This habit is found in other bog plants and is probably related to the deficiency of nitrate in boggy soils. The deficiency is made up by breaking down protein in the insects' bodies. The upper surfaces of sundew leaves bear hairs surmounted by glands. When an insect lands on a leaf it is trapped in sticky secretions, the hairs of the plant bend towards it and secrete fluids that digest it. The products of digestion are then absorbed by the plant. The caterpillars of *Trichoptilus* feed on sundew leaves, and presumably in some way avoid being caught and digested, but it seems to be as precarious a way of life as living on man-eating tigers.

| phylum | **Arthropoda** |
|---|---|
| class | **Insecta** |
| order | **Lepidoptera** |
| family | **Pterophoridae** |
| genera & species | **Orneodes hexadactyla** *many-plume moth* **Oxyptilus periscelidactylus** *grapevine plume moth* **Platyptilia gonodactyla** *triangle plume moth, others* |

*Unspectacular adults that have remarkable larvae, male (above) and female processionary moths, **Thaumetopoea pityocampa**. Note the male's plume-like antennae. In most moths these are used to locate the females, being sensitive to extremely low concentrations of the scent given off by the females (×4).*

# Processionary moth

Also known as processional or procession moths, it is the caterpillars of these moths that have stolen the limelight. The caterpillars form processions which almost every writer on the subject has been so taken with that he has failed to say anything about the moth itself.

There are two species in southern Europe, the oak processionary and the pine processionary, and others in the Old World. The male of the oak processionary moth is just over 1 in. across the wings, the forewings brown-grey with dark bars, the hindwings grey with indistinct dark bars. The female 1¼ in. across the wings is lighter in colour. Both rest on bark during the day with the wings folded and fly among the tops of oaks at night from August to September. The eggs are laid on the trunks of oaks and the following late spring the caterpillars hatch out. They are dark bluish-grey, whitish on the sides with rows of rusty-red hairy warts on the back and they grow to 1¾ in. The caterpillars spin a communal web, usually at the base of a tree, and go out at night in a procession to feed on the oak leaves. They pupate at the end of June in the communal web, the brownish pupae forming tight groups.

The pine processionary moth is similar but 1½ in. across and is on the wing from May to July. The eggs are laid on pines. The caterpillars are 1½ in. long, greyish-green with a dark back stripe and yellowish-red warts. The caterpillars cluster by day but have no permanent communal nest and they pupate individually, deep in sandy soil.

△ *Gathering of pine processionary caterpillars. These larvae feed on pine shoots, sometimes to the extent of becoming a pest.*

▽ *An orderly troop of* **Ochrogaster** *larvae. It is from this unusual 'follow-my-leader' habit that the adult moth gets its name.*

## Round and round interminably

The habits of the processionary are best illustrated by the well known story told by the famous entomologist JH Fabre. He persuaded the leader of a line of caterpillars to walk onto the rim of a tub 5 ft in circumference. When enough caterpillars were on the rim to form an unbroken circle he removed the rest and he cleaned away the trail of silk they had left behind. Steadily marching round and round the rim, the head of each touching the rear end of the one in front, the caterpillars continued for 8 days until some of them, either from exhaustion or accident, fell from the rim and the spell was broken. They had circled 335 times, stopping at intervals for a rest.

## Two kinds of processions

The pine processionary travels in a single line and as many as 300 have been counted stretching for 40 ft. The oak processionary travels in shorter groups with a single leader followed by two, then three and so on to make a wedge-shaped column. Each caterpillar lays a thread of silk as it goes, so the trail is marked by a substantial carpet of silk. This was the trail Fabre removed. It used to be thought that in some way the silk helped the caterpillars follow each other. This proved not to be so although the silk trail is used for returning to their communal web. Since the caterpillars are blind and are said to lack a sense of smell it is reasonable to suppose they merely have the impulse to push the head against the rear end of one of their fellows. If one of them is pushed out of line the whole procession stops until that one is back in its place, then all set off again. Apparently there is no question of a leader. It is quite accidental which one starts the procession, and any one of the column can act as a leader.

## Nettle-backs

At first glance it would seem that this extraordinary behaviour must lay the caterpillars open to dangers greater than usual. They have, however, very subtle defences. First, we are told, they are sensitive to approaching storms and all make for their home web. Secondly, they have a rude sur-

prise in store for living enemies. Along the back each caterpillar has 'mirrors' normally hidden by folds of the skin. These are the warts. When the caterpillar is alarmed the folds are withdrawn and the mirror is exposed. Its surface is covered with nettle-hairs, short hollow bristles with poison glands at their bases. Around each mirror are longer branched bristles which, when touched, brush against the nettle-hairs breaking them away from their moorings so they form a sort of poison dart: one of the many examples of chemical warfare in the animal kingdom. These tiny poison darts produce an intense skin irritation.

## Breaking up the procession

In a letter to *African Wild Life* of September 1958, Brian B Hobbs described an adventure just north of Satara, South Africa. He saw a line of caterpillars crossing the road, each light brown, hairy and 1¼ in. long. Before he realized they were there he had driven over them. 'Those on the passenger side of the car continued moving into the grass, while those between the wheels remained where they were; those on the driver's side also ceased moving forward. In each case the leader of the last two groups kept nosing about, trying to regain contact with his fellow in front, who had been obliterated. His hind-quarters remained rigid and those caterpillars behind him remained quite still. It would appear they are all blind . . .' Hobbs remained on the spot for 20 minutes and the two leaderless sections still had not moved forward.

## Meaningless circles?

The habit of the processionary moth caterpillar may seem odd to us. Indeed, to see a circle of these caterpillars moving endlessly round and round is one of the most comical sights imaginable. Yet in spite of the kind of hazard Mr Hobbs described, the follow-my-leader behaviour must have great advantage to the species. For one thing, by using the silk trails they lay down, and by following each other, these caterpillars are sure of reaching their feeding grounds and of returning to the security of their communal web after feeding. But what are we to say of the nymphalid butterfly *Atella phalenta* of Mauritius which flies in immense numbers to the east across the mountain Trou-aux-cerfs, then around the foot to the starting point in an endless ring that has no beginning and no end. Alexander B Klots, the American entomologist, remarks that this makes less sense than Fabre's processionary caterpillars—this is an understatement.

| phylum | **Arthropoda** |
|---|---|
| class | **Insecta** |
| order | **Lepidoptera** |
| family | **Notodontidae** |
| genera & species | ***Ochrogaster contraria*** *Australian processionary* ***Thaumetopoea pinivora*** *pine processionary* ***T. processionea*** *oak processionary, others* |

# Purple emperor

*A large, showy and sometimes rare butterfly, the purple emperor is named after the purple iridescence on the wings of the male, which can only be seen when viewed from a particular angle. Otherwise they are dark-brown, almost black, with a line of white patches and an inconspicuous eyespot on each hind wing. The white patches are very occasionally missing and such purple emperors are known as the variety* **iole**, *much sought after by collectors. The underside of the wing has an intricate pattern of brown and grey with bands of white. The female is very much like the male but lacks the iridescence and is slightly larger. Her wingspan is 3 in. compared with $2\frac{1}{2}-2\frac{3}{4}$ in. of the males.*

*Purple emperors are found locally in many parts of Europe and Asia.*

## Two plants needed

Purple emperors' preference for oak woods is one factor which limits their distribution since these woods become scarcer year by year due to man's activities. Purple emperors do, however, survive in woodlands that have been stripped of all tall trees. They are on the wing in July and the first half of August but even in bright weather and in places where they are known to live they are not easy to see. They are not attracted to flowers like so many other butterflies and spend most of their time around the tops of oak trees. The dull coloured females are easier to find because they descend to lay their eggs in sallow bushes. The males spend their time perching on leaves and periodically flying high across a clearing or soaring up almost out of sight on their powerful wings. Sometimes several males may be seen chasing each other in circles.

## Slug-like caterpillar

Purple emperors lay their eggs on the upper surfaces of sallow leaves. Each female ranges over a considerable area, laying one egg on each leaf, although she may revisit a bush later and so lay another egg on a leaf already bearing one. Other females may also use that leaf, so it is quite possible to find several eggs on one leaf. The egg is like a minute blancmange, $\frac{1}{25}$ in. high, almost hemispherical with about 14 radially arranged ridges. At first it is green, then the base becomes purple, and just before hatching it turns black. The caterpillar emerges about a fortnight after the egg is laid. It is yellow with a black head and measures just a little over $\frac{1}{10}$ in.

After 10 days of eating the sallow leaf on which the egg was laid the caterpillar sheds its skin. It is now green, the same colour as the sallow leaf, and it looks very much like a slug, with a pair of horns projecting from the head and a body tapering to a point at the rear end.

The caterpillar continues to feed through the summer and into autumn. It grows to $\frac{1}{2}$ in. and changes to brown, so matching the autumn leaves. When not feeding it lies along the midrib of the leaf so that it is very inconspicuous. In October the caterpillar retires to a twig or a fork between two twigs, and spins a mat of fine silk on which it rests for the winter. In the following April the caterpillar changes colour back to green, and starts feeding on the fresh leaves, growing to $1\frac{3}{4}$ in. before pupating in June. Pupation takes place on the underside of the sallow leaf where it lays a mat of silk and runs more silk up the leaf stem to the twig, presumably to act as an anchor. The chrysalis hangs from the silk mat by a number of small hooks. Just before pupating the caterpillar changes to a very pale green, matching the underside of the sallow leaf, and making the chrysalis very difficult to find. The adult butterfly emerges in about 3 weeks.

## Lured to the ground

Although male purple emperors spend most of their short lives in the tops of the trees, they do sometimes come down, feeding on the sap that oozes from wounded trees and sometimes on the honeydew of aphides (page 13). They also descend to the ground to drink at puddles or to feed on animal carcases or horse droppings. At one time purple emperors were caught by placing the rotting corpse of a rabbit or other animal in a woodland ride, but this method is not successful now, probably because the

*Brilliant beauty—a purple emperor sunning itself on a sprig of oak leaves. This attractive butterfly is, unfortunately, not very common and is seen even more rarely than one would expect as it spends most of its time at the tops of oak trees. Although it can survive in young oak plantations, mature oak woods are becoming fewer and fewer.*

*The butterfly's purple colouring, possessed by the male only, is normally seen only on one wing, as in this picture. In some lights both wings are iridescent, the purple scales changing colour with the incidence of the light. There are also dark scales caused by melanic pigment.*

purple emperor has become so rare. They can also be attracted by bright objects and there are several stories of male purple emperors coming down to settle on car radiators, and even flying headlong into cars as they are being driven along.

| phylum | **Arthropoda** |
| --- | --- |
| class | **Insecta** |
| order | **Lepidoptera** |
| family | **Nymphalidae** |
| genus & species | *Apatura iris* |

# Puss moth

*The puss moth is a member of the family of prominent moths whose body is covered with fluffy hairs recalling the hair of a cat. The family is named after the prominent tuft of scales on the rear margin of the hindwings. The wings and body are whitish, the thorax is marked with dark spots and the abdomen with broad transverse bands. The wings have yellowish veins with black branches and the forewings have patterns of wavy lines. Puss moths are about 1⅓ in. from head to the tip of abdomen, the females being larger and with darker hindwings. Puss moths are found in most of Europe, across Asia to Japan and in North Africa.*

*Closely related to the puss moth are the kitten moths, smaller than the puss moth with darker bodies and more heavily patterned forewings.*

### Inconspicuous cocoon

Like all prominent moths, the puss moth is a night flier. It is readily attracted to light and can be found in May and June, in places where poplars, sallows and willows grow. The reddish-brown hemispherical eggs are laid on the leaves of these trees. They are placed, usually in pairs, on the upper surfaces of the leaves where they hatch in June.

When small the caterpillars are black with a pair of long 'tails' that give them a catlike appearance and also their common name. As they grow they develop a pattern of green and brown and when full grown, these grotesque caterpillars are 2–2½ in.

▽ *The elegant back view of a puss moth, a moth discreetly and tastefully patterned compared with its garish larva.*

long. While feeding the body appears hunch-backed, rising to a sharp peak just above the legs. Four pairs of prolegs support the rear part of the body and from either side of the tip of the abdomen rise the two long tails, broad near the base, with whip-like tips. Along the head and back runs a broad band of purplish brown edged with white which forms a saddle in the middle of the body. This pattern is an example of disruptive coloration, breaking up the outline of the caterpillar so that it is difficult to see among the leaves and is easily mistaken for a withered leaf.

The caterpillars feed throughout July and August, and sometimes into September. Then they select crevices in the bark of the trunk or branches of the tree in which they were feeding. As the caterpillar weaves its cocoon of silk it incorporates small scraps of bark and chewed wood into the matrix, making the cocoon hardly distinguishable from its background.

### Cutting its way out

The cocoon is a tough structure and the caterpillar leaves the skin at the head end thinner than the rest so that the adult moth can escape the following summer. To assist its emergence the moth has two mechanisms for opening the cocoon, one mechanical, one chemical. When it bursts out of the pupa case or chrysalis within the cocoon, a small part of the case remains attached by hooks to the moths' head. This bears two sharply pointed spikes which are used to cut a hole in the cocoon. After the moth has climbed through the hole it pushes this cutting tool off its head with its legs. Cutting is made easy by the secretion of a weak solution of caustic soda from the mouth which softens the tough wall of silk.

▽ *Lobster moth larva in its threat attitude—another member of the puss moth's family, renowned for its striking caterpillars.*

### Red for danger

The bizarre caterpillar of the puss moth is remarkable for having two kinds of protective coloration. As already described the pattern of brown and green disrupts the outline of the caterpillar making it difficult to find. This is a passive form of protection, and does not help if the caterpillar is found by accident. Once disturbed, however, it rears up presenting a terrifying picture; the head is drawn in and the 'shoulders' hunched displaying a bright scarlet ring, with two black spots above it. This looks very much like a face and its sudden appearance probably scares enemies.

The scarlet ring is a warning. If further molested a burning 40% formic acid solution is squirted from thoracic glands.

Other moths of the prominent family possess similar means of defence. Many have protective coloration and one species secretes strong hydrochloric acid when disturbed. Stranger in appearance than the puss moth caterpillar is that of the lobster moth. This is found on beech, hazel, oak and birch from Britain to Japan. The caterpillar is brown, has two pairs of very long legs and the tip of the abdomen is raised vertically. When annoyed, the lobster caterpillar rears up and waves its long legs.

| phylum | **Arthropoda** |
| --- | --- |
| class | **Insecta** |
| order | **Lepidoptera** |
| family | **Notodontidae** |
| genera & species | ***Cerura vinula*** *puss moth* <br> ***Harpyia*** *kitten moths* <br> ***Stauropus fagi*** *lobster moth* |

▷ *'Shoulders' hunched, and a terrifying 'face' appears; the caterpillar of the puss moth in its defence posture.*

# Robber fly

*Robber flies, or assassin flies, like the horse flies (page 105), have dagger-like mouthparts for piercing and sucking the blood of their prey, but robber flies attack insects whereas horse flies suck the blood of mammals. Some robber flies are no doubt killed under the impression that they are horse flies. They are strong fliers that can generally be recognised by their hairy bodies, long, spindly legs and, usually, long abdomens. Asilus crabroniformis, which is over 1 in. long and has a yellow and black abdomen, looks quite dangerous. The hairs covering the body and long legs give some robber flies a spider-like appearance, while others have coloured abdomens and look like bees or wasps. Some robber flies, for example, Bombomima, have broad, hairy bodies with black and yellow stripes and look very like bumble bees. This mimicry may have two advantages. It may protect robber flies from birds and other predators that avoid bees and it may allow the robber flies to approach the bumblebees on which they prey without arousing suspicion—a sort of 'wolf in sheep's clothing'. These bee mimics may even buzz in flight like a bumblebee. Robber flies form a world-wide family of over 4 000 species.*

## Lying in wait

Robber flies can be found in grassland, heaths or forest clearings crouching motionless on bare earth or sand or on a perch such as a stem of grass or the leaf of a bush. They are not resting but lying in wait for their prey, with their long legs drawn up ready to pounce. When an insect comes near, the robber fly leaps out, and seizes it with its forelegs. A large robber fly may leap up to 20 in. to reach its prey. Some robber flies attack insects that land near them while others catch insects as they fly past.

Although robber flies do not appear particularly strong or agile, they prey on remarkably large insects. Large robber flies, such as *A. crabroniformis*, capture grasshoppers, dragonflies, beetles and even bees and wasps. Small ones limit their attacks to flies, bugs and other small insects. Robber flies are able to overcome other large insects, which are often well equipped to defend themselves, by the suddenness of their attacks and, probably, by a poison which quickly quietens their victims. Not only do they avoid the jaws of dragonflies and the stings of bees but robber flies seem unaffected by the body fluids of milkweed butterflies and others which are usually distasteful to other insect predators.

Surprisingly, robber flies themselves fall prey to spiders, tiger beetles, hunting wasps and other small predatory animals.

## Perilous mating

Male robber flies have one particular foe —the female robber fly. As sometimes happens with spiders and a few other arthropods, the female is likely to attack her mate, so courtship is perilous. Successful mating seems, therefore, to depend on the male being able to approach the female cautiously, perhaps when she is busy feeding. The female is recognisable by her sting-like ovipositor, through which she deposits her eggs in earth, rotten wood, or dung according to the species. The larvae are similar to those of horse flies, pale maggots pointed at each end; having hairs on the head and tail and along the back. Robber fly larvae are not entirely carnivorous like horsefly larvae. They live in fairly dry places, under dead leaves and bark or in rotten wood, where they feed mainly on decaying plant tissues.

## Wooing with presents

The male of a related family of predatory flies, the Empididae, have the same courtship problems as the robber flies. In some species mating takes place in flight and it seems that this presents the male with greater problems of survival since he often presents his prospective mate with a small insect such as a midge for her to consume, apparently to take her mind off him during mating. Some species wrap the insect in silk secreted from glands in the legs which requires more attention by the female to unwrap it. Such behaviour immediately calls to mind human parallels, even to 'gift-wrapping' but some of these flies go so far as to act under false pretences. They hand the females an empty package of silk and mate with her as she is examining it.

| phylum | **Arthropoda** |
|--------|----------------|
| class | **Insecta** |
| order | **Diptera** |
| family | **Asilidae** |

△ *A big catch.* **Alcimus tristrigatus** *straddles a painted lady butterfly while devouring it.*
◁ *Two* **Stenopogon sabandus** *shown mating.*

▽ *Dual purpose disguise.* **Bombomima** *mimics a bee it feeds on. The disguise may also ensure some protection from insect predators.*

# Rove beetle

There are over 20 000 species of rove beetles. Most of them are small and some are minute, one of the smallest being only $\frac{1}{20}-\frac{1}{10}$ in. long. When you talk of having got 'a fly in your eye' it is likely to be one of these. A larger example is Devil's coach-horse, a name given to different rove beetles in various countries. The British Devil's coach-horse **Ocypus olens** is all black but the Australian species **Creophilus erythrocephalus** has a red head. A characteristic of rove beetles is their very short wings which do not cover the abdomen, so they look like earwigs but without the characteristic forceps.

Rove beetles are active and can run fast. Most of them fly well, some by day and others by night. When disturbed they cock their tails up and secrete an offensive vapour, hence their other name of 'cocktail' beetles. Although some rove beetles have taken up unusual ways of life, the majority live in damp places feeding on carrion or decaying plants.

### Strange places for beetles

Some rove beetles have unique habitats. The beaver beetle *Platypsyllus castoris* is found only in the fur of beavers, both in Europe and North America. It has no wings or eyes and only minute jaws and nothing is known about its feeding habits. *Leptinus testaceus* has been found on small rodents and birds, as well as in the nests of ants and bumblebees, but how it lives is quite unknown. A few of the very small rove beetles live on the seashore, some wandering about in tidepools, staying submerged for several hours. Some beetles of the genus *Bledius* are restricted to a narrow strip of land just above the high water mark. They burrow in the sand making complicated galleries, detectable by the casts of very fine soil which are thrown up. *Bledius* beetles are also unusual among beetles in being gregarious.

### Varied diets

Rove beetles are generally scavengers or hunters. They can be found in dung, fungi and rotting vegetation or feeding on oozing sap. *Oxytelus tetracarinatus* feeds on cast up seaweed. Some are parasites: *Aleochara* parasitises flies which breed in seaweed. Carrion beetles, such as *Ablattaria laevigata* and *Phosphuga atrata*, attack snails. They bite the foot of the snail which retreats into its shell and attempts to seal the entrance with slime. The beetle follows the snail into the shell, continually biting it and squirting a fluid from the tip of its abdomen until the snail is overcome.

### Ant guests

A few rove beetles of the families Staphylinidae and Clavigeridae enjoy a relationship with ants and termites as close as that of aphides (page 13). *Claviger testaceus* lives in the nests of the yellow ant *Lasius flavus*. Superficially it looks more like an ant than a beetle. It is wingless, eyeless and the mouthparts are very small and useless. This

is no disadvantage because the beetle is fed by the ants who regurgitate food for it. The ants feed and cosset the beetles with such care that their own offspring sometimes suffer, for the beetles secrete a substance to which the ants are very partial. This is secreted from a hollow at the base of the abdomen which is filled with tufts of golden hairs.

Some of these ant guests move from one host to another. In both North America and Europe some rove beetles spend the summer with wood ants and move to the nests of carpenter ants *Camponotus* in the autumn. The ants rear the beetle larvae, so the beetles are completely dependent on them, and some even live with army ants, following the colony as it moves about.

One very striking rove beetle, a relative of the Devil's coach-horse, is called the mahout beetle. It is one of many that take food from termites and give nothing in return. This minute beetle sits on the broad head of one of the termite workers, as a mahout sits on the neck of an elephant. When the worker termite meets a fellow worker the two exchange food. The mahout beetle just moves forward and takes food as it is passed from mouth to mouth.

### 'Camphor beetles'

In damp, boggy ground, especially near waterfalls there live small beetles that are $\frac{1}{4}$ in. long and black with orange legs. They

△ *Its eggs and newly hatched larvae* ($\times$ 4).
▷ *Devil's coach-horses in threatening pose with hind bodies raised and jaws open wide* ($\times$ 6).

have no common name but belong to the genus *Stenus*. If thrown into a pool they shoot unerringly to the nearest bank. This is not a blind dash for the beetles deliberately steer for the bank which they recognise by the contrast between the darkness of the banks and the brightness of the sky. They can easily be fooled by hanging a piece of black board in the water.

*Stenus* beetles have a remarkable method of propulsion which is similar in principle to that of toy boats driven by camphor. The camphor lowers the surface tension of the water behind the boat so it is drawn forward by the high surface tension in front. The beetles secrete a fluid that has the same action as camphor and so they can skim effortlessly across the water.

| phylum | **Arthropoda** |
|---|---|
| class | **Insecta** |
| order | **Coleoptera** |
| families | **Staphylinidae** |
| | **Clavigeridae** |
| | *others* |

# Sawfly

*The sawflies are named after the sawlike tip of the ovipositor with which the female drills holes in plants to lay her eggs. Sawflies are related to ants, bees and wasps but can be distinguished from them by not having a narrow 'wasp waist'. Some, however, have striped bodies like bees and wasps and the long ovipositor may be mistaken for a sting. The black and yellow horntail, which is ¾ in. long, may in particular cause needless alarm. Some sawflies, including the horntail, are called wood wasps because they lay their eggs in wood rather than leaves and the other soft parts of plants.*

*The larvae of sawflies are easily mistaken for caterpillars, and no doubt they are often collected in the hope that they will turn into butterflies. Close examination shows that, as well as the three pairs of true legs, they have more pairs of false or prolegs than the caterpillars of moths and butterflies. Sawfly larvae have only one pair of minute eyes, whereas caterpillars have a cluster of 4–6 on each side of the head.*

## Drilling for a living

Adult sawflies are very short lived, the males dying shortly after mating and the females surviving only long enough to lay their eggs. The eggs are laid in slits made in plants by the ovipositor. The ovipositor is made up of two thin rigid blades, protected when not in use by a pair of sheaths. The lower parts of the blades are notched to form saws or rasps. The two blades work alternately, moving to and fro as they drive into the plant tissue. The larvae of sawflies feed on many plants, including pines, turnips, roses and apples and are consequently often serious pests.

The larvae are found in a number of places such as in leaf galls, inside wood, in the open on leaves or living socially in silken webs. Those that live on leaves either scrape away the cuticle covering the leaves, forming conspicuous patterns, as may be seen on roses, or, like the pear sawfly, reduce the leaves to skeletons. The larva of the pear sawfly is often called the slug-worm, and may be mistaken for a slug. The similarity is increased by the shiny slime it secretes, apparently as a deterrent to insect-eating birds. The pear sawfly larva assumes the usual form of a sawfly larva for only a short time before it pupates.

The larva of the palisade sawfly, which lives on poplars, erects a strange barricade around itself. It lowers its mouth to the leaf and exudes a drop of saliva. As the head is raised, the drop is drawn out and immediately sets to form a fine, shiny post. The action is repeated until the larva is surrounded by a fence. Having eaten the leaf within its enclosure, the fence is eaten

◁ *Close up view of destruction. Hordes of* **Nematus** *larvae devour a sallow leaf, reducing it to a skeleton; often the leaf veins are eaten.*

and the larva moves to another leaf and erects another palisade. The fence is so flimsy it is hard to see how it could give any protection.

### Strange antics

Sawfly larvae may take several years to mature. Some drop to the ground and burrow to pupate while others spin a cocoon attached to a leaf or twigs. Larvae that feed in the wood pupate in the tunnels they have made. The strangest life history among the sawflies is that of the jumping-disc sawfly which pupates in a cocoon that also serves as a parachute. The larva lives in sycamore leaves and feeds on the tissue of the leaf without damaging the upper or lower cuticle. When full grown it cuts a series of perforations in the upper cuticle to form a circle. Then it weaves a silk hammock from the inside of this circle. The hammock does not touch the lower cuticle. Once safe inside, the disc of upper cuticle separates and drops to the ground with the larva attached by its hammock. When it has landed the larva works its way into a sheltered space by jerking its disc along.

Many sawfly larvae are strikingly coloured —black and white, black and yellow and so on. This is apparently a warning coloration as some sawflies can squirt irritating fluids from glands on their undersides. The pupae, however, are hunted by birds and rodents. In the United States it was found that the proportion of pupal cocoons that were damaged was a good indication of the size of the local mouse population, and in Britain 100 pupae were once found in the stomach of a red squirrel. Both larvae and pupae are parasitised by ichneumon wasps, such as *Megarhyssa* whose ovipostor can bore through 3 in. of wood.

### Controlling sawfly

Many sawfly larvae are serious pests and have spread beyond their native homes. The wheat-stem borer has, for instance, been carried to North America and several wood wasps have been spread, perhaps in imported timber. In the early 1940's the European spruce sawfly reached eastern Canada and became a serious threat to forests there. A search was quickly made for predators, such as ichneumons, which could be imported to combat it.

Another wood wasp reached Australia in about 1947. Apart from holes made by the larvae, it caused great damage because the females injected a fungus with their eggs. Several ways of killing the wood wasp are being tried. Ichneumons have been introduced, as have certain nematode worms which sterilize female wood wasps so they lay eggs packed with young nematodes, which also eat the destructive fungus.

| phylum | **Arthropoda** |
| --- | --- |
| class | **Insecta** |
| order | **Hymenoptera** |
| super family | **Tenthredinoidea** |
| genera & species | *Gilpinia hercyniae* European spruce sawfly *Cephus pygmaeus* wheat-stem borer *Urocerus gigas* horntailed sawfly *Eriocampa limacina* pear sawfly *Nematus compressicornis* palisade sawfly *Phyllotoma aceris* jerking-disc sawfly |

Caught in the act on an apple tree. **Tremex columba** drills a hole for her eggs with her ovipositor. The larvae tunnel for about two years, causing considerable damage to the wood. The pigeon tremex, as it is commonly called in America, is often parasitised by large ichneumon wasps.

# Scale insect

Some scale insects are among the most serious pests to crops, yet no family of insects has provided more raw materials for human use. Together with mealy bugs they make up a family of insects related to aphids and cicadas. The clue to their appearance lies in the two common names. All are flattened and degenerate and are covered with a secretion of wax or resin which in most forms is mealy or cottony. In addition some are covered with a scale and look like tiny limpets on the twigs of trees and bushes. Most of them are small, the largest of the family are only 1 in. long. Scale insects are found all over the world, apart from the polar regions, and some species are worldwide, having been carried about on plants or on parts of plants by man.

◁ A mealy bug blight. Hundreds of **Pseudococcus** cover a hibiscus tree. They are tended by ants who eat the sweet white secretion the white scale insects produce.

▽ Adult and young purple scale insects (× 11) **Chrysomphalus aonidium**, looking like limpets, are covered by a hard, dark, circular scale.

▷ Suffocating beauty. **Ceroplastes** suck the sap from a branch, slowly killing it, while ants eat their waxy pink secretion.

*Adult and juvenile cottony cushion scale insects (× 3) with their fluted secretions. The young are less degenerate than the adults and are not covered by the secretion which is produced as they grow.*

## Prey to plant feeders

Although ladybirds and other predatory insects are the main enemies of scale insects and mealy bugs, there are many other enemies which are, in a sense, accidental predators. These are the many insects that feed on the surface tissues of plants, chewing the tissues with their jaws. They are known to take animal food readily even though they are basically vegetarian, so they will chew any scale insects that happen to lie in their path.

## Multiple uses

The earliest recorded use made of the secretions of scale insects is of the quantities of sweet honeydew given out by the genus *Trabutina* in Palestine. This solidifies on the leaves and on the ground beneath and forms the manna on which the Children of Israel were supposed to have fed for 40 years. Also well known and used since the 16th century is the resinous secretion given out by *Laccifera lacca*. This feeds on banana, fig and other trees from India to the Philippines and Formosa. It was doubtless in use long before that, but it was first brought to the west in the 16th century and has been used in shellacs, varnishes, polishes and sealing wax, and for making inks, buttons, gramophone records, pottery, linoleum, aeroplane coverings, and electrical insulation, to name just some of the main products. This long list of uses alone underlines the enormous numbers in which this one species exists. It takes 150 000 insects to produce a pound of lac and, until synthetic products began to take its place, anything up to 90 million pounds of lac was collected each year. Another well-known product from scale insects is cochineal, at one time used in dyes, medicines, cosmetics and confectionery. The North American Indians used to make a kind of chewing gum from the wax given out by a scale insect; the Chinese used the wax from another species for making candles, and among uses made of scale insect secretions by different peoples were the beads, known as ground pearls, worn in South Africa and the Bahamas. Each bead was the bronzy cell of wax with which the immature female *Margarodes* surrounded herself.

## Degenerate insects

The greatest damage is done by female scale insects which are apt to infest vegetation in very large numbers. All females are wingless and many are quite degenerate as adults, lacking legs and eyes. The males are more normal, although some are wingless, and the others have only one pair of wings, the second pair being very small and slender with one or two hooks to fasten them to the front wings. All males, however, lack mouthparts and therefore do not feed, and they are never present in such numbers as the females. In some species there are two kinds of males, winged and wingless, which alternate from one generation to the next. In most species, however, males are rare and the females reproduce by parthenogenesis. In many species males are numerous on one host plant, rare on another.

## Devastating pests

Like all bugs the scale insects have a proboscis which is a sucking tube. In their case it is pushed into the tissues of the leaf or root of a plant, to suck up sap. This is harmful to the plant and when scale insects occur in large numbers the results can be devastating. The best-known example is of the cottony cushion scale introduced into California from Australia and New Zealand in 1868. It wiped out hundreds of thousands of orange trees in the next quarter of a century and its numbers were controlled only by introducing its natural predator, a

ladybird, from Australia. The elm scale of Europe and North America is another well-known pest. It kills the trees by sucking the sap from the undersides of branches. Some species, like the pine leaf scale, of North America, attack just one or a few types of plants. The heath scale of Britain forms galls on heaths. Others, like the mussel scale, feed on 130 different kinds of trees and bushes. The damage they do is best assessed by remembering that one female may produce 30 million offspring in a year.

## Well-protected eggs

Some scale insects lay eggs, others give birth to living young, as in aphides (page 13). In both cases the larvae are flattened and oval in outline, and therefore not easily seen on stems or leaves. At first they have the usual number of legs and crawl about actively, but in many species these are soon lost, and in all species the larvae soon settle in one spot, covering themselves with the secretions characteristic of their species. A feature of scale insects is that the eggs are not laid in the open but underneath the female's body or under the scale, or else they are covered with the cottony or mealy secretions. In some species the eggs do not hatch until the female is dead and her body protects them during the winter. In one subfamily, the Ortheziinae, each female is covered with a number of small white waxy plates and has a special wax scale covering the eggs at the end of her abdomen.

| phylum | **Arthropoda** |
| --- | --- |
| class | **Insecta** |
| order | **Hemiptera** |
| family | **Coccidae** |
| genera & species | ***Chionaspis pinifoliae*** <br> *pine leaf scale* <br> ***Dactylopius coccus*** <br> *cochineal insect* <br> ***Ericerus pe-la*** <br> *Chinese wax insect* <br> ***Eriococcus devoniensis*** <br> *heath scale* <br> ***E. spurius*** *elm scale* <br> ***Icerya purchasi*** <br> *cottony cushion scale* <br> ***Lepidosaphes ulmi*** <br> *mussel scale* <br> *others.* |

# Scarab beetle

The most famous of these beetles is the sacred scarab of Egypt. It and its immediate relatives are scavengers, and most of them are dung beetles. They collect and bury dung in a variety of ways, but the best known is by trundling a ball of it along the ground. This has led to their name of 'tumblebug' in the United States; and has also inspired the most complete and graphic account of their dung-burying behaviour by the celebrated French writer Henri Fabre. The sacred scarab is only one of more than 20 000 species in the family. Others include the May bugs (page 128) and the largest beetles in the world: the goliath beetle, 4 in. long, the equally large rhinoceros beetle, and the hercules beetle. The scarabs and dung beetles are mostly medium-sized, about ½ – 1 in. long, with heavy rounded bodies, oval or almost oblong in outline, and a bumbling flight. They are beautifully coloured in metallic hues of black, purple, blue, green, bronze or gold, usually iridescent. Their legs are short

△ Two scarab beetles share the task of rolling a ball of dung which they will later bury and eat.

and the middle joints flattened and broadened. The antennae are short but the head and thorax often bear ornamental spines or spikes.

There are dung beetles in every continent except Antarctica but the number of species in each continent varies. In Australia and South America, where the large mammals are fewer than in Africa, the number of species of scarab beetles is also proportionately smaller.

163

## Large-scale food transport

The typical scarab, on finding a pile of dung, separates a portion of it, compresses it and moulds it into a ball much larger than itself and then starts to roll it away. An inch-long beetle may make a ball 3–4 in. diameter. Taking position behind it the beetle places its hindlegs on the ball and, with its body inclined downwards and front feet pushing on the ground, it proceeds to roll the ball along. It may be joined and helped by another of its species, even one of its own sex. Having taken the load a distance, the beetle or beetles dig a hole under it until it drops down and is buried. They feed on this, eating more than their own weight in a day. Then they return to the surface for a fresh supply.

Not all dung beetles are ball-rollers. Most of them bury small portions near the place where they find the dung or drag pellets, as in the case of sheep droppings, a short way to a previously excavated hole.

## Taking care of the young

When about to breed the scarabs come together in pairs and the pattern of the dung collecting changes. The two combine to roll a large ball to a selected site where they bury it. When it is underground the female shreds the dung and moulds it into a solid pear-shaped mass, tamping its surface hard. The neck of the 'pear' is left hollow and an egg is laid in the cavity. A hole is left at the top, where the stalk of a pear would come out, and this is loosely filled, allowing air in. The adults leave the cavity, filling in the tunnel behind them as they go up to the surface. When the larva hatches it feeds on the 'pear' until only the hard outer rind is left. The larva then pupates and, when rain softens the earth above, the new beetle emerges from the pupal skin and makes its way to the surface.

The larva has complete protection in its underground larder so only a few eggs, usually 2–4, are laid in one season. Other species of dung beetles use less elaborate methods, burying smaller quantities of dung in egg-shaped, globular masses or in cylinders, and *Geotrupes*, the dor-beetle, digs a vertical shaft 8 in. deep with a plug of dung at the end. All these species lay more eggs. In a European species *Copris hispanus* the female stays underground constantly walking around the several balls of dung she and her mate have accumulated in one cavity. Each ball contains one egg and the mother works incessantly keeping the surfaces of the balls clear of moulds and sealing any cracks that may develop in them. This is because they have not been tamped and hardened as in the sacred scarab and others. Indian scarabs of the genera *Heliocopris* and *Catharsius*, for example, coat the large balls of dung with clay and bury them 8 ft down; and when these were first dug up they were thought to be ancient stone cannon balls. In spite of the care taken by such species as *Copris hispanus* the parental devotion ceases as soon as all the young beetles have hatched and have found their way to the surface.

The larvae of many scarabs and related dung beetles stridulate, and the adults of some species are also known to make similar sounds. The purpose of this is not clear.

## Enemies winter and summer

*Geotrupes stercorarius* is known in Britain as the lousy watchman because it is so often infested with mites. These push their sucking mouth-parts through the soft skin at the joints of the beetle's armour and suck blood. Larger enemies include shrews, hedgehogs and similar insect-eaters. Within the last few years it has been found that hibernating horseshoe bats wake at repeated intervals throughout the winter and fly out to feed on dung beetles.

## Doubly deserving deity

The Ancient Egyptians figured the scarab on their monuments, bas-reliefs, jewellery and seals so frequently that we can be sure it held a high place in their esteem. It seems they assumed that some gigantic celestial scarab kept the Earth revolving like the humble scarab made its ball of dung revolve. On the front of the sacred scarab the head is drawn out into a number of spines which to the Egyptians symbolized the sun's rays, giving an even greater significance to the beetle. It was also thought the beetle

▷ *The scarab beetle was held sacred by the ancient Egyptians who thought it represented the sun. This relief shows the beetle between the gods Isis and Nepthys, and surrounded by amulets—symbols of good luck.*

▽ *Head of a male rhinoceros beetle* **Oryctes nasicornis**. *For all its impressiveness the horn is relatively useless as a weapon. During a skirmish between rival males, one may lift an opponent up with the horn, carry him off, then drop him; a female may also be dealt with in the same way. This has given rise to the idea that the male may carry the female away to a suitable place for mating. However, this behaviour would be very un-insect-like.*

buried its ball of dung for 29 days and on the 30th cast it into the Nile, so rounding off the month. The Egyptians also credited the scarab with a total of 30 joints, 5 to each of its 6 legs, which is the same number as most of its relatives have; but in fact the sacred scarab has only 20.

There could have been other, even more solid reasons for deifying the scarab, such as their all-important task of sanitation, at the same time making the ground fertile. Fabre found that an inch-long beetle with a volume of $\frac{1}{4}$ cu in. buried 60 cu in. of dung a night, 240 times its own bulk, and repeated this process night after night.

| phylum | **Arthropoda** |
|---|---|
| class | **Insecta** |
| order | **Coleoptera** |
| family | **Scarabaeidae** |
| genus & species | *Scarabaeus sacer* <br> *sacred scarab, others* |

△ *Panorpa germanica on a buttercup.*

▽ *Like the adults, scorpion fly larvae are carnivorous: this one feeds on a dead elephant hawk-moth.*

# Scorpion fly

*Although scorpion flies belong to a small order containing less than 300 species they are descended from a very ancient line. The earliest known endopterygote fossils—that is, of insects with a complete metamorphosis—are of scorpion flies allied to those of the present day family Choristidae of Australia. The insect is named after the appearance of the genital organs of the males of the family Panorpidae. One well known member of this family is the common scorpion fly* **Panorpa communis.** *The genital organs at the tip of the abdomen are turned upward and forward resembling the stinging apparatus of a scorpion although they are quite harmless. Few scorpion flies are more than one inch long although the extremely long legs of some species make them look larger. Their most distinctive characteristic is the curious head, the front part being elongated to form a prominent downward-pointing beak at the end of which are the biting mouthparts. The antennae are long and threadlike. There are four slender wings with rounded ends which in many species are colourless and transparent. In some, however, they are blackish or blue-black*

*with white patches or they may even be yellowish with dark spots.*

*The members of the genus* **Boreus** *of the closely related family Boreidae of Europe and North America are only about $\frac{1}{16}-\frac{1}{4}$ in. long. Their wings are vestigial or entirely lacking and they look rather like tiny grasshopper nymphs as they crawl or hop about.*

*There are six families of scorpion flies. Two are worldwide, two are found in Australia, one is found in Europe and North America and one is limited to the New World continent. Scorpion flies are related to doodle bugs (page 70) and lacewings (page 114).*

## Beneficial insects

Most scorpion flies are considered beneficial because of their predatory and scavenging habits. They are found mainly in damp woodlands and hedgerows where they feed on small insects, dead animal matter or plant debris. The members of the genus *Bittacus* of the family Bittacidae have very long slender legs the last joints of which can snap back against the preceding joints like a trap. These legs form efficient but not very strong prehensile organs, used in catching prey as well as in holding onto a perch. Scorpion flies sometimes hang from a leaf or twig holding on with one or two feet while the other legs wave in the air ready to seize at any small insect.

## Curious courtship

Scorpion flies indulge in a curious form of courtship. The male spits out small globules of sweet sticky saliva onto the leaf where a female is sitting. While she turns to feed on this the male seizes the end of her abdomen and mates with her. It has been suggested that if she is fed in this way she will be less likely to devour the male once mating has been completed. This is a ruse used by several predatory insects, such as the empid flies, as well as by spiders, in which the predacious females are liable to kill and eat a potential mate.

The larvae of most species of scorpion fly look rather like caterpillars but are not often seen, as they burrow in loose soil or debris coming up to the surface only to feed. Like the adults they are carnivorous. They have the same kind of biting mouthparts at the end of a long proboscis, like tongs, and they take much the same food. They pupate in the ground in the burrows they have dug, the pupae moving up to the surface just before the adult insects are ready to emerge. Unlike those of any other scorpion fly the larvae of the members of the family Nannochoristidae, found in Australia, are almost certainly aquatic.

## Snow flies

As has already been said the scorpion flies in the genus *Boreus* have no wings. They live especially where there is much moss-covered ground, and on a sunny winter's day they can often be seen in large numbers crawling or hopping about on the snow and have thus earned the name of 'snow flies'. In place of wings the males have a pair of finely toothed spines and the females a small pair of scale-like lobes. They have the long antennae and long legs of most other scorpion flies but they lack the clawed genital organs at the tip of the abdomen. In spite of sometimes being called 'scorpion snow flies' they are quite harmless and live on the forest floor feeding on dead vegetation and possibly on springtails, small primitive wingless insects which also come out onto the snow when the sun shines. Being small and dark, either greenish, bronzy or black, snowflies are unlikely to be noticed except against the white background of snow. Moreover their larvae feed and pupate underground, in much the same way as those of other scorpion flies.

| phylum | **Arthropoda** |
|--------|----------------|
| class  | **Insecta**    |
| order  | **Mecoptera**  |

◁ *Hanging down to hunt.* **Bittacus** *catches its prey with its long slender legs. These form efficient prehensile organs; the last joints can snap back on the preceding joints like a trap. The scorpion fly hangs from a twig or leaf by one or two legs, the other legs being waved about until a small unwary insect passes. The prey is seized and then killed by the biting mouthparts which are almost as remarkable as the legs in that they are long and drawn out into a beak-like structure.*

# Shieldbug

*Shieldbugs are also called stinkbugs— and for good reason. They represent a group of plant-bugs comprising four families of the suborder Heteroptera. All are flattened in shape and some have an outline like that of an heraldic shield. Most are ¼—½ in. long, but the colourful red, black, orange and blue* **Oncomeris flavicornis** *of Australia, is 2 in. long. Shieldbugs are included in the great order of insects called the Hemiptera, which include the true bugs and cicadas, all of which are characterised by mouthparts formed for piercing and sucking. They also grow into adults by incomplete metamorphosis.*

*Most shieldbugs have a superficial resemblance to beetles, but these develop by complete metamorphosis, involving distinct larval and pupal stages, and they have biting mouthparts. They also resemble beetles in using the hindwings for flying and the forewings as a protective covering for the hindwings. Not all shieldbugs can fly and most of those that can, do so only in hot weather. In the shieldbugs each forewing is divided into two parts, a thick leathery basal part and a thin membranous area towards the tip. This results in the backs of these insects being broken up into patterns of triangles, which is the most noticeable feature distinguishing them from beetles.*

*Shieldbugs are mainly insects of warm climates and are most numerous nearer the tropics. For example, less than 40 species occur in Britain, many more are found on the continent of Europe, especially towards the south, and, of course, the number increases greatly in tropical Africa.*

### Useful and harmful selection

Almost all shieldbugs are found crawling about on the foliage of trees or bushes or in low herbage, and many of them are found attached to particular species of plants on whose sap or fruit they feed. The birch, hawthorn and juniper shieldbugs take their names from their food plants and the last two types feed mainly on the berries. As might be expected some of them are pests of agriculture. One of the tortoise bugs *Eurygaster integriceps* is a serious pest of wheat in the USSR and Near East. The green vegetable bug *Nezare viridula* has a world-wide distribution in the warmer countries, including southern Europe, and does great damage to beans, tomatoes and other vegetables. It is sometimes encountered in imported vegetables in Britain and other northern European countries, but does not seem to be able to establish itself in these countries.

▷ *The bright colours of Australasian* **Catacanthus punctum** *warn predators; like most shieldbugs it can emit a foul-smelling liquid.*

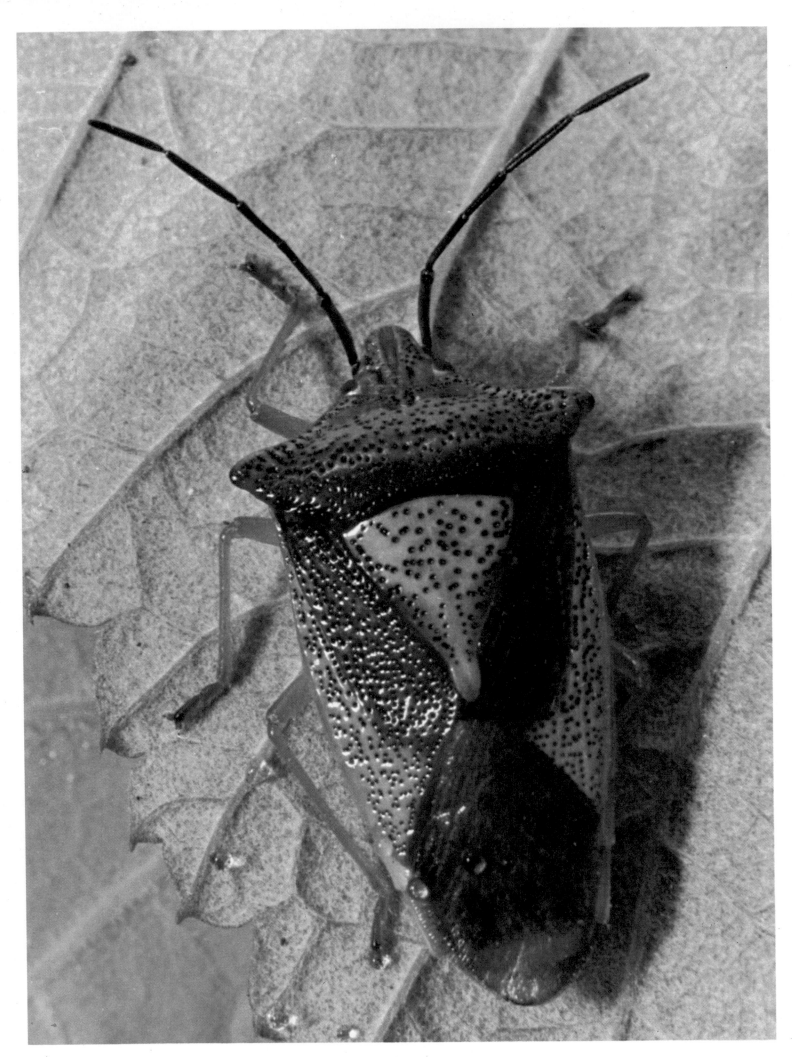

*◁ The hawthorn shieldbug **Acanthosoma haemorrhoidale** prefers the berries to the leaves; it will also feed on whitebeam and oak.*

Some of the shieldbugs are predatory and may be of service in destroying harmful insects. The North American genus *Podisus* is a useful enemy of the Colorado beetle.

## Broody shieldbugs

Shieldbugs lay their eggs either on their food plant or on the ground. The eggs are laid in batches and look rather like those of butterflies and moths. They are usually developed in the insect's body 14 at a time and the batches often comprise multiples of this number. A few shieldbugs develop their eggs in dozens and lay them in two neat rows of six, lying side by side. In many species the eggs hatch by the opening of a definite lid on the top, so that under a microscope the egg cases look like little empty barrels.

The young grow by stages, changing their skins usually five times before reaching full size. Although the development is gradual there is often a startling change in colour and pattern when the adult stage is reached. *Sehirus dubius*, an interesting species quite common in continental Europe, is variable in colour. In one form of it the young are black on the forepart of the body, and red with black markings on the hinder part. After the last skin-change the adult is at first brilliant red, but it only retains this coloration for a couple of hours; its colour then darkens until it assumes its final livery of steely black.

A number of the shieldbugs are known to brood their eggs, attending and protecting them up to the time they hatch. The parent bug *Elasmucha grisea*, which lives in birch woods, goes further than this. The female lays a batch of about 40 eggs on a birch leaf, the egg-mass being diamond-shaped and compact, the right shape for her to cover with her body, and she broods the eggs rather as a hen does, for 2—3 weeks until the young hatch. The mother and small larvae stay around the empty egg shells for a few days and then move away together, in search of the birch catkins which form the main part of their diet.

## Why stinkbug?

Many of the shieldbugs have glands from which they can eject an evil-smelling and ill-tasting fluid if molested. Anyone picking a berry and not noticing the shieldbug on it may get an unpleasant taste in the mouth. A bug held in one's fingers will usually resort to this same mode of defence, and the smell is so strong and offensive that 'stinkbug' is used, especially in North America, as an apt alternative name for the shieldbugs. Some kinds feed on fruits and berries and render any they touch inedible. The forest bug *Pentatoma rufipes* sometimes infests cherry orchards and spoils a great deal of the fruit in this way. It can be prevented from climbing up the trunks of the trees in spring by grease-banding the trunks.

Some species having this defence capacity are conspicuously coloured, usually black with white, yellow or red patterns. They are undoubtedly examples of warning coloration. By making themselves conspicuous to predatory enemies, especially birds, they derive protection from the fact that a bird, once it has tasted one of the bugs, will remember its distinctive appearance and avoid trying to eat others of the same species. The individual suffers but the species benefits.

Shieldbugs not protected in this way are preyed on by birds, especially tits, which seek out the hibernating bugs in winter. Far more serious enemies are the tachinid flies, whose larvae live as parasites inside the bodies of the developing bugs, killing them just before they reach maturity. These predators are in no way deterred by the bugs' repugnant fluids or lurid colours.

| phylum | **Arthropoda** |
|--------|----------------|
| class | **Insecta** |
| order | **Hemiptera** |
| suborder | **Heteroptera** |
| families | **Acanthosomidae** **Cydnidae** **Scutelleridae** **Pentatomidae** |

*Patterns on a leaf, **Lyramorpha** and its young. The harlequin-like young grow by stages, changing their skins several times before the adult stage.*

# Silk moth

*The silk moth (also known as the silkworm moth) used for the commercial production of silk is the mulberry silk moth* **Bombyx mori**. *It is a medium-sized, light-coloured moth of Chinese origin. Related species, belonging to the family Bombycidae, are found in eastern Asia and in Africa, but none in Europe. It is the only completely domesticated insect: none of the many strains or races of domestic silk moths could possibly fend for themselves or exist in the wild. The species is now entirely unknown in the wild state.*

*The natural food of the larva is mulberry leaves, and when it is ready to pupate it spins a thick, strong silken cocoon formed from a single continuous filament of pale yellow silk about a thousand feet long, which can be spun or reeled off as a single strand. The strains of silk moth which appear to be nearest to the ancestral form have one generation a year, passing the winter as eggs.*

### Silk moths in domestication

In the silk industry the larvae are called silkworms and the eggs 'seed'. The eggs are stored during winter at a low temperature. As soon as mulberry leaves become available they are removed to surroundings at a temperature of 18°C/65°F and this is slowly increased to about 25°C/77°F. After they hatch the larvae are kept at this temperature and feed for 42 days, changing their skins four times, each skin change involving 24 hours of inactivity when they do not feed. When fully grown they stop feeding altogether and begin to make side-to-side weaving movements with their heads. They are then given bushes to climb up and they spin their cocoons among the twigs. The cocoons are then exposed to steam or hot air to kill the pupae contained in them, before the silk is reeled.

An ounce of eggs or 'seed' will produce about 30 000 larvae and with good management they should produce 12 lb of silk, consuming a ton of mulberry leaves in the process. A silkworm increases its weight about 10 000-fold from the time it hatches to the time it is full grown.

Selective breeding has been directed towards production of larger cocoons and better silk, and also towards more docile

◁ *The beginnings of an industry. The flight-less silk moth sheds its seeds, as its eggs are called in the silk industry.*

△ *Developing the industry in the home. The newly-hatched caterpillars are transferred to boxes with strips of mulberry leaves to feed on.*

△▷ *A fully-grown larva, about 2 in. long, has retired to a corner to spin its cocoon.*

▷ *The weaving process: the larva, still visible, surrounds itself in an ever-thickening cocoon of pale yellow silk in which to pupate.*

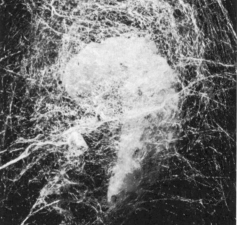

and manageable behaviour on the part of the insects. The silkworms now have no instinct to wander or hide themselves, but can be kept in open trays. As every lepidopterist knows, the larvae of all wild moths must be carefully caged in captivity. Silk moths have well-developed wings, but they cannot fly. Domestic silk moths of this kind have existed in China for many hundreds of years, so it is no wonder that the wild stock became extinct there. In the early period of domestication there must have been frequent accidental crossings of wild moths with escaped or discarded domestic ones, with the result that the wild stock became degenerate through genetic contamination of characters useful in a domesticated insect but dangerous or fatal in a wild one. It is surprising that the ancestral silk moth has not survived in some part of

central Asia remote from the Chinese silk-producing areas. It may still survive and is yet to be discovered by entomologists.

## Keeping your own silk moths

Silk moths are less interesting to keep and breed than other moths and butterflies, but are easier to manage due to their inbred docile nature. The eggs are best obtained in the spring when the mulberry tree comes into leaf. If they are purchased before this, they should be kept in a refrigerator until the time is convenient for them to hatch. Then, the tiny caterpillars should be put in a cardboard-box lid or tray made of newspaper with mulberry leaves cut into strips; this provides more leaf edges from which the larvae can feed. They will do well at the usual indoor temperature of a house, but will grow rather more slowly than

the commercially reared stocks. Slightly wilted lettuce leaves can be used as food for silkworms, but they will not thrive as well as on mulberry, and if started on mulberry leaves, they will not take to lettuce.

When a larva stops feeding and stays in one place on a leaf or the bottom of the tray, it is preparing to shed its skin. If it is disturbed or moved during this period, which lasts about 24 hours or so, it will probably die. It is well worth keeping the caterpillar under constant observation in order to watch the actual process of skin shedding, which is very interesting and takes only a few minutes.

When they reach full size, about 2 in., keep a lookout for larvae that get into corners and weave their heads about with a searching movement. Each one should be put separately in a rolled and pinned paper cone, and will then proceed to spin its cocoon. After about ten days gently shake the cone; if it rattles there is a pupa inside the cocoon. This is the time to reel the silk off. A cocoon from which the moth has hatched is useless because the moth cuts its way out of the cocoon at one end and so severs the continuous thread of silk in many places.

To reel the silk, take the cocoon and pull off all the loose outer fuzz until the cocoon is smooth and firm, then soak it in warm water for half an hour. Then by gently pulling away the silk from the sides a few strands at a time, you will soon find yourself pulling off a single strand, which is the continuous thread. This can be wound on to a reel or piece of cardboard. It is a good idea to reel the silk from several cocoons simultaneously as this gives a bigger yield at the end. Leave the cocoons tumbling about in the water as you wind. Not all the silk will come off because the first spun, innermost part of the thread is more firmly glued and felted together than the rest of the cocoon. If you have been skilful you will end up with a loop or skein of lustrous pale yellow silk. Treated in this way the pupae are not injured and can be kept until the moths hatch from them.

## The history of silk
The silk industry originated in China, and the traditional story is that it was first given official recognition by the wife of the Emperor Huang Ti about 2140 BC. The secret appears to have been guarded for over 2000 years, but in the 3rd century AD it reached Japan by way of Korea. A little later cultivation of silkworms was established in India, and as it started in the northeast, in the Brahmaputra valley, it seems likely that it came overland, direct from the Chinese Empire.

Around the beginning of the Christian Era silk from Asia was one of the most costly items in the trade between the Roman Empire and the Orient. The Emperor Justinian (c482–565) reserved the monopoly of the silk trade for himself and sent two Persian monks, who had resided in China, to bring the means of producing silk to Constantinople. They succeeded in doing so, smuggling the eggs in a bamboo tube in 550 AD. From that time on the silk industry was established in Europe, and it was widely spread in the 8th and following centuries by the conquering Arabs or Moors, who carried it both east into Asia Minor and to western Europe. In Europe, France and Italy have always been the leading producers.

In recent years natural silk production has suffered severely from competition with artificial fibres, and now the only important industry is in Japan, where it is kept alive by a combination of hard work and efficient factory production methods.

## Other silk moths
None of the other species of *Bombyx* has been used with any success for silk culture, but several moths quite unrelated to the mulberry silk moth, and belonging to the emperor and atlas moth family Saturniidae (see page 20) have formed the basis of minor silk industries in India, China and Japan. The most important of them are the producers of tussore and muga silk, large moths of the genus *Antheraea*. These include *Antheraea pernyi*, *A. mylitta* and *A. paphia* and the Japanese species *A. yamamai*. Another Indian silk producer is the Eri silk moth *Attacus ricini* a relative of the giant atlas moth.

In recent years these large and beautiful moths have become an object of interest to dealers in Europe and North America who import them and sell the eggs or pupae to naturalists to rear for the pleasure of seeing the magnificent moths and their extraordinary larvae. Locally available food plants can generally be found for them: most species of *Antheraea* will feed on oak. Many other exotic Saturniids are imported and all are known collectively as giant silk moths, though most of them have never been concerned in any way with the production of usable silk, and they bear no affinity or resemblance at all to the real silk moth.

| phylum | **Arthropoda** |
|---|---|
| class | **Insecta** |
| order | **Lepidoptera** |
| family | **Bombycidae** |
| genus & species | *Bombyx mori* |

*The end of the line: a continuous strand of lustrous, pale yellow silk surrounds the larva. The cocoon is exposed to steam or hot air to kill the larva before it hatches by cutting its way out through the single strand of silk. The silk is then carefully wound off onto a reel.*

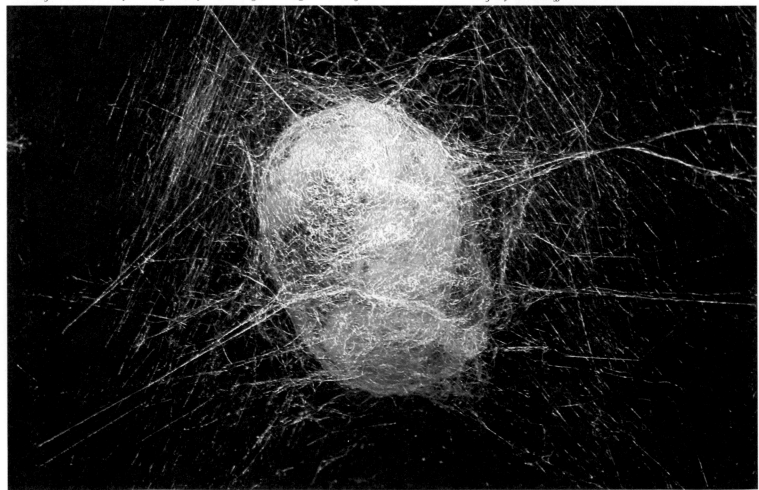

*A South African skipper, **Coliades forestan***

# Skipper

These butterflies are characterised by their rapid darting flight, which has given them their name. They form a family of butterflies, the Hesperiidae, which are quite distinct from all other butterflies, and there is some doubt whether they should be called butterflies at all or whether they are 'in between' butterflies and moths. They fly by day, however, have clubbed antennae and are generally more like butterflies than any of the Lepidoptera that are traditionally regarded as moths. The antennae almost always have a slender extension beyond the club, which is usually hooked. The wing venation is primitive and the body thick and hairy. The head is wider than the thorax and the eyes are large and protruding.

Most of the skippers are small, but three groups of them have a wing span of about 3 in. Two of these inhabit the American tropics and subtropics, the other is found in eastern Asia. Of the former, the members of the genus **Pyrrhopyge** have extremely rapid and accurately controlled flight and are among the hardest of all butterflies to catch. Included in a separate family, the Megathymidae, **Megathymus** is a very peculiar genus of skippers confined to Mexico and the southern United States. In India and southeastern Asia some species of **Gangara** and **Erionota** also have a 3in. wing span. They are unusual, as they fly at dusk and sometimes even come to artificial light after dark, just like moths.

Brown and tawny yellow are the most usual colours displayed by skippers, but some of the tropical species have bright metallic blues and greens. The species of **Argopteron**, found in South America, have the underside of the wings a solid metallic golden colour.

## Flimsy silken cocoons

Skippers' larvae taper at both ends and are in most respects primitive in structure. They fasten leaves together with silk to form a shelter to live in, and pupate in rather flimsy silken cocoons or in rolled leaves fastened with silk. Many of the larvae feed on grasses. One of the large Asian species *Erionota thrax* lives on the leaves of banana and is sometimes abundant enough to damage the plants. The larvae of the peculiar American genus of giant skippers *Megathymus* lives on yucca plants.

## Moth or butterfly?

One of the features that distinguishes butterflies and moths is the presence in most of the latter of a peculiar structure on the underside of the wings that joins the fore and hind wings together. The component on the hind wing is called the frenulum and that on the forewing is called the retinaculum. For some reason unknown it often differs in male and female and is often the easiest way of telling a male moth from a female moth.

In Australia, the home of primitive survivals, skippers make up about one third of the continent's butterfly fauna. One of them, known as the regent skipper *Euschemon rafflesiae*, is unique among the Lepidoptera because the males have a well-developed frenulum and retinaculum and the females lack both. It is a beautiful insect, metallic blue with white spots on the wings and marked with bright red on the head and tail. In appearance, habits and life history it is clearly a skipper, and it demonstrates in an illuminating way the fact that there is really no clearly marked dividing line between moths and butterflies.

Those who like to compare human inventions with what is found in animals see in the frenulum and retinaculum the equivalent of the hook-and-eye fastening. The comparison is reasonable, if we may judge by the words of Dr EB Ford, in his book *Moths*, where he says of them 'this structure was invented at an early stage in the evolution of the Lepidoptera'.

| class | **Insecta** |
|---|---|
| order | **Lepidoptera** |
| family | **Hesperiidae, Megathymidae** |
| genera & species | ***Pyrrhopyge, Megathymus, Gangara, Erionota, Argopteron, Erionota thrax*** banana skipper ***Euschemon rafflesiae*** Regent skipper ***Hesperia comma*** silver-spotted skipper ***Ochlodes venata*** large skipper ***Pyrgus malvae*** grizzled skipper ***Carterocephalus palaemon*** chequered skipper others |

◁△ *A small skipper* **Thymelicus sylvestris,** *its clubbed antennae clearly establishing its claim to classification as a butterfly.*
◁ *With their long probosces — tongues — uncoiled, a grizzled skipper (left) and a blue suck up moisture around a dead leaf.*

*The outsize proboscis of the convolvulus moth.*

*Convolvulus moth feeding from the nectar of night-flowering sweet tobacco.*

# Sphinx moth

*Sphinx moths—also called hawk moths—make up the family Sphingidae, large, thick-bodied moths found throughout the world. Most of the 900 species are tropical and only 23 are known in Europe.*

*Sphinx moths have a thick, torpedo-shaped body, long narrow forewings, small hindwings and large eyes. The tongue or proboscis is well developed and sometimes remarkably long. The larvae are stout and usually have a spike or horn at the hind end of the back. Many of them when molested rear up in a characteristic way which reminded early entomologists of the Sphinx of Egypt, which explains the name of the family.*

### Swiftest of insects?

The sphinx moths all have powerful, well controlled flight and most of them can hover like hummingbirds when feeding from flowers. The little hummingbird moth looks remarkably like a tiny bird as it hovers in front of flowers; honeysuckle, jasmine and valerian are particularly attractive to it. Some of the larger species are probably the swiftest fliers of all insects, but since almost all of them fly by night their speeds are extremely hard to measure. The fastest speeds so far measured for insects are for dragon-flies. Speeds of 45, even 55 mph have been reported for some dragonflies, but sphinx moths have even thicker and more muscular bodies and their wings and flight muscles are more efficiently designed than those of dragonflies. So although only 33 mph has been recorded for a sphinx moth the chances are that they achieve greater speeds than this.

A sphinx moth found at rest usually cannot fly immediately because its body tem-perature is too low. If one of them is disturbed when at rest it will rapidly vibrate its wings for a minute or more, and then take to the air. This raises its internal temperature to the point at which it can fly.

As might be expected, the sphinx moth's powerful flight is associated with migratory habits. The convolvulus hawk is a huge grey moth with a very wide range, from Africa and Europe across Asia to Australia. It breeds in Africa and regularly flies north-wards, crossing the Alps with ease and appearing in Britain in late summer and autumn; it has even been recorded from Iceland. The equally large and more heavily built death's-head hawk is seen far less frequently in Europe, but occasionally flies from North Africa in swarms.

### Feeds on potato poisons

Sphinx moth caterpillars feed on the leaves of plants and trees and the various species usually confine their attention to a fairly narrow range of plants related to each other.

*Head-on view of the large elephant hawk **Deilephila elpenor**.*

*Elephant hawk after emergence from pupa.*

*Through the last barrier: out comes the adult moth after the completion of pupation.*

*Sphinx moth heavyweight, the death's-head moth gets its name from the eerie 'skull' pattern on the back of its thorax. These buccaneer moths plunder beehives of their honey.*

Both their Latin and English names often indicate the food plant, as in poplar hawk moth, lime hawk moth and privet hawk moth. The huge caterpillar of the death's-head hawk, 5 in. long, feeds on plants of the family Solanaceae, most of which are poisonous to us and other animals. Potatoes are one of these and at one time the caterpillars were common in potato fields, but spraying against blight has made them very rare. If you do find a death's-head caterpillar, remember that the pupa requires warmth if it is to produce a moth. The pupae cannot survive in the open in northern Europe, so even when the caterpillars were more common they lived in vain, never completing their life history.

The caterpillars of many sphinx moths are big enough to look rather like snakes. Some tropical species have false eyes and other markings on the front part of the body and these, with appropriate movements and postures, give the caterpillar a vividly snakelike appearance which is probably effective in scaring off hungry birds, as are the conspicuous 'eyes' on the fore part of the elephant hawk moth caterpillar.

Most of the sphinx moth caterpillars pupate underground in an earthen cell, but a few, including the two elephant hawks, spin an open-mesh cocoon among debris or under herbage on the surface of the ground. In those species in which the proboscis is greatly developed it is contained during the pupal stage in a curved or coiled sheath at the front of the pupa. This is present in the pupa of the privet hawk and is very conspicuous in that of the convolvulus hawk.

### Adults suck nectar

Almost all of the adult moths feed on nectar, hovering and probing the flowers with the long tubular proboscis, which is coiled like a watch-spring when not in use. That of the convolvulus hawk is extraordinary: when fully extended it is about 4 in. long, and can take nectar from flowers, such as those of tobacco plants, with very long corolla tubes.

This species has, however, by no means the longest tongue of all sphinx moths. In 1862 the English naturalist Charles Darwin noticed that there was an orchid native to Madagascar, with its nectaries situated at a depth of 10–13 in. No insect was known that could reach them and so act as a pollinator, and Darwin predicted that a sphinx moth would be found that could do this. In 1903 just such a moth was discovered in Madagascar with a proboscis 11 in. long. It was named *Xanthopan morgani* and received the appropriate subspecific name *predicta*.

The death's-head hawk has a short, stiff proboscis, quite unsuitable for delicately probing flowers, and it robs bees' nests and hives of their honey. Most modern hives are designed to prevent its entry, but the beekeepers of a century and more ago knew it well, and the early entomologists called it

*Putting a bold face on it: tropical sphinx caterpillars have disconcerting 'eye' patterns.*

*One of the most striking and attractive sphinx moth caterpillars is that of the privet hawk **Sphinx ligustri**, looking like a cross between a pantomime horse and a heraldic monster.*

△ *Poplar moth laying eggs. The following sequence shows the development of another prominent hawk — **Acherontia atropos**, the death's-head.*

△ *The last moments in the egg; inside the shell the head and jaws of the infant caterpillar can be clearly seen as it prepares to break out.*

△ *Take it slowly: out comes the head followed by the front segments.*
▽ *A last look at the old home? Not at all — this is its first meal!*

△ *Progress quickens with the front legs out and getting a good grip.*
▽ *Leave no litter: a methodical nibble round the edge of the shell.*

*Narrow-bordered bee hawk **Hemaris tityus**.*

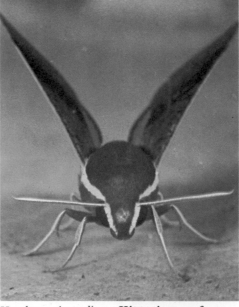

*Handsome Australian—**Hippotion scrofa**.*

*Living up to its name: lime hawk on lime leaves.*

the 'bee tyger'. Its modern name is based on a rather fanciful resemblance in the markings on its thorax to a human skull. Another curious feature of it is the ability to squeak quite loudly, both as a caterpillar and as a moth. The caterpillar stridulates, but the adult moth squeaks by forcing air out through an opening at the base of the proboscis. Beekeepers long ago suggested the squeaks quieted the bees, who took it to be their queen squeaking, so making it easier for the moth to take their honey. In recent years it has been possible, using very small microphones, to listen to the queen bee.

## Fake eye trick

When mounted in a collection the eyed hawk seems one of the most beautiful of British hawk moths. The elegantly shaped forewings are marbled in shades of violet-grey and on each of the pink and ochreous hindwings is a sharply drawn blue-and-black 'eye'. However, an eyed hawk moth sitting at rest, with the hindwings covered, looks very like a chance arrangement of curled-up dead leaves. If discovered by the sharp eyes of a searching bird and pecked, it immediately reacts by lifting the forewings and revealing what appears to the enemy to be a pair of lurid, staring eyes of a size to suggest a cat or an owl. Experiments have been carried out in which a bird was persuaded to attack an eyed hawk, and the bird always started back in alarm. The 'eyes' seem to be essential, if the hindwings are rubbed and the pattern obliterated the moth will go through the same performance as usual, but the birds will always kill and eat it. The two bee hawks, with partly scaleless and transparent wings, look very much like bumblebees and so may gain some protection.

| phylum | **Arthropoda** |
|---|---|
| class | **Insecta** |
| order | **Lepidoptera** |
| family | **Sphingidae** |
| genera & species | ***Acherontia atropos*** *death's-head sphinx* |
| | ***Deilephila elpenor*** *elephant sphinx* |
| | ***Hemaris fuciformis*** *broad-bordered bee hawk* |
| | ***H. tityus*** *narrow-bordered bee hawk* |
| | ***Herse convolvuli*** *convolvulus hawk* |
| | ***Laothoe populi*** *poplar hawk* |
| | ***Macroglossum stellatarum*** *hummingbird hawk* |
| | ***Mimas tiliae*** *lime hawk* |
| | ***Sphinx ligustri*** *privet hawk* *others* |

*Like the aptly-named hummingbird hawk moth the elephant sphinx looks amazingly like a small bird as it hovers in front of a flower to feed.*

*Incredible birth: this **Bactrododema aculiferum** has just hatched from its tiny egg shell, having first pushed off the top of the egg, the operculum.*

# Stick-insect

*Stick-insects are today more commonly kept as pets than probably any other insect. They are sluggish and live among the foliage of trees and bushes or in low-growing herbage, relying for protection on their resemblance to their surroundings. They are always long and very slender, usually with smooth bodies, although some species are spiny. The larger kinds look like twigs and may be green or brown; the small species and the young of the larger ones are usually green and resemble the midribs of leaves or the stems and blades of grass. Some are very large and the Asian species **Palophus titan** is the longest living insect, sometimes exceeding a foot in length.*

*Some stick-insects have wings but many are wingless, a condition that enhances their resemblance to twigs.*

*Stick-insects, with the leaf-insects, comprise an order, the Phasmida, once included in the Orthoptera together with the grasshoppers, mantids, cockroaches and others, but this group has now been divided into several separate orders. About 2 000 species of phasmids are known, the majority being found in the Oriental tropics. One species, **Bacillus rossii**, is native to Europe, ranging as far north as central France. Two kinds of stick-insects from New Zealand have become established in the extreme southwest of the British Isles: the prickly stick-insect **Acanthoxyla prasina** in Devonshire and on Tresco in the Scilly Isles, and the smooth stick-insect **Clitarchus**

hookeri also on Tresco and on an island off County Kerry, Eire. The so-called laboratory stick-insect **Carausius morosus** is an Oriental species often kept in schools and laboratories and more generally as a pet. It is a very easy insect to keep and breed and can be fed on leaves of privet, ivy or lilac. It cannot, however, survive out of doors through the cold winter in northern Europe and it is important that it is kept inside during this period.*

## Dazzle and hide

Most stick-insects feed and move about only at night. By day they remain motionless and often appear to be 'feigning death'. In fact they pass into a hypnotic or cataleptic state during the day. When they are in this condition the limbs can be moved into any position and will stay there, rather as if the joints were made of wax. Some of the winged species are active by day. In many of these the hindwings—which are the only ones developed for flying—are brightly coloured but are entirely concealed when the insect is at rest. If it is disturbed the wings are suddenly unfolded and the resultant flash of bright colour is confusing to a searching predator. Then, when the wings are closed again, the bright colour suddenly disappears, so the exact position at which the insect has alighted is effectively concealed. This is a well-known protective device and is called 'flash coloration'.

All stick-insects are plant eaters and occasionally they become numerous enough to defoliate areas of woodland. In Australia there are two species which occur in swampy areas but also feed on agricultural crops where they sometimes cause serious damage.

## Eggs like raindrops

All the phasmids lay rather large, hard-shelled eggs which look very like seeds. In some cases they closely resemble the actual seeds of the plant on which the insect feeds. The eggs are dropped by the females at random. The tap of falling eggs is often heard from the cages of captive stick-insects and a North American species *Diapheromera femorata* is sometimes so numerous that the sound of thousands of its eggs falling on the forest floor is as loud as that of rain.

Several hundred eggs are usually laid, a few each day, and they take a long time to hatch. Those of the laboratory stick-insect hatch in 4—6 months at ordinary room temperatures, but this can be speeded up to 2 months by extra warmth or retarded to 8 months by cold conditions such as an unheated room in winter. The eggs of the Madagascar stick-insect *Sipyloidea sipylus* will hatch in as little as one month if kept at 24°C/75°F—27°C/80°F, but at lower temperatures may lie dormant for up to a year.

The young look very like the adults in all except size and, in the case of the winged species, in lacking wings, which develop gradually during growth.

Many stick-insects reproduce by parthenogenesis, that is the females lay fertile eggs without mating. In these species the males are usually rare; in cultures of the laboratory stick-insect, for example, they number about one in every 4 000 females. Of the two New Zealand species already mentioned, the male of the prickly stick-insect is unknown and possibly does not exist. In New Zealand, males of the smooth stick-insect are almost as common as females, but no males have been found in the small British colonies of the same species and the eggs develop without fertilisation.

179

## Odd colours

The laboratory stick-insect occurs in various colour forms ranging from green to shades of brown. The colour is determined by green, brown, orange-red and yellow granules in the cells of the surface layer of the skin. Pure green individuals cannot change colour, but the others regularly change, becoming darker at night and paler by day. The change is brought about by movement of the pigment granules within the cells. Brown pigments may move to the surface and spread out, making the insect dark in tone, or they may contract into lumps and move to the inner part of the cell so the insect becomes pale. The orange-red granules can also move about in this way, but the green and yellow ones are unable to move about at all.

The alternation of colours becomes established by exposure to normal day and night, but once established it continues as a rhythm governed by the time cycle of 24 hours. A stick-insect conditioned to normal light change and then kept in permanent darkness will continue for several weeks to change colour every 24 hours, just as it did before. If it is kept in the dark by day and exposed to artificial light at night a reversed rhythm will develop in response to these conditions. This also persists for some time when the insect is kept continually in darkness with no light at all.

| phylum | **Arthropoda** |
| --- | --- |
| class | **Insecta** |
| order | **Phasmida** |
| families | **Bacteriidae** |
| | **Phasmidae** |

△ *Remarkable camouflage: head of* **Bactrododema aculiferum** *with its ear-like projections looking very like broken-off twigs.*
▷ *Rare shot: 7-inch* **Clemancatha regale**.
▽ *Precarious upside-down mating of* **Gratidia spp**. *The female holds onto the stem as the male clasps her — both beautifully camouflaged.*

△ *The beauty of this Japanese swallowtail* **Papilio maackii** *is indescribable, but it is easy to see how this butterfly got its common name.*

# Swallowtail

*Swallowtail butterflies get their name from the 'tails' on their hindwings which recall the forked tail of the swallow. They all belong to one family, the Papilionidae, but not all members of the family have 'tails'. There is, however, another feature which is more peculiar and is found in all members of the family. It is the possession by the larva of a protrusible Y-shaped organ, the osmeterium, situated just behind the head. It is usually orange or yellow and is normally hidden but can be suddenly pushed out if the larva is disturbed. It is connected with glands in the thorax of the caterpillar and when pushed out it disseminates a strong scent, which varies with the different species. This organ is also present in the larvae of the Apollo butterflies (page 15) which although members of the Papilionidae are not usually regarded as swallowtails.*

*The 600 species of swallowtails are found everywhere except in the Arctic and Antarctic regions. Most are tropical: North America has 20 – 30 species, Europe only five or six. Britain has one,* **Papilio machaon,** *which has a very wide range from western Europe through the whole of temperate Asia to Japan, and is represented by numerous races or sub-species. One of these,* **Papilio machaon britannicus,** *is the form native to Britain*

and is now confined to the Norfolk Broads.

*Another species* **Graphium podalirius** *is called the 'scarce swallowtail' on the strength of a few specimens captured in southern England; it is common in France, Germany and other parts of Europe.* **Papilio hospiton** *is remarkable in being entirely confined to Corsica and Sardinia.*

### Gathering at 'salt licks'

Swallowtails range widely in their choice of habitat; races of a single species may have markedly different habitats. The British race of the common swallowtail, for example, is strictly confined to marshes and fens; the French subspecies is an inhabitant of open country, especially chalk downs. In the tropical rain forest many swallowtails fly high in the treetops and some of the early collectors used to overcome the difficulty of catching them by shooting their specimens down with dust-shot. Another feature of butterfly life in the rain forest, in which swallowtails feature prominently, is the habit of gathering in closely packed crowds on sand or gravel beside rivers and streams. If these butterflies are carefully watched they can be seen to be eagerly sucking up moisture with their long tongues. It is now known that most of these congregations gather where the urine of animals that come to drink at the water-side has soaked into the sand. Organic salts appear to be the attractant, and butterflies also gather at mineral springs and wet ashes. A curious feature of these congregations is that they consist entirely of males; the females feed

only on the nectar of flowers and seldom come down to ground level.

### Snake-like and poisonous caterpillars

Swallowtails have a typical butterfly life history. The larva feeds on the leaves of plants, the food plant of the common swallowtail being milk parsley and fennel in the wild; it can be reared on the leaves of carrot. One group of mainly tropical species confine themselves to the poisonous creepers of the genus *Aristolochia*. The poison taken in from this plant renders the caterpillars inedible to birds and as it persists in the pupa and the perfect insect, these also are protected against predators.

Another curious form of protection in many swallowtail larvae is the eye-spots on the forepart of the body, which give the larva a snake-like appearance. In the tropics tree snakes are among the most deadly enemies of lizards and small birds, and merely to be reminded of a snake may well be enough to alarm them and so discourage attack. The scent of the osmeterium is undoubtedly defensive in function, and may be directed against parasitic wasps and flies.

The swallowtail pupae are attached by the tail to a leaf or twig. They face head upwards and are supported by a silk girdle.

### Mimicry

Many swallowtails profit by looking like other more unpalatable species. The poisonous *Aristolochia*-feeding species, already mentioned, are protected from predation because they have a distinctive appearance, and birds quickly learn to recognise them as poisonous. In the course of evolution other swallowtails, acceptable as food for birds, have come to resemble the poisonous species and so gain protection by 'flying false colours'. One of the best-known mimetic species is the Oriental *Papilio memmon*. The male is a large blue-black butterfly with little tendency to vary, but the female appears in a number of varieties or forms, some with 'tails' others without, each of which is a copy of one of the species of *Aristolochia* swallowtails. From the fanciful idea that he possesses many different wives. *P. memmon* is called the 'Great Mormon' by collectors in India and the Far East.

Another famous mimic is the African *P. dardanus*. Here again only the females are mimetic (the males are plain black and pale yellow), but they appear in a bewildering multiplicity of forms all of which mimic, not other swallowtails, but distasteful butterflies of various other families. In most parts of Africa a female *dardanus* will almost always prove to be a mimic of some poisonous species occurring in that particular locality. Only in Ethiopia and Madagascar is this butterfly non-mimetic; in these regions the females resemble the males.

### Glorious butterflies

The swallowtails include some of the most brilliant and magnificent of all butterflies. Finest of them are the birdwing swallowtails of southeast Asia, New Guinea and tropical Australia. These are described in an article under Birdwing (page 27); it can

recalled here that the female of one of these, *Troides alexandrae* from New Guinea, has a wing-span up to 10 in. and is the largest butterfly known. *Drurya antimachus* of tropical western Africa is another enormous swallowtail, orange-brown with black markings and spanning 8 in. Here the male is considerably larger than the female, a condition contrary to that seen in the large birdwings. The species that swarm on contaminated sand in tropical Asia are mostly kite swallowtails of the genus *Graphium*, many of which are black barred or spotted with brilliant green or blue. The Bhutan glory *Armandia lidderdalei* of Assam and the royal swallowtail *Teinopalpus imperialis*, found in the same region, both have three tails on each hindwing, and both are sufficiently beautiful and remarkable to be known by English as well as Latin names. The small Asian *Leptocircus* have tails longer than the span of the forewings and their flight is as quick and strong as that of a hawk moth. No real idea of the splendour and diversity of swallowtails can be given unless a book is devoted to them.

△ *Complete metamorphosis: the swallowtail exposes its blue-banded wings to the daylight and gets ready to make its maiden flight; the empty chrysalid is still held by a silk girdle.*

| phylum | **Arthropoda** |
|--------|----------------|
| class | **Insecta** |
| order | **Lepidoptera** |
| family | **Papilionidae** |

▽ *A peculiar habit of male swallowtails is to gather at places where an animal has urinated beside a river or stream and to suck up the moisture-containing organic salts from the sand. In this such gathering are three species of kite swallowtails. The females feed on the nectar of flowers.*

# Tachina fly

Tachina is from the Greek for swift. Although the family name for tachina flies is Tachinidae an alternative sometimes used is Larvaevoridae, or larvae eaters. This describes the flies even better because all pass their larval stage as parasites in the larvae of other insects including butterflies and moths, bees and wasps, bugs and grasshoppers. Some also parasitize spiders, centipedes and woodlice.

Adult tachinid flies are not easy to tell apart except by those who make a special study of them. They are mostly the size of houseflies and bluebottles, are coloured grey, brown or black and are very bristly. Many have a characteristic attitude at rest, with the wings half open and so at right angles to each other. They also have a fussy, inquisitive sort of flight that has been compared to a small dog questing to and fro to pick up a scent. This, indeed, is exactly what the females are doing when they are searching for victims in which to place their offspring. Tachinid flies are closely related to the Calliphoridae, the family including blowflies (page 34) and bluebottles, and members of the two families can only be distinguished by reference to obscure details of anatomy.

Tachinid flies have a world-wide distribution and are very numerous. The adults fly actively, some in sunshine, others in shady places. Many feed on nectar, helping to pollinate the flowers they visit. One species **Dexiosoma caninum** a long-legged, bristly yellow and brown fly, is often to be seen in summer in woods in Britain sitting on bracken, and seldom anywhere else. They are of great importance as a natural check to the numbers of the insects which they parasitize. Many of them are not at all particular in their choice of host and deposit their eggs or their larvae in a wide range of insects' larvae belonging to many different orders. Some, on the other hand, seem to have narrow preferences. The species of one genus **Crocuta,** for example, confine their attentions mainly to the 'leatherjacket' grubs of craneflies.

△ A tachina fly investigates a moth's cocoon.
▽ Life and death in the insect world: a tachina fly larva emerges from the body of a moth caterpillar that was about to pupate.

## Several ways, only one end

The female tachinas lay their eggs in four different ways. In some species they scatter the eggs over plants in places where they are likely to be eaten, accidentally with its normal food, by a caterpillar or some other plant-eating insect. These eggs must be minute and very numerous to be swallowed undamaged; one female may lay up to 6 000 eggs. These hatch in the intestine of the host. In other species the eggs are laid in places likely to be frequented by the host. They hatch quickly into active larvae which bore their way into the skin of any suitable insect that comes along. While waiting, these minute larvae are protected from drying up by a covering of hard plates. The third way is for the female to lay her eggs on the skin, or stick them to the hairs, of the host. When the larvae hatch they bore through the skin into the host. In the fourth method the female tachina punctures the skin of the host and lays an egg which hatches as it is laid, so that a newly hatched larva is easily introduced into the host's tissues.

The last method comes very close to the way in which the ichneumon wasps insert their eggs into the host by means of an ovipositor. Tachinas which use the third and fourth methods lay relatively large eggs, up to 200 in number. In some tachinids only a single larva develops inside each host.

Inside the host the tachina larva is faced with the problem of how to breathe. When very small it can absorb oxygen through its skin from the host's blood, but later it must make a hole in the victim's skin or perforate one of its main tracheae or internal breathing tubes, to gain direct access to air. The parasite then attaches its rear end to the breathing hole so made.

### Parasite eats parasite

Among the enemies of tachinid larvae are other insect parasites. An ichneumon wasp may lay its eggs in a host already infested by a tachinid larva. Usually the ichneumon grub eats the tachina larva as well as devouring the vital organs of its doubly parasitized host. There are even some chalcid wasps (page 48) that can only develop in a tachina larva already feeding inside a caterpillar.

### Biological control

Tachinid flies, as well as chalcid and ichneumon wasps, are the living tools for biological control so often advocated as a desirable alternative to the widespread use of insecticides. Some have already been cultured artificially to control the numbers of insect pests, especially those that have been introduced into parts of the world where they are not native. Two European species of tachinids, *Compsilura concinnata* and *Sturmia scutellata*, have been imported into North America to help control the numbers of the gypsy and brown-tail moths, themselves both accidental introductions from Europe, and pests of trees. Control of the brown-tail has been particularly successful.

| phylum | **Arthropoda** |
|--------|----------------|
| class | **Insecta** |
| order | **Diptera** |
| family | **Tachinidae (Larvaevoridae)** |

▽ *A gruesome sight: tachnid larvae devour a* **Ceratogyrus** *spider which was initially paralysed by a pomalid wasp as a host for her eggs, but a tachina fly laid her eggs on the spider before the wasp could bury it.*

# Termite

Termites, often incorrectly called white ants, resemble true ants in their way of life, although less so in appearance, and the two are very distantly related. Ants are related to bees and wasps and termites are near relatives of cockroaches. Most of the 1 700 species live in the tropics, but a few are found in southern Europe and 55 in the United States. They are absent from northern Europe and are the only important order of insects not represented in northern Europe.

Fossil termites date back at least 250 million years. One very primitive genus **Mastotermes**, surviving in Australia, is very similar to a cockroach in the form of

its hindwings and also in the way the female lays her eggs, these being arranged in groups of 16 and 24 in two rows.

Termites and ants often resemble each other in being social insects living in colonies numbering hundreds or thousands of individuals. In both, the colonies consist of large numbers of 'workers' and 'soldiers' which are non-reproductive, and a few, or even just one, reproductives, the 'kings' and 'queens', which are the parents of all the others and may be very long-lived. In both, the non-reproductives are wingless, but the functional males and females have wings and fly in swarms from the nest. Before founding new colonies, or re-entering existing ones, they break off their wings. Both ants and termites have the habit of trophallaxis or mouth-to-

Harmonious community (above). A winged reproductive termite, two soldiers and two white workers: **Calotermes flavicollis** ($\times 15$).

Nest of activity (right), harvester termites **Trinervitermes trinervoides**. Note the long snout on the head of each soldier which can secrete a toxic liquid to repel enemies ($\times 6$).

mouth feeding. The 'royal' individuals are fed entirely in this way. Termites and ants are also alike in having some species that cultivate fungi underground for food.

The life histories of the two insects are, however, very different. In ants there are distinct larva and pupa stages and the larvae are helpless and have to be fed by the workers. In termites the young hatch as minute replicas of the adults and do not change their form as they grow. They

*are first fed by trophallaxis, but soon learn to feed themselves and can take an active part in the work of the nest long before they are fully grown. Ant workers and soldiers are all non-reproductive females; in a termite nest all the castes are composed of both sexes. The queen ant mates only on her nuptial flight and is not joined by the male when she founds a colony. The king and queen termite, on the other hand, cooperate in founding the colony and live together in the nest, mating at intervals and being fed by the workers.*

### A termites' nest

One of the most intensively studied of all termites is the black-mound termite *Amitermes atlanticus*, investigated by Dr SH Skaife in the Cape Province of South Africa.

The nests consist of black, rounded mounds, 2 ft or less in diameter. The nest is made of a cement of the termites' faeces. It is watertight and very strong; a pickaxe or hammer is needed to break it. When broken open it has a sponge-like appearance, consisting of innumerable cells an inch or less in size connected by openings just big enough for the termites to creep through. The inhabitants of the mound live in a perpetual warm, moist fug, with 5—15% of carbon dioxide always present in the air. A man confined in such an atmosphere would soon lose consciousness. The temperature varies far less than that of the outside air. In extremes of heat and cold the termites huddle to the centre; when the sun re-warms a chilled nest or the summer dusk cools an overheated one, they crowd to the periphery. The king and queen black-mound termites are not confined to a 'royal

chamber' as in some termites, but move about from cell to cell through temporary enlarged openings made by the workers.

The outside crust of the nest consists of sand grains stuck together with faecal cement, and any break in it is quickly repaired with this same material. During the spring months of August and September the nest is enlarged about an inch all round.

### Division of labour

The queen is $\frac{1}{2}$—$\frac{3}{4}$ in. long, depending on her age, which may reach 15 years. The king measures only $\frac{1}{4}$ in. Both had wings and flew at one time, but they broke their wings off when founding the colony. In addition to these 'primary reproductives' there are 'secondary reproductives', individuals of both sexes with rudimentary wings, which can produce fertile eggs if the primary pair meet with an accident or become infertile with age. They are stimulated to do so by special feeding, but are never as prolific as a primary queen, and her place is taken not by one but by a number of female secondaries. In some nests a third, wholly wingless type of reproductive is found, but these are rare. The non-reproductives are either workers or soldiers. These go out at night for food, which in this species consists of decaying vegetation. The soldiers are simply a bodyguard against attack by ants, the arch-enemies of termites. They cannot even eat the natural food themselves but are fed, as the reproductives are, by the workers. A black-mound termite nest may last 40—50 years.

## A two million termite tower

The more primitive kinds of termites, including *Mastotermes* and the family Kalotermitidae, live in wood, excavating galleries and chambers in it and feeding on it. Their natural role is to break up fallen timber and return it to the soil, but when they turn their attention to the timbers of buildings or to stored wooden crates and boxes they work havoc and are a serious problem in all tropical regions. Some of the more advanced types of termites make immense nests, towering as much as 20 ft above the

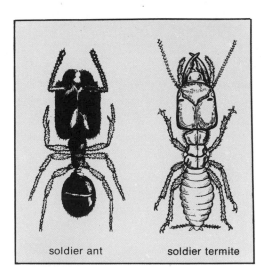

soldier ant      soldier termite

ground and containing perhaps a couple of million inhabitants. When ground is being levelled in tropical Africa for cultivation or building, the large termite nests sometimes defy even bulldozers and have to be destroyed with explosives. In northern Australia the remarkable compass termite *Amitermes meridionalis* makes termitaria 10—12 ft high. They are shaped like a flat wedge with its edge uppermost and stand in an exact north and south position, with the flat sides facing east and west. It is not certain how this arrangement benefits the termites, or how they manage to build with such exact orientation, although it has been suggested that the termites build to make full use of the sun's warmth.

Some termites make underground nests with little or no visible superstructure, others build carton nests of chewed wood pulp in trees, very like wasps' nests.

## Need help to digest

Termites are primarily vegetarians. Those that live in wood and feed on it have microscopic protistans in their intestines which break down the cellulose of the wood, enabling the termites to digest it. The subterranean and mound-building termites subsist on various kinds of vegetable matter,

◁ *Comparison between a soldier ant* **Pheidole instabilis** *(left) and a soldier termite* **Archotermopsis**. *Both social insects, ants and termites live in colonies, each member or caste of the colony with a specific job. The soldiers, as their name implies, defend the colony. The most notable difference between these two soldiers is that the abdomen of the ant is waisted.*

▽ *Rulers of the colony, king and queen termites,* **Macrotermes natalensis,** *the longest lived members of the society. The king looks a mere weakling beside the queen who has her abdomen swollen disproportionately with eggs. Once fertilised she does nothing but lay eggs, the king staying with her, which is unusual among social insects, to help expand the new colony (approx × 2).*

living, dead and decaying. The fungi which are invariably present in decaying wood or leaves are probably important to many if not most termites, and some cultivate fungi in large chambers underground, just as the leafcutter ants do (page 119).

In a termites' nest of the black-mound type nothing is wasted. The bodies of the dead are devoured and excrement is eaten over and over again until every particle of nourishment is extracted from it. The paste that remains is used for building.

## Free-for-all feast

When the winged males and females swarm out of the nests every insectivorous creature is their enemy. Birds, small mammals, lizards, toads and even some sensible opportunists among humans have a feast. Only a tiny fraction of the fragile fluttering princes and princesses live to become kings and queens. A few highly specialised mammals, such as anteaters, pangolins, the aardvark, and aardwolf, can break into the termitaria using strong claws and sweep up the termites with long sticky tongues. The termites' arch-enemies are, however, ants; a permanent state of war exists between the two insects. Termite soldiers are really specialised ant fighters. Some have powerful jaws which can snap an ant in two. Others have no jaws but instead the head is drawn into a spout-like snout from which an intensely sticky liquid can be squirted that effectively gums up any ant it touches. In spite of their seemingly effective armament, however, no termites are a match for ants in open battle, and they rely on the massive defences of their nests for their continued existence.

## The long-lived queen

Most people know what a queen termite looks like—a great sausage-shaped egg-factory. Queen termites are unique among insects in growing after their last moult. The skin between the abdominal segments stretches, leaving the original segmental coverings as brown islands on the pale, bloated back. The queen black-mound termite can live 15 years; others, of larger and more highly developed species, may live longer. In Australia, in 1872, the top of a large termite nest had to be broken off to allow telegraph wires to pass over. In 1913 and again in 1935 the nest was examined and was found to have a flourishing population, although the broken top had not been renewed. No secondary reproductives have ever been found in nests of this species *(Eutermes triodiae)*, so the original king and queen, founders of a nest already 14 ft high in 1872, were probably still alive in 1935. It is possible the original population had died and the nest had been recolonised, but it was more probably a case of an insect living as long as a man.

| phylum | **Arthropoda** |
| --- | --- |
| class | **Insecta** |
| order | **Isoptera** |

# Tiger moth

Not all tiger moths have markings like a tiger but all their caterpillars are hairy and so are called woolly bears. For this reason the whole family is known as the Arctiidae, from the Greek **arctos**, meaning a bear. This family also includes the footman or ermine moths which lack the very bold markings and coloration characteristic of the true 'tigers'. In continental Europe the moths themselves are called 'bears' rather than 'tigers', by reference to their larvae.

The most typical members of the group belong to the genus **Arctia**, one of which is the common and gaudy garden tiger moth **Arctia caja**. The garden tiger is 1 in. long with a wingspan of nearly 3 in., the males being slightly smaller. The forewings are cream coloured with bold dark brown to black markings and the hindwings are red with large black spots with deep blue centres. Not all garden tigers have markings recalling those of tigers but they are very variable and in some individuals the markings are tiger-like. This is even more true of other species of tiger moths. So variable are the markings that no two individuals of a species are quite alike, and on any individual the pattern of the wings will be different.

Another common species is the cream-spot tiger *A. villica. A. quenseli* lives in the Arctic and also high up in the Alps and *A. hebe* is a southern European moth. The Jersey tiger **Euplagia quadripunctaria** and the brilliantly coloured scarlet tiger

△ Cloaked in the long brown, black and white hairs that have given it its name, a garden tiger moth caterpillar nibbles a nettle leaf. These larvae are less fussy than most in their diet and will eat almost any succulent plant leaves —a few will eat leaves of woody plants.

**Panaxia dominula**, another European species, are sometimes placed in a separate family, the Hypsidae.

A few true tigers, including **Arctia caja**, are found in North America, but the characteristic tiger moths of the region belong to the genus **Apantesis**, which is almost confined to that continent. These occur in great variety and on the forewings of almost all of them they display a distinctive pattern of pale streaks on a dark background.

## Wandering ravenous larvae

The caterpillars of most tiger moths feed on low-growing plants of various kinds, and that of the garden tiger is content with almost any fairly succulent leaves that it encounters, such as weeds and cultivated plants. When they are ready to pupate, these very hairy larvae, and also those of the allied ermine moths, always wander for several hours before settling down to spin their cocoons. They may often be seen crossing roads and, for caterpillars, they travel remarkably fast. The moths themselves also run over the ground and do so fast enough to be sometimes mistaken at first glance for a mouse. Often a kitten will play with one, so drawing its owner's attention to the moth. The wandering habit of the caterpillars was noticed in England as much as 400 years ago and this is recorded in Topsell's *Book of Serpents*, published in 1608. At that time they were called 'beare-worms' and also 'palmer worms', by reference to the palmers or mendicant friars, 'which doo wander and stray hither and thither and consume and eat up that which is none of their owne'—a description which fits the caterpillars equally well. In the United States the name 'palmer worm' is given to *Ypsolophus pometellus*, a relative of one of the clothes moths which also wanders and sometimes causes considerable damage to fruit trees.

The pupa is enclosed in a cocoon of silk in which larval hairs, shed at the time of spinning the cocoon, are mixed.

The hairs of these larvae may cause some irritation, but do not have the poisonous and urticating properties of some of the other hairy caterpillars, notably those of the tussock moths, Lymantridae. They are, however, sufficient to deter almost all birds from eating them, the exception being the cuckoo, which swallows them without hesitation, ejecting the hairs from time to time in the form of pellets.

*Idly resting on a leaf, a male garden tiger moth of the darker variety, displays the individual and distinctive brown and white markings on its wings.*

## Artificial tiger moths

The extremely variable wing markings of the garden tiger has led to unusual effects. The forewings are occasionally entirely white or entirely dark brown, and the blue-black spots on the red hindwings may be almost absent or may spread, so the red is masked altogether. The moth is easy to rear as the larvae can be fed both in summer and winter on cabbage, and will breed continuously, generation after generation, if kept warm. Some of the more unusual individuals have appeared only in captive broods and so are really artificial productions, like fancy pigeons or breeds of cattle. Since their characters are usually inherited according to the precise laws of heredity, these varieties are of value in the study of genetics.

## Stinging moths

The gaudy colours of the tiger moths play a definite part in protecting the insects from birds, as they advertise the fact that the moth is distasteful or even poisonous. If a resting garden tiger moth is molested or irritated it raises its forewings, displaying the bright red hindwings, and at the same time exposes a fringe of red hairs behind the head. These are not empty threats for a substance resembling the poison acrylycholine is secreted in glands in the thorax and another dangerous poison can be extracted from its body fluids. If a tiger moth is roughly handled the sharp spines or spurs on the legs may become contaminated with the poison and act as a sort of sting, but only people with very delicate skin are affected.

| phylum | **Arthropoda** |
| --- | --- |
| class | **Insecta** |
| order | **Lepidoptera** |
| family | **Arctiidae** |

*A warning from a female garden tiger moth as she exposes the fringe of red hairs behind her head and displays her boldly marked hindwings.*

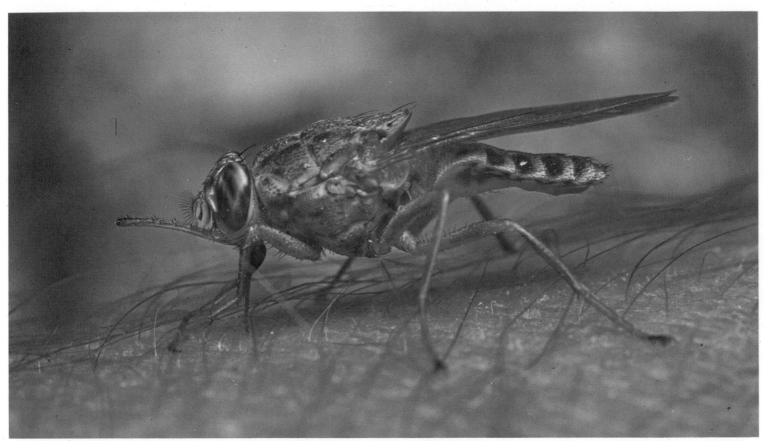

△ *Before:* **Glossina morsitans** *inserts its proboscis into a man's arm . . .* ▷ *and after: gorged with blood. Tracheae show through distended abdomen.*

# Tsetse fly

*Tsetse is the name, probably of Bantu origin, of a genus of flies,* **Glossina**, *endemic to Africa south of the Sahara. Tsetse flies are notorious as carriers of the disease known as nagana in cattle and horses and also of sleeping sickness in man. They feed by piercing the skin with their mouthparts and sucking the blood of the mammals, birds and reptiles. Unlike mosquitoes in which only the female sucks blood, both sexes of the tsetse fly feed in this way. About 20 species are known. They are a little larger than houseflies but they differ more especially in the way they fold their wings, scissor-like, over their backs when at rest.* **Glossina** *belongs to the same family as the housefly and is quite closely related to the common European biting stable fly* **Stomoxys**. *The mouthparts of both these are modified to varying extents for piercing and sucking, in the same way as those of the tsetse fly.*

### Blood-sucking flies

Each species of tsetse fly has its own habitat preference. *Glossina palpalis*, the most important carrier of sleeping sickness, prefers dense forest bordering rivers and lakes. It lives largely on the blood of reptiles such as crocodiles and monitor lizards, and also on that of the marshbuck or sitatunga antelope; it also bites people. In open forest or savannah *G. morsitans* and some related species depend upon game animals for food. These are the carriers of the nagana cattle disease and also of one type—the Rhodesian form—of sleeping sickness.

### Almost a marsupial fly

Compared with the breeding habits of other insects, those of the tsetse fly are peculiar. Most insects lay large numbers of eggs to compensate for the heavy mortality suffered by their young, which are usually larvae, fending entirely for themselves, without the power of flight to escape from their enemies. The tsetse flies produce their offspring rather as the mammals do. The female develops only one egg at a time and it hatches inside her body. The larva stays inside the mother and is nourished by a secretion produced by glands which open by a nipple near the larva's mouth. They are, in effect, milk glands. The female maintains the supply of this fluid by constantly taking meals of blood. The larva breathes by means of a pair of black knobs which reach to the exterior through the opening of the female fly's oviduct. When it is fully grown the larva is extruded or 'born'; it falls to the ground and immediately pupates in the soil. A female tsetse fly may live for about 6 months and give birth to not more than 12 larvae during her life. This breeding rate is slower than that of the rabbit!

### Tsetse flies and disease

Sleeping sickness is a terrible disease which runs a slow course, from a few months up to several years, and ends in coma and death. It is caused by infection from single-celled organisms, or protistans, known as trypanosomes. The transmission of the disease is cyclical. That is to say, the trypanosome undergoes part of its cycle of development in the blood of the vertebrate host and another part in the fly. There are two distinct forms of sleeping sickness. That known as the Gambian form is caused by *Trypanosoma gambiense*, carried mainly by *Glossina palpalis*, and the Rhodesian form, caused by *Trypanosoma rhodesiense*, which is conveyed mainly by *Glossina morsitans*. Rhodesian sleeping sickness first appeared in 1909 in Rhodesia and is more severe, often causing death in a few months.

### Effective control

Gambian sleeping sickness can be controlled by felling riverside vegetation or by catching and trapping the flies in paths and clearings. The disease retreats as a matter of course as the increase of human population leads to agriculture replacing waterside forest. As tsetse flies find their victims by sight, dark-coloured models of large mammals, crudely made and therefore cheap to set up, can be used to lure them into open country. They settle on the model and can then be destroyed. They can also be persuaded to deposit their larvae on prepared sites where the pupae can then be destroyed. The flies are attracted by dark colours, while white clothing is effective in repelling them. Fly screens on buildings, vehicles and river boats are also useful. The disease can be cured if diagnosed in good time, and several months' protection against infection can be given by injection of a drug called pentamodine. In Rhodesia, wholesale slaughter of game animals has, not surprisingly, been effective in controlling the Rhodesian sleeping sickness.

The cattle disease nagana is far more difficult to control. Several kinds of trypanosomes are involved, *Trypanosoma brucei* and *T. congolense* are the most frequent, being carried by several species of tsetse flies which attack a great variety of animals, birds and reptiles. In these circumstances extermination of wildlife is impracticable as well as being horrible to contemplate.

▽ *Marshy savannah—ideal breeding grounds for* **Glossina**. *They feed on the abundant game, such as these red lechwe, which become disease reservoirs.*

## Why they walked

In the early exploration of Africa by white men it was not always possible to use horses or mules for transport. The familiar picture is of the white explorer walking in front, followed by a long string of porters with boxes and bundles on their heads. This was because of the tsetse fly. Moreover, the impossibility of keeping cattle in large areas of Africa has led to their remaining un-populated by people to whom cattle are not a food source, but a status symbol.

Efforts are now being made to persuade the pastoral Africans to abandon their miserable cattle and to make intelligent use of the indigenous animals, which are im-mune to nagana. The deeply rooted tradi-tion of cattle breeding will, however, be hard to eradicate.

A rather unconventional attitude towards the tsetse fly has been well expressed by Professor VB Wigglesworth in his book *The Life of Insects*: 'But there are those who con-sider the tsetse fly to be the one great saviour of the African soil. By ignorant procedures, or by ruthless exploitation for short-term gains, so much of the soil surface of this planet has been squandered, and vast areas of Africa reduced to semi-desert, that it is possible to regard any insect which bars the way, and conserves the soil for the more enlightened cultivators of the future, as a true friend of man.'

| phylum | **Arthropoda** |
| --- | --- |
| class | **Insecta** |
| order | **Diptera** |
| family | **Muscidae** |

△ *Upper surface of a pinned specimen of **Chrysiridia madagascarensis,** a brilliant urania moth.*
▽ *Magnificent from all aspects: the underside shows similar colouring — an unusual moth feature.*

▽ *Production of iridescent colours in moth and butterfly scales through interference by thin plates. The detail shows sections across the scales; 'urania type' left, 'morpho type' right.*

# Urania moth

*In Greek mythology Uranus was the husband of the Earth goddess and the father of the planet Saturn. The scientist who called a genus of moths **Urania** was almost certainly moved by the thought that he was dealing with a heavenly being living on earth. The name was first given to New World moths but it has been extended to include all the moths of the family Uraniidae. They are almost entirely limited to the tropics. Some are large, conspicuous day-flying moths, brilliantly coloured and bearing 'tails' on the hindwings like those of the swallowtail butterflies (page 182), which the urania moths greatly resemble in appearance.*

*The genus **Urania** is centred on tropical America. The South American **U. leilus**, like most of the moths of this genus, is brilliantly coloured iridescent green and blue with a long tail and broad white fringes. It has a slender body and a wingspan of 3 in. The largest and most brilliant member of the family is **Chrysiridia madagascarensis** of Madagascar which has been called the most magnificently coloured of all animals. Its wings are black, banded with metallic green which changes to blue and gold according to the angle of the light and the hindwings have a patch of glowing copper and purple, and long white fringes around their tailed and deeply scalloped margins. As well as being so spectacular this moth is a classic mystery: why is it in Madagascar when its nearest relatives seem to be the South American uranias rather than any African or Asian moths?*

*In the Indo-Australian region the species of **Nyctalemon** and **Alcides** are similarly 'swallow-tailed' and some are beautifully coloured with bands of pale blue, green and yellow. The common **Nyctalemon patroclus** of India is banded with brown and white and may be seen sitting on trees and buildings with its wings outspread, as if the whole group of moths were spread out in a display cabinet.*

## Dazzled into ignorance

It seems almost as if the very brilliance of these moths has taken the collectors' minds off their habits and life histories. Except that the caterpillars feed on leaves and the moths fly by day, little more seems to be known. The females tend to lay eggs on shrubs and bushes of the *Euphorbia* type.

The caterpillars are very diverse in shape and appearance. That of *Chrysiridia* has black spatulate spines and in the northern Indian species *Epicopeia polydora* the caterpillar is covered with white cottony filaments. When the caterpillars pupate they spin a loosely woven silken cocoon. Possibly another reason why so little can be said about the life histories of these moths is that study has been concentrated on the colours of their wings.

## Structural coloration

Iridescent or metallic colours that in nature change with the angle of the light are always known as structural colours. This implies that they are not due to pigments which absorb certain wavelengths and reflect others, but to very minute structures which refract and reflect the different wavelengths in different directions. In the wings of butterflies and moths two types of structural coloration are recognised, both depending on 'interference'. This is the physicist's term for colour effects produced when two or more very thin layers or films of a substance are separated by a medium of different refractive index. The 'rainbow colours' shown by a film of oil on water afford an instance of this. The brilliant metallic colours on the wings of some butterflies and moths are produced by interference structures in the scales, and two types are recognised, the 'morpho type' and the 'urania type'. In the former the longitudinal ridges on the scales have extremely minute plates or lamellae projecting from their surfaces (see page 140). In the urania type, named after the moths under discussion, either the upper or the lower part of the scale is thickened by a number of superimposed layers actually lying in the thickness of the scale and not on ridges standing up out from it. Although the morpho type is named after a butterfly and the urania type after a moth the two types are not characteristic of butterflies and moths respectively, for the glorious bird-wing swallowtail butterflies, for example, have the urania type of coloration, rather than the 'morpho type'.

| phylum | **Arthropoda** |
| --- | --- |
| class | **Insecta** |
| order | **Lepidoptera** |
| family | **Uraniidae** |

△ *Specimen of* **Urania leilus**, *a day-moving species that flies faster and is more brilliantly coloured than most butterflies.*
▽ *In complete contrast,* **Nyctalemon patroclus** *from New Guinea exhibits the sombre colouring more associated with moths.*

# Vanessids

*The Vanessids include some of the most colourful butterflies in the northern hemisphere, and some of these have a wide distribution. The scientific name, **Vanessa**, is now restricted to the Red Admiral, although this species, and all the others here included in the popular name Vanessids, are in the same family ( Nymphalidae). Vanessids have the front pair of legs reduced in size, only the rear two pairs being used for walking. They are fairly large butterflies, with a powerful flight. Most of the species resident in northern Europe pass the winter hibernating as butterflies, others are continuously brooded in the subtropics and migrate northwards in summer. Their caterpillars bear an armature of branched spines and the pupae, or chrysalises, which are suspended by the tail, are ornamental with shining metallic spots. It was the ornamentation of these pupae which led the early butterfly collectors to call them aurelians', from the Latin **aureus,** golden. 'Chrysalis' has a similar derivation from the Greek chrysos also meaning golden.*

*Species of Vanessid are found on all continents. Generally, they are large powerful fliers. Many of the tropical species feed on ripe fruit or even on the rotting carcass of a dead animal.*

## Peacock

This beautiful butterfly ranges from Britain eastwards to Japan. It is resident in Britain and spends the winter hibernating in dark sheltered places, often in attics and outhouses. It is quite easy to breed peacock butterflies, by keeping them in a cage in a cool, dark room for the winter. They can then be 'tamed' before releasing them in the spring, so they will remain in the garden and will come to be fed on sugar-water. They have only one generation a year, and the habit of hibernation results in the butterfly having an unusually long life in the winged state. A peacock butterfly in captivity lived for 11 months. Its food plant is nettles.

## Red Admiral

The red admiral is the popular name for a butterfly which has several subspecies. One found in Europe, Asia and the Canaries, is the familiar European one. Formerly it was believed to occur in the United States but a distinct subspecies occurs there. This is found from Canada to Mexico and on some West Indian Islands and has been introduced to Hawaii. There is even one distinct species of Red Admiral which is known only from Hawaii. Other species of Red Admiral are found in India and the Far East.

## Map butterfly

There are many species of Nymphalids known as Map butterflies from the appearance of the pattern on the wings. The European Map butterfly is widespread in France and elsewhere in Europe. Attempts to introduce it to Britain have failed. It is remarkable in being represented by two distinct seasonal forms. Unlike most vanessids it overwinters as a pupa, and the butterflies which hatch in May are chequered tawny and black and look rather like fritillaries. The larvae from the eggs of these spring butterflies feed and grow rapidly, pupate and produce in July a generation of black-and-white butterflies totally unlike their parents. The length of day during the larval stage determines which form the mature butterfly shall assume. By exposing the caterpillars to long or short 'days', using artificial light, successive generations of either form can be bred. Its food plant is entirely nettles.

## Camberwell Beauty

This butterfly is known as the mourning cloak in North America. It is, like the red admiral, distributed all over the northern hemisphere, and it also goes down the Andes, in South America. In spite of its wide distribution it is a great rarity in Britain. It appears to need the severe continental winter to induce proper hibernation. It feeds on willow, poplar and birch.

## Small tortoiseshell

This gay little butterfly ranges right across the Eurasian continent to Japan. It is one of the commonest species in Britain and can be seen in gardens throughout most of the spring and summer as it goes through two generations in a year. The butterflies of the second generation hibernate and reappear in spring. Its food plant is nettles.

## Large tortoiseshell

Up to the first two decades of this century this butterfly was not uncommon in southern England, but it has suffered a decline and is now by far the rarest of the resident vanessids in Britain. It is still occasionally seen in Essex and Suffolk and is common in central and southern Europe. Its food consists of elm foliage.

△ *Mourning cloak—a vanessid that hibernates as an adult, feeding on the sugar-rich sap from trees when it emerges in early spring.*
△ ▷ *Bird's eye view of a small tortoiseshell.*
▷ *The most widespread butterfly in the world— the painted lady. In the spring it migrates in vast numbers from North Africa to Europe.*
◁ *The rich-hued vanessid of European summer— each year the red admiral flies north from the Mediterranean to lay its eggs.*
▽ ◁ *Peacock butterflies on a spray of* **Buddleia,** *a favourite food plant of adult butterflies.*
▽ *The tattered look of the comma provides excellent camouflage when the wings are folded.*

## They taste with their toes

As already mentioned, all the nymphalid butterflies (vanessas, fritillaries, emperors and others) are 'quadrupeds', the forelegs being stunted and not used for walking. Those of the males have only two terminal joints and are brush-like. In the females these legs are more slender with four terminal joints and are only sparsely haired. They are used as sense organs, the end joints serving as organs of taste. A red admiral can distinguish, by touching with its forefeet, between pure water and a sugar solution $\frac{1}{200}$ of the strength required to be detected by the human tongue.

## Spare the nettles

Farmers and people obsessed with the idea of 'tidiness' wage a relentless war on nettles, spraying them ruthlessly wherever they grow. But nettles should be allowed to grow in places that are not needed for cultivation or pasture. Five of the vanessid butterflies described here depend on nettles for their larval food. If those who aim to exterminate this plant had their way we should see much fewer gaily coloured butterflies.

## Comma butterfly

The recent history in Britain of this very attractive butterfly is in curious contrast to that of the large tortoiseshell. Up to about 1920 it was confined to a small area in South Wales, but about that time it began to spread over southern England and the Midlands and has maintained this wider distribution. Like the other resident British vanessids it hibernates as a butterfly, but remains in the open in woods and hedges, sheltering under leaves instead of seeking shelter in natural hollows or buildings. When its wings are closed the coloration and irregular outline make the butterfly look like a withered leaf. Without this the butterfly would never survive the hunting of winter-hungry birds. It goes through two generations in the summer and the larva feeds on nettles and elm.

## Painted Lady

This is known as the thistle butterfly in North America. It has the distinction of being the only butterfly with a world-wide distribution, without the formation of any well defined races or subspecies. The reason for this is that the urge to migrate is so powerful and persistent in this butterfly that its populations are subject to constant mixing, which of course prevents the formation of local races. In Britain and northern Europe the painted lady is a summer migrant of the same type as the red admiral. The main breeding ground of the European painted ladies is North Africa, and travellers there have witnessed the hatching of thousands of pupae among the sand dunes and the start of the butterflies' massed flight towards the Mediterranean. Its food plant is thistles.

| phylum | **Arthropoda** |
| --- | --- |
| class | **Insecta** |
| order | **Lepidoptera** |
| family | **Nymphalidae** |
| genera & species | **Aglais urticae** *small tortoiseshell* **Araschnia levana** *map butterfly* **Nymphalis antiopa** *Camberwell beauty, or mourning cloak* **N. io** *peacock butterfly* **N. polychloros** *large tortoiseshell* **Polygonia c-album** *comma* **Vanessa atalanta** *red admiral* **V. cardui** *painted lady or thistle butterfly, others* |

# Vapourer moth

The most distinctive feature of the vapourer moths is the great difference between the males and females. The males are active little moths, with a wingspan of just over 1 in. They fly mainly in sunshine, although they are recorded as coming to an artificial light at night. Most of the females, and certainly all those of the European species, are wingless and look like fat six-legged spiders, and they are so inactive that they never leave the cocoons which enclose their pupae. The larvae feed usually on the leaves of various trees and bushes, but that of one European species lives on heather.

The name, Vapourer, was first given to the species **Orgyia antiqua** in 1782. A vapourer then was the term for a braggart or a tongue-wagging talker. The male of the vapourer moth is reddish brown and almost the only decoration on its wings is a white eye-spot on the rear of the forewings; there is no white mark at the tip of the wings. There is nothing to boast of in this, so the name may have been suggested by the male moth's fluttering flight.

The vapourer is one of the tussock moths and its common name was later given to related species, such as the scarce vapourer and the heather vapourer. There are other related species in temperate Asia and a closely related North American species is the white-marked tussock moth.

△ *Confined for life: the common vapourer female lays her eggs on her cocoon. Her life history is simple — she develops and mates in her cocoon, lays her eggs on it and then dies.*

## Wind-blown caterpillars

The common vapourer moths hatch from the pupae in late summer. The females remain in their cocoons where the males seek them out, guided by their scent. Even dead and preserved females have been known to attract males into a room with an open window. Having mated the female lays her eggs on the surface of the cocoon and then dies. The young larvae are covered with very long hairs and have the habit, in common with many small caterpillars, of letting themselves down on silken threads when alarmed. They are then easily blown about by the wind, like thistledown, and may travel long distances. This is, in fact, the only means of dispersal they have, apart from the larva's limited powers of crawling, since the female is completely sedentary.

## Male and female caterpillars

The grown larvae are prettily coloured, and ornamented with tufts and strands of hair. If a cocoon covered with eggs is found and the larvae are hatched and reared in captivity a curious activity will be seen. About half of them reach maturity and pupate while the rest feed for about ten days longer and grow to a much larger size before spinning their cocoons. Then, on opening one of the earlier cocoons and one of the later their respective pupae will be seen to differ both in size and appearance.

The smaller ones are males and the larger ones females. This is one of the rare instances in which the sex of a caterpillar can be recognised. The males are the first to appear after pupation. The females, however, begin to emerge long before the last of the males, so the time lag is less marked than it was in the pupating stage.

## A grisly cradle

The three European species show an interesting sequence in the degree to which the females become inactive. The female common vapourer comes right out of the cocoon and lays her eggs on its outside. The female scarce vapourer lays them between the inner and outer layers of the cocoon, while the female heather vapourer stays

right inside the cocoon for mating and dies there as well, her eggs overwintering in her dead, dried-up body. In a South African species *Bracharoa dregei*, closely related to the vapourer moths, the female behaves rather like that of the heather vapourer, but her eggs hatch soon after mating and the larvae make their first meal of their mother's still-living body.

The North American white-marked tussock moth is similar to the European vapourer in appearance and habits. It is sometimes a minor pest of trees and shrubs. In a Japanese vapourer the male is a normal vapourer moth but there are two forms of the female, one fully winged and resembling the male but larger, and one with vestigial wings.

## Why no wings?

There are a number of species of moths with wingless females, but in almost all cases they are species in which mature moths emerge in winter. The winter moth, a notorious pest of orchards, is an example. It has been suggested that if the females of such species had wings, winter gales might blow them far away from the place where they lived as larvae, perhaps even out to sea, where they would perish.

No such explanation can be given for the vapourer females, and the reason for their wingless condition remains a mystery. All that can be said is that there is a tendency for the females of all tussock moths to show a reluctance to fly. The female gypsy moth, for example, never flies although she is fully winged, and the larvae of gypsy moths are known to be dispersed by wind like those of the vapourers. It is of interest that the Japanese vapourer has both winged and wingless females.

| class | **Insecta** |
|---|---|
| order | **Lepidoptera** |
| family | **Lymantriidae** |
| genera & species | *Orgyia antiqua* common vapourer *O. ericae* heather vapourer *O. leucostigma* white-marked tussock *O. thyellina* Japanese vapourer *O. recens* scarce vapourer others |

△ *Bizarre but beautiful: the caterpillar of the common vapourer moth displays its ornamental tufts and strands of hair. When handling this larva care must be taken as the hairs can cause severe skin irritation.*
◁ *The sluggish female and winged male common vapourer moths on their cocoon. The male's only attributes are the white eye-spots on his wings. They occur practically over the whole of Europe, and also in northeast Asia Minor, Armenia, Siberia and North America.*

# Velvet ant

Velvet ants are some of the biggest frauds in the animal kingdom. Although called ants they are, in fact, solitary wasps. Their common name is due to the marked difference between the male and female. The female is wingless and is therefore forced to run about over the ground. The male is winged and so attracts little attention among other wasps that fly around.

The bodies of velvet ants are covered with a pile of short velvet-like bristles, often patterned in black, bright orange

and scarlet. Even the antennae are covered with these short hairs. The 3 000 species are all much alike in colour, and most of them live in the hotter, drier parts of the world, and especially in America. A few live in temperate latitudes, even including northern Europe. All velvet ants are parasitic on the larvae and pupae of other insects, including bees and wasps. There are even velvet ants that parasitize other solitary wasps, the hunting wasps, that themselves prey on other insects. Some of the desert species have a thick covering of long whitish hairs. The smallest velvet ant

*Mutilla lilliputiana* is $\frac{1}{8}$ in. long and the largest, **Dasymutilla occidentalis**, of the southeastern United States, is 1 in. or more long and is known as the cow-killer or mule-killer. The so-called large velvet ant of Britain **Mutilla europaea** is only about $\frac{1}{2}$ in. long. In many species the male is nearly twice the size of the female, but in three of these species the females are slightly smaller than the males.

▽ *Wasp parasitzes wasp: a South African velvet ant lays her eggs in the nest of a mud-dauber wasp; on hatching the larvae will eat the host's eggs. (Approx × 15.)*

## Well armed and defended

Velvet ants are equipped for entering the nests of bees and other wasps; they are not only armed but armoured. They have unusually thick and hard outer coverings and entomologists report having difficulty in pushing a steel pin through the thorax of a dead velvet ant when adding a specimen to their cabinet. The males are without a sting and can be handled with impunity. The female, however, has a long and formidable sting, although the power of its venom has often been exaggerated. There is no reason to suppose, for example, that it could cause the death of a large quadruped such as a mule or cow. The female can, however, sting the hand painfully, if handled carelessly, and it is presumably lethal to the insects, such as bumble-bees, whose nests the velvet ants parasitize.

Both male and female of the large velvet ant make a squeaking sound by stridulation, using a file-and-scraper type of organ which is situated about halfway along the upper surface of the body.

The female velvet ants are usually encountered running actively on the ground near the nests of the species which they victimise, or they may be found actually in the nests if these are opened up. The males visit flowers and are generally noticed only by entomologists with specialised knowledge.

## Rough mating

In temperate regions males and females appear and mate in spring. Professor HM Lefroy, in describing the mating of tropical species, spoke of the males as powerful insects. When one finds a female he 'seizes the female by the thorax and flies off; on some convenient spot he mates with her, clasping her firmly to him by his forelegs and standing erect on the others . . . in the frequent intervals the male shook the female with a twisting motion as we would shake a bottle whose contents we desired to mix.'

## Feeds on honey store

After mating, the female runs about, probably covering considerable distances, until she finds an established bumble-bees' nest, or the nest of whichever kind of insect she battens upon. Then she enters. She is well equipped to resist any attempts to evict her, and remains in the nest, feeding on the bees' store of honey, and eventually she lays her eggs in the pupal cells or cocoons of the bees, one egg in each cell. The larvae from these eggs feed on the host pupae, then they themselves pupate, coming out later as adult wasps. In temperate latitudes they pass the winter as pupae in the bees' nest, which is abandoned by the bees at the end of the summer.

There is a record of a bumble-bees' nest dug out of the ground containing 76 velvet ants and only two bumble-bees. This is probably an abnormally high number but it illustrates how effective the female velvet ant

must be in coping with the efforts of the female bumble-bee, the rightful owner of the nest, to drive her out.

## Coat for coolness

The female 'velvet ant' wasp, by her appearance, tricked the ordinary person into giving her the misleading common name. The behaviour of both the females and the males made it difficult for scientists to study them. As a result not a great deal is known about them, and nobody seems to have carried out precise experiments to test why they should have such unusually hairy bodies. We can only guess that it serves as an insulating layer, the clue being that these insects are essentially desert and semi-desert dwellers. The camel's coat keeps in the heat during the cold nights in the desert and it also keeps out the heat of the sun by day. The female velvet ant, being wingless and forced to run over the hot sand by day, probably needs the insulating layer against the heat from the ground as well as from the sun. Her mate, in the case of most species of velvet ants, can keep cool by flying or perching in cooler air, but there are some species in which even the males have only degenerate knob-like wings, or are completely wingless.

| phylum | **Arthropoda** |
| --- | --- |
| class | **Insecta** |
| order | **Hymenoptera** |
| family | **Mutillidae** |

▷△ *Fur-coated in the desert: the hairs on the white desert velvet ant* **Dasymutilla gloriosa** *probably act as an insulating layer against the intense heat in the Arizona desert.*
▷ *A closer look shows that despite its ant-like attitude, its mouthparts are more typical of wasps.*

# Vine pest

When Columbus discovered America he started a chain of events that nearly ruined the vineyards of France. Native to North America, the vine pest is a tiny insect related to the well-known aphides, also known as plant lice, greenfly and blackfly. The vine pest is called the vine phylloxera, sometimes referred to as the graperoot louse, although it also feeds on a wide range of other plants.

Except that the vine pest threatened to wipe out the vine-growing industry in France and elsewhere towards the end of the last century, there is little that is remarkable about it, other than its complicated life history. The vine pest was introduced into Europe between 1858 and 1863, when vine growers were experimenting with species of vines imported from America. By 1885 it had reached Algeria, Australia and South Africa. It also reached California about the same time, probably taken there on vines from other parts of the United States east of the Rocky Mountains that had been imported from Europe.

## Nearly vineyards' doomsday
From time immemorial only one species of vine has ever been used for wine-making in Europe. This is *Vitis vinifera*, a native of the region bordering the Caspian Sea, and it has proved extremely susceptible to attacks of the introduced vine pest. The presence of the aphid on a vine is shown first by the stunting of the plant itself and then in the reduction in the size and number of the leaves. In some cases the leaves become discoloured and galls form on their lower surfaces. At the same time knot-like swellings are found on the smaller roots. These turn from yellow to black and cause the roots to die and decay. The growth of the grapes is arrested and the fruits become wrinkled. When at its worst this pest ruined 2½ million acres of vineyards in France.

## A complicated life history
After mating the female vine pest aphid lays her egg on the bark of the vine. Each egg passes the winter on the bark and in spring hatches, producing a wingless female called a fundatrix, or foundress. This female crawls into a leaf bud where she causes a gall to develop on the young leaf. Inside the gall she lays a number of eggs which develop into further wingless females called gallicolae, or gall-dwellers. These multiply during the summer, giving further gall-forming generations that in turn infest other leaves. Later in the season they produce another kind of wingless female, the radicicolae, or root-dwellers, which go down to the roots. After producing several generations of their own kind these radicicolae give rise to winged females which, in late summer, fly to other vines where they lay two kinds of eggs: small ones which produce males and large ones which produce females, both sexes being again wingless.

The mouth-parts and digestive systems of this latest batch are not developed so they do not feed, but they mate and each female lays a single egg. These are the eggs which overwinter and which form the start of a new generation of fundatrix females which start the whole complex series again.

This is the typical, complete life history of a vine pest on its natural and native American host plants. When transferred to European vines the radicicolae are the principal form and they seem to be able to hibernate through the winter and reproduce their own kind indefinitely.

## How it is controlled
The French vineyards are, happily, still productive. They were saved by intensive entomological research. There are many species of vine native to North America and these have varying degrees of resistance to the vine phylloxera. If European vines are grafted on to stocks of these resistant American plants the radicicolae are unable to thrive on their roots and the *Vitis vinifera* scions escape the effects of the pest. *V. riparia*, *V. rupestris* and *V. berlandieri* are American species of vine that are suitable for grafting, and hybrids between them and *V. vinifera* are also extensively used.

In the American grape-growing industry *V. vinifera* is cultivated on resistant stocks, as in Europe, and some resistant species of vines, producing fruit of different kinds and flavours, are also grown, including *V. labrusca* and *V. rotundifolia*.

△ △ *Healthy grape vines in Yugoslavia.*
△ ◁ *Ugly galls on lower surface of a dried vine leaf, destructive work of the vine pest.*
△ *The culprits, wingless and winged females.*

## Simple life
Aphides in general, and the vine pest in particular, have specialized mainly in the simple life. As insects go they are simple in structure, having few specializations other than the general features of the Hemiptera, the order to which they belong. Their food is simple and so is their method of feeding: they simply push their proboscis into the skin of a plant and suck. So, apart from enemies, life would be idyllic. By contrast, their methods of reproduction are highly complicated. Some pests have even more complicated life histories. The oak phylloxera, *Phylloxera quercus*, has no fewer than 21 different forms in its life history.

Complicated life histories, coupled with a high rate of multiplication, tend to be the rule for parasites. This can mean only one thing: that a complex reproductive cycle is needed for the species to survive.

| phylum | **Arthropoda** |
|---|---|
| class | **Insecta** |
| order | **Hemiptera** |
| family | **Phylloxeridae** |
| genus & species | ***Phylloxera vitifoliae*** *vine pest* |

# Wasp

To most people a wasp recalls the black-and-yellow insect often abundant enough in summer to be a nuisance, but in its broader sense the term 'wasp' includes any of the stinging Hymenoptera that is not a bee or an ant.

The common wasp *Vespula vulgaris* and the German wasp *V. germanica* are equally common in Europe, and so alike that the workers are difficult to distinguish, though the queens can be separated by the pattern of their yellow and black markings. Except to entomologists these two are just 'wasps', without any thought of there being more than one species. Almost all that is said here jointly concerns both.

Their nearest European relative is the hornet *Vespa crabro* (page 103), and they are more distantly related to the paper wasps **Polistes** (page 146). Their American equivalents, with similar habits, are known colloquially as 'yellowjackets'.

Four other species of **Vespula** are found in Europe, all very similar in appearance to the two common kinds. The red wasp *Vespula rufa* also nests underground, but the tree wasp *V. sylvestris* and the Norwegian wasp *V. norvegica* hang their nests in trees and bushes. Finally there is the cuckoo wasp *V. austriaca* whose queen enters the nest of a red wasp, kills some of the workers and supplants the queen. The parasitic invader's brood is reared by the red wasp workers, the offspring of the parasite consisting entirely of fertile males and females.

▽ *Lover of liquids – a wasp feeding.*
*Adult wasps feed on nectar, fruit and tree sap.*

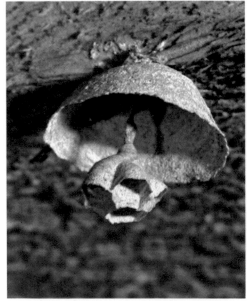

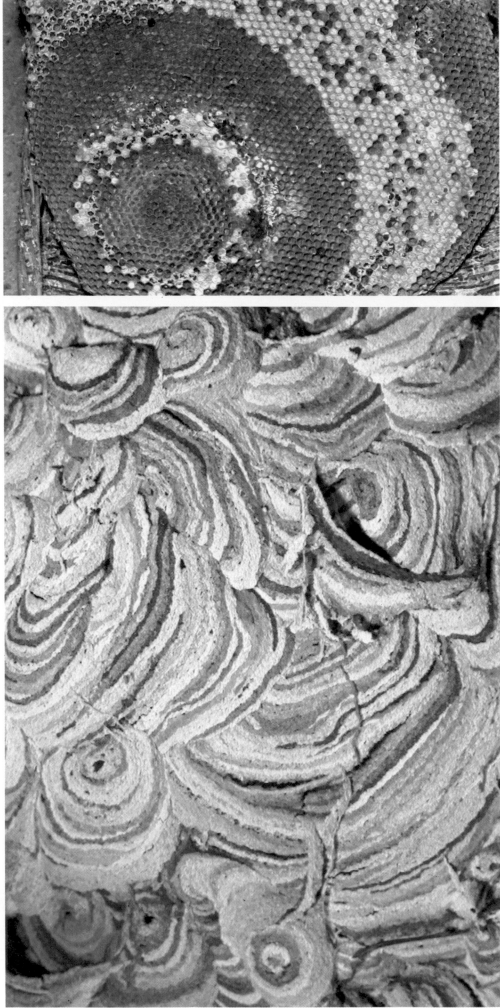

△ *Built by a queen: the finely sculptured first cells of the common wasp are suspended by a stalk from a delicate paper canopy.*
△ ▷ *The underside of a layer of cells from the upper storey of a common wasps' nest. The white cells contain larvae which prior to pupation spin a cocoon and seal off the mouth of the cell with a layer of tough silk.*
▷ *Whorled and circular design: detail of the outside of a wasps' nest formed by the laborious efforts of the queen. Pieces of wood are rasped with the mandibles, worked up with saliva and masticated to form a substance which when dry has a paper-like consistency.*
▽ *Stratified: part of a section through a common wasps' nest shows the different layers of comb supported by tiny props.*

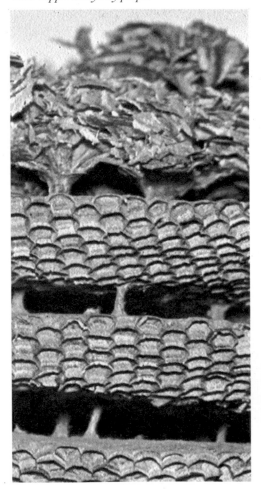

*Fear-inflicting German wasp. Wasps usually sting only when annoyed or if their nest is approached.*

## Elaborate paper building

The history of a wasps' nest really begins in the autumn of the year previous to its construction, when the big queen wasps leave the nests where they were hatched, mate and then hide themselves, to pass the winter in hollow trees, sheds and attics. The queen finds a rough beam or piece of sacking, clamps her jaws onto a fibre and hangs unconscious for six or seven months. She emerges in late spring and seeks a crack in the ground or an old mouse's hole running under a tree root. Just below this she digs out a chamber, removing the earth in her jaws. Then she flies repeatedly to and from a fence post or dead tree, each time bringing home a little pellet of paste made by rasping away the wood and moistening the resultant material with saliva. This substance is plastered on to the underside of the root, where it hardens to form a kind of cardboard or paper. A little curved canopy is fixed onto this foundation and a paper stalk is made, pointing down from the centre of the canopy. A cluster of hexagonal cells, also of paper, is then made round the stalk, with their open ends downward. The queen lays an egg in each then encloses this first comb in a bag of paper about as big as a golf ball, with a hole at its lower end.

## Building a city

All this time the queen has been feeding on nectar. When the eggs hatch into small white larvae she divides her time between feeding them on the juices of chewed-up insects—they are growing and so require a protein diet—and adding more cells to the comb, enlarging the enclosing bag as she does so. By the time the larvae from the earliest eggs have passed through the pupal stage to produce the first workers, she may have added a storey to her house, built below the first and hanging by little stalks of paper. To make room for the growing nest the queen may have to excavate more earth and carry it away.

When the worker wasps, which are non-reproductive females, appear in quantity, they take over from the queen the job of extending and enlarging their home. New storeys are added, one below the other,

increasing to the maximum diameter of the nest and then decreasing again to give it a roughly spherical shape. Quantities of earth are removed by the workers and wood pulp is brought back for construction. The anchorage to the root is strengthened as the bulk and weight of the nest increases, and struts and stays are made between it and the surrounding earth. The queen stays at home, fed by her sexless daughters, who must also bring home animal food for all the growing larvae. As each cell is completed she places an egg in it until a population of as many as 5 000 wasps, or more in very big nests, is built up and maintained. The total number of the queen's offspring that hatch, live and die in the service of the nest throughout a summer may be five times this number.

## Make do and mend

When complete the nest is a hollow sphere 8–9 in. wide, containing 6–10 horizontal combs which extend more or less right across it. The nest is comparable to a house built of bricks and mortar, yet there is a difference: although the nest has a basic external form, the inside is continually being nibbled away and repulped to be added, together with fresh pulp, to the outside and to the expanding combs, so the whole structure is constantly changing.

At the end of the summer a generation of males and functional females is produced. The latter are the queen wasps, similar to workers but larger; the males are about the same size as the workers but have much longer antennae. Eggs which produce workers and queens are always fertilised by spermatozoa from the store which the queen acquired at mating and keeps in her body. Males are produced from unfertilised eggs, from which the queen withholds sperm as she lays them. After mating the males soon die and the queens hibernate. At the end of the summer the workers become lazy and cease to maintain the economy of the nest, and they and the old queen die with the first frosts of autumn.

The workers feed on nectar and fruit juices and also accept drops of liquid exuded by the larvae. The larvae and queen are fed

by the workers on the juices of captured insects; wasps destroy great numbers of bluebottle flies.

The larva is a white legless grub and it maintains its position in the upside-down cell by pressing its body against the sides. When fully grown it closes the cell by spinning a papery cover across the mouth. During its life its excrement accumulates at the end of the intestine and is voided all at once in the last larval skin when it changes into a soft white pupa. The wasp emerges 3–4 weeks after the eggs were laid.

## Guests and parasites

A hoverfly *Volucella* enters wasps' nests and lays its eggs without any interference from the wasps. Its curious prickly larvae play a useful part in the nest as scavengers, living in the midden below the nest, where dirt and dead bodies accumulate, and also entering vacated cells and cleaning out the deposits of excrement. This helps in making the cells available for re-use. The larvae of the moth *Aphomia sociella* also live as scavengers in wasps' nests. Late in the season, when the nest is 'running down', these invade the combs and devour the grubs and pupae. The larva of a rare beetle *Metoecus paradoxus* lives parasitically on the grubs of wasps in underground nests. It is at first an internal parasite (like the larva of an ichneumon or a tachina (page 184) fly), but later emerges and devours its host. It is a remarkable fact that *Metoecus* apparently invades the nests of only the common wasp, never those of the German wasp, although to our eyes the two species look exactly the same.

## The wasp's sting

This formidable weapon is really an ovipositor or egg-laying organ that has become transformed into a tiny hypodermic needle connected with a poison gland. The eggs are extruded from an opening at the base of it. Wasps sting if they are squeezed or restrained, as when they accidentally crawl inside someone's clothing. They also attack and sting if the nest is interfered with or even simply approached. The inhabitants of large, well-populated nests are more aggressive than those of small ones. The two main constituents of the venom are histamine and apitoxin. Old-fashioned remedies such as washing soda and ammonia were based on the mistaken idea that the venom is an acid of some kind, and they are ineffective except in giving reassurance. Genuine relief is given by the application of antihistamine to the site of the sting and by taking antihistamine tablets.

| phylum | **Arthropoda** |
| --- | --- |
| class | **Insecta** |
| order | **Hymenoptera** |
| family | **Vespidae** |

# Water beetle

*Fresh water would not remain fresh for long if it were not for scavengers like the water beetles that feed on decaying vegetation. There are 2 000 species in the worldwide family, most numerous in the tropics, known as water beetles, or sometimes as water scavenger beetles, to avoid confusion with another family, the diving beetles (page 69). The name is not wholly appropriate because not all species live in water, some living in damp places among vegetable rubbish, others in dung.*

*Many water beetles look very like the diving beetles because both are dark brown or black and oval in outline. The former are, however, stouter, less flat, and differ in their habits, especially in the way they swim and breathe. The silver water beetle is one of the best known and largest. It is nearly 2 in. long, black and smooth above. Under water it appears bright silvery underneath due to a covering of very fine short hairs which trap a thin layer of air. Usually hidden under the head, the antennae are short and clubbed, and are used in breathing. There are much-elongated palps on the maxillae which look like a second pair of antennae, and in many species these function as such.*

## Awkward swimmers

Water beetles live in shallow weedy ponds, in pools in marshes, some mainly on damp land, a few live in brackish water or in running water where there are plenty of algae. They swim awkwardly with alternate strokes of the legs, very different from the efficient rowing action of more truly aquatic beetles such as the great diving beetles. The first pair of legs are not adapted to swimming and the beetle uses first the middle and hindlegs of one side, then those of the other. These are flattened and fringed. When the silver water beetle submerges it carries a silvery film of air on the underside and a bubble between the body and wing-cases. The beetle replenishes its store in a peculiar way, coming to the surface headfirst, not tail first like the diving beetles,

turning on one side and piercing the surface film with one of the antennae. This forms a funnel which puts the outside air in continuity with the two stores of air the beetle carries. This species, like other members of the family, also flies at night and is attracted to artificial light.

The adult beetle feeds on water plants, including algae, or on decaying matter, seldom on living animal prey, although the larvae are more often predatory. Where the larvae live in dung they are maggot-like, feeding on fly maggots found there. In some parts of the Far East water beetles are used to combat the larvae of other beetles which damage sugar cane and banana stems.

## Carnivorous larvae

The female silver water beetle spins a large silken cocoon and attaches it to the underside of a leaf of floating vegetation. A vertical 'chimney' projects above the water surface, allowing air to reach the 50 – 100 eggs laid inside. Sometimes the cocoons are spun independently of any support and they float like small brown balloons at the surface,

with the chimney looking like a mast. In a few species the female carries the cocoon about with her, held between her hindlegs. When these hatch the larvae swallow some air and then bite their way out of the cocoon. The object of swallowing the air seems to be to make the larvae buoyant so they can rise to the surface to breathe. Unlike the adults they are carnivorous, but confine their attentions mainly to water snails. The jaws are asymmetrical and are apparently designed for holding and cutting through the shell of a snail. Well-grown larvae also prey on tadpoles. The soft body of the prey is eaten normally, not externally digested as in the case of the diving beetle larva.

The larva is nearly 3 in. long when fully grown. At this time it leaves the water to pupate in an earthen cell.

## An aquarium favourite

It is not surprising that such a large, handsome and well-behaved insect as the silver water beetle should be a favourite with aquarium keepers. It is rather rare and at one time it was thought that over-collecting

△ *The silver water beetle, so-called because of the shiny layer of air on its underside.*

for aquaria was a threat to its existence. This is probably no longer the case, but it is now in far greater danger than before from modern agricultural operations involving filling up ponds and the mechanical dredging of drainage ditches in country that was formerly marshland. This, added to the way the beetles or their larvae serve as food for birds, fish, frogs and toads, may be too much for the water beetles.

| phylum | **Arthropoda** |
|---|---|
| class | **Insecta** |
| order | **Coleoptera** |
| family | **Hydrophilidae** |
| genus & species | *Hydrous ( =Hydrophilus) piceus others* |

▽ *Bottom up: diving beetle* **Dytiscus** *fills the air reservoir trapped behind its wing cases.*

▽ *Antennae raised, water beetle* **Octhebius** *renews the air store under its body.*

# Water scorpion

*Water scorpions are bugs and therefore have nothing to do with the more familiar land scorpions, and they are far less dangerous to people. They are water insects, called scorpions because of the shape of their front legs, which are modified for grasping prey, and the presence of a long, slender 'tail', which resembles to a very slight degree a scorpion's tail. The larger kinds of water scorpion can pierce the human skin with their tongues with painful but not serious effects. In Australia people are attacked often enough to have earned for the insects the name 'toe-biter' or 'needle bug'.*

*Water scorpions are flat, blackish-brown insects, the largest being no more than 1—2 in. long. They live on the bottom around the edges of muddy ponds and ditches and are difficult to see on account of their resemblance to water-logged dead leaves. The more or less oval outline of the body is made more leaf-like because the 'tail' looks so like a leaf-stalk. They are poor swimmers and seldom venture into open water, but may climb about on water weeds to get to the surface to breathe air. For this they use the tail, which consists of two half-tubes closely applied to each other and held together by interlocking bristles to form a 'snorkel', the tip of which is pushed above the surface.*

*The family which includes the water scorpions is a small one, with only about 150 species, but these are well distributed over the world. The water stick insect is in the same family.*

▽ *Predacious pair: water scorpions in weeds.*

## Wings hide evolutionary secrets

When the wing-cases of a water scorpion are raised a pair of very delicate hind-wings are revealed. These are never used, however, as the insect has lost some of the principal wing muscles and cannot fly. The wings are pink with bright red veins and the part of the hind body over which they lie is brick-red with black bands. This permanently concealed splendour must have had a function at some time, so it must be supposed that this loss of the use of the wings has occurred rather recently in its evolutionary history. Another feature that is revealed when the wings are lifted is a group of three pairs of false spiracles on the surface of the abdomen below the wings. The spiracles of insects are primarily breathing pores, but in the water scorpion only those at the base of the breathing tube are used for this. The three pairs on the upper surface of the abdomen are balancing organs. Experiments have shown that these spiracles are extremely sensitive to water pressure, which will be very slightly greater on the side of the insect which is tilted downwards from the horizontal position.

## Predacious bugs

Water scorpions are predatory, seizing small tadpoles, insects and other animals with their forelegs, each of which is hinged like a clasp knife, so the end portion can fold back into a groove along the basal part. The piercing beak, a feature characteristic of the whole order Hemiptera—bugs—is plunged into the victim, which is killed and consumed by external digestion. In this type of feeding digestive juice is pumped down the beak and into the victim, thus dissolving the tissues, which are then sucked back in liquid form. As well as being digestive the injected juice is also poisonous and quickly paralyses and kills the prey—even large victims, like young fish, are quickly subdued.

## Chains of eggs

Water scorpions lay their eggs in spring, among aquatic plants near the surface. At one end of each egg is a bunch of seven long filaments. These become entangled and the eggs cling to each other in chains. The newly-hatched young are like their parents, except in size.

## Water stick insects

Water stick insects are larger than most water scorpions. They are long and slender with long legs, rather like the familiar stick insects after which they are named. The breathing siphon is nearly as long again as the rest of the body, which is light ochreous in colour, and its mode of feeding is similar to that of the water scorpion. Water stick insects live in still waters among water weeds and standing reeds. Unlike water scorpions they have functional wings and will fly in search of a new habitat if their pond or ditch dries up. Their eggs are most peculiar. They are inserted into floating leaves, such as those of water lilies, the female having a saw-like ovipositor for cutting the leaves and fixing the eggs in position.

Perhaps the most remarkable thing about this unusual family is that the two types of insects have come to look like vegetation. One has come to look like leaves, the other like stems, and all within the one family.

| phylum | **Arthropoda** |
|---|---|
| class | **Insecta** |
| order | **Hemiptera** |
| suborder | **Heteroptera** |
| family | **Nepidae** |
| genera & species | ***Nepa cinerea*** *water scorpion*<br>***Ranatra linearis*** *water stick insect* |

▽ *Diagonally placed: water stick insect with legs and breathing siphon extended is about 2 in. long.*

*Shadow and symmetry—even the water strider's leg hairs make a beautiful pattern on the water. A perfectly balanced water strider spreads its legs out on the glassy surface of the water.*

*Grappling iron? Water strider's leg with water resistant hairs and a claw for catching prey.*

# Water strider

*Water striders, or pond skaters, are the familiar insects that can be seen floating or skimming swiftly over the surfaces of ponds, streams and flooded ditches. Their bodies are flat, narrow, and $\frac{1}{4} - \frac{3}{4}$ in. long. They appear to have only two pairs of legs, but the front pair are short and held close to the head, just behind the antennae. The rear two pairs are long and the tips are fringed with hairs, which rest on the surface of the water. Some species are wingless, others have small wings while a few have fully developed wings. Water striders develop through a series of moults from a small nymph. An adult bug can usually be distinguished from a nymph by its fully developed wings, but adult water striders are not so easily recognised because one with small wings could be a nymph or an adult, depending on the species.*

*While true water striders belong to the family Gerridae, other bugs that float on the surface of water are sometimes called water striders. These include the water measurer, or water gnat, family Hydrometridae, which has a curious long, narrow head and the water crickets of the family Veliidae. There are also the pondweed bugs of the family Mesoveliidae. One member is terrestrial, living among fallen leaves in the forests of New Guinea.*

### Running on water

Water striders often gather in groups along the edges of ponds and lakes, scuttling over the water when disturbed and then re-grouping. They are propelled by the long pair of middle legs and steered by the hindlegs. When moving slowly, each flick of the legs sends the water strider sliding several inches over the surface of the water, but they also hop across the water, rising an inch or so at each bound. Water plants present no obstacle and water striders walk over floating weed and even over dry water lily leaves.

Water striders prey on dead or dying insects which fall on to the water, grasping with their front legs and piercing the bodies of the prey with their mouthparts and sucking them dry. Cannibalism is common. Prey is detected by sight or by vibrations picked up by sense organs on the legs. One European species lives in estuaries and is also found around the coasts of the Baltic Sea. Water striders of the genus *Halobates* are among the very few marine insects. They live in tropical and subtropical seas, sometimes hundreds of miles from land, skimming over the waves and feeding on floating dead animals.

### Adult hibernation

In temperate regions there are one or two generations of water striders each year, depending on the species. The second generation hibernates on land, but occasionally takes to water on warm winter days. In the spring and early summer they return to water and mate. About 100 eggs are laid in groups on submerged or floating plants and covered with mucilage. They hatch in about 2 weeks, depending on the water temperature, and a month later the nymphs finally change into adults.

### Invisible support

The best time to watch water striders is on a sunny day. The tip of each leg can be seen to be in a dent in the water surface. If the water is shallow the shadows of the water striders can be seen on the bottom, and each leg is surrounded by a round shadow made by this dip. It is caused by the weight of the water strider pressing the legs into the water, but it does not sink because the force of surface tension is counteracting this weight. The surface tension is due to a film of closely linked water molecules on the surface of the water which acts like a very fine rubber sheet. It is a very weak sheet and normally we do not notice it. It is this force of surface tension that holds a drop of water in a globule on a polished surface instead of spreading out in a film. The capacity of surface tension to keep objects afloat can be demonstrated by floating a cigarette paper in a glass of water and gently placing a needle on it. Eventually the paper becomes waterlogged and sinks, but the needle remains afloat—held up by surface tension.

Water striders sometimes enter the water completely but can refloat themselves because the undersides of their bodies are covered with a dense pile of hairs that traps air and prevents the body from becoming wetted. It has been said that a marine *Halobates* becomes wetted and drowned if a drop of rain lands on its back, but if this is so it is surprising that they have not been wiped out by tropical storms.

| phylum | **Arthropoda** |
|---|---|
| class | **Insecta** |
| order | **Hemiptera** |
| family | **Gerridae** |
| genus & species | *Gerris lacustris* *G. thoracicus* *G. remigis* others |

# Weevil

Insects form the most numerous and diverse class in the animal kingdom, and the beetles, which include the weevils, are the largest insect group. Entomologists have already described and named about 40 000 species of weevils and every year several hundred new ones are discovered — and no doubt there are hundreds still unknown to science.

Most weevils are small, ⅛ in. or so long. A few attain ½ in. and there are tropical weevils of up to 3 in. They are generally very compact, with the head drawn out into a snout, called the rostrum. In some species the rostrum is long, slender and downward curving, and it is longest in the females; in other species it is quite short. The jaws are at the end of the rostrum. Often the antennae arise from a point halfway along the rostrum and are elbowed at the end of the first joint so that they can be folded back into a groove on each side of the rostrum. Many weevils are wingless and few of them fly much.

## Problems of egg-laying

All weevils are plant feeders, both as larvae and adults. The female uses her snout, with its terminal jaws, to drill a hole in a stem, bud or fruit. She then turns round and extends a long egg-laying tube or ovipositor from inside her body and deposits an egg at the end of the tunnel. Sometimes a female weevil can come to grief doing this. As she is boring into a nut or acorn her feet may slip and she is then left poised on her embedded nose, her legs waving helplessly in the air. She has no means of extricating herself from this situation and remains there until she dies. The larvae, little white legless grubs, usually live inside the plant tissues. Some pupate within their larval habitat, while others gnaw their way out and pupate in the soil.

## Old World weevils

The majority of weevils feed on some particular species or genus of plant, and often on a special part of the plant, and there are few plants without their associated weevils. This accounts to a great extent for the remarkable diversity of this family of beetles. The following are examples of weevils attached to particular plants.

The female nut weevil, of the Old World, bores into hazel nuts while they are still green and lays an egg in each one. The larva feeds on the growing kernel until the nut falls in the autumn, when the mature larva gnaws its way out and pupates in the soil. The proverbial 'bad nut' is a hazel nut either containing or vacated by a little white legless grub.

▽ *Glossy black weevil:* **Liparus coronatus** *a European species that feeds on carrots shows the downward-pointing head rostrum and clubbed antennae typical of weevils. This group of the Coleoptera contains more species than any other animal group: many are notorious as pests on fruit and vegetables.*

The figwort weevil is a small brown beetle with a black dorsal spot. The larvae are unusual in feeding openly on the leaves. They are covered with slime and pupate attached to the plant in cocoons formed of hardened slime. These very closely resemble the seed capsules of the figwort and they therefore no doubt derive protection from insectivorous birds.

The eggs of the gorse weevil are laid in batches of a dozen or so in the seed pods of the gorse plant. The larvae feed on the seeds and pupate inside the pods, hatching on dry days in summer when the gorse seed is ripe and the pods are splitting. In this plant the pods split or dehisce suddenly with a cracking sound and the seeds are scattered quite widely. Infested pods dehisce in just the same way, but in this case it is beetles instead of the seeds that are hurled around.

So the weevils are spread as far as the gorse seeds on which they feed. This weevil has been introduced to New Zealand to control the spread of introduced gorse.

One of the largest European weevils is the large pine weevil, about $\frac{1}{2}$ in. long, blackish with patches of short yellow hair. It lives on coniferous trees, especially pine, and the adult beetles do serious harm to young pines by feeding on the tender bark of the shoots and on the buds. The larvae are comparatively harmless boring into the old stumps and roots of felled trees.

## Curse on cotton

The close attachment of particular weevils to particular plants has of course led to some of these beetles becoming agricultural pests. A weevil feeding on a wild plant that is brought into cultivation will almost certainly multiply enormously when its food plant, normally scattered among many other kinds of wild flowers, extends, uninterrupted, for hundreds of square miles. The pine weevil is a pest in forestry plantations of young pine, but for a weevil whose depredations are economically really impressive we must turn to the southern United States, where the cotton boll weevil costs the American cotton industry between one and two million dollars a year.

This notorious insect first invaded southern Texas from Mexico in 1892 and rapidly spread to all the cotton-growing regions. It is a typical weevil, compact, brown in colour, $\frac{1}{4}$ in. long, and it has a stout, down-curved rostrum. Its eggs are laid in the buds or, later in the season, in the fruits of the plant, one in each, and a single female may lay 100—300 eggs. The life cycle

*Cosmopolitan pest:* **Calandra oryzae** *attacks stored grain products. In a rice grain only one larva develops but a maize seed may contain several.*

*A cyclamen root infected with the larvae of* **Otiorrhyncus sulcatus.** *The larvae damage the roots of many garden plants, the adults attack foliage.*

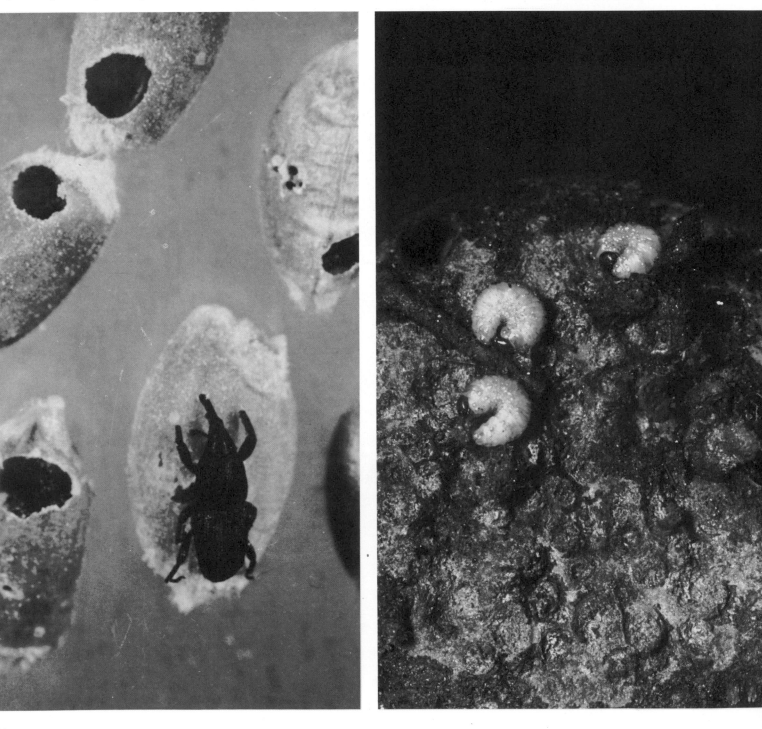

takes only 3 weeks and in some localities there may be ten generations in a year. The bolls that are infested are rendered useless, and once inside the bud or fruit the larva is largely protected from sprayed or dusted pesticides. Carefully timed applications of insecticides are partly effective, and burning debris, in which the adults overwinter, is an important control measure.

From one point of view the boll weevil can be regarded as a benefactor of the southern United States. Before it invaded the area agriculture was concentrated on two crops, cotton and tobacco, and so was very vulnerable to price fluctuations. The weevil forced the farmers to diversify their agriculture and the economy of the American South has undoubtedly benefited from this. One city has acknowledged indebtedness to the boll weevil by erecting a statue to it.

## Infestation of flour

The Anglo-Saxon word *wifel*, from which weevil is derived, referred to the grain weevil which has infested stored grain since prehistoric times. The egg is laid, and the larva lives inside cereal grains of all kinds, hollowing them out and causing serious damage if uncontrolled. It can be destroyed by fumigation in suitably constructed stores. It also infests any foodstuffs prepared from flour, and is the weevil that we read about in the stories of sailing ship days. The staple food on board was a sort of thick, hard biscuit in which the grain weevil thrived. Fastidious sailors broke their biscuits and tapped them on the table to dislodge the little grubs and beetles; others ate them as they were and were possibly better nourished as a result of eating the insects contained in them, which are harmless to man.

| phylum | **Arthropoda** |
|---|---|
| class | **Insecta** |
| order | **Coleoptera** |
| family | **Curculionidae** |
| genera & species | ***Anthonomus grandis*** *cotton boll weevil* ***Apion ulicis*** *gorse weevil* ***Cionus scrophulariae*** *figwort weevil* ***Curculio nucum*** *nut weevil* ***Hylobius abietis*** *large pine weevil* ***Sitophilus granarius*** *grain weevil* *others* |

*Tunnels bored by the larvae of the sugar beet weevil* **Temnorrhinus mendicus** *make this vegetable useless for marketing.*

*A major pest of apple:* **Anthonomus pomorum** *is found especially where orchards adjoin woods, providing favourable hibernation conditions.*

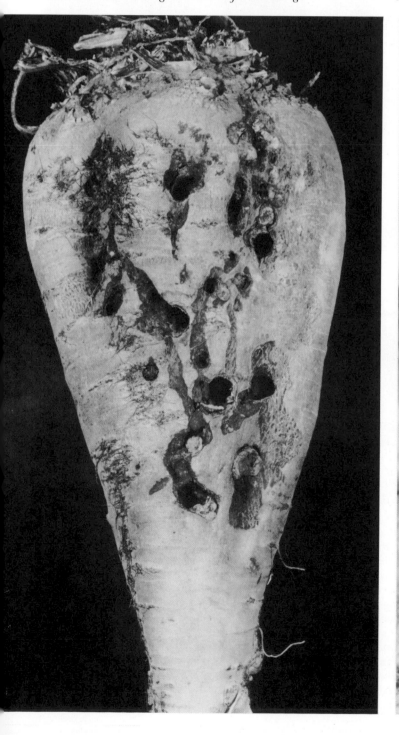

211

# Whirligig beetle

The small beetles that gyrate rapidly on the surface of the water on ponds and canals are called whirligig beetles. The name dates from the 15th century and originally a whirligig was a toy that spun. Most of them belong to the genus **Gyrinus** and are shiny blue-black or dark bronze in colour. They swim with the second and third pairs of legs only. These legs have their segments flattened and fringed with hairs, making them effective oars. The first pair of legs are slender and quite normal, and they take little or no part in swimming. The antennae are short and clubbed and the eyes are remarkable in being divided into separate upper and lower compound eyes on each side of the head. Whirligig beetles have wings and fly readily and will quickly escape from an open aquarium.

Ten species of **Gyrinus,** all very similar in appearance, are found in Europe and some species of whirligig beetle are almost cosmopolitan. In one member of another genus, **Orectochilus,** the upper surface,

*Surface swimmers — whirligigs* **Gyrinus natator.**

instead of being shiny, is clothed with thick yellowish-grey hair. It is known as the hairy whirligig and lives in running water, gyrating on the surface only at night. By day it hides under the bank. It is the only species of its genus found in Europe: one other kind of hairy whirligig is known from Africa and a number from Asia. The Gyrinidae is a relatively small beetle family, containing a total of about 400 species, as compared, for example, with the 40 000 species of weevils.

212

## Semi-submerged skaters

Their capacity for scooting about like tiny speed boats, weaving around in dense crowds but never colliding, is the whirligigs' most characteristic feature. They do not float on the surface film like pond skaters. The undersurface and legs are wettable and are immersed in the water but the shiny or hairy upper surface repels the water and remains dry. The antennae are held actually in the surface film and are believed to be sensitive to changes in its curvature, thus enabling the beetles to avoid collision with each other. Each beetle makes a dimple in the film around it and throws up little bow waves in front. The two pairs of swimming legs do not rely only on their fringe of hairs for propulsion, as do those of most other water insects. The flattened joints fold up like a fan on the forward movement and then open up for the backward propulsive stroke.

## Maintaining position

A group of whirligigs can be seen to maintain its position on a pond, or even in slowly flowing water, without simply scattering, as would perhaps be expected from the maze-like movements of the individuals. The two separate pairs of eyes are so positioned that one is under the water and the other above, and there is little doubt that their facets or ommatidia are adapted respectively for aquatic and aerial vision. There seems to be only one possible means by which the beetles can maintain their position when swimming. They must keep a constant pattern of objects on the bank in view. The fact that they can do this while weaving about in elaborate convolutions implies a remarkable degree of co-ordination of movement and vision.

Whirligigs can swim well under water and dive readily when alarmed. They always carry a bubble of air attached to the hind end; this bubble is probably used for respiration when the beetles rest clinging to underwater plants.

They make no attempt to hide themselves at any time and seem to be an easy prey for

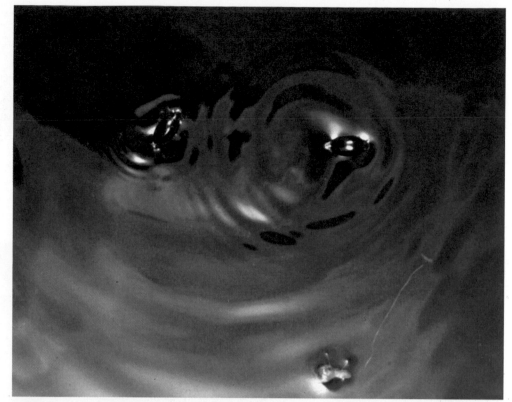

*Ripples on a pond:* **Gyrinus natator** *whirl around on their specially flattened mid- and hind-legs.*

birds and fishes, for all their active movement. They are probably protected by their power to exude a milky fluid when molested. This is variously described as smelling 'disagreeable', or, in one American whirligig, *Dineutes americanus*, 'like apples', but it is likely to function as a repellent in all cases.

So far as is known whirligigs feed on small insects that fall onto the water surface, which they seize with their long, mobile front legs.

## Aquatic larvae

Whirligigs over-winter as adults and the females lay their eggs in spring, end to end in rows on submerged water plants. The larvae hatch and grow rapidly. They swim in a wriggling manner or creep about the bottom feeding on other insects and to

some extent on vegetable matter. Their pointed jaws are hollow for sucking the juices of their prey. When fully grown the larva is very slender and over $\frac{1}{2}$ in. long. The joints between the segments are deeply indented and there is a row of feathery gills along each side of the body, one pair on each abdominal segment except the last, which has two pairs. The last segment also has two pairs of hooks which are said to be used for climbing about on water plants. About the end of July the larvae climb up the stems of emergent water plants and spin cocoons above the surface. The adults appear a month or so later and it is at this time, in late summer, that whirligigs are extremely abundant.

The larva of the hairy whirligig is found among gravel in shallow flowing water, and keeps out of sight, like the adult.

## Aquatic all-rounder

A whirligig beetle is unusual in enjoying the best of three worlds. Although it spends much of its time sculling about on the surface it can easily take off and fly, skimming over the surface to look for a fresh feeding ground. Then it noses over into a steep dive, using its wing cases as a parachute, and lands gently on the water. It can then, if necessary, shut its wing-cases, trapping a bubble of air under them, and submerge like a submarine or, better still, a skin-diver.

*The best of both worlds: divided compound eyes allow a whirligig to see both above and below water.*

| phylum | **Arthropoda** |
|---|---|
| class | **Insecta** |
| order | **Coleoptera** |
| family | **Gyrinidae** |
| genera & species | **Gyrinus natator** *whirligig* **G. marinus** *whirligig* **Orectochilus villosus** *hairy whirligig, others* |

# White butterflies

The term 'white butterflies' is sometimes used to cover the whole of the great butterfly family Pieridae, but many pierids, especially tropical species, are brilliantly coloured yellow, orange and red, so this usage is rather misleading. The European white butterflies comprise the members of the subfamily Pierinae, exclusive of the 'orange-tips' and those of the Dismorphiinae, one of which is the wood white. The pierine whites are the familiar cabbage white butterflies. In the New World

one species, accidentally introduced from Europe, is a serious pest of cultivated plants of the cabbage family. This is **Pieris rapae**, the small white or (in America) the European cabbage butterfly. There are also a number of indigenous American species of **Pieris**. Another North American pierine is the pine white, the larva of which feeds on pine, an unusual diet for a member of this family of butterflies. Some species of whites range up to 18 000 feet or more, the highest habitat known for any butterflies. These include species of **Phulia** and **Piercolias** in the Andes and **Baltia** of central Asia.

The whites, and all other members of the Pieridae, pupate like the swallowtails. The pupa is attached by the tail, usually to a vertical surface, and has an anchoring girdle of silk surrounding it at midbody. It is thus suspended rather like a telephone linesman at work. The eggs are bottle-shaped and ribbed and stand upright on the leaves when laid. The larvae are often elongate and green but show considerable diversity of form.

▽ Marbled mating of a pair of meadow whites **Pontia helice**. Close relatives of the Bath white, they live throughout South Africa.

## Crop pests

The large white and the small white are notorious pests of cabbage and other brassica crops, on which their larvae feed. The large white is generally less numerous but it sometimes migrates in huge swarms, which occasionally cross the Channel to southern England. Its bristly larva is dull green and yellow with blackish mottling. It has an unpleasant smell and is distasteful to birds, although they eagerly search for and eat the pupae during the winter. The larva is heavily parasitised by the small ichneumon wasp *Apanteles glomeratus*. It is often found feeding on 'nasturtium' *Tropolaeum* as well as on cabbage.

The very abundant small white also migrates in swarms, but less frequently. Its larva is not protected by any distasteful properties, but is well camouflaged by its green colour. It also suffers heavily from parasites. In both species the sexes are distinct, the black markings of the females being heavier and always including a pair of black spots on the forewing. Both have a spring and a summer brood, of which the latter is more strongly marked with black in both sexes.

The small white has spread widely over the world, probably by accidental conveyance of pupae. It reached Quebec about 1860 and in the next 25 years spread all over temperate North America. It appeared in New Zealand in 1929 and in southern Australia some years later, reaching Tasmania about 1940. In these regions biological control has met with some success. The agent used is a chalcid wasp (page 48) *Pteromalus puparum* which lays its eggs in the newly formed pupa.

## Harmless white butterflies

The third common European white butterfly, the green-veined white, is similar in size and appearance to the small white, but differs in having the veins of the wings bordered with greenish-grey scales on the underside. The sexes and the spring and summer generations differ in much the same ways as the large and small whites. The larva feeds on various wild Cruciferae, such as hedge mustard and cuckoo flower, and does not attack cultivated crops. This is one of the butterflies in which a distinct race or subspecies has evolved in Ireland. It is more strongly marked than even second brood butterflies from Great Britain. The black-veined white has no distinct markings except an outlining in black of the wing veins. It is common in continental Europe. The larva feeds on sloe, hawthorn and plum, hibernating through the winter in a communal web.

## Historic butterflies

The Bath white is distinctively marked, having areas of both wings dappled with greenish-black. Its English name is a piece of whimsy derived from the circumstance that at some time during the 18th century a young lady of Bath executed a piece of needlework in which the butterfly was depicted. It is also interesting to note that a specimen of it, collected and preserved in 1702, shortly after Queen Anne came to the English throne, is preserved in the Hope Department of Entomology at Oxford. It is

△ *Small white butterflies congregate around a patch of mud to drink.*
◁ *Pupae of the large white overwinter on a tree trunk. The pupal stage involves a great amount of internal rearrangement from the caterpillar to the adult butterfly.*
*Metamorphosis of insects into different forms is controlled by hormones produced in the brain—the pupa develops when the epidermal cells are exposed to a relatively large amount of moulting hormone and a small amount of juvenile hormone. The adult butterfly develops when no more juvenile hormone is produced. To complicate matters the whole sequence of events is genetically controlled. The pupa, common to many insects, represents a protective transitional stage, and must have had selective value in the course of evolution.*

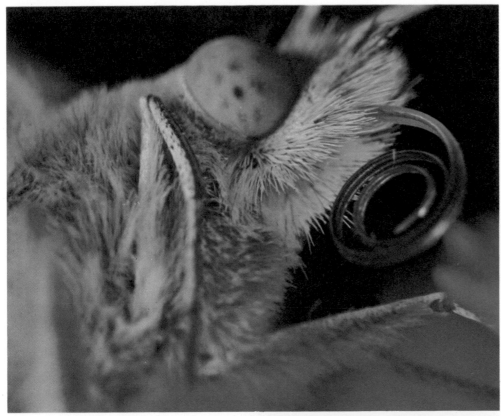

| phylum | **Arthropoda** |
|---|---|
| class | **Insecta** |
| order | **Lepidoptera** |
| family | **Pieridae** |
| genera & species | *Aporia crataegi* black-veined white |
| | *Leptidea sinapis* wood white |
| | *Melanargia galathea* marbled white |
| | *Neophasia menapia* pine white |
| | *Pieris brassicae* large white |
| | *P. napi* green-veined white |
| | *P. rapae* small white |
| | *Pontia daplidice* Bath white |
| | others |

◁ *Large white–close up : the coiled proboscis is formed by the highly modified maxillae held together by interlocking spines.*
▽ *A colourful white–the purple tip **Colotis danae,** a butterfly of the low African veld.*

common in continental Europe but a rare summer visitor to Britain.

The wood white and two other related species are remarkable in being the only Old World representatives of the subfamily Dismorphiinae, which is otherwise entirely confined to South and Central America. In that region about 100 species are known, many of them brightly patterned.

## Butterfly pigments

In many of the most brilliant butterflies the colours are produced by the effect known as 'structural coloration' (page 140). In the Pieridae, of which the 'whites' are a sober coloured minority, we find bright colours, red, orange and yellow as well as white, which are due to chemical pigments produced by the insect and deposited in the scales of its wings during its period of development.

These pigments are known as pterines; the white substance in the scales of the common white butterflies is a particular pterine called leucopterine, which chemically resembles uric acid and was formerly confused with it. The marbled white butterfly has wings checkered with white and black, but is a relative of the meadow brown (page 133) not of the true whites. If a preserved specimen of a pierid, say a large white, and one of a marbled white are exposed together to ammonia vapour the large white will remain unchanged but the colour of the marbled white will deepen to a yellow tint.

This is because its white pigment is of a wholly different nature; it is a flavone or anthoxanthin, a type of pigment derived from the food plant. The fact that the scales of the wood white also contain flavone pigment does not mean that it is related to the marbled white, but it does underline its quite remote relationship with the other more typical pierid butterflies.

# Whitefly

*Whitefly are not flies at all but extremely small bugs very closely related to the aphids (page 12) and scale insects (page 160). They are seldom more than ⅛ in. long and many are less than this. The adults look like minute white moths as they fly actively around. Their colour is due to a fine waxy powder which covers the body and wings. This is given out from the anus, which lies in a cavity overlaid by a tongue-shaped flap, or lingula, the cavity itself being covered by a lid, or operculum. Originally, the wax was probably given out as a waste substance, as in some other bugs, but in whiteflies this 'waste' is put to use, possibly as a protective covering. The majority of known whiteflies are tropical and they would largely escape notice but for the fact that some are serious pests of crops. Indeed, it is highly likely that the majority of whiteflies living today have yet to be discovered. The cabbage whitefly infects cabbages in practically all temperate countries, and the greenhouse whitefly is a tropical insect which establishes itself in glasshouses, attacking tomatoes, cucumbers and many other plants. It is believed to have come originally from Brazil. A third species, the citrus whitefly, is a pest of citrus fruits in the southern United States.*

## Harmful sapsucker

The cabbage whitefly congregates when young on the undersides of cabbage leaves where it breeds throughout the summer. In autumn the adults rise in clouds when disturbed and settle again like tiny snowflakes. Both the greenhouse and citrus species discolour and weaken the plants they infest by sucking their sap, in the same way as aphids, and like the aphids they cover the plants with sticky honeydew. On citrus fruit the honeydew promotes the growth of a fungus, the sooty mould *Meliola camelliae,* which so discolours the fruit that, even if it is not spoiled altogether, it has to be expensively washed for marketing. The reason why whiteflies and other bugs take in so much sap, in excess of their need for carbohydrates, is that they need other nutrients such as amino-acids, which are less concentrated in the sap.

## Eggs laid in circles

The eggs are laid on the undersides of leaves, sometimes in a double layer, and are usually arranged in an arc or a circle, because when laying the female keeps her head in one place and moves her body round it. Each egg has a stalk and is laid upright, a batch of eggs looking rather like a group of minute pegs. The larvae are tiny and scale-like. They move about, feeding on the sap and excreting honeydew. They cast their skins three times and after the third moult the larva develops rods or filaments of wax all around itself. Then it stops feeding and settles down in a condition resembling that of the pupa of a

higher insect. After a longer or shorter period of rest, varying with the species, the winged insect emerges fully developed.

The stalks of the eggs actually pierce the outer layer of cells of a leaf and, as they are hollow, they draw moisture from the leaf by capillary action. So long as the plant is well supplied with water, development of the eggs proceeds normally. If the leaf withers, however, the development of the egg is arrested; and if the plant wilts during a drought the egg goes into a resting stage until more sap is available. Sometimes whitefly eggs go into a resting stage for no obvious reason. All these are almost certainly adaptations to life in the tropics.

The characteristic way in which all bugs develop is by a series of instars, or stages separated by skin changes. In the course of these the insect gradually takes on the characters of the adult and continues to feed and move about throughout its life without a break, contrasting with, for example, the pupa of a moth. The false pupa of the whiteflies is an interesting departure from the normal way in which bugs develop, and it closely parallels the true pupa of such insects as butterflies, bees and beetles. The differences are that the false pupa has much the same shape as the previous larval stage and it keeps feeding. It is also decorated with wax rods.

## Imported parasites

The greenhouse whitefly can be effectively controlled by the use of another exotic insect, the minute chalcid wasp *Encarsia formosa*, which probably also came from the tropics, although nobody is sure of its precise point of origin. This wasp is a parasite of the whitefly and was first noticed in

△ *A congregation of whitefly of the family Aleyrodidae. They are not, in fact, flies, but hemipteran, sap-sucking bugs.*

a greenhouse at Elstree, in Hertfordshire, England, in 1926. A stock of it was bred up and was found to be effective in wiping out whitefly in greenhouses. Consignments of it were sent out all over Britain and also to Canada and Australia.

The parasite reproduces by parthenogenesis, that is, by the development of unfertilised eggs. The males are rare and apparently do not mate even when they occur. The female wasps lay their eggs in the larvae or 'scales' of the whitefly, and those that are parasitised turn black; this is useful as an indication that the parasite is being effective. To introduce the wasp, bunches of tomato leaves bearing parasitised scales are obtained and hung up in the greenhouse. Blackening of the scales is generally noticed 2−3 weeks after the introduction of the parasitised material. A night temperature of about 13°C/55°F is needed to maintain the wasps.

| phylum | **Arthropoda** |
|---|---|
| class | **Insecta** |
| order | **Hemiptera** |
| suborder | **Homoptera** |
| family | **Aleyrodidae** |
| genera & species | **Aleyrodes brassicae** *cabbage whitefly* **Dialeurodes citri** *citrus whitefly* **Trialeurodes vaporariorum** *greenhouse whitefly others* |

# ARACHNIDS

## Introduction

Spiders, along with scorpions, mites and ticks are grouped in the scientific class Arachnida. The Arachnida owe their name to that of Arachne, a maiden in Greek mythology who rashly challenged the goddess Athene to a contest of weaving—and won it. With the total lack of sportsmanship that the ancient Greeks seemed to expect of their gods Athene tore up Arachne's tapestry and turned her into a spider, condemned to spin and weave forever.

Spiders (order Araneae) are by far the most conspicuous and familiar arachnids. They are uniform in their external body structure, and in their development they resemble the primitive insects. All of them start life as tiny spiders and, by the normal arthropod process of successive ecdyses, grow up into larger spiders. Their bodies are divided by a waist into two parts; the fore part bears the eyes and mouth and also six pairs of appendages, the back four pairs being the eight walking legs. It is these eight legs which distinguish a spider immediately from any insect. The other two pairs are the chelicerae or jaws on each side of the mouth and the pedipalps, often called just palps, outside them. These six pairs of appendages are characteristic of all arachnids. All spiders, without exception, are predatory and their jaws have the form of poison fangs for killing their prey. The palps of male spiders are used in mating, the sperm being transferred to them before it is administered to the female.

The rear part of the body, the abdomen, contains the digestive and internal reproductive organs. At its hind end are the organs called spinnerets with which the spider produces silk. The dominant sense of most spiders is that of appreciating and interpreting tension in the threads and webs of silk with which they surround themselves. They not only spin webs to catch their prey, but line their burrows with silk and enclose their eggs in silken cocoons. Some very small spiders pay out strands of silk which catch the wind and eventually cause the spider to be blown away like a thistle or dandelion seed. This action helps them all to find new homes.

Spiders kill their prey with a poisonous bite and the venom of a very few is dangerous to man. They feed by chewing the victim up in the chelicerae and continually injecting and sucking back digestive fluids which dissolve the soft parts. The skeleton, usually that of an insect, is discarded when nothing soluble remains. It could be said that spiders feed entirely on pre-digested liquid.

Among the other orders, the scorpions (order Scorpiones) include the largest arachnids, and most of them are tropical or subtropical. They have the pedipalps enlarged to form finger-and-thumb claws and carry a venomous sting at the end of the tail. The sting of some scorpions is dangerous to human life.

The tiny false scorpions or pseudoscorpions (order Pseudoscorpiones) also have long chelate pedipalps, but lack the 'tail' of the scorpions and have minute fangs on their claws. They are widespread but never abundant and not often seen.

The harvesters, or Daddy long legs, (order Opiliones) are often confused with spiders, but can be distinguished by the round, apparently undivided head and body. Many of them have immensely long, slender legs. They are common wherever there is plenty of vegetation.

Other arachnids described in this book include the Pedipalpi, a rather varied artificial assemblage of mostly tropical animals, the desert-living solfugids or sun-spiders (order Solifugidae), and the mites (order Acarina). Almost all mites are small, many microscopic, and they are the most numerous of all land arthropods. An investigation gave an estimate of 666 millions of mites to an acre of grassland. Most mites are ground dwellers, but some live in fresh water and quite a large number are parasitic.

Very curious mating behaviour is found among some of the arachnids, especially the spiders, scorpions and false scorpions. It arises from the fact that the animals are predators and that the female is usually larger than the male. Therefore, unless the male quickly convinces the female that he has come to mate, she will catch and eat him. The male spider usually performs an elaborate courtship dance and, when accepted, he injects his sperm with his pedipalps, thereby still keeping some distance from her. Both scorpions and false scorpions 'join hands' as a preliminary to mating, and the courtship dance of scorpions has been immortalised in Walt Disney's film 'The Living Desert'.

# Bird-eating spider

*Among the largest of living spiders are the so-called bird-eating spiders of the family Theraphosidae. The largest, from the Amazon basin, can attain a length of $3\frac{1}{2}$ in. with a leg span of 10 in. The body and legs are hairy and the hairs have an irritant effect on the human skin. The theraphosids, which belong to the suborder Mygalomorphae, differ from the more numerous and generally smaller Araneomorphae in having four lungs instead of two, four spinnerets instead of six, and jaws that work vertically instead of sideways.*

*There are over 600 species, all living in the tropics. A number of other spiders, in related families, have also been called bird-eaters, and there are others, only distantly related, that are referred to by this name.*

*The bird-eating spiders are sometimes referred to as tarantulas, especially by American writers. The true tarantula, however, is a wolf spider, **Lycosa tarentula**, found in Southern Europe. Some trapdoor spiders, for example, will kill small birds and there are a number of spiders of the genus **Nephila** that spin such a stout web that small birds are trapped and accidentally eaten.*

## Hairy night-hunter

During the day the bird-eating spider hides in a rock crevice or a hole in a tree and comes out into the Amazon jungle at night to hunt. With its legs spreading $7\frac{1}{2}$ in. or more (as wide as the span of a man's hand) it does not spin a web but runs down its prey or seizes it by a sudden silent dash, to catch small mammals or drag humming-birds from their nests. In spite of its size and the revulsion most people feel on seeing this spider, it is not especially dangerous to humans. It is not easily provoked into attack and its venom is usually no more trouble-some than a bee sting. On the other hand the whole body and legs are covered with fine hairs which can be very irritant. A curator of the insect house at London Zoo was once injured so badly by handling one of these spiders that his hand was red, swollen and painful for several days and one of his fingers remained permanently crooked.

## Fangs for stabbing prey

Once the prey is captured it is instantly stabbed by the sharply-pointed hollow fangs and a fluid injected. It is not clear whether this fluid is a venom or merely the first of a series of injections of digestive juices. It is said to be very mild as a poison, neither kill-ing nor paralysing the prey and yet it can cause a painful local reaction in man, which suggests that it could be a protein-splitting digestive enzyme. Most spiders digest their prey by injecting powerful digestive juices which liquefy the victim's body and then they suck out the contents. Early stories of bird-eating spiders tell of them chewing their food as well as liquefying it, but it is now known that movements once mistaken for chewing are really repeated insertions of the fangs to liquefy more of the victim's body during the lengthened feeding process.

## Female spider guards her babies

The bird-eating spider's instinct to attack and eat any moving thing it can manage is so strong that the male has to approach the female very cautiously during the brief courtship. To avoid being eaten he grasps her fangs with his front legs and after mat-ing he eases himself away from her, then hastily retreats. It is not known whether he finds his mate by smell or touch but his sight is poor.

Each female lays 500 – 1 000 eggs in sum-

△ *The fangs of the bird-eating spider are sharply pointed and hollow. As soon as the prey has been caught and quickly stabbed, a fluid is passed down the hollow fang. It is not clear whether this fluid is a venom or merely the first of a series of injections of digestive juices.*

mer, in a loose cocoon, which she guards by resting with her front feet on it or sitting on it as a hen broods her eggs. If disturbed, she spreads her fangs in a threatening pos-ture. After three weeks white baby spiders hatch from the eggs but stay in the cocoon for up to five weeks. When they leave the cocoon, they are brown with a black spot on the abdomen. They stay near the cocoon for a further 3–12 days, then they scatter.

Baby bird-eating spiders feed at first on very small, slow-moving insects, and grow from 4 mm to 16 mm in the first three years, and increase in weight from 0·0052 gm at birth to 0·8 gm. When adult these large spiders have been known to fast for nearly two years; and they can live for 30 years. They moult about 4 times in each of the first

**Bird-eating spider**
*(family Theraphosidae)*

219

three years, twice in each of the fourth and fifth years, and after that once a year. During the moult the senses of sight, hearing and touch are suspended, and the spider remains motionless for several hours.

## Enemies

The bird-eating spider has few enemies, largely, it is claimed, because of the irritant nature of its hairs, which it is said to scrape from its abdomen with its hind legs so releasing a cloud of fine hairs which blind and stifle its pursuer. Its main, and probably the only effective, enemies are the hunting wasps, against the paralysing sting of which it is defenceless. The most the spider can do is to rise high on its legs and spread its fangs, in a threat display, which the wasp ignores.

In spite of the parental care enjoyed during the first weeks of life, it has been estimated that not more than 0·2% of bird-eating spiders reach adulthood.

## An artist vindicated

The first person to record the carnivorous habits of the bird-eating spiders was Maria Sibilla Merian who, in 1705, published in Amsterdam, a large book called *Metamorphosis Insectorum Surinamensium.* She was an artist and worked in what was then Dutch Guiana. In her book, which was mainly devoted to insects, was a picture showing a large spider dragging a hummingbird from its nest. Beside it was an account of how these spiders take small birds from their nests and suck their blood. No one believed her and in 1834 WS Macleay, an Australian zoologist, made a vitriolic attack on Madame Merian's book, and it was not until 1863, when HW Bates watched spiders killing finches in the Amazon Valley, that Merian's account was fully accepted.

| phylum | **Arthropoda** |
|--------|----------------|
| class  | **Arachnida**  |
| order  | **Araneae**    |
| family | **Theraphosidae** |
| genus  | *Theraphosa,* others |

△◁ *The bird-eating spider has few enemies, largely it is assumed, because of the irritant nature of its hairs. The main and probably only effective enemy of this spider is the hunting wasp whose sting paralyses it.*
◁ *Mother with baby bird-eating spider hatched at the London Zoo in October, 1966. The parents were brought back from Guyana earlier in the year. The female laid over 50 eggs in cocoons she had woven and hidden amongst the vegetation in her cage. On hatching, because of the danger of cannibalism between the young, they were each put in a separate glass tube where they were fed on fruit flies (life size).*

# Crab spider

*Crab spiders are so called because of the length and curvature of their legs and the way they scuttle rapidly sideways, like the true crabs of the sea shore. Crab spiders are all much alike wherever they are found. Many are found in flowers, the colours of which they often match to perfection. They make no web but lie in wait for their prey. They are represented in Britain by 41 species, many rare or of local distribution, and they range from very tiny to not much more than ¼ in. All but one of these belong to the family Thomisidae, there being a single representative of the family Sparassidae, the beautiful, green **Micrommata virescens** which is comparatively large, the female being ½ in. long, the male ⅓ in.*

### Beauty lies hidden

Crab spiders' colours or marks blend with their surroundings and this helps in capturing prey. Some spend most of their time in flowers, others lurk among leaf litter or low vegetation, and some lie along the stems or leaves of plants, head-downwards with the legs on each side held together in the same plane as the piece of foliage. Many combine effective camouflage with considerable beauty. *Thomisus onustus*, for example, is often a bright pink, blending perfectly with the flowers of the bell heath or certain orchids. Another, *Misumena vatia*, sometimes called the 'white death', occurs only in white or yellow plants, the white forms being found in flowers like the butterfly orchis, yellow varieties in mullein and gorse. If one of these spiders is transferred to a flower of a different colour, it quickly leaves it and seeks out another flower to match its own hue.

### Danger in a flower

As the crab spider seizes its prey it pumps a poison into the victim's body along ducts in its sharp-pointed jaws. This quickly affects the insect's nervous system or its blood, or both at once. The paralysed prey is then drained of its body fluids through the cuts made by the jaws. The husk is discarded. A wide variety of small insects and other invertebrates is taken.

Those crab spiders which lurk in flower heads often take insects like hover-flies, bees and butterflies which visit the flowers for nectar. Sometimes the prey is bitten in a non-fatal part, such as the abdomen, in which case the spider manipulates it until it is able to administer the *coup de grâce* in the head or thorax where the central nervous system can be more directly reached.

### Captive courtship

A few days before the male undergoes his final moult he builds a small band of web on which to discharge a drop of seminal fluid. This he takes up into each of his two palps and then goes in search of a mate. There is little preliminary courtship, only tentative caressings with the legs which enable the two partners to recognise each other and which stimulate the female to

*An example of crab spider technique on a flower in the Transvaal veld: sudden death for a honey bee. In this case the spider has selected a flower in which its own colour will not be noticed by the victim until too late. Crab spiders kill by striking at the victim's head and thorax.*

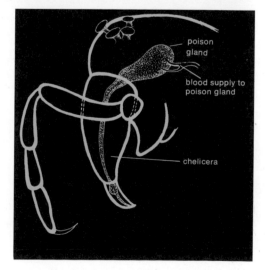

▷ *The crab spider's hypodermic. The venom is held in the sac-like gland, which is covered with secretory cells. Muscle fibres encircle the gland; when they are contracted, venom is forced down the long duct running through the chelicera (fang).*

△ *The face of an assassin: head-on view of a crab spider showing groups of eyes and pedipalps hiding the chelicerae or poison fangs.*
▽ *Female crab spider, with male. Like other spiders, mating is fraught with peril for the male crab spider, for the female will often seize and kill the male. In one species the male ties down the female until mating is completed and he can make good his escape.*

accept the male. Grasping the female by a leg the male inserts the sperm into her genital aperture. If she has already mated she will not allow the male to approach but menaces him by raising her front legs and jerking her body. If he persists she may well seize and kill him. Mating may last for less than a minute or go on for several hours.

In one species *Xysticus cristatus* the male employs a device to prevent the female from seizing him. He binds her legs to the ground with threads of silk, after caressing her into accepting his initial advances. When mating is over the female is delayed just long enough in freeing herself from her bonds to allow the male to make good his escape.

Most crab spiders lay their eggs in early summer. The female makes a silken saucer into which to lay her eggs. This she then covers with another silken layer, forming a cocoon. It may be built between leaves lying on the ground or among foliage. Sometimes the female makes a silken tent within which she sits guarding the eggs. Many females eat nothing during the period of incubation, becoming extremely emaciated. Others capture prey as usual, though never straying far from their eggs. Young crab spiders are hatched as miniatures of their parents, though often differing considerably in colour. As in other spiders they grow by shedding their skins at regular intervals.

## Many enemies

Spiders have many enemies. Small mammals, birds, reptiles and amphibians eat them, as do beetles, ants, and centipedes. Certain species of wasps and ichneumon flies lay their eggs in living crab spiders. Not least, considerable spider mortality is caused by different species of spider killing and eating one another. Indeed, it is likely that spiders indirectly play a major part in controlling their own numbers.

WS Bristowe, distinguished student of spiders, once estimated that the spider population of England and Wales alone was probably of the order of $2\frac{1}{5}$ billions (2 200 000 000 000) at any one moment—or some 40–50 thousand times the human population of Britain! If each spider eats only 100 insects a year, a conservative estimate, then the value of the service spiders render us in keeping insects down to a reasonable level is obvious. On a world scale it is incalculable.

△ *The crab spider's sharp-pointed jaws inject paralysing venom. It then drains the helpless victim of its body fluids.*

▽ *Crab spiders specialise in camouflage; this species is a perfectionist, even matching the flower's yellow-pointed stamens.*

| | |
|---|---|
| phylum | **Arthropoda** |
| class | **Arachnida** |
| order | **Araneae** |
| family | **Sparassidae** |
| genus & species | ***Micrommata virescens*** |
| family | **Thomisidae** |
| genera & species | ***Thomisus onustus*** ***Misumena vatia*** *others* |

# False scorpion

*The false scorpion is a very small animal, rarely exceeding ⅓ in. in length, related to the true scorpions but differing in a number of important particulars. The best known, and the one used here to typify all the false scorpions is **Chelifer cancroides**, sometimes found in old books and so known as the book scorpion. About 1000 species of false scorpions are known, ranging throughout the world except for the polar regions. In addition to their small size and the way they manage to keep out of sight, they are inconspicuous because, unlike so many other animals, they usually keep quite still when disturbed. Their name indicates a superficial resemblance to the true scorpions but they lack the well-known 'tail' with the sting in the end.*

*Occasionally one or other of the false scorpions may be seen clinging to the leg of a fly, so obtaining free transport. Another peculiarity of the false scorpion is its ability to run backwards, especially if it brushes against another animal representing a potential danger. Few animals can move backwards as quickly as they can go forwards, and the false scorpion belongs to an even more select few that can do so more rapidly.*

### Makes an igloo to moult in

The normal habitat of false scorpions is under bark or stones or in heaps of vegetable rubbish, but one species, the book scorpion proper, which is cosmopolitan, lives in human buildings. In spite of its name it may be found in houses, in stables or outhouses, especially where there is hay or straw.

The first pair of appendages, the chelicerae, possess glands, but whereas in spiders similar glands secrete venom, in false scorpions they give out silk, which is used for making nests used for shelters during the period of moult; a false scorpion moults four times in the course of its 2 or 3 years of life.

Having selected a site the animal collects tiny fragments of wood and sand grains and arranges these in a circle around itself. On this it lays down a layer of silk in which the debris finally becomes embedded. Then more sticks and stones are laid on this and more silk added to cement them until finally a silken igloo results, its wall reinforced with building materials. In the later stages the opening of the igloo is very small yet the animal manages to climb in and out to collect building materials. When complete the false scorpion is fully imprisoned. It then gives the shelter a final lining of silk. The igloo is just large enough for the animal to be stretched out to moult, hibernate or lay eggs. When these things are finished the animal has to break through the wall of the shelter to be free again.

### They leave no remains

The second pair of appendages, the pedipalps, are greatly enlarged to form a pair of pincers, which are not unlike those of true scorpions. The book scorpion's prey is minute insects, especially springtails, and mites, seized with the large pedipalps and chewed. Unlike other small animals, such as spiders, a false scorpion eats the whole of its prey, leaving no remains at all.

### Elaborate courtship

Mating is preceded by an elaborate courtship in which the male approaches the female waving his claws and wriggling his abdomen. Should she move he stays dead still. If she remains quiet he moves close to her, the two of them facing each other, head on. Now the male lowers his body to the ground and as he raises it a vertical thread is left on the ground bearing at the top a drop of seminal fluid. The male retires and gives a particular signal with his claws, whereupon the female moves forward until she is over the seminal fluid. At this point the male comes forward, seizes her with his claws and rocks her from side to side with a downward movement so that the fluid is inserted into her genital opening, and fertilises her.

When the time comes for her to lay eggs, the female secretes a liquid from glands in her abdomen that hardens to form a membranous capsule for the eggs. This remains attached to her body. When the larvae hatch they cling to the mother by short beaks and drink from her a nutrient fluid formed by the degenerating tissues of her ovaries. They remain attached until the first moult. After this they leave the capsule, and eventually leave the igloo to feed themselves. They moult three times more, to become adult at the age of a year.

### Skilled hitch-hikers

There are a number of small animals that use slightly larger animals as their means of transport. This enables them either to reach new feeding grounds or to find suitable places in which to lay their eggs. Certain two-winged flies are somewhat given to this, and their aerial transport is supplied by dung beetles. Another example is the blister beetle (page 31). This is a kind of benign, one-sided partnership. The host is not harmed by it, so it cannot be called parasitism. The animal using the transport draws no other benefit than that of being carried from place to place. Consequently, a special name has been given to it: phoresy or phoresia. It is the earliest known form of an airliner.

Certain species of false scorpions frequently use this form of air travel. One of them may grab the leg of a housefly or bluebottle and be carried off, holding on by one pincer. The large spider-like harvester is also used by false scorpions, but this is a bus service rather than air service. As many as 8 false scorpions have been seen riding at one time on the legs of a crane fly.

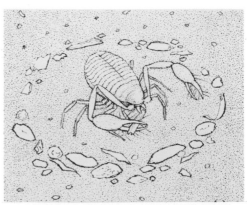

△ *Arranging the foundation circle of debris.*

12 × natural size

△ *False scorpion makes a kill on a fruit fly.*
▷ *Glossy adult has no sting-tipped tail, unlike the true scorpions.*
▽ *Hitch-hiker in action: a false scorpion takes it easy on the abdomen of a myrmicine ant.*

4 × natural size

| phylum | **Arthropoda** |
| --- | --- |
| class | **Arachnida** |
| order | **Pseudoscorpiones** |
| genus & species | *Chelifer cancroides* others |

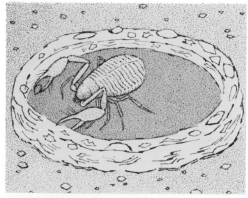
△ *Binding together the debris with silk.*

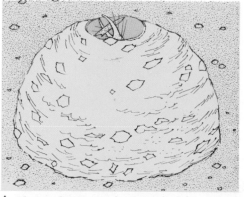
△ *Closing the ring at the tip of the igloo.*

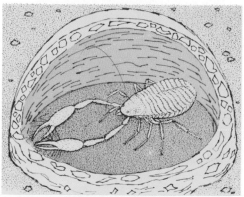
△ *Finished: room for moulting and breeding.*

13 × natural size

# Harvester

*Although often called harvest spiders, harvesters or harvestmen are not true spiders but belong to a separate order, the Opiliones. Both belong, however, to the same class, the Arachnida. Harvesters differ from spiders in several important respects. They have only two eyes, 'back to back', on turrets on the thorax, whereas spiders have up to eight eyes arranged in a group on the 'head'. In addition, while all spiders have the abdomen sharply marked off from the thorax, harvesters have no such 'waist'. Unlike spiders, harvesters never spin webs. Other differences are in their habits. Generally speaking, male and female harvesters are difficult to tell apart except that the male usually has longer legs and a smaller body. In some species, however, notably in the common* **Phalangium opilio**, *the pedipalps of the male are long, giving the impression of another pair of legs. About 3 000 species of harvester are distributed all over the world except for the polar regions. Only 22 are found in Britain.*

*In the United States harvesters are known as daddy long-legs, a name sometimes used for them in Britain but which is more properly applied to the cranefly (page 63).*

### Losing legs

Mainly drab and inconspicuous, harvesters are nevertheless familiar to most people. They live in woods and among long grass and other low-growing vegetation but being largely nocturnal we more often see them under flowerpots and beneath window sills. The gardener turning over a pile of rubbish or compost, or perhaps an old sack lying on the ground, may see one of the larger species scuttling away on its long, thread-like legs. Sometimes in making its escape one of its legs is lost. The leg is thrown off at a breaking point between the first two segments. After coming away the leg may twitch and quiver for some seconds. Harvesters appear to suffer little inconvenience from the loss, but cannot regenerate a lost limb. This is a further point of difference from spiders which can regrow their legs.

Harvesters have been found still moving around with only two legs. The second pair of legs, usually the longest, carry sense organs. They are used to feel the way over obstacles or, held in the air, to detect vibrations. They seem also to carry a sense of taste or smell. Loss of this pair of legs slows a harvester down very considerably.

### Feeding on scraps

Harvesters are largely carnivorous, feeding on a variety of small invertebrates, such as insects, spiders and mites. They do not in-

▷ *Hitch-hikers all aboard! Red mites are often found on harvesters as passengers taking rides from one place to another. The larval mites shown here are parasitic.*

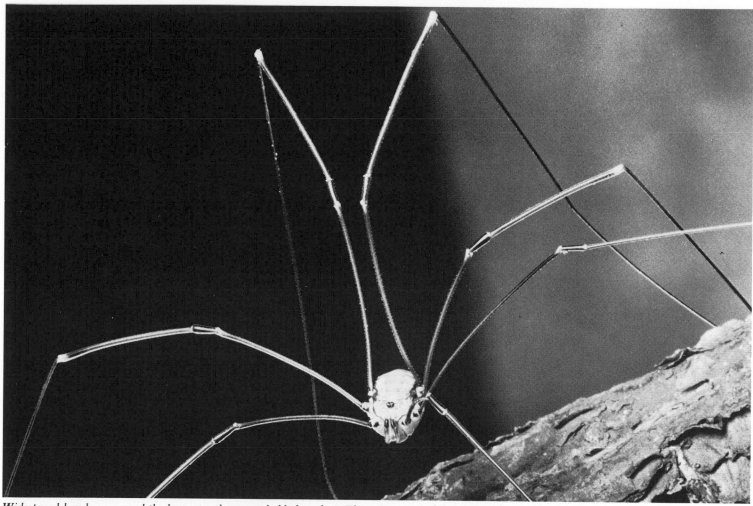

*Widespread legs have earned the harvester the name daddy long-legs. They often wave their sensitive legs in the air which has given rise to the old bit of folklore which claims a farmer can tell where his cows are by watching a harvester's legs and seeing in which direction they point.*

ject poison into their victims, as spiders do. Instead, they have large and powerful beak-like jaws, or chelicerae, with which to pierce the prey and suck out its juices and soft tissues. They also eat some of the more juicy forms of plant life. They are in fact omnivorous. In captivity they can be fed on almost anything edible, from bread and milk to meat; this is probably the reason why they are so common in garden rubbish heaps. If a bottle containing scraps of meat and fat is placed with its opening level with the soil and left overnight, this will often contain one or more harvesters in the morning. Harvesters also need to drink at frequent intervals to keep in good condition. They cannot endure the long periods of starvation that spiders can and lack of water for drinking soon makes them stiff and torpid. A drink, however, quickly restores them.

### Three months of life

Mating is by internal fertilisation and there is no courtship. Matings are frequent, the same male mating several times in rapid succession with the same partner or with other females. The female lays her eggs, which are less than $\frac{1}{5}$ in. diameter, in the soil or in crevices in the bark of trees, usually in late summer or autumn using an ovipositor. In some species, the eggs overwinter, young harvesters being hatched the following year. In others, the eggs hatch fairly quickly but the young hibernate through the winter. Apart from size, there is little or no difference between adult and

young harvesters. In some species, males are exceedingly rare and reproduction is largely by parthenogenesis. This is especially true of *Megabunus diadema*, found on mountains in Britain. It is silver, green and black. One count showed only one male to over 400 females.

Growth is by ecdysis, or moulting, the whole skin being shed. There may be seven or eight such skin changes during a harvester's lifetime, with about ten days between each, the moult usually taking place at night. The gossamer-light sloughs, complete in every detail, intact down to the thinnest portions of each leg, may sometimes be found attached to low growing vegetation to which the harvester usually anchors itself for the moult. The old skin splits and the body is drawn out from it. Then each long leg must be removed from its old casing. For this the harvester uses its jaws.

### Anaesthetic defence-measure

Harvesters are preyed upon by centipedes and the larger spiders, as well as being taken by the smaller insectivorous birds. Their only defence is to cast a limb which may twitch and wriggle like a living thing, so catching the attention of the predator long enough for the harvester itself to make good its escape, or to discharge an offensive, volatile fluid from glands near the eyes. This fluid seems to affect even harvesters themselves if a group of them are placed in a closed container. They seem to be anaesthe-

tised by it, but if taken out and exposed once more to the air they quickly recover.

### Water—essential but hazardous

Having so many sense organs on its legs a harvester must keep them cleared of dust and dirt, so its toilet is carried out with great care. Always after feeding and at other times as well each leg in turn is held in the jaws and slowly pulled through them. By the time this is finished the leg has curved almost into a circle. Then comes the need for cleaning the jaws themselves, and for this the harvester must go to water, rest the front pair of legs on the surface film and dip its face in the water. Sometimes the legs break through the surface film and the animal cannot regain its balance and is drowned. Water for harvesters is a dire necessity for drinking and washing, and also a natural hazard.

| phylum | **Arthropoda** |
|---|---|
| class | **Arachnida** |
| order | **Opiliones** |
| family | **Phalangildae** |
| genera & species | *Phalangium opilio* *Megabunus diadema* |

# Mite

*Mites are minute relatives of spiders and scorpions. They are the small members of the order Acarina, the largest being the blood-sucking ticks which will be described later. The body is rounded, usually about ½ mm long, with no visible division into two parts as there is in the bodies of spiders. As in spiders, there are four pairs of many-jointed legs with claws at the tips, and a pair of chelicerae. These may be sharp and able to pierce the bodies of other animals and plant tissues. In spiders the chelicerae are the poison fangs.*

*On each side of the chelicerae are two short limbs called pedipalps, which are not pincers as in scorpions or false scorpions (page 224) but are leglike and carry many sensory hairs.*

*The total number of mites is not known but there may be in excess of a million species. There are relatively few scientists studying mites compared with the thousands studying insects, yet in 1966 descriptions of 1 000 new species and 150 new genera of mites were published. Little is known of the habits of many mites and new mites are being discovered all the time. Some, however, have as great an economic importance as insects, and are responsible for the transmission of certain diseases in plants and animals.*

△ *The giant red velvet mites* **Dinothrombium** *are, as their name suggests, large, about 1 cm long. They are in fact the largest of the Acarina. Their bodies have the exact texture of velvet. They are mainly found in desert and semi-desert areas and also in some humid parts of the tropics. After heavy rains they emerge in such great numbers that they cover the ground and can be counted in their thousands.*

### Mites almost everywhere

Mites are found in all sorts of odd places and have a great diversity of habits but they are readily overlooked because of their small size. They are found in the nostrils of seals, among the gills of crayfish and the hearing organs of moths. Others cause plant galls, a few live in the sea and many eat decaying matter, such as the cheese mite that feeds on decaying cheese. Mites are also found in the Antarctic where they feed on fungi and decaying plants in the scanty patches of moss and algae. Perhaps the best known mite is the harvest 'bug' or harvest mite. The larval stage of the harvest mite waits in matted vegetation or low bushes and clings to warm-blooded animals as they pass. The larvae of harvest mites have only six legs: they are white to orange-red and about $\frac{1}{100}$ in. long—just visible to the naked eye. They pierce the skin of the host with the chelicerae, which is painless, but a fluid is injected to break down the cells of the skin to allow liquid food to be sucked up. This causes quite severe irritation and small inflamed pimples. As the harvest mite sucks up food its body stretches until it is three or four times its original size. The larval mite then drops to the ground and completes its life cycle, changing first to an eight-legged nymph, then to the mature adult.

The harvest mite is picked up by people without adequate protection from clothing when they walk or sit in vegetation where these mites are abundant. Another mite that attacks humans is the itch mite which burrows in the skin. The eggs are laid in the burrows and larvae emerge 2—3 days later. Scratching the sources of irritation increases the risk of infection. Some mites transmit disease directly, such as scrub typhus, and some very minute mites that live on dandruff and sloughed skin trigger asthmatic attacks when they are inhaled with household dust.

## Not always dangerous

Infestation by mites often causes little or no harm to the host except the loss of some body fluid. Some mites infest the 'ears' of certain moths, such as the army worm moth a severe pest in North America. They rupture the eardrum of the moth, lay their eggs on the ear duct and pierce its wall to suck the moth's blood. No doubt the 'ear' is put out of action, but in a study of army worm moths it was found that only two out of every 1 000 had mites infesting both ears. No-one knows why all the mites should head for only one ear but it does prevent the moths becoming deaf.

## Gradual growing up

The mating behaviour of mites is very similar to that of spiders, in that the male transfers a bag of sperm, the spermatophore, to the female. In one species studied in the laboratory, the male climbs onto the female, feeling with his legs and pedipalps, then turns her onto her back and exudes a spermatophore. This is transferred to her genital opening and gradually drawn in.

Mites lay large eggs one at a time at long intervals. The mite that lives in the 'ears' of moths lays eggs almost half its own size at intervals of 2 hours or more until about 90 have been laid. Before laying the female mite scrapes a patch on the lining of the 'ear' on which she sticks the egg. Each time an egg is laid the process is repeated until there are several neat rows of eggs.

The larvae that emerge from the eggs have only three pairs of legs or, in the case of the gall-forming species, two pairs. At

△ *A common sight.* **Parasitus coleop-tratum** *nymphs clinging to the underside of a dor beetle which is struggling to turn itself the right way up. These mite nymphs, each one about $\frac{1}{20}$ in. long, are only using the beetle as a means of transport, and do not do any harm to the beetle.*

▽ *Not quite the colour you might expect: adults of a red spider mite* **Metatetranychus ulmi***, eggs and hatched egg cases on the underside of an apple leaf. It is a pest of gardens and orchards; infestation is easily recognizable from the loose webs covering leaves on which the eggs are laid (30 × life size).*

intervals the larvae shed their skins and each time they emerge they look more like the mature adults.

## Pesticides cause pests

One of the drawbacks to the powerful pesticides developed in the last 20 years or so is that they sometimes 'backfire' by making new pests. This does not mean, of course, that new animals are created. A pest is an animal that causes sufficient damage to man's property or person to be of economic importance. Such a pest is the red spider mite, which attacks fruit trees and other crops. The red spider mite weaves sheet webs on plants that look like opaque cellophane. The mites live in large numbers within the webs, sucking the plants' juices. At one time it was not a pest because the damage it did was negligible. Then the widespread application of powerful pesticides killed off the red spider mites' enemies, resulting in an astronomical increase in these mites.

As a result pesticides had to be employed against the red spider mites, but unfortunately they became immune and even larger amounts had to be used. Such enemies as were left, if they did not succumb immediately to the poisons, died from eating poisoned mites.

There is now hope that the red spider mite may be rendered innocuous again. The answer seems to be in biological rather than chemical control. The red spider mite is a very serious pest of cucumber and other greenhouse crops, but experiments have shown that their numbers can be drastically reduced by introducing a predatory mite *Phytoseiulus riegeli*. Paradoxically it is sometimes necessary to infect a greenhouse with red spider mites to ensure an adequate supply of food for the predators. The system works well, it is apparently 10 times cheaper than chemical control, and there is the advantage that an animal cannot become immune to another that eats it.

| phylum | **Arthropoda** |
| --- | --- |
| class | **Arachnida** |
| order | **Acarina** |
| genera & species | *Tetranychus urticae* red spider mite |
| | *Trombicula autumnalis* harvest mite |
| | *Tyrophagus putrescentiae* cheese mite, others |

# Orb spider

*Orb spider is a collective name for those spiders belonging to the family Araneidei that spin an orb-shaped web, sometimes called a cartwheel or geometric web. These spiders, with their bodies large by comparison with their legs, are entirely dependent on their webs to catch their prey. The most numerous and studied orb spider in Europe, is the European garden spider,* **Araneus diadematus** *also known as the diadem or cross spider.*

*The female is ½ in. long, excluding the legs, the male is about half this, although the sizes reached by males are variable. The colour of the body may vary from a drab pale fawn to a rich brown. It may have little patterning on the abdomen or it may be marked with spots, blotches and lines in white, yellow or shades of brown. The most characteristic of the markings is, in its simplest form, a group of five whitish spots forming a cross. This pattern may be extended into a series of spots or oval markings.*

## How the web is built

All spiders live by eating other animals, usually insects. Most of them construct some form of snare made of silk threads given out from a group of spinnerets on the underside near the tip of the abdomen. In orb spiders the web or snare starts with an outer scaffolding. The first thread laid down is known as the bridge thread. It is horizontal and uppermost. Then two side threads are joined to it and, often, a fourth to complete the rectangle. This last thread may be missing when, as sometimes happens, the spider builds a triangular or polygonal frame. A set of radial threads is then laid down, from the frame to a hub in the centre. At the hub a closely woven platform is made from which a spiral of temporary scaffolding is run outwards. All this is made of non-sticky silk and the snare itself is laid down on it. Using the non-sticky threads to walk on, the spider, working from without inwards, lays down the close spiral of sticky threads, distinguished by the beads along each thread. As the spider is making the sticky snare it cuts away the temporary scaffolding as it goes.

It is a popular idea that the silk is liquid when first given out of the spinnerets and that it hardens on contact with the air. In

△ *Jewelled abdomen—the unmistakable markings on the abdomen of the garden spider show clearly why it is often called diadem spider and cross spider.*

▷ *Spiders' webs shimmer with dewdrops which will soon evaporate to leave the traps invisible.*

▽ *Looking like a discarded candyfloss this delicate yellow ball is in fact a silken cocoon containing about 600 garden spider eggs.*

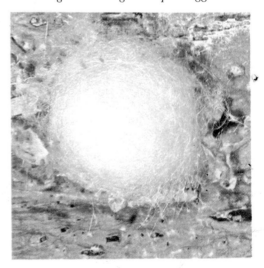

△ *Bejewelled diadem. A garden spider in the centre of its dewdrop-laden web, having every reason to be proud of its geometric magnificence. When the web is complete, the spider usually hides somewhere nearby; when an insect flies into the web and struggles it rushes out to secure its victim.*

fact it coagulates as it is being squirted out and becomes strong and extensile as the spider pulls on it.

### Webs as fishing nets
When the web is complete the spider retires to a hiding place, perhaps under a leaf, somewhere on the outer scaffolding. When an insect flies into the web and struggles the spider is alerted by the vibrations and runs out to secure its victim, usually swathing it in silk. At the same time it injects poison into it from its fangs (chelicerae) which not only paralyses the prey but acts as a digestive juice liquefying the contents of the body.

Although insects are the main prey of spiders the larger species may catch small birds in their webs. Tropical species of *Nephila,* for example, spin webs between trees and these may be as much as 8 ft across and made of thick, tough silk. In parts of southeast Asia the local peoples have used these webs for fishing nets, bending a pliable stick into a loop with a handle

and passing this through a web so it comes away attached to the loop.

### When spiderlings leave home
Eggs are laid in autumn in silken cocoons of a dingy golden-yellow colour, more or less oval, 1½ in. long, each cocoon containing 600—800 eggs. The cocoons are fastened under large leaves, a window sill, plank or inverted flower pot, anywhere that offers a secluded corner. The eggs hatch the following June and the spiderlings, as soon as they are hatched, spin an irregular mass of almost invisible strands of silk in which they cluster in a ball. When disturbed they rush about in all directions coming together again in a ball once things have settled down. They stay together in this way for a few days then they start to scatter once again.

As each arrives on a new site it spins a small orb web about 2 in. across similar to the familiar 'cartwheel' but much more irregular. At this time there is little difference between male and female, but after a

while the females begin to grow more quickly.

They do not mature until the following summer, and then growth in size is very rapid, the females outstripping the males and making webs 2 ft across. This is why the orb webs seem suddenly to appear in late summer. The spiders have been there all the time, but they and their webs have suddenly grown large. The majority do not survive the first frosts and by the end of November even the hardiest of adults have died. A few pass the winter in sheltered spots and occasionally a diadem spider will stay in a house.

### Climate the worst enemy
In temperate latitudes at least the weather is the spider's worst enemy, especially drought and excessive rain. The orb spinners are less preyed upon than those spiders living nearer the ground but there are many small birds that include spiders in their normal diet. Insects such as the parasitic wasps and ants also prey on them. There is

a certain amount of cannibalism as well, the best known of which is when the female eats her mate.

## Does she eat her mate?

Many people tend to think that once the male has mated he is eaten by the female, but experts have declared that this is a great exaggeration.

The leading British expert on spiders, WS Bristowe, in *The World of Spiders*, writes: 'Having survived the threats of starvation, climate and enemies the male spider, if he is a web-builder, abandons his web, and spends his time searching for females and courting them, often with little effort devoted in between whiles to feeding himself. His remaining span of life is usually short, and post-mortem investigations would show that death was in most cases due to exhaustion and under-nourishment rather than to slaughter by the females as is commonly supposed. Such tragedies do occur but are comparatively rare.' The mere fact that a male usually mates with more than one female should be proof enough that the popular notion of 'the female spider eating her husband' is unfounded.

| phylum | **Arthropoda** |
|---|---|
| class | **Arachnida** |
| order | **Araneae** |
| genus & species | ***Araneus diadematus*** *European garden spider* |

▽ ***Argiope****, a South African orb spider swathes a butterfly in silk to disable it.*

▽ *Signature spider is the local name for* ***Argiope*** *as it makes a silk zig-zag in its web.*

▽ *Silken canopy, but the beauty is deceiving for this is a snare for unsuspecting victims.*

▽ *Experienced tight-rope walkers: the male garden spider (left) makes his first tentative advances towards the lady of his choice (right).*

# Pedipalpi

*The pedipalpi are an assemblage of animals, now regarded as belonging to three separate orders within the Arachnida. The members of two of these groups are both known as 'whip scorpions' but for different reasons: The 'whip' in one group, the Uropygi, is a long thin tactile tail at the end of the abdomen, while the other whip scorpions, the Amblypygi, carry two 'whips' in the form of a pair of very long, flexible legs. All three groups use the first pair of legs as feelers rather than for walking, but in the Amblypygi the length is particularly exaggerated. The members of the third group, the Schizomida, are small and retiring and not well known. In all three, the body is in two parts, a combined head and thorax, or cephalothorax, and an abdomen of 12 segments. They vary in length from $1-2\frac{3}{4}$ in. The cephalothorax bears the legs and, at the*

*front, a short pair of appendages called chelicerae followed by the well-developed pair which names the group pedipalps.*

### Frog-eating tail-rumps . . .

The powerful pedipalps of the scorpion-like Uropygi are armed with claws for the capture of cockroaches, grasshoppers and other insects, as well as slugs and worms–or even small frogs and toads in the case of the largest species *Mastigoproctus giganteus*, of Mexico and the southern United States. At the base of each pedipalp is a large semicircular toothed structure used for crushing the prey. There are 8–12 feeble eyes arranged in 3 groups on the cephalothorax, but the first pair of legs are more important as sense organs. In any case, the Uropygi are nocturnal hunters, hiding during the day under logs and stones, or in burrows. *M. giganteus* spends several days digging its burrow with its pedipalps and when it is finished the tunnel may be 4 in. long. The prey is usually devoured here.

There are about 700 species of Uropygi

△ *At death's door? This whip scorpion* **Damon variegatus** *traps and kills insects with its large spiny pedipalps and then dismembers them with its sharp, curved chelicerae. Two pairs of tiny eyes can be seen on top of the cephalothorax.*

(literally tail-rumps) living in southern North America and northeastern South America as well as in India, Malaya, eastern Asia and Japan.

### . . . split middles . . .

The members of the small group, the Schizomida, are $\frac{1}{4}$ in. or less long with at most only a knob for a tail. The carapace of the cephalothorax, divided in this order alone into three parts, carries only one pair of eyes. The pedipalps end in spines instead of in claws and they move up and down instead of sideways as in the Uropygi. There are three genera and the group occurs sporadically in tropical regions, appearing sometimes also in botanical gardens such as that at Kew. The Schizomida feed at night, probably on insects and hide by day, though not in any fixed home. When disturbed,

they make their escape by a quick backwards leap and can run fast. Little more is known of their habits.

### ... and blunt-rumps

The tail-less Amblypygi, (literally blunt-rumps) have very flattened bodies suitable for getting through narrow cracks and the two halves are joined by a slender stalk. There is one pair of median eyes and three pairs of lateral eyes as in some of the Uropygi. The pedipalps are spined, powerful and sometimes very long, and each ends in a movable hook. There are fewer than 100 species, $\frac{1}{4}-1\frac{3}{4}$ in. long, and they are found in humid tropical and subtropical regions: the southern half of Africa, America, India, Malaya, Borneo and New Guinea.

Nocturnal like the others, the Amblypygi cling by day to the undersurfaces of rock crevices, logs and stones. Some species, with less need for dampness, have become commensal with man and in some parts of the world few houses are without them. When exposed to light, their first reaction is to freeze, but they will run fast if touched.

Usually they walk sideways and then, as well as while at rest, they are continually searching around with the tips of their long legs. One of the two families consists mostly of small cave-dwellers and these, unlike the others, can run around under the ceilings of caves or even up polished glass. The prey, mostly insects of various kinds, are held in the spiny pedipalps while the chelicerae remove pieces for chewing.

### Courtship dances

Courtship and breeding have not been observed in many of the pedipalpi, but at least it is clear that the groups differ. In the Uropygi the courting male holds the long front legs of the female in his pedipalps and chelicerae and walks backwards with his mate following. She responds by lifting her abdomen which the male strokes with his front legs. The sperm is transferred in a spermatophore which is held against the female genital opening for some hours. The pregnant female digs a burrow where she stays several weeks and lays, in one species at least, 20–35 yellowish eggs which are

retained in a transparent membrane under her abdomen. The young cut their way out of this by means of special spines on their legs and cling to the upper side of the mother's abdomen or to the bases of her back legs until they reach the adult form, at the first moult. They then leave the mother whose strength is nearly spent and become adult after three more yearly moults.

In the single member of the Schizomida studied, the mating pair promenade with the female holding the end of the male's abdomen with her chelicerae. He then deposits a spermatophore and cements it to the ground. From the top of this, the female gathers the sperm. Later she builds a little nest with cemented walls under the soil. The Amblypygi court at night, with much tapping of the front legs and threatening with the pedipalps, but no grasping. The male deposits a slender transparent spermatophore on the ground while facing away from the female and then turns towards her and loads it with sperm. As he steps back and quivers, she collects the sperm, leaving the spermatophore for him to eat. She also

carries her eggs in a sac under her abdomen. △ *Uropugid whip scorpion* **Thelyphonus caudatus.** ▽ *Amblypygid pedipalp* **Damon variegatus.**

## Exaggerated reputation

With the scorpion-like tails of one group and the exaggerated legginess of the other, whip scorpions are unfailing objects of horror. In fact, they have neither stings nor venomous bites and the Amblypygi, at least, are harmless. Nevertheless, the large *Mastigoproctus giganteus* of southern North America, where it has the local name of 'grampus', is generally feared for its supposed venomous properties. In fact it can inflict a wound with the spines on its pedipalps and, like others of the Uropygi, can discharge a protective cloud into the air from glands near the base of the tail which can be very irritating to the mucous membranes. The secretion of some species smells of formic acid or chlorine, but in *M. giganteus* it is acetic acid.

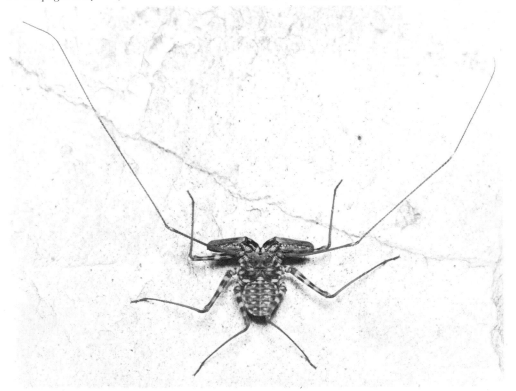

| phylum | **Arthropoda** |
|--------|----------------|
| class | **Arachnida** |

# Scorpion

Scorpions are notorious for their stings, the venom of which, in some species, is fatal to man. They range in length from ¼ in. to as much as 8 in. in **Scorpio viatoris** of Africa. The body is segmented and bears a pair of powerful chelicerae or pincerlike claws similar to those of a lobster. The thorax has four segments each with a pair of walking legs on the undersurface and the abdomen has six segments tapering to a single sharp sting at the end with a small opening supplied by two relatively large venom glands. Such animals as the 8in. African scorpions have a very large sting and venom dangerous to humans.

The lobster-scorpion of Sumatra is even larger but as it lives in dense forest it is not often encountered by man. Although the United States has about 40 species, only two, the 2–3in. **Centruroides sculpturatus** and **C. gertschi**, have venom which can be fatal.

The 650 species are found in all the warm regions of the world. They are particularly abundant in deserts but are found only sparsely in the temperate zones. In America they are found as far north as British Columbia, and they also live in southern Europe. They are extremely adaptable and can stand fierce heat.

## Dangerous in the house

One of the main dangers from a scorpion is its habit of living in human dwellings, crawling into beds, furniture, under carpets and into shoes. Away from houses they hide by day under logs or rocks, or in holes in the sand which they dig with their middle legs. Scorpions lead solitary lives, being very hostile to other scorpions, the females may even devour the males after mating.

## Tearing their victims to pieces

Scorpions hunt by night. Their prey consists almost entirely of insects and spiders. They seize a victim with their large claws and tear it to pieces or crush it, extracting its body juices. If it offers any resistance the scorpion may then, and only then, use its sting by bringing its abdomen forward over the body and thrusting the poison-bearing tip into its prey. The prey is then slowly eaten, an hour or more sometimes being spent in consuming a single beetle. Scorpions can survive long periods without eating and it is said that they never drink, getting all the moisture they need from their food or from dew. This is not true. In captivity they will readily take water. The usual method of supplying a scorpion with water is to put a wad of wet cotton-wool in its cage, which it will visit regularly to drink.

▷△ *The sting, with its poison-bearing tip, is stabbed into any victim which puts up a fight.*
▷ *Young scorpions ride on their mother's back for nearly a week. These miniature adults are born alive over a period of several weeks.*

Some species of scorpions stridulate, or 'sing', by rubbing the bases of their clawed limbs against the bases of the first pair of walking legs. In some there is what is known as a rasp at the base of each claw with a 'keyboard' on the walking legs. In others the 'keyboard' is on the claw. Scorpions do not stridulate for the same reason as grasshoppers do. Their 'song' is used as a preliminary to attack or as a defensive warning. It is interesting that the positions of the claws differ: in the attack posture they are held wide apart with the claws open and pointing upwards, while in the defensive position the claws are held low and in front of the head. Only the pseudoscorpions have similarly enlarged pedipalps or claws.

## Courtship 'dance'

Like spiders, scorpions indulge in a form of courtship before mating. Normally when the female is responsive the male first grasps her with his claws and then manoeuvres to face her, gripping her claws with his own. Sometimes when the female is not submissive and tries to pull away, the male raises his sting almost straight above his claws and the female does the same. It happens very rarely and then only for a few seconds. Having grasped the female the male drags or pushes her to a suitable place where he scrapes away the soil with his feet and deposits his spermatophore. Then, still holding her by her claws, he manoeuvres her over it so she can take up the sperma-

tophore with her cloaca. The two animals remain together for about 5 or 6 minutes before breaking away.

Development in scorpions is especially interesting because the entire order is either ovoviviparous or truly viviparous. The young scorpions are born alive, one or two at a time, over a period of some weeks. In some species a placenta-like tissue is formed in the mother's body through which food is passed to the growing embryo and waste products removed. After birth the baby scorpions ride around on their mother's back. Only after their first moult do they leave the mother and become independent. Some scorpions are known to live for as long as 5 years.

## Danger when provoked

The ferocity of scorpions has probably been much exaggerated although there is no doubt that some species are very dangerous. They will not, however, use their sting against humans unless considerably provoked. The danger lies in their coming into houses and, where they are common, this can make living hazardous unless special precautions are taken. In the United States and Mexico it is estimated that more people are killed by scorpions than by snakes. In a town in Brazil, with a population of only 200 000, in 1954 alone nearly 200 people needed emergency hospital treatment for scorpion stings. It is much the same story in other tropical parts of the world and in some places the number of scorpions is amazingly high as shown by a report from Bombay in India. There, what was described as a casual hunt revealed nearly 15 000 scorpions in an area inhabited by only 13 000 people, and the writer of the report suggested that a closer search might have revealed even more.

A sting from one of the more dangerous species is often followed by collapse, profuse perspiring and vomiting, and the skin becoming cold and clammy. Even when drugs and oxygen are administered the patient has difficulty in breathing, with a profuse frothy fluid coming out of the mouth and nostrils. Even with modern medicines this usually ends in death.

| phylum | **Arthropoda** |
|--------|----------------|
| class | **Arachnida** |
| order | **Scorpiones** |
| genera | *Ospistobuthus* *Buthus* *Scorpio* *Tityus* |

▽ *Battle in the sand. The triumphant victor of these two* **Centrurus** *grasps its overturned opponent's claw. The last two sections of the large pedipalps are modified and enlarged to form claw-like pincers. The overturned scorpion displays its segmented abdomen and the arrangement of legs on the thorax.*

# Solifugid

*These relatives of spiders probably have the strongest jaws, in proportion to their size, of any animals. Perhaps it is because they have so many names, such as false spiders, sun spiders, wind scorpions and camel spiders, that zoologists usually refer to them collectively as solifugids. There are also zoologists who speak of them as solpugids because the order to which they belong is variously known as the Solifugae or the Solpugida. This question of classification is relatively unimportant because they are fairly unknown.*

*Solifugids look like hairy spiders but differ from them in many ways. They seem to have very large heads because of the powerful jaws and the large muscles needed to work them. The thorax consists of three separate segments and the abdomen is also segmented. They appear to have five pairs of legs but the first pair are pedipalps which are long, powerful and very hairy, and each has a sucker at the end, used in climbing smooth surfaces. The chelicerae are held high up while the animal is moving and are used to seize prey. Behind them are four pairs of walking legs, each ending in a sharp pair of claws, but the first pair are normally held up off the ground, like antennae. The hind pair of legs each bear five racquet-shaped organs. These may be used to detect movements of their prey.*

*The 600 species of solifugids are usually yellow, brown, or sometimes black. A few have stripes along the body. They vary from $\frac{1}{2}$—2 in. in length, and the larger species span 6 in. with their legs. They are especially numerous in the desert regions of Africa and Arabia but are found as far east as Celebes. In Europe they occur only in southeast Spain. In North America they are found in Florida, in the deserts of the southwest United States and around hot springs as far north as southwest Canada. They also live in Central America and in the coastal areas of northern, eastern and western South America.*

## Sand plough

The name solifugid means 'fleeing from the sun' and most of the species are nocturnal. There are the others, however, which earn the name of sun spiders (*arañas del sol* in Spanish). They all run quickly and the diurnal solifugids have been described as looking like balls of thistledown blown over the sand as they run about, hence the name wind scorpions. A solifugid will suddenly stop and quarter the ground as if it has sensed the presence of prey. Because they are so active solifugids need a more efficient breathing system, so instead of the lung books of spiders, they have a tracheal system like insects. When attacked they bend the abdomen up, recalling a scorpion's tail, but the solifugid does this only to keep its abdomen out of harm's way. The nocturnal

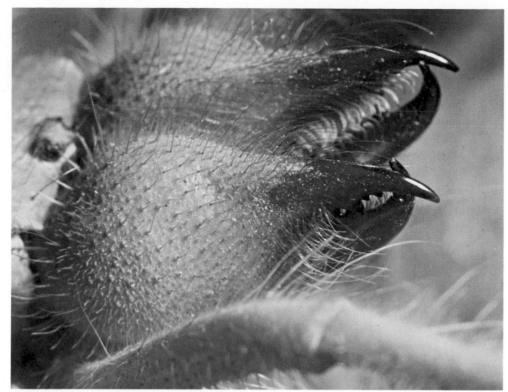

△ *For its size the solifugid's chelicerae are massive. Each is composed of two parts which form a pair of strong pincer-like jaws that are used to kill the prey.* ◁ *Opposite: At the kill—G. arabs devours a young gecko. Solifugids have voracious appetites and will attack any small animal.*

species hide under stones by day or bury in the sand, using their stout jaws to plough into the sand or scraping the sand backwards with their second pair of legs.

The female is more aggressive than the male towards other animals of their own size. The male will run from a scorpion, dodging the stabs from its sting. A female will attack, seizing the scorpion by the tail just behind the sting.

## Real gluttons

Solifugids are wholly carnivorous. They eat insects, spiders, scorpions and smaller solifugids as well as small mice, birds and lizards. The prey is held and passed to and fro through the jaws by the pedipalps which chew it to a soft pulp. After this it sucks up the juices. A solifugid never drinks, probably because it gets all its moisture from its food. So long as there is food it will gorge itself until it can hardly move.

## Trance-like state

The males are lighter in colour, smaller, more active and have longer legs than the females. They also have narrower heads and smaller jaws, which may be why they flee, in contrast to the female which will stand her ground and fight. In courtship the male taps the female's body and strokes her, until she is in a trance-like state, when he can approach without danger of being attacked. The male then opens her genital orifice with one of the chelicerae, discharges a drop of sperm which he catches with the other chelicera and places inside the female. After this he scuttles away before she 'comes to'. The female goes into a deep burrow to lay her eggs, and stays beside them until they hatch. She then goes out to hunt for food for her offspring which she feeds until they are old enough to leave the burrow.

## Biblical mice

Where solifugids are numerous there is a general belief that they are venomous. The fact is they produce no poison although they can inflict painful bites with their powerful jaws. These are normally reserved for their prey but sometimes people are bitten and one species living in parts of the North African desert is said to inflict particularly painful bites. JL Cloudsley-Thompson tells us that the Egyptians believe solifugids 'crawl in one's bed at night, bore into the crutch and lay their eggs'. The people of Baku, on the Caspian Sea, believe the local solifugids to be especially poisonous when they first come out of hibernation in the spring. The cure is to rub the wound with another solifugid—after steeping it in boiling oil—to neutralize the effects of the venom. It has been suggested, according to Cloudsley-Thompson, that the Hebrew word translated as 'mouse' in the Old Testament refers to some form of Solpuga, and that the sores from which the Philistines suffered were from their bites. He adds that their rapid movements and hairy bodies give an illusion of mice and 'they have been known to attack travellers asleep in the desert at night'.

| phylum | **Arthropoda** |
|---|---|
| class | **Arachnida** |
| order | **Solifugae** |
| genera & species | *Galeodes arabs* *Rhagodessa cloudsleythompsoni* *others* |

# Tarantula

*Although everyone knows that the tarantula is a spider, few people are sure of its exact type; great confusion exists over the name. Originally, it referred to a small spider, belonging to the family of wolf spiders living in southern Italy. Its name was derived from the town of Taranto where legend stated that its bite was fatal unless the patient danced until exhausted, and the poison had been sweated from the system. The dance became known as the tarantella. All this happened in the Dark Ages, possibly earlier, and long before Columbus discovered America. Soon after that discovery the large bird-eating spiders of South America were called tarantulas. Their large size and, to most people, repulsive hairiness epitomized the popular horror of spiders and the image in many people's minds of the dreaded spider of southern Italy. Setting the seal on the confusion, certain harmless whip-scorpions that are not even spiders have been placed in a family named the Tarantulidae.*

*There are nearly a dozen species of the genus **Tarentula**, including the one that started all the fuss. This used to be known as **Tarantula inquilina**, then **Lycosa narbonensis** and now it is named **Tarentula narbonensis**. Its long, somewhat narrow, grey body is just over 1 in. in length, with dark spots, and its legs are hairy and about the same length as the body. Other European species are similar but only just over ½ in. long, or less, and one, **T. fabrilis**, has a dark, dagger-shaped mark on its abdomen. The tarantula of southern Europe is **Lycosa tarentula** (pages 219 and 248).*

*A tarantula attacking a grasshopper. Tarantulas kill insects by injecting them with a poison.*

## Poison investigated

Tarantulas are found in different habitats according to the species, from lowlands to mountains up to and above 2 000 ft, on open country such as moors, heaths and grassland, and also in woodlands. They live in short burrows in the ground and spin no web but, like wolves, run down their prey which is mainly small insects. They kill these by injecting a poison. Henri Fabre, the famous French entomologist, found this was instantly fatal to insects, but he went further to investigate the potency of the poison in relation to the legend. He found the tarantula would bite a sparrow but that a young sparrow took 3 days to die, and a mole died in 36 hours. From this he concluded that the bite could be troublesome to people and that measures to counteract the poison should be taken.

## Male tarantula dances

As in all spiders the courtship is elaborate, and, fittingly, in these species the male does a dance. WS Bristowe, in his *Comity of Spiders*, has given a detailed description of what happens in some of them. In two species the male moves his palps up and down, slowly at first, then more quickly, and he begins to pulsate his abdomen. Then he walks around the female with jerky steps, with his front legs bunched up and pulsating both his palps and his abdomen, the latter making a tapping sound on the ground. In a third species the male paws the ground in front of him with his front legs, in the manner of a horse, and then starts to circle the female, getting slowly closer and closer to her. He rears up with his palps pointed upwards and his first pair of legs raised in a curve. He then jerks them upwards before lowering them, trembling, to the ground. The female eventually becomes receptive and the male transfers the packets of semen first from one palp, then from the other, to the female.

So far as we can see, these strange convolutions eventually bring the female into a mood to mate, and it is not without profit to recall that the human victim of the tarantula's bite, dancing to cure himself, infected those who watched. In his case, however, he produced a kind of mass hysteria, which has been called tarantism.

The female, like other wolf spiders, carries her eggs in a silken cocoon attached to the tip of her abdomen. When the 40 or so spiderlings hatch they ride in a crowd on the back of the mother's abdomen.

## Disease and remedy

The bite of the tarantula was supposed to bring on a general melancholy which in the end proved fatal. The only thing for the victim to do was to call for one or more musicians who, with their pipes and fiddles, would play a succession of tunes until they hit upon one that set the patient dancing, slowly at first but with more and more speed and vigour—rather like the male tarantula's wooing—until the patient finally fell sweating profusely, exhausted but cured. By that time all of his neighbours might be affected and they would take up the dance, and this might spread to other communities.

It sometimes happened that mass hysteria would break out and spread across Europe. The tarantula was blamed for this. By contrast we find Robert Burton, in his *Anatomy of Melancholy* (1621), recommending hanging the spider in a nutshell around the neck as a cure for the ague (malaria). He says he got this cure from his mother but seems to have been doubtful of its value until he found it had been recommended by Dioscorides, Matthiolus, Aldrovandus and other authors of high standing from the days of the Ancient Greeks onwards.

▷ *Tarantula: the spider that started all the fuss. **T. narbonensis**, poised menacingly above its burrow. Its long, hairy legs and body and beady stare make it easy to see why many people find it so repulsive.*

| phylum | **Arthropoda** |
|---|---|
| class | **Arachnida** |
| order | **Araneae** |
| family | **Lycosidae** |
| genus & species | ***Tarentula barbipes*** <br> ***T. cuneata*** <br> ***T. pulverulenta*** <br> *others* |

△ *Black hairy monster* **Pachylomerus
nitidulans** *waits at its doorstep for prey.*

▽ *In her lady's chamber: silk-lined tunnel of*
**Bothriocyrtum californicum** *in cross section.*

▽ *Seen in action:* **Cteniza caementaria**
*seizes a millipede, paralyses it and retreats.*

# Trapdoor spider

*The trapdoor spiders are related to the large
hairy bird-eating spiders that are sometimes
wrongly called tarantulas. Instead of
being hunters like the bird-eating spiders,
trapdoor spiders have specialized in
a remarkable way and have brought the
building of a secure retreat, using the crafts
of spinner and builder, to a fine art.*

*Trapdoor spiders are an inch or more
long in the body with relatively short legs
as compared with the bird-eating spiders.
The bristles or 'hairs' on the body and legs
are short, inconspicuous, and often sparse.
The spiders themselves are mainly dull in
colour, usually some shade of brown. Their
most characteristic features are the large
jaws, each with a long fang, and the row
of horny teeth along the underside of them.*

*The true trapdoor spiders live in tropical
and subtropical countries but related
species, known sometimes as trapdoor
spiders, but more correctly called purse-
web spiders, are found in temperate
latitudes.*

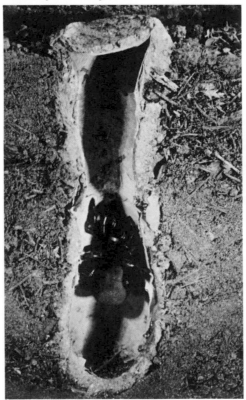

## Life in a closed box

Trapdoor spiders dig a shaft in the ground which may be as much as 1 ft deep and 1–1½ in. diameter. The teeth on the underside of the jaw as well as the fangs are used to loosen soil and then to grip it and carry it away. The walls of the shaft are made firm by soil reinforced with silk, so when completed the shaft is lined with a continuous tube of silk. The entrance is secured with a trapdoor made of layers of silk and soil which form a circular, solid lid. This is coated on the outside with moss or any other readily available plant matter. Thus, when completed and in position, the trapdoor is beautifully camouflaged. Inside the lid are two holes into which the spider can fix its feet to hold the door tight down to keep out intruders. At one point there is a silken hinge and on the outside, above the hinge, there is sometimes a ridge which acts like a counterpoise.

There is nothing especially remarkable about the spider burrowing or lining the shaft with silk. Several kinds of other spiders dig in the ground and line their tunnels with silk. The masterpiece of construction is the lid or trapdoor. In some species it is toothed to give an exact fit. WS Bristowe has described a species of *Nemesia*, in Majorca, which hardens the rim of the door, then shapes it into teeth with its fangs. The rim of the shaft is treated in the same way, but reinforced with earth. When the trapdoor is pulled down, the teeth on the lid fit between the teeth on the shaft rim. The spider is fastidious also in the material it uses. 'Only fine earth was employed, the gritty particles were held in the chelicerae (jaws) and then sharply flicked away with the palps and front legs.'

## Surreptitious feeding

A hungry trapdoor spider must leave its retreat to forage. Some people say it raises the lid of its burrow slightly and watches through the crack for a passing insect. Then it lets the lid spring up, rushes out and pounces, paralysing its prey with poison from its fangs and, holding it, retreats backwards into its burrow, pulling down the trapdoor after it. Other writers say it hunts at night, but there is little information on the way trapdoor spiders feed. The poison is not dangerous to people although some species can give a painful bite; the advice given to anyone bitten by Australian trapdoor spiders is to treat their bites with as much respect as snakebites.

## Underground nursery

Small, secretive animals are especially hard to study and their breeding habits particularly tend to remain unknown. The best that can be said of trapdoor spiders is that the females lay their eggs in their burrow, enclosed in a silken cocoon fixed to the wall of the shaft. The young ones stay with the mother until they are 8 months old.

## Why build a trapdoor?

In fashioning such an ingenious trapdoor the spider ensures that its retreat is not filled in with dust and vegetable rubbish. It is a guard also against changes in air temperatures and heavy rain. Most of all, however,

△ *Primitive spider* **Liphistius batuensis,** *suborder Liphistiomorphae, outside her home in the Batu Caves, Malaya. The radiating lines spun by the trapdoor spider are ingenious trip lines for prey. Compare the thin pliable door of this spider's home with the thick 'cork' doors on the opposite page.*

the trapdoor gives protection from enemies, particularly from their main predator, the hunting wasp.

## Purse-web spider

Not all trapdoor spiders use the elaborate methods described here. The lid, for example, may be paper-thin or it may be as thick as cork; it may be merely a flat circular lid or it may be elaborately scalloped or toothed. The shaft may be of varying degrees of perfection. The retreats of some of the less skilled trapdoor spiders come very near to those of the purse-web spiders, which is one reason why the latter are sometimes called trapdoor spiders. One purse-web spider *Atypus affinis,* of the family Atypidae, lives in Western Europe, from the British Isles to Denmark and Hungary and southwards into Algeria. It digs a more or less horizontal tunnel in a bank, up to 1 ft long and about ½ in. diameter. In this is a long silken bag with an inch or so lying free beyond the entrance to the tunnel. The bag is sealed at both ends and the spider inside gets its food without ever coming out. When an insect walks over the free end the spider runs to the spot and pushes its fangs through the silk to hold its victim. Then, using one jaw to hold the prey, it cuts a slit in the silk with the row of teeth along the underside of the other jaw. The fang of this jaw then holds the victim while the other jaw cuts a parallel slit close to the first. The prey is

then pulled in, carried down into the tube and secured with silk threads. The spider then goes back and repairs the slits, after which it can return to eat its prey.

The male, ⅓ in. long, as against the ½ in.-long female, courts her by tapping on the free end of her silken bag. If the signs are favourable he enters and mates with her. This happens during September–October but her 100–150 eggs are not laid until the following June–August, the young hatching in August and September. They remain with the mother until the following March or April. A period of 18 months elapses between mating and the time when the spiderlings leave home.

| | |
|---|---|
| phylum | **Arthropoda** |
| class | **Arachnida** |
| order | **Araneae** |
| suborder | **Orthognatha** |
| family | **Ctenizidae** |
| genus & species | ***Cteniza californica*** *American trapdoor spider* |
| family | **Barychelidae** |
| genus & species | ***Blakistonia aurea*** *Australian trapdoor spider* *others* |

# Water spider

*Although many spiders can live temporarily underwater, or even voluntarily enter water, there is only one species that lives more or less permanently below the surface. It does so by constructing a diving bell.*

*There is nothing unusual about the appearance of the water spider. It is small-* bodied and long-legged, the front part of *the body light brown with faint dark markings, the chelicerae reddish brown and the abdomen greyish and covered with rather short hairs. An unusual feature is that the females are usually smaller than the males, the size range being 8—15 mm although females of up to 28 mm long— just over an inch—have been recorded.*

*The water spider ranges across temperate Europe and Asia.*

△ *A male water spider, usually larger than a female, crawls over some water vegetation. Only the* **Argyroneta** *species of spiders spend their entire life in the water.*

### Stocking up with air

Although it lives permanently in water, the water spider is dependent on air for breathing. It rises to the surface and hangs head-down from the surface film with the end of its abdomen pushed up into the air. With a sudden jerk of the abdomen and the hind pair of legs a bubble of air is trapped on the spider's underside. The spider then descends, swimming down or climbing down the stems of water plants, to its thimble-shaped bell of silk, holding the bubble of air between its hindlegs. It enters and, with its head directed towards the top of the bell, the bubble of air slides forward under the spider and the front part of it is released, to rise to the top of the bell. The spider then turns round, directing the tip of the abdomen upwards, and releases the rest of the air, stroking the abdomen with the rear legs if necessary to brush it off. The spider then goes to the surface and swims down with another silver bubble, this being repeated until the bell is filled with air.

## Building the bell
The bell is made by first spinning a platform of silk between the stems or leaves of water plants, with strands running out from the spider to the vegetation around. Wherever the spider goes it lays down a guide line of silk and this may serve other purposes than guiding the spider back to its home. The thread accumulation probably helps to secure the silken bell, and insects bumping into them probably alert the spider to the approach of prey. Once the platform of silk has been spun the spider releases air beneath it, making the silk web bulge upwards. As more and more air is added the web takes on the shape of a bell or thimble.

## Lying in ambush
During the day the spider remains inside the bell, with the front legs pushed beyond the mouth of the bell, into the water. Any small animal, particularly an insect or its larva, passing near will make the spider dash out, seize it and return to the bell to eat it. An insect falling on the surface of the water will also set up vibrations to which the spider is sensitive, sending it to the surface to seize the insect and take it down to the bell to be eaten. By night the spider leaves its bell to hunt, but it will always return to the bell with its prey.

## Eggs laid in bell
Mating begins in spring or early summer with the male loading his palps with sperm and setting out to visit a female in her bell. If she is ready to mate only a brief courtship ensues, otherwise she lunges at him, making him retire. Having mated with her he may remain in her bell for a while and even mate a second time. The female lays 50—100 eggs in a silken bag that takes up the upper half of the cavity of the bell. The eggs hatch in 3—4 weeks, the spiderlings biting their way through the bag into the bell where they stay for a few weeks, moulting twice during that time. Some of the brood stay in the same pond, but many go to the surface, climb out, spin threads of silk onto the wind and float away—to find a new pond or die.

## Predators preyed upon
There is probably a heavy mortality as the young spiders disperse. Even after this stage of the life cycle has been safely passed, enemies are numerous. They include dragonfly larvae, backswimmers, water stick

insects, beetles and their larvae, frogs, fish and possibly larger members of their own species. Whether cannibalism occurs in the wild or is, as so often has been demonstrated, the result of being in captivity, would be hard to say.

As winter approaches, water spiders go to a lower level in the pond and spin a winter bell, stocking it with air. Some will use an empty water snail shell lying on the bottom. The one bubble of air will last 4—5 months, since the spider is completely immobile and using almost no energy while in its submerged winter quarters.

## Other spiders can submerge
Among other spiders that voluntarily submerge in water, one species has been tested experimentally. It is unrelated to the water spider, belonging to the family Pisauridae, and is named *Dolomedes triton*. WH McAlister, of the University of Texas, found that this spider requires a solid surface to push itself into and out of the surface film, and while submerged needs a solid support to cling to as an anchor. So it is fair to say that the spider deliberately enters water. In addition it was found to remain submerged voluntarily for 4—9 minutes, exceptionally up to 30 minutes. While being tested it was found to survive sustained immersion for up to 180 minutes, which is 10 times as long as most terrestrial spiders.

People often find a spider in the bath. Many are strongly averse to spiders yet are equally averse to killing one, so solve the problem by washing it down the wastepipe. They often ask—having perpetrated the foul deed—whether the spider dies from this. Most spiders tend to trap some air among the hairs on their bodies when immersed, and from McAlister's experiments it would seem that most spiders can stand up to 10 minutes' immersion, some can stand more than this, which should give them time to get out of the water to safety —provided the water used to wash them away is not hot.

| phylum | **Arthropoda** |
|---|---|
| class | **Arachnida** |
| order | **Araneae** |
| family | **Agelenidae** |
| genus & species | *Argyroneta aquatica* |

▽ *A water spider inside its bell of air, which is still in the early stage of construction.*

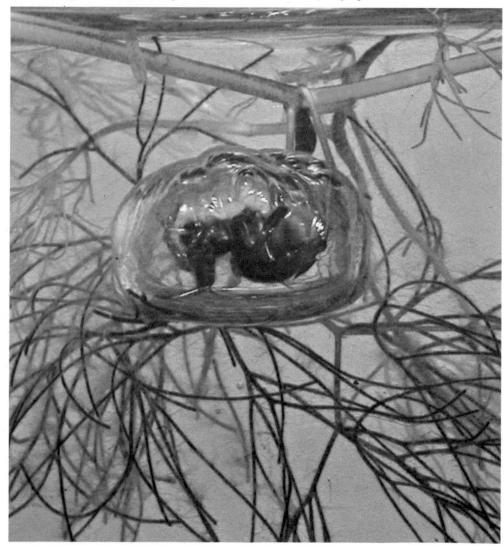

# Wolf spider

*Wolf spiders, like the carnivores after which they are named, run their prey down instead of making a silken snare like so many other spiders. There are, however, a few species that use silk to line their burrows or make silk tubes from which to pounce on their prey.*

*They are small to medium-sized spiders, the largest being less than 1 in. long in the body with legs also 1 in. long. They are dark or drab in colour, and their bodies are covered with a pile of short bristles. They have strong jaws. Their most characteristic feature is the three rows of eyes on the head; four small eyes in front, just above the base of the jaws, then two larger eyes in each of the two succeeding rows, all simple, as in other arachnids.*

*Wolf spiders are widespread across all the continents except Antarctica. The total number of species is hard to estimate: there are about 125 in North America, and 50 in Europe. The tarantula of southern Europe Lycosa tarentula is a wolf spider.*

## Wolf-like in many ways

Wolf spiders are often numerous, especially among leaf litter. They tend to be more active at night or under overcast conditions, but they can sometimes be seen in large numbers by day, running over dead leaves, probably because they were disturbed by someone walking over the litter. They shelter by day in small burrows dug in soft earth. Some species line the burrow with silk, while others also have a silken tube running out a short way from the mouth of the burrow. The silk is never used as a snare, but more as an ambush. The food, as with most spiders, is small insects, which the wolf spiders pursue and grab with their strong jaws. They then chew their prey to a pulp and suck the juices through a very small mouth, too small to admit any but the smallest particles.

## Wooing by waving

Wolf spiders have relatively keen sight and courtship is conducted by visual signals. A male ready to breed sets out in search of a female. He stations himself in front of her and begins to wave his long palps up and down like semaphore arms. These are usually black and are conspicuous against the drab body. In some species, parts of the

△ *Beloved burden: the female nursery web spider – this one is* **Pisaura mirabilis** *– is very attached to her cocoon and will substitute some other similar object if it is removed from her care.*

front pair of legs are also black and these are also held up and waved. The males of many species vibrate this front pair of legs; in other species the male may tremble in the legs and the abdomen. If the female is not receptive at first she may be induced to respond later by the sight of these movements in the male. She may then face the male and signal back in like manner. Finally the two mate by the male placing his sperm, previously deposited in the pedipalp, into the female's genital pore.

The female lays her eggs in a spherical or lens-shaped silk cocoon, specially spun for the purpose. She attaches this cocoon to the rear end of her abdomen and carries it around with her wherever she goes. Should the cocoon become detached she turns and retrieves it, fastening it again to her abdomen. In experiments, designed to test her devotion to the cocoon, it was found that if the cocoon is taken away and a small white object such as a pith ball, or a pellet of screwed up blotting paper, placed on the ground near the spider she will retrieve this.

## Spiderlings travel on mother's back

When the eggs hatch the spiderlings remain for a short while in the cocoon until it splits, under favourable weather conditions. They then climb onto the mother's back and are transported by her. In some species the brood is so numerous the spiderlings cover the mother's back several layers deep. So far as we know the spiderlings do not feed during this time. Should one fall off the mother does not halt for it to regain its position on her back, or do anything to assist it. The spiderling must either quickly climb up one of her legs, to reach her back, or be left behind to perish. This is in sharp contrast to the solicitude she shows for the eggs in the cocoon. She will seek shelter when it is raining, to preserve the cocoon, and should it get wet she will, at the earliest opportunity, tilt her head and body downwards to hold the cocoon up to the sun to dry it. 'Solicitude' is probably the wrong word because there is nothing intelligent or deliberate about these acts. They are all automatic responses to circumstances.

## Two deadly enemies

The drab colouring of wolf spiders, their mainly nocturnal habits and their use of burrows into which they can retire gives them a fair degree of immunity from enemies. There are, however, two important enemies. The first is the mantisfly, which preys on the eggs while they are still in the cocoon. Hunting wasps are the second danger. They paralyse the spiders and use them to feed their larvae. These hunting wasps fly low over the ground on a zigzag course, searching for prey. When a wasp is over the burrow of a wolf spider it lands and starts to dig. Once the wasp is inside the burrow the spider becomes easy prey.

WS Bristowe has described how he touched a wolf spider *Arctosa perita* sitting at the mouth of its burrow with the tip of a fine grass stem. The spider grabbed the silk on one side of the opening and pulled it across, like a curtain, until only a small slit was left, which it then closed by spinning silk criss-cross over it. We can suppose this is what it would do to keep out a wasp.

## Good vision important

The eyes are more important to wolf spiders than to web-spinning spiders. When a female is loaded with her brood of spiderlings they spread in a solid layer, or layers, across her back and onto her head. Yet you never see any of the babies covering the mother's eyes. This seems like some remark-

△ *About hatching time, in June or July, the female **Pisaura mirabilis** detaches her cocoon and spins a tent over it, by which she stands guard. Clustered together inside, the young complete the final stages of development, including two moults, and then disperse.*

able instinct which makes the spiderlings draw back when in danger of covering their mother's eyes. When we watch carefully, however, we see that every now and then one or more spiderlings are pressed forward by the mob, so almost blindfolding the mother. The moment this happens the mother passes one of her palps over her head, like someone brushing back their hair, and casually pushes the erring spiderlings away from her eyes.

| phylum | **Arthropoda** |
|---|---|
| class | **Arachnida** |
| order | **Araneae** |
| families | **Lycosidae** **Pisauridae** |

# Index

## Acknowledgments

This book is adapted from 'Purnell's Encyclopedia of Animal Life', published in the United States under the title of 'International Wild Life'.

Photo Sources:
AFA; A. C. Wheeler; F. G. H. Allen; Heather Angel; Toni Angermayer; Ron Austing; Barnabys; Bavaria (Sune Berkeman, Bleuler, W. Harstrick, Chr. Lederer, B. Leidmann, H. Pfletschinger,

Klaus Meier-Ude, A. Niestle, Novoflex, Hans Wagner) S. Beaufoy; Carlo Bevilacqua; S. C. Bisserot; J. D. Bradley; J. Breeds; British Museum of Natural History; Colin G. Butler; N. A. Callow; Carolina Biological Supply Co.; James Carr; Richard Cassell; Lynwood Chace; J. M. Cherrett; Michael Chinery; Arthur Christiansen; John Clegg; M. J. Cole; F. Collet; J. A. L. Cooke; Gene Cox; James Cross; Crown Copyright; Cyr Color Agency; W. T. Davidson;

R. B. Davies; Herman Eisenbeiss; Robert Fletcher; J. B. Free; Friedel Schöx; G. S. Giacomelli; H. Lou Gibson; John Goddard; J. A. Grant; W. D. Haacke; Peter Hill; M. J. Hirons; W. Hoflinger; E. O. Hoppé; Chris Howell-Jones; A. K. Hyatt; G. E. Hyde; Jacana (Yves Lanceau); Walter Jarchow; Palle Johnsen; Keystone; Hille Kleinstra; H. Klingel; A. Klots; Yves Lanceau; Wolfgang Lummer; Mansell; Aldo Margiocco; John Markham; Micro-colour

Int (Gene Cox); The Murphy Chemical Co; Natural History Photographic Agency; L. Hugh Newman; NHPA (F. Baillie, Anthony Bannister, N. A. Callow, Stephen Dalton, R. Foord, F. Greenaway, Brian Hawkes, Alice Hopf, C. McDermott, W. J. C. Murray, L. Hugh Newman, Brian O'Donnell, G. Temple, W. Zepf); Okapia; Klaus Paysan; Lawrence Perkins; Photo Library Inc (Roy Pinney); Photo Res (Jane Burton, S. C. Bisserot, C. Ciapanna,

Russ Kinne, Peterson, Graham Pizzey, Louis Quitt, Edward Ross, H. W. Silvester); Picturepoint; Graham Pizzey; Joyce Pope; Popperfoto; Walker Van Riper; Heinz Schrempp; W. M. Scott; Shell Photo; Fritz Siedel; M. T. Tanton; Ron Taylor; Sally Anne Thompson; M. Tweedie; USDA Photo; J. J. Ward; Peter H. Ward; Constance P. Warner; Birgit Webb; We-Ha; J. A. Wilson; John Norris Wood after Savory; ZEFA (Jack Novak).